HOMELAND INSECURITY

HOMELAND INSECURITY

THE ARAB AMERICAN AND MUSLIM AMERICAN EXPERIENCE AFTER 9/11

LOUISE A. CAINKAR

Russell Sage Foundation • New York

The Russell Sage Foundation

Library of Congress Cataloging-in-Publication Data

Cainkar, Louise A.
  Homeland insecurity : the Arab American and Muslim American experience after 9/11 / Louise A. Cainkar.—1st ed.
     p. cm.
  Includes bibliographical references and index.
  ISBN 978-0-87154-048-5 (alk. paper)
  1. Arab Americans—Social conditions. 2. Muslims—United States—Social conditions. 3. September 11 Terrorist Attacks, 2001—Influence. 4. Civil defense—Social aspects—United States. 5. National security—Social aspects—United States. 6. United States—Race relations. 7. United States—Ethnic relations. I. Title.
  E184.A65C35 2009
  305.8927073—dc22

                              2009003523

Text design by Suzanne Nichols.

RUSSELL SAGE FOUNDATION
112 East 64th Street, New York, New York 10065
10 9 8 7 6 5 4 3 2 1

To Janet Abu-Lughod and
Anwar, Ryan, and Carmen
Young women: lead the way,
reflect, uphold justice.

Contents

About the Author

Louise A. Cainkar is assistant professor of sociology at Marquette University.

Acknowledgments

MANY PEOPLE have crossed my path and shared my journey during the data collection, analysis, and writing stages that culminated in this book. I am grateful to all who have given me support in the multiple ways humans desire and need. I want to especially thank the individuals who provided research assistance on this project: Sandra Del Toro, Maha El-Nur, Dwan Kaoukji, and Samira Ahmed. I also want to thank Eman Hasabella, Aalia Khawaja, Savera Iftikhar, Mariyam Hussain, Assia Bandaoui, Tahani Hassan, and Ayesha Akhtar, who provided research assistance on other related projects. Opportunities to thank these women who have been eager to forge out and ask questions of others on behalf of my research projects are limited, so thank you! I would also like to thank friends and colleagues who read drafts of various chapters, including Kristine Ajrouch, Jan Abu-Shakrah, Dawne Moon, and David Cole. Thanks also to Kay Wade, from whom I received technical support, and to Cindy Serikaku, my incredible, indefatigable bibliographic assistant.

Kind gratitude goes to Stephanie Platz, formerly of the Russell Sage Foundation, whose backing of the ideas behind this research project helped to make it a reality, and to the Foundation as a whole for providing me with generous grant support. I also want to recognize the persistent collegial support of David Perry, director of the Great Cities Institute at the University of Illinois–Chicago, where this project was housed during much of the data collection stage. Several institutions provided me with the scholarly settings, colleagues, and intellectual support for the ongoing cultivation of my thinking and the opportunity to incessantly check my interpretations of data, including the Carnegie Corporation, which awarded me a Carnegie Scholar Award, the Social Science Research Council, the France–Stanford Center for Interdisciplinary Studies, the Minda de Gunzburg Center for European Studies at Harvard University, and the Chicago Council on Global Affairs.

My commitment not only to rigorous scholarly work but also to social justice has found a welcoming home at Marquette University, where I moved in 2006. I want to recognize my colleagues there for their support and encouragement while I wrote this book. In addition to great college basketball at Marquette, my welcome in Milwaukee has been made a thousand times warmer by the friendship and kindness of Sandra Edhlund and Art Heitzer.

My daughter Anwar lived with this project through her youngest years and has, I believe, developed remarkably well despite its relentless grasp of my time and attention, a state my husband Hassan and son Walid readily tolerated with ongoing patience.

Thanks to everyone named and unnamed who has made my life richer and my work more meaningful.

Finally, thanks to the members of the Arab American and Muslim American communities who have opened their doors and lives to me. I am evermore grateful for your trust in me and your confidence in the integrity of my work.

Chapter 1

Introduction

THE TITLE for this book emerged from research data showing that during the three years following the attacks of September 11, 2001, a majority of Arab Muslim Americans reported feeling unsafe and insecure in the United States.[1] This sense of insecurity, which was not only articulated in narratives but was palpable, was an outcome of their treatment by the American government and some members of the American public and by portrayals of them in the mainstream American media, which proffered constructions of reality that repeatedly supported notions of the collective culpability of Arab and Muslim Americans for the attacks. Throughout the two-year period of interviews for this study—2003 to 2004—a majority of the persons interviewed said in various ways that they were not confident about their personal safety, that they felt vulnerable, and that they were uncertain about their ability to live freely in the United States, fearing that they might face expulsion from the country or incarceration en masse in camps. These fears of collective quarantine or banishment weakened as time passed, perhaps because Bush administration policies had shifted from the incarceration and expulsion of Arabs and Muslims to their registration and monitoring. But many remained fearful of their fate should another attack occur in the United States for which, while not of their doing and not under their control, they might be held responsible.[2]

This book provides an analysis of Arab Muslim American experiences after 9/11 as documented by a sociological and ethnographic study of Arab Muslim Americans in metropolitan Chicago. Its account of that critical period of American history is perhaps not as positive as some might wish, but also not as negative as others might expect. It is compiled neither from the observation of encouraging and heartening events nor from an inventory of discouraging and shocking incidents, but rather from the detailed accounts of a wide range of immigrant and native-born Arab Muslim Americans, who overwhelmingly felt that their experiences could only be understood in the larger context of Arab and Muslim American

1

history, a perspective shared by the author. Indeed, a principal argument of this book is that the negative treatment of Arabs and Muslims in the United States after 9/11 was caused not by the 9/11 attacks themselves, but by preexisting social constructions that configured them as people who would readily conduct and approve of such attacks. These social constructions did not emerge on 9/11 but were the culmination of processes of labeling and interpretation transmitted by interested actors through major American social institutions over the latter decades of the twentieth century. These interpretations, which sought to explain the reasons for violence and turmoil in the "Middle East" (itself a social construction) through the use of essentialized notions of human difference, set the stage for Arab and Muslim American communities to be held collectively culpable for the 9/11 attacks by the government, the media, and the citizenry. As I show in chapter 3, for decades prior to the attacks Arabs and Muslims had been represented in American culture as monolithic groups that had an inherent proclivity to violence, with "pathological cultures" (Abu-Lughod 2007) and a morally deviant religion that sanctions killing. They were socially constructed as "others," as people not like "us," an interpretation shown to be widely accepted in public opinion polls long before 9/11.

Notions of inherent human differences imply something akin to biology in American culture, and are often interpreted and acted upon as race. Sociologically and anthropologically speaking, Arab Americans had been racialized in American society—set off from the body of mainstream Americans as "others"—through social processes that bore many similarities to those experienced by other racialized groups, but also with significant differences (see chapter 3). The most important difference was that the racialization of Arab Americans inhered not from domestic interests but from the global political and economic interests of a rising American superpower. This difference explains not only the distinct timing of the racializing processes for Arab Americans (coming much later than for African, Native, Latino, and Asian Americans) but also the unusual circumstance that Arabs were once positioned in a structurally more favorable status in the United States as whites (and they are still officially considered white). With the end of the Cold War, and during a time of massive immigration to the United States, Arab Americans could easily be reinvented and reimagined as new immigrants and as people we really did not "know"—although hundreds of thousands of them had lived in the United States over the previous one hundred years.

For their part, long before 9/11 Muslims were widely represented in American culture not only as an inherently volatile group that threatened American global allies and interests but also as a group that potentially threatened American culture itself, in particular its core values of democracy and personal liberty. As shown in chapter 7, the content of these charges against Muslims in the United States is strikingly similar to the claims of anti-Catholic nativists in the nineteenth-century United States (Higham 1955). After the 9/11 attacks, some Americans would latch on to these ideas about Islam's cultural threat to justify the harassment and assault of Muslim women in *hijab* (head scarves).[3] Overall, by the time the 9/11 attacks occurred, Arab and Muslim Americans were well positioned in both government group-think and the public's mind to be held culpable for them. Much the same had happened during the period following the Pearl Harbor attacks in 1941: the attacks alone did not explain why the government, the media, and much of the public supported the internment of Japanese Americans in camps; rather, it was the ways in which Japanese Americans had been socially constructed prior to the attacks that facilitated their representation as potential co-conspirators and produced social support for these collective measures. This treatment of Japanese Americans as the "threat within" has been widely acknowledged as unjustified and was the subject of a formal government apology in 1988.

Interviewees' sentiments about "homeland insecurity" referred to a collective status and were expressed to an equal degree by the American-born and foreign-born Arab Muslims interviewed in this study: whether the United States was a native or adopted homeland, it had ceased to be a place where members of these communities felt safe and protected. A majority of study participants described their citizenship as an inferior one that excluded guarantees and rights accorded to other citizens. A state of uncertainty and peril more common to refugees living on the borders of war zones and global migrants without documents was induced in citizen and resident Arabs and Muslims, largely because of post-9/11 federal government policies, which were deeply informed by notions of unvarying, monolithic, and threatening Arabs and Muslims. Thousands of Arab and Muslim noncitizens were deported from the country for visa violations, at least one thousand were jailed for extended periods of time without charge, tens of thousands of Arab and Muslim U.S. citizens and residents were interviewed by the Federal Bureau of Investigation (FBI), and hundreds of thousands were watched. Arabs and Muslims in the United States lived with a lurking fear that any impropriety committed at any time in their lives might be brought forth to impugn them. Their behavior needed to meet a standard of perfection reserved for profiled groups: full stops at all stop signs, turn signals on all turns. Chapter 4 offers an inventory of many of the government's policies after 9/11 and shows their measurable impacts on Arabs and Muslims living in the United States. The American government alleged and then vigorously pursued efforts to find connections between Arabs and Muslims living in the United States and the 9/11 hijackers, but failed to do so. The attorney general argued that coercive policies were necessary to locate the terrorist sleeper cells hiding within Arab and Muslim American ("their") communities, thereby threatening "our" communities. Despite the use of its full resources and aggressive tactics unlimited by the Constitution or rule of law, the government actually uncovered very little, as shown by the data presented in chapter 4. When the Nixon Center policy analyst Robert Leiken (2004, 136) argued for targeting the "haystack" if "the needle resists discovery," he used a metaphor that captures well the systematic criminalization of Arabs and Muslims that occurred during this period of American history.

While the grounding of Arabs and Muslims in the United States was destabilized by the collective targeting of federal government policies, "go back to your country" was a frequent exhortation of the American flag–wavers in their midst. "De-Americanization," according to Bill Ong Hing (2002), relies on the symphonic collaboration of citizenry and government, where the latter sets the stage for the former's outcasting work—public performances informed by notions of intrinsic group differences and differentiated rights of national belonging. In the first months after the 9/11 attacks, "I want to kill you" was often shouted by the more violently oriented, and angry neighbors and co-citizens yelled, "Osama!" as Arab and Muslim Americans were symbolically attached to the 9/11 hijackers. The status of outsider and its concomitant position of insecurity were reinforced at the everyday local level by egg-throwing, spitting, hijab-pulling, garbage-dumping, "bomb in your briefcase" jokes, ethnic slurs, religious affronts, hate graffiti, hand signals, removal from planes, and, in some cases, assault and murder. Battered in the grounded spaces of their daily lives, in the media, and in the fundamental arenas of rights and citizenship, listening to coworkers' tales of Arab and Muslim barbarism, asked to explain the reasons for the attacks or to apologize for them, facing discrimination in the workplace, at airports, and in schools and banks, it is no surprise that Arabs and Muslims felt the chill of homeland insecurity. "There was something in the air," said one interviewee—something that seemed to make it permissible to say or do anything to Arabs and Muslims in the United States. Chapter 5 provides a narrative account of many of these widely shared post-9/11 experiences as described by Arab Muslims living in metropolitan Chicago.

The aggressive and hostile public responses to Arabs and Muslims after 9/11 are often described in the literature in generalities; these accounts lack an analysis of perpetrators or local context, partly because the data collected focus on victims and narrow events. The writers often assume that the relevant explanatory social context is a national one—because the 9/11 attacks were interpreted as attacks on the nation, because the media's treatment of Arabs and Muslims was largely unvarying across the nation, and because the government policy context was national. The experiences related in chapters 4 and 5 did have this general character: they occurred in a wide array of places, were perpetrated by a range of people, and were experienced by a broad variety of Arab Muslims. This study also found, however, that there were variations in Arab Muslim post-9/11 experiences by place. Chapter 6 examines these variations in detail and explains why one community with a significant Arab Muslim population experienced calm and solidarity within a few months of the attacks while another, similarly settled by a significant Arab Muslim population, was characterized by years of hate acts, aggression, and outcasting. The heightened and prolonged character of the attacks in the latter area is explained by preexisting sentiments that the growing Arab and Muslim population was becoming a cultural threat to the moral order of the area; these sentiments were ignited by the spark of the 9/11 attacks. The attacks provided a justification for the hate-mongers who moved into action after 9/11, as if they were neighborhood defenders on a moral crusade (Levin and McDevitt 2002). A social geography of spaces of varying interpretation emerges from this comparative spatial analysis. Local-level social relationships are shown to have held the power to add a layer of noise between the dominant national discourses of Arab and Muslim American culpability for the 9/11 attacks and the public interpretation of these discourses; they also had the power to make these dominant discourses even noisier. This finding makes sense, because the post-9/11 treatment of Arab and Muslim Americans was not about the attacks themselves but about the *social construction of their relationship to the attacks.* As a social construction, alternative interpretations, grounded in local context, become possible. This study found that where positive intergroup relationships were well developed prior to the 9/11 attacks because of community-organizing efforts, Arab Muslims experienced relative safety at the neighborhood level.

Information about the type of threat that Arabs and Muslims were said to pose to American society was widely available in the United States, and it was used to guide perpetrators' selection of targets for hate acts and harassments after 9/11.[4] The notion that Muslims posed not only a security threat to American society but also a cultural one helps to explain why, as this study found, twice as many Arab Muslim women reported experiencing hate acts and harassment as Arab Muslim men. If fear of terrorists had been driving hate acts, then one would expect that men would have been the principal victims. As it turns out, post-9/11 repercussions for Arab and Muslim Americans were quite gendered, with men positioned as the security threat managed largely by the government and women as the cultural threat dealt with by the public.[5] While men took the brunt of government security measures, such as incarceration, registration, interrogation, and removal (chapter 4), women took the brunt of public rage, especially women in hijab (chapter 7). That women in hijab were interpreted as symbols of the foreign cultural threat posed by Muslims explains why the overwhelming majority of women experiencing hate acts were either wearing hijab or in the company of a woman wearing hijab when victimized, as were many of the men. Hijab was imbued with meaning as a countersymbol to personal freedom, an interpretation that exposed its alleged threat to American culture. Hijab symbolized force—or perhaps even more threatening to American culture, the choice of American Muslim women to *reject American freedom.* As a representation of the foreign, the actual citizenship status of women in hijab had little bearing on their experiences. Men had the exact opposite experience: for them, citizenship status was key to their differential experiences with the federal government.

This symbolic meaning of hijab had been invested in for some time by a wide range of interested parties—mostly non-Muslims, but also a small proportion of Muslims—and was cashed in domestically to garner popular support for the U.S. invasion of Afghanistan after 9/11, when the connection between hijab and oppression was prime-time American culture talk (Abu-Lughod 2002). While some might argue that it was simply the visibility and easy identification of women in hijab that explained their victimization, this explanation is weakened upon contextualization of these acts: women in hijab were most likely to be assaulted and verbally abused in neighborhoods where Arab Muslim men were readily identifiable. These were the suburban neighborhoods where a substantial number of people held implicit understandings about the American way of life, symbolized not by diversity but by a white, middle-class, Christian culture that had motivated most residents to move to them in the first place. Chapter 7 describes the gendered repercussions of the 9/11 attacks on Arab Muslims, explores the cultural meaning of hijab that was grounded in nativist notions of the Muslim threat, and examines the popular war on difference fought by neighborhood "cultural snipers." This contextualization of the meaning of hijab helps to explain why the value of religious freedom strongly embraced in American society and by religious parties backing the Bush administration protects Muslim women's right to wear hijab and undergirds government support for this right, but does not protect Muslim women wearing hijab in public.[6]

The book concludes with an analysis of how Arab Muslims said the 9/11 attacks and their aftermath affected their religious faith. The study found that the majority of practicing Muslims reported a deepening of their religious faith and that many formerly nonpracticing or secular Muslims joined religious congregations and began practicing their religion during this period. Persons in both groups spoke of a thirst for greater knowledge about Islam, driven by both the use and abuse of religion by the 9/11 hijackers and the vilification of Islam in American culture, often referred to as "Islamophobia." Study participants said that they needed to understand Islam better—not only for their own sakes but because they could not explain or defend Islam to others when their state of knowledge was inadequate. Chapter 8 also examines data on how Arab Muslims see their future in the United States. The majority of study participants saw the future in a positive light, framing their current predicament as similar to that experienced by other negatively racialized and persecuted religious groups in American society. They felt that, just as those other groups had been able to struggle and win the battle for social inclusion, so too would they. The post-9/11 challenge they faced was to carry on with their lives despite all the components of homeland insecurity and to assert agency to change this country into one more tolerant and less easily impelled by hatred. Recognizing that active efforts were required to produce positive outcomes, many were encouraged by the surge they saw in Muslim American activism and by the defense of their rights taken up by American civil society groups. Despite formidable resistance from certain quarters and a global context in which some would place them on the other side of a Manichaean divide, there is evidence of significant post-9/11 mainstream engagement of Arab and Muslim Americans and their domestic issues. Indeed, if religion could be disentangled from issues of foreign policy, American Muslims as a religious group might fare better in the battle for inclusion than Arab Americans, because American society is one in which religious freedom has proven more attainable than equal treatment for racialized groups.

The findings reported in chapters 4 through 7 point to the crucial importance of bridging social capital—the social ties that link people together across a cleavage—to "homeland security."[7] Organized social relationships with persons from outside the group offer protection from harassment and assault and from the excesses of an overbearing government, while they mitigate the power of those engaged in discourses of demonization. This formidable power, which is embedded in knowing others and being "known," holds true for defense in individual legal cases, for relationships within the neighborhood, and for the design of federal policies. Arab and Muslim Americans could not change their social conditions in the United States alone, a fact highlighted in chapter 3, which shows that Arab American invisibility and absence from the table of subordinated groups allowed their vilification and social and political exclusion to continue unfettered for decades. Without this pre-existing condition of social exclusion, post-9/11 calls by members of the Bush administration and other American leaders for the American public to be watchful of all Arabs and Muslims living in the United States would have largely fallen flat.

Data presented in chapters 4 through 8 show that Arab and Muslim Americans recognized the challenge before them rather quickly after the 9/11 attacks and vigorously stepped up to the plate. The data also show that the excessive measures engaged in by the government and the violence perpetrated by some members of the American public produced their own counterforce: mobilizations of non-Arabs and non-Muslims ready to join with Arab and Muslim Americans to challenge these actions. These joint mobilizations in turn launched social processes that would produce greater social and political integration of Arab and Muslim Americans.[8] Indeed, much has changed in the United States since the 9/11 attacks, and some of these changes, discussed further in the final chapter, have been positive for Arab and Muslim Americans. The mobilizations, coalitions, and solidarities that emerged after 9/11 to defend Arab and Muslim Americans, as well as the launch of local-level homeland security "community roundtables," effectively transformed their predominant social status in many U.S. locations from socially excluded "outsiders" or "unknown" communities to embraced, civically engaged, and known. Similarly, Arab and Muslim Americans have become more deeply woven into the fabric of an extensive range of American activist, policy, and watchdog organizations, and many of their own community and faith-based organizations have been strengthened. Philanthropists and foundations that were formerly reluctant to support Arab and Muslim American organizations came forward with financial support after 9/11 because the emergency circumstances outweighed normative pressures to hold back.[9] This material support, in turn, increased Arab and Muslim American institution-building and leadership development. All of these positive social changes make it now far more politically difficult than in the first few years after the 9/11 attacks for the American government to implement policies that openly and *visibly* target Arab and Muslim Americans en masse.

This study shows that when weighed against each other, the American people provoked much less fear among Arab and Muslim Americans than did the federal government—the Bush administration, to be precise. Although popular violence against Arab and Muslim Americans and persons perceived to be members of these groups surged after the attacks, it settled down in most areas within a few months. It nonetheless remains a persistent, if episodic, national problem, subject to varying levels of latency and manifest encouragement. As this study confirms, popular violence against Arab and Muslim Americans is indicative of and stimulated by far more complex matters than simple indiscriminate outbursts of post-9/11 revenge. Indeed, the 2008 U.S. presidential campaign showed that anti-Arab and anti-Muslim sentiments continued to hold enough currency in the United States to be easily ratcheted up for political benefit without any critical event taking place. Longtime U.S. representative Ray LaHood (R-Illinois) told the press on October 10, 2008, that while he supported the Republican presidential ticket, he was profoundly dismayed by crowds shouting "Terrorist!" and "Kill him!"—assumed to refer to Democratic presidential candidate Obama, whose biological father was a

Muslim—during rallies for Republican vice presidential candidate Sarah Palin. Republican presidential candidate John McCain took a step to subdue these emotions, which were intentionally incited by members of his own party, by responding to a supporter at an October McCain rally who claimed Obama was an Arab, "No, ma'am, no ma'am, he's a decent family man, citizen, that I just happen to have disagreements with on fundamental issues"—inadvertently implying that Arabs cannot be "decent" or perhaps even American.[10] Responses to McCain's comment were swift, revealing the other side of the post-9/11 sociopolitical environment for Arabs and Muslims in the United States as, for example, the prominent actor Ben Affleck noted on national television that " 'Arab' and 'good person' are not antithetical to each other."[11] Referring to the overall climate of anti-Arab and anti-Muslim baiting that had been whipped up for partisan benefit, former Secretary of State Colin Powell said on *Meet the Press:*

> Well, the correct answer is, he's not a Muslim. He's a Christian, and he's always been a Christian. But the really right answer is: What if he is? Is there something wrong with being a Muslim in this country? The answer is no, that's not America. Is there something wrong with some seven-year-old Muslim American kid believing that he or she could be president?[12]

The closing months of the 2008 presidential campaign evidenced a contemporaneous surge in anti-Muslim violence in Chicago's heavily Republican western suburbs. October reports included anti-Muslim graffiti spray-painted on a Muslim American woman's college locker (*Chicago Sun-Times*, October 10, 2008) and the vandalizing of the west suburban Villa Park mosque for the fourth time in two months (*Chicago Tribune*, October 10, 2008).[13] It is indeed notable that these hate crimes did *not* happen in the southwest suburbs, which are both heavily Arab and Muslim and heavily Democratic, lending support to my argument that local context matters profoundly. While hate activity against Arab and Muslim Americans still rises and falls, subject to interpretations of world events and intentional political manipulation, more subtle discrimination against Arab and Muslim men and Muslim women wearing hijab reveals a pattern of consistency.

The religion scholar Diana Eck (2002, xv) wrote in late 2001, "Statistically, one would have to say that benevolence outweighed the backlash." She notes, for example, that the murder of a Sikh man brought on donations of hundreds of flowers and that acts of vandalism and arson often unleashed streams of flowers, cards, and offers of support. Eck concludes: "Americans would not condone indiscriminate violence against neighbors of any faith or culture" because the "multireligious and multicultural fabric of the United States was already too strong." Since most Americans did not engage in physical violence against Arabs and Muslims in the United States, perhaps Eck is correct. I argue, however, that it took the severe public backlash of murders, assaults, arsons, and vandalism to generate its counterforce, the social change that would see much of the American public embracing Arab and Muslim Americans as "fellow" Americans, quite a few for the first time. Such gestures of inclusion were few and far between in the years of stereotyping, harassment, and hate crimes prior to the 9/11 attacks. There may be a number of sociological explanations for this phenomenon, but it is certainly clear that the strong wave of popular violence against Arab and Muslim Americans and those perceived to be Arab or Muslim served as the spark that moved many Americans from inaction to action, including symbolic efforts that proclaimed their opposition to acts driven by hatred. This dramatic dialectic provoked by hate, stimulating its counterforce, may partly explain why poll data show that American attitudes toward American Muslims were more favorable in November 2001 than six months prior and four months later.[14] Although Eck's observation is meaningful for what it says about American society, it had little meaning at the time to the people about whom this book is written. To each individual Arab and Muslim, one murder was potentially *their* murder, or their spouse's or child's murder, and the ripple effect of each attack required a range of altered behaviors described in various chapters of this book.

Voices that had long before 9/11 connected all Arabs and Muslims to violence and terrorism and effected their social marginalization reached a crescendo after the 9/11 attacks; then their near-dominance was shattered, because these messages of intolerance proved utterly useless to Americans looking for ways to build cooperative social relationships in shared space.[15] Scholars have observed significant shifts in American popular culture and its representations of Arabs and Muslims in the years since the 9/11 attacks; their work offers further evidence that the cultural hegemony of anti-Arab, anti-Muslim essentialist discourses has been broken. Shifts have been observed, for example, in American television programs, including an increase—from a historic handful—in the number of Arab and Muslim *American* characters and the mainstreaming of sympathetic and humanizing portrayals of Arabs and Muslims, a rarity before 9/11 (Alsultany 2008). Some scholars argue, however, that the new discourses and representations are only slightly more complex than the old ones, in that they promote simplistic good Muslim–bad Muslim dichotomies (Mamdani 2004). Evelyn Alsultany (2008) argues that while more recent television plots evoke sympathy for the plight of Arab and Muslim Americans, they also reaffirm the right to be suspicious of them during times of national crisis.[16] Despite the changes we have seen for the better, Arab and Muslim stigmas remain in place in American culture. While there is much evidence of this stigma, it is perhaps best evidenced by the efforts noted earlier to smear Democratic presidential candidate

Barack Obama by calling him an Arab and a Muslim, by Republican presidential candidate John McCain's rejoinder that Obama was not an Arab but a good man and an American, and by Obama supporters' incessant assertion, "He is not a Muslim!" as if being either Muslim or Arab is still considered un-American.[17] Colin Powell was the first major American public figure after 9/11 to publicly make the statement that many Arab and Muslim Americans had been waiting for: going well beyond Bush administration requests that Americans not physically attack Arabs and Muslims, Powell suggested that their youth too could dream of moving out of the margins and into the mainstream of American society.

Study Methodology and Sampling

This book unpacks the "homeland insecurity" articulated by Arab Muslims using data collected in metropolitan Chicago between 2002 and 2005 for an ethnographic and sociological study of Arab/Muslim post-9/11 experiences. The study methodology included participant-observation that spanned this three-year period and interviews with 102 Arab Muslims—male and female, native-born and immigrant—from a range of social classes and countries of national origin and ancestry conducted in 2003 and 2004. In selecting interviewees, using purposive stratified and snowball sampling techniques, I was guided by my in-depth understanding of Arab American demographic patterns in metropolitan Chicago. All of the 102 interviews were conducted face to face using an extensive protocol of open-ended questions. Initially, interview notes were handwritten (thanks to Howard Becker for this skill) to enhance the interviewee's sense of safety—these were very difficult times characterized by seemingly arbitrary arrests—but over time a larger proportion of the interviews were recorded and then transcribed. I conducted about 80 percent of the interviews, all of which were in English. The remaining interviews were conducted in Arabic or English by research assistants. Table 1.1 provides a summary of study sample demographic characteristics.

Table 1.2 identifies the interview sample by location of residence in metropolitan Chicago. Interviews were conducted with Arab Muslims who resided throughout the city and its suburban areas. Care was taken to reflect the range of Arab American residential patterns while also sampling more heavily from areas of residential concentration. Arab Americans have two concentrated areas of residence in the southwest corridor of the Chicago metropolitan area: on the southwest side of the city, and in the nearby southwest suburbs. These areas are discussed in detail in chapters 6 and 7. Arab Americans also live in significant numbers on the north side of the city, although they are more broadly dispersed across a range of neighborhoods and are more likely to be Christian than

Table 1.1   Demographic Statistics of the Study Sample (N = 102)

	Percentage
Female	45
Income	
Poor or low-income	18
Middle-class	62
Upper-middle-class and wealthy	20
Age	
Nineteen to twenty-nine	30
Thirty to forty-nine	56
Fifty or older	14
Education	
High school or less	14
Some college or BA/BS degree	43
Postgraduate	42
Born in the United States[a]	30

Source: Author's calculations.

[a] Includes for sociological reasons persons who migrated to the United States before age ten.

Arab Americans on the southwest side. The majority of Iraqi refugees in Chicago were resettled in the 1990s on the north side, in the Albany Park neighborhood close to a large Assyrian community originally from Iraq. The Arab Americans dispersed throughout the north, northwest, and western suburbs are more likely to be Egyptian, Lebanese, and Syrian than Arab Americans on the southwest side and in the southwest sub-

Table 1.2   Interviewees by Residence in Chicago Metropolitan Area

	Number
City: north side	16
City: south side	2
City: southwest side	19
City: unspecified	14
Southwest suburbs	24
Northwest suburbs	11
Western suburbs	8
Northern suburbs	4
Other	4
Total	102

Source: Author's calculations.

Table 1.3   Interviewees by National Origin and Age at Migration or by Parents' National Origin if U.S.-Born

Country of National Origin	Total	Age Ten to Seventeen (1.5ers)	Under Ten	Foreign-Born Over Seventeen	U.S.-Born
Algeria	1			1	
Egypt	9		1	2	6
Iraq	7			7	
Jordan	7			6	1
Lebanon	2			2	
Lebanon-Syria	1			0	1
Libya	1		1	0	
Morocco	4			4	
Palestine[a]	44	7	7	20	10
Saudi Arabia	2			1	1
Somalia	5			5	
The Sudan	13			12	1
Syria	5	2		1	2
Yemen	1			1	
Total	102	9	9	62	22
Percentage of sample		9	9	61	22

Source: Author's calculations.

[a]See table 1.4 for countries of birth for Palestinians.

urbs; the latter are predominantly Palestinian, with smaller numbers of Jordanians (majority Christian), Yemenis, and members of other Arab nationalities.[18]

Arab Americans from thirteen countries of national origin are represented in the study, with a few of mixed national backgrounds. Table 1.3 identifies study participants by country of national origin, age at migration to the United States, and, for the U.S.-born, parents' national origin. Immigrants in the study most often came to the United States as adults, but slightly more than 10 percent of them were "1.5ers," defined as persons who migrated between the ages of ten and seventeen. This group is often highlighted in the immigration literature as a special type because its members were socialized in two cultures during their formative years (see Hurh 1998). Another group accounting for slightly less than 10 percent of all interviewees came to the United States as children under the age of ten, a group that sociologists have found to be more similar in perspective and life course to second-generation children of immigrants than to immigrants themselves. As I show here using immigration data,

Palestinians are the dominant Arab population in metropolitan Chicago, and have been so historically. Indeed, in my estimation, metropolitan Chicago may be home to the largest concentration of Palestinians in the United States. Owing to their large numbers and tendency to concentrate in enclave-like settings among other Palestinians, Palestinians are 43 percent of the study sample: 45 percent of the American-born and 42.5 percent of the foreign-born.

Persons familiar with Arab culture and history know that in the Arab world Arabs tend to identify with their ancestral place of origin regardless of where they were born and raised. Thus, Iraqis born in Yemen will most likely see themselves as Iraqi, regardless of their place of upbringing, passport, or citizenship. The same applies to Egyptians born in Saudi Arabia or Palestinians born in Kuwait. For this reason, I use the terminology and codify study participants by "country of national origin" rather than country of birth. Not understanding this sociological phenomenon results in flawed data analysis. For example, Palestinians—who live with this dualism more than any other Arab group because of their diasporic state—have been miscoded as Kuwaitis or Saudis by researchers who use country of birth or last permanent residence as indices of nationality. Country of citizenship or lack thereof further complicates this messy picture for Palestinians.[19] The U.S. Census Bureau has contributed its share to the problem of identifying Palestinians by recoding persons who indicate Palestine as place of birth and by doing so in a different way with every decennial census (see Cainkar 1988). These issues are quite salient for researchers of areas with large Palestinian populations. Table 1.4 indicates the countries of birth of the Palestinians interviewed in the study. Thirty-four percent were born in the West Bank or Jerusalem area, 20 percent in Jordan, 23 percent in the United States, and the remaining 23 percent in a range of countries.

Egyptians make up 9 percent of the study sample, followed by Iraqis and Jordanians at 7 percent each. Table 1.6 in the next section suggests that the proportion of Egyptian immigrants might be slightly low, but that the U.S.-born segment is probably about right. Sample proportions for Iraqis and Jordanians are adequate when one considers that the majority of these groups in the Chicago area are Christian and that this is a study of Muslims. Sudanese and Somalis were oversampled in this study (with reference to the immigration data in table 1.6) in an attempt to measure any differential impact of race or blackness. The study found, however, that their experiences were quite similar to those of the other Arabs interviewed.[20] Like other Arab groups, Sudanese and Somali men reported facing or fearing special measures by the American government because of their origin in Muslim-majority countries. Sudanese and Somali women who wore hijab reported harassing incidents similar to those experienced by other Arab Muslim women in hijab. The major distinction found in

Table 1.4   Palestinians in Sample by Place of Birth and Age
at Migration (N = 44)

| | Migrated to United States (Foreign-Born) | | | | |
Place of Birth	Over Age Seventeen	Under Age Ten	1.5er (Age Ten to Seventeen)	U.S.-Born	Total
West Bank/ Jerusalem	8	5	2		15
Israel	1				1
Jordan	7	1	1		9
Kuwait	3		3		6
Libya	1				1
Puerto Rico		1			1
United Arab Emirates			1		1
United States				10	10

Source: Author's calculations.

interviews with Sudanese and Somali men was in vulnerabilities related
to the occupation of taxi driving.

The Sampling Context: Recent Arab Migration to the United States and Chicago's Arab American Communities

Between 1965 and 2000, more than 630,000 persons immigrated to the
United States from the Arab world; most were Arabs, but some were
Assyrian, Armenian, Chaldean, or Kurdish.[21] Six Arab countries—
Lebanon, Jordan, Egypt, Iraq, Syria, and Yemen—and Palestine accounted
for 81 percent of these immigrants (see table 1.5). Except for Egypt, these
are the same places from which Arab immigrants came to the United States
one hundred years ago. The remaining 19 percent came from a wide range
of Arab countries, including the Sudan, Morocco, Libya, Bahrain, Oman,
Tunisia, Algeria, Kuwait, and Saudi Arabia; much smaller numbers came
from other Arab countries. Mirroring the Arab migration pattern of one
hundred years ago, Lebanese were the largest Arab immigrant group in
the post-1965 period, although Illinois is exceptional in this regard because
it is one of only a few states in which persons of Lebanese and Syrian
descent are outnumbered by other Arabs, notably Palestinians, Jordanians,
and Iraqis (U.S. Bureau of the Census 2000). Table 1.5 provides immigration numbers and percentages for the major Arab immigrant groups
over the thirty-five-year period since 1965. The problem of counting
Palestinians affects this big picture; if they could be accurately counted,
their numbers in table 1.5 would surely surpass those for Egyptians.

Table 1.5   Major Arab Immigrant Groups to the United States by Country of Birth, 1965 to 2000

Country of Birth	Number of Immigrants	Percentage of Major Arab Immigrant Groups
Lebanon	122,291	24
Egypt	114,812	22
Jordan and Palestine[a]	113,117	22
Iraq	87,499	17
Syria	62,610	12
Yemen	9,959	2
Total	510,288	100

Source: U.S. Immigration and Naturalization Service, country of birth data, 1965 to 2000.

[a]Jordan and Palestine are combined here for a number of reasons, the most important being that some 80 percent of Jordanians migrating to the United States are Palestinians. Other reasons have to do with passports and complications with regard to how Palestinians are counted. See Cainkar (1988) for a more detailed explanation.

The 2000 census counted about 1.2 million persons of Arab ancestry in the United States; the research and polling firm Zogby International estimates that the real number is closer to 3 million. According to 2000 census data for the United States as a whole, persons of Arab ancestry had higher levels of education than the overall American population. The proportion of persons of Arab ancestry age twenty-five or over with at least a high school diploma was 84 percent, as compared to 80 percent of the total U.S. population. The proportion of Arab Americans with at least a bachelor's degree was also higher than that of the total population (41 percent compared with 24 percent), and this was true for each individual Arab group. Some 42 percent of employed persons of Arab ancestry age sixteen or older worked in management, professional, and related occupations (compared with 34 percent of the total population), and another 30 percent worked in sales and office occupations (compared with 27 percent of the total population).

During the period 1965 to 1999, 44,633 immigrants from Arab countries declared to the Immigration and Naturalization Service (INS) that Illinois was their place of intended residence. Eighty-five percent of these immigrants were from the major countries of Arab migration listed in table 1.5, including 15 percent of all combined Palestinian/Jordanian immigrants and 13 percent of all persons born in Iraq. Of those intending to reside in Illinois, 33 percent were Palestinian or Jordanian, and 25 percent were Iraqi, most of whom were Assyrian (see table 1.6).[22] During some years, 20 percent of all Palestinian/Jordanian immigrants to the United States and 25 percent of all Iraqis chose Illinois as their initial location.

Table 1.6   Cumulative Patterns for Arab Immigrants Intending to Settle in Illinois, 1972 to 1999

Country of Birth	Number of Immigrants to Illinois	Percentage of Group to Illinois	Group as Percentage of Main Arab Immigrants to Illinois	Group as Percentage of All Arab Immigrants to Illinois
Jordan and Palestine	14,701	15	39	33
Iraq	11,247	13	30	25
Syria	4,043	6	11	9
Lebanon	3,763	3	10	8
Egypt	3,626	3	10	8
Yemen	737	7	2	2
Total selected countries	38,117	7	100	85
Total all Arab countries	44,633	8		100

Source: U.S. Immigration and Naturalization Service, country of birth data, 1972 to 1999.

Table 1.7 shows that among Arab immigrants declaring their intention to settle in Illinois, Palestinians and Jordanians were the principal group throughout the entire post-1965 period, although in the early 1980s and, to a lesser degree, the mid-1990s they were followed relatively closely by Iraqis (including Assyrians, Arabs, and Kurds). During other periods, however, Palestinians/Jordanians stood alone in their dominance, accounting for some 39 to 45 percent of all immigrants from Arab countries intending to settle in Illinois. These figures are even larger when we add the 3 to 4 percent of "Kuwaitis" (largely Palestinians born in Kuwait) to the Palestinian numbers. Table 1.7 also indicates that Arab migration to Illinois has become more diverse since the 1990s: the five main Arab groups fell to 71 percent of all intended immigrants by 2000.

Arab Americans living in Illinois are largely an urban population connected to the greater Chicago economy, with the exception of the historic Lebanese communities in and around Peoria. Eighty-five percent of the persons of Arab ancestry in Illinois counted by the 2000 census lived in the nine-county Chicago primary metropolitan statistical area (PMSA) (Paral 2004). The Arab American Institute's report on persons of Arab ancestry in Illinois (which includes Assyrians from Arab countries), based on the 2000 census, places 72 percent in Chicago-centered Cook County and another 11 percent in bordering Lake and DuPage Counties. Table 1.8 shows that the median household incomes for persons who reported Lebanese, Syrian, or Egyptian ancestry in Illinois were above

Table 1.7   Arab Immigrants Intending to Resettle in Illinois, Selected Years (National Group as a Percentage of All Arab Immigrants Intending to Resettle in Illinois)

Country of Birth	1972	1980	1986	1995	2000
Jordan and Palestine	45%	36%	39%	31%	31%
Iraq	16	35	15	26	16
Egypt	15	10	12	9	6
Lebanon	10	8	11	8	5
Syria	6	6	9	5	10
Kuwait	—	2	3	4	4
Total	97	97	89	83	71

Source: U.S. Immigration and Naturalization Service, country of birth data, 1972, 1980, 1986, 1995, and 2000.

the state median and Iraqi-ancestry households were slightly below, followed by Palestinian, Arab/Arabic (mostly Palestinians), and Jordanian households. Poverty rates were highest among Iraqis, Palestinians, and Jordanians, with levels above the state norm. Palestinians and Jordanians in metropolitan Chicago were largely middle-class, with some very wealthy households and some very poor households. Non-Assyrian Iraqis, on the other hand, tended to be either wealthy professionals who had been in the United States for decades or low-income refugees.

Just how many Arabs live in metropolitan Chicago is a topic of much discussion among scholars, community members, and national organizations. The city of Chicago ranked fourth among "places with the largest Arab population" in the 2000 census, following New York; Dearborn, Michigan; and Los Angeles, with a count of 14,777. The 2000 census counted 40,196 persons of Arab ancestry in Cook and DuPage Counties. Zogby International has estimated that at least 182,000 people from Arabic-speaking countries live in Cook, DuPage, and Lake Counties, including Assyrians, Somalis, and Sudanese, whom the Census Bureau counts separately from Arabs (Arab American Institute Foundation 2003). In 1998 the Advisory Council on Arab Affairs of the Chicago Commission on Human Relations estimated the metropolitan Chicago Arab population at about 150,000, plus about 65,000 Assyrians (see Cainkar 1998). These large discrepancies between official data and community estimates are not new; the true number lies somewhere in between them. As indicated earlier, the problem of numbers in metropolitan Chicago is complicated by the large Palestinian presence.[23]

The problem of Arab American numbers beleaguers scholars—who identify issues of ambiguous categories, sampling error, and fear—as well as community organizers, who need numbers to obtain grants for com-

Table 1.8   Arabs and Assyrians in Illinois: Median Household Income and Poverty Rates

Group	Median Household Income	Percentage of Persons Below Poverty Level
All Arabs	$46,595	15.8
Lebanese	57,656	7.2
Syrians	57,422	9.2
Egyptians	56,944	7.9
Assyrians	49,027	8.3
Iraqi	45,991	19.9
Palestinians	39,804	18.3
"Arab/Arabic"	39,349	20.5
Jordanian	32,703	17.6
All Illinois	46,590	10.7

Source: The 2000 U.S. census, as tabulated by Rob Paral (2004).

munity services. On the U.S. census, Arabs are enumerated as whites, a category that many Arabs say they do not identify with given their experiences (see chapter 3). For community workers, official Arab whiteness has meant that schools, police departments, domestic violence and homeless shelters, and a slew of other agencies have no data to offer them to demonstrate need. Detailed profiles of Arab Americans are based on the census long form, sent to a sample of the U.S. population, and depend on responses to the open-ended ancestry question. These data have the issues associated with smaller populations. Finally, studies have shown that some Arabs in the United States—Palestinians in particular—are uncomfortable with government reporting mechanisms (see chapter 3; Suleiman 1999b; Cainkar 1999). To counteract both undercounting and fear, a large mobilization was undertaken in Arab American communities across the United States for the 2000 census. Community activists encouraged Arab Americans to perform their census duty and assured them that they had nothing to fear. A 2004 request by the Department of Homeland Security (DHS), however, for a Census Bureau report with Arab ancestry data organized by zip code only reaffirmed this fear among Arab Americans (Clemetson 2004). According to the Electronic Privacy Information Center (EPIC), a research center focused on civil liberties,

> The tabulations apparently include information about United States citizens, as well as individuals of Arab descent whose families have lived in the United States for generations. One tabulation (pdf) shows cities with populations of 10,000 or more and with 1,000 or more people who indicated

they are of Arab ancestry. For each city, the tabulation provides total population, population of Arab ancestry, and percent of the total population
which is of Arab ancestry. A second tabulation (zip), more than a thousand
pages long, shows the number of census responses indicating Arab ancestry in certain zip codes throughout the country. The responses indicating
Arab ancestry are subdivided into Egyptian, Iraqi, Jordanian, Lebanese,
Moroccan, Palestinian, Syrian, Arab/Arabic, and Other Arab.

The data-sharing on Arabs between DHS and the Census Bureau was dis-
closed by a Freedom of Information Act (FOIA) request submitted by the
EPIC.[24] According to documents it received from that request, EPIC reports
on the government's communications regarding this matter as follows:

> The heavily redacted documents show that in April 2004, a Census
> Bureau analyst e-mailed a Department of Homeland Security official and
> said, "You got a file of Arab ancestry information by ZIP Code Tabulation
> Area from me last December (2003). My superiors are now asking ques-
> tions about the usage of that data, given the sensitivity of different data
> requests we have received about the Arab population."

A DHS Customs and Border Protection (CBP) official sent an explanation the same day:

> At U.S. International airports, U.S. Customs posts signage informing var-
> ious nationalities of the U.S. Customs regulations to report currency
> brought into the U.S. upon entry. . . . My reason for asking for U.S. demo-
> graphic data is to aid the Outbound Passenger Program Officer in iden-
> tifying which language of signage, based on U.S. ethnic nationality
> population, would be best to post at the major International airports.

The Decennial Census Advisory Committee called these actions by
the Census Bureau and Homeland Security "the modern day equivalent
of the pinpointing of Japanese-American communities when internment
camps were opened during World War II" (Lipton 2004). The Census
Bureau subsequently revised its policy on sharing statistical information about "sensitive populations" with law enforcement or intelligence
agencies, as did the CBP regarding sensitive requests. The problem of
census data and counting Arab Americans will probably continue into
the future because of these actions.

The Social Context of the Study Interviews

At the time when the interviews were conducted for this study, between
early 2003 and late 2004, a significant segment of Arabs and Muslims in
the United States perceived that their social, political, and civil rights situation was unstable. This sentiment was discussed in meetings and con-

ferences attended by the author and in newspaper articles, magazines, newsletters, and blogs and on websites; it was the topic of casual conversation among members of these communities, and it comes through strongly in the data from this study. During this period, Arab and Muslim males who had entered the United States on a visitor's visa were being subjected to special registration, and many thousands whose immigration papers were out of order faced voluntary departure or deportation. Arab and Muslim Americans reported being visited at home and at work by FBI agents who "just wanted to talk," in the process stigmatizing them in the face of their neighbors and coworkers. Topics of daily conversation included reports of searches of homes and businesses that seemed to lack probable cause and arrests that appeared to lack legitimate charges. The cases of the L.A. Eight and of Mohammed Salah, a resident of Chicago's southwest suburbs, which had been pending from the late 1980s and the mid-1990s, respectively, were resurrected for prosecution by the federal government. James Yee, a Muslim military chaplain at the Guantánamo Bay detention center, had been falsely imprisoned as a spy. Six Muslim charities were shut down on allegations of terrorist support in the context of legislation that permitted the government to press charges against charitable donors whether or not they were aware of any alleged wrongdoing by the charity. The USA PATRIOT Act, a series of intelligence provisions that Arab and Muslim Americans felt were intended to target them, was passed by Congress. The FBI announced that it was focusing its intelligence work on mosques, and it was revealed that the Department of Homeland Security had requested the zip code list of areas of Arab concentration from Census Bureau staff. It seemed to many Arabs and Muslims at the time that simply being Arab or Muslim was enough to legitimate government actions against them that they believed ran counter to democratic practice. And then there was Guantánamo Bay, which loomed in the background as a potential nightmare world with its hundreds of orange-suited prisoners living incommunicado in wire cages.

These were tough times, compounded by media treatment that Arabs and Muslims found largely derogatory. There were also reports of job discrimination, removal from airplanes, delays in immigration processing, and sporadic hate crimes and harassment. Chapters 4 through 7 reconstruct this general climate based on interview data. Although this book is my best effort to create a readable narrative of that period as seen through the eyes of Arab Muslim Americans, I believe that no amount of writing can ever fully reconstruct the flavor of those times for Arabs and Muslims in the United States. We can look back at the period now and breathe a sigh of relief; we can be thankful that the worst fears of Arab and Muslim Americans were not realized. We can focus on the positive gains for Arabs and Muslims in American society, despite continued voices of intolerance, and on the generally better social and economic status they enjoy compared to most Arabs and Muslims living in many European countries. But we have once again learned an old lesson: that social constructions applied to entire groups of people can be extremely damaging to them, especially when a government uses such ideas to guide its policies.

I wish to express my deepest gratitude to every single person who allowed me to interview him or her during this period. Most of the interviewees did not know me; I respect the bravery it took to talk with me, and I remain extremely thankful for the trust in me that inspired it. This book is written from the analytic perspective of a sociologist who has spent her career as a scholar of Arab American and Muslim American communities and as an ethnographic researcher in these communities. My perspective is informed by the body of findings of other scholars as well as by my own prior work. My attempts to distance myself from the poignant findings of this study and from the emotional impacts of this period of history are sometimes unsuccessful. I am no less a scholar because I am also human.

Chapter 2

Little Is Monolithic:
Five Oral Histories

T HE FOLLOWING oral histories take readers in-depth into the lives of eight Arab American Muslims: four members of an Arab American family and four individuals, two of them men and two of them women. Three of the interviewees were born in the United States, one immigrated as a young child, and the rest were adult immigrants. Their roots are Egyptian, Palestinian, Iraqi, and Yemeni, and they were selected to represent some of the diversity of national origins among Arab Americans in metropolitan Chicago. Corresponding to the residential patterns associated with these identities, two of them live in Chicago's southwest suburbs, two live on the city's north side, and the Egyptian family lives in the northwest suburbs. All of them are Muslims by birth, and in their different ways each understands and practices his or her faith. I selected these interviewees not because they were Arab American superstars or notable victims, but rather for their capacity to represent the mundane humanity of everyday life. While the study data presented in the rest of this book speak from the analysis of a representative sample, the aim of this less representative chapter is to compensate for the truncated perspective that emerges when data are analyzed and sorted by variables and whole persons cease to be seen or heard.

These interviews were conducted during the summer of 2008. Unlike the interviews conducted with the 2002 to 2004 sample, they were done without a protocol of questions, their focus was much larger than the immediate post-9/11 historical period, and they were driven in sequencing and topic largely by the interviewee. Interviewees spoke about their own life histories, their joys and challenges, and the issues and experiences that were personally relevant in the summer of 2008. Readers will note that the post-9/11 era was still quite alive to these Arab American Muslims, both as memory and as present-day lived experience. These interviews will introduce readers who do not know any Arab or Muslim

Americans personally to a few new people. They will show that unlike the charges of those who tell us to be suspicious and watchful and the claims of those who promote intolerance and hatred—in their insistence that Arabs and Muslims think and act alike and march to the beat of inherent proclivities, feverish emotions, and religious mandates—herein lies the humanity that we all share.

The Kulthum Family

Samir and Nora Kulthum live in a large, well-appointed home in a somewhat secluded northwest suburban subdivision. A number of Egyptian families live in the area, some of whom are Nora's brothers and sisters and their families. On the day of my visit, Samir and Nora were heading to a picnic at the nearby mosque and community center purchased through donations from Egyptians living in Chicago's northwest suburbs. Samir and Nora have two sons and two daughters, all born in the United States and all now married and building their own families.

Samir and Nora emigrated from Egypt to the United States in 1973, shortly after their marriage. Samir, who completed a bachelor's degree in engineering at an Egyptian university, says that they migrated to the United States for a new life. At that time, recalls Samir, "Egypt was comfortable." There was no political repression, and life was economically manageable. They were not dying to come to the United States and had not given a lot of thought to how life would be different for them. According to Nora, they migrated to be near her family, most of whom had been living in the United States since 1969, when her father left Egypt because he did not want to participate in the corruption and bribery that were a part of his job. Most of Nora's family stayed in the United States; her mother returned to Cairo after her husband's death. Now almost everyone in Nora's family lives in the Chicago area, and only her mother and sister remain in Egypt.

Upon migration, Samir found work within three weeks at an engineering firm where his brother who preceded him also worked and where he has worked ever since. Nora spent her time homemaking, raising their four children, and doing volunteer work. The children went to public schools and on Saturdays attended Islamic religion and Arabic classes, which changed locations during their tenure from libraries or rooms at public schools to the Islamic College on Irving Park Road in Chicago.

Thinking panoramically about their lives in the United States, Nora says that family and friends are what has made it good:

> To me, the relationship between family and friends is the bond that holds us to the U.S. I was young when I left Egypt, twenty-one years old. Being near family and friends is the most significant aspect of life in the U.S.

Samir feels that they have been blessed in the United States; except for the deaths of his father and brother, his recollections are all positive:

> We feel that living in the States is an advantage from the point of freedom. People have the freedom to practice their faith. The big event in our life is that we raised our children. We had a long trip; it was not easy. But with the grace of God, our kids are safe. They are all educated. They graduated from college, got married, have kids. My life in the U.S. has been blessed. Even my mother was here with us for a while. I lost my father in 1977. I have two sisters in Egypt. My brother passed away in Egypt.

Their daughter Samia relates a more difficult experience growing up in the United States. Born in northwest suburban Chicago, Samia describes being one of the few "minority children" in her elementary school, along with a few Indians and African Americans.

> It was not a very good experience. Kids teased us. For me, there was a separation between school and after-school. I had a lot of cousins here. That is what saved me. It was two totally different experiences. If I had to deal with school alone, I'd be in a worse state. [*What was the source of discrimination at school?*] The source of discrimination at school was race, not religion, even though technically we are not a minority. Also, I was an overweight child, and that was part of it. Although I would dread the day someone would see my mom at Jewel. They would say, "We saw your mom, and she wears a turban," and make fun of me.
>   I didn't start covering until the middle of sixth grade. I don't know why I did it. I just did it. That's when things got a little better. And seventh grade was a lot better than elementary school.

Samia's family moved to Asia for four years for her father's work. The new social context in which she experienced eighth grade through junior year changed her life. The narrow perspectives and racial prejudices of kids in the Chicago suburbs were replaced by a more global community of young students with broader worldviews, and with that came an acceptance of herself.

> It was totally different. I was in an international school. Kids were much more open-minded. I had been intimidated by white people. But in this country, all the foreigners hung out together. The white kids who would have never been my friends in Chicago were my friends there. It opened our minds and gave us a global perspective.

Samia returned to the United States for her senior year of high school, which, thankfully, passed quickly enough.

> I came back, and I did not know anyone. I did not have a driver's license. I was the senior on the bus. It was tough. I made some friends, Muslim

and Indian. It went fast. And then I moved on to college, which was a completely different experience. It was great.

Samia found peace with her identity while attending the University of Illinois at Chicago (UIC).

That's when you finally grow into wanting to be a Muslim. That's where I met all my Muslim friends, when I first became good friends with non-Arabs. College was what defined me. That's where I asserted my Muslim identity more. I shed some of my Egyptianness. You go through phases, and I went through all of them. I found myself. It was good. But it was tough for my parents.

Samia became active with the Muslim Student Association (MSA), and a whole new life emerged for her, with friends, after-school meetings, parties, and travel connected to the MSA. Life became "dichotomous" between school and home. While her mother never stopped her from these activities, she worried about Samia staying out late, driving alone after midnight, being alone in hotel rooms. According to Nora, "She traveled with the MSA. I did not agree, but she went anyway. I would not give her a ride to the airport or pick her up. . . . She was an adult. I was just worried about her." Her father was more lenient. "I felt, she is responsible," says Samir. "Why not? We trust her." Nora adds, to show she was not opposed to Samia's work with the MSA, "To work with Muslims, I was never against it. I used to cook for the MSA. I was just worried about her traveling alone."

Samia graduated from college, found a job at the same university, and then started her master's degree. She is still contemplating what she plans to do in the future, whether she will work in her field or continue on to a PhD. Meanwhile, two years ago she married Hassan, a man from Egypt who had been living in North Carolina and was related to her sister-in-law. Her parents chuckle that they passed on responsibility to him and that he too lets her go to meetings alone. Samia says that she "went through a few fixed-up situations" in the search for a spouse, and they did not go well. She decided that she wanted a good person, a requirement that, along with religious faith, was more important to her than social standing. And then there was not smoking.

According to her husband Hassan:

It started four years ago. A relative told Samia about me, and when they told her I smoked, she said, "No." [Samia interjects, "I did not want someone who smokes."] One year later I quit smoking, and they told her about me again. When Samia replied, "He smokes," they said, "No, he quit."

Now a nonsmoker, Hassan finally met Samia, and the chemistry worked well. Eventually they got engaged and then married. Although he loved North Carolina, Hassan, who has a degree in accounting, moved to the Chicago area because Samia had a stable job and was in graduate school. Hassan immediately found a job working with Samia's uncle. But his ongoing search for a new job has been hampered by discrimination:

> I am looking for a job, but when they see my name on a résumé, there is no response. When I call and check the status of my application and they ask for my name, they say, "We have no openings right now." I saw one of those jobs advertised in the paper again, and I called. After I gave them my name, they repeated that they had no openings. I went to [another company], and I was told that they had immediate openings and if I had no criminal or driving record I would 100 percent be hired. But no one called.

Samia interjects that Hassan is a pacifist. He never complains about bad treatment. "If we get bad service at a restaurant, he won't say anything." Samia reports that she gets better service in restaurants since she got married, now that she is accompanied by Hassan, while Hassan says his service experience has deteriorated since marriage. "I never got the 'service with a smile,'" says Samia, inferring that her hijab brought on reduced customer service—a common complaint of women who wear hijab. Hassan says that it is because they are recognized as Muslims, but in Samia's view, "I don't think it is because we are Muslims, I think it is because we are different."

But experiences of difference occur over and over. For example, when she takes the Metra train to the Loop, Samia says that she is the last person other passengers will sit next to. "Only if the train is packed will someone sit next to me. And when someone does, it is usually an Indian. You get over it after a while. These are the kind of things you get used to."

Recently, however, Samia and Hassan had what they consider "one of our worst experiences since 9/11" while bowling in a northwest suburb:

> There was a country music song playing. The lyrics were about the USA, red, white, and blue, the flag. There was a part that went something like "If they don't like it, we're going to shove them with our boots." When they came to that part of the song, they blasted that little section, almost blew the bowling alley speakers out, and then they cut the lights out on our lanes. We were only on the fifth frame. When we went up to the desk, they would not let us play more games. Actually, the guy was not nice from the beginning. He said they don't take credit cards under seven dollars, and we said we'd spend more than seven dollars, and he said sorry. We left with our tail between our legs. My coworkers said we should do something about it. Call a lawyer. One of my white coworkers apologized for the incident. It was so immature.

Samia was particularly surprised by this experience because it occurred in a suburb that was heavily Latino; she had thought that neighborhoods characterized by diversity brought a kind of safety from these types of experiences.

> It is the media. It is the effect of the media on other people. There is always a negative association with Islam on the news. That is what has affected our life the most. Imagine you're somewhere where there is a television, and they are all over the place, and something comes up about Islam, and then all the eyes are on you. You feel so exposed. We went to see *Syrianna*. It's a good movie. But when it opened with the *adhan* [call to prayer], I sunk in my seat. Oh, Lord.

What is this feeling Samia and Hassan are describing? Is it fear? Samia responds:

> It's not really fear. I mean, I don't think someone will do something to us. It is more that someone will say something. It's a vulnerability. You know what is behind the look. When people leave the theater and you are among them and they might be angry.

Samia was at UIC when 9/11 occurred. She says that the university body was very diverse and that "people reached out to us." Samir, Nora, Samia, and Hassan all agree that things are not worse now than they were right after the 9/11 attacks, but they also feel that they are not getting better. Samir thinks that the events of 9/11 and their aftermath brought a positive dialogue about Islam into play. But then he mentions a number of specific efforts across the country to halt this dialogue and to prevent students from reading about Islam.

Nora and Samir's positive memories of three decades of life in the United States are punctuated by 9/11. After that day, Nora and Samir agree, "everything changed." Although they say they have not personally experienced any problems, they have not been subject to any harassment, and their neighbors are nice, the negativity surrounding Islam in the American media has changed their American experience. Nora says:

> The big event that happened, 9/11, changed things. Everything changed in our lives here. We never really had any problems, but through the media. The media are against Muslims. They only show Muslims as terrorists. I cannot believe Muslims did 9/11. No way. I wear a scarf, and I get up at night to pray, and I know that to kill innocent people you go straight to hell. A good Muslim . . . no way would do this.

Samir interjects:

> We were not subject to harassment. Here in the States, it is the best. Even with the racism, when you compare it to the Middle East, you can practice your faith the way you want. I am not a bearded guy, but if I was, I

would be subject to many checks in Egypt. In the U.S., we are more free. But the media pushes this idea of Islamic terrorism. They are very biased. Look at how they talk about Barack Obama. That he is a Muslim. It is like tainting him with something so bad!

Samir and Nora proceed to explain the psychological effects of the negative portrayals of Muslims and Islam in the American media. According to Samir,

It affects us psychologically. We are not comfortable. It's like if something is done by a black person, and you are black . . . the comparison between being black and being Muslim. We feel that if anything bad happens overseas, in the U.S., in England, we are going to be treated badly. You get scared to be a Muslim. People treat you bad, look at you bad. We are scared for our safety. I get scared that if something happens they will come attack us here in our home. We all know what happened to the Japanese in World War II. They were Americans. But they put them in camps.

Nora is more explicit:

My son the doctor sometimes says, teasing, "I am going to be the doctor in the concentration camp." We are scared from that. This is the only thing that really scares me.

Samir adds:

I always tell my kids, "This is your country. I was not born here. I feel this is my country, but you were born here. Your parents are from a different culture. But this is your country. You have to fight for your rights like any American." Sometimes they say they are Egyptian, and I say, "No, you are an American." They have to fight for their rights like any other American.

I ask if any of them would like to live in Egypt. Samia, who was born in the United States and feels that "here is home for me," says that she would like to. Recalling her very positive experience in Asia, she would like to provide her children (if she is blessed with them) with a similar international experience, although she grants that Egypt may not be the place. Samia's husband Hassan says he would love to go back to Egypt but cannot do so as long as so many people are suffering under the weight of poverty. He says he cannot bear to see the sharp cleavages between rich and poor, a sensitivity no doubt influenced by having spent the first two-thirds of his life in an Arab Gulf country where there was little poverty (his father was a teacher). The Egyptian middle class is disappearing, they all agree. Samir says he would not go back except for a month or two.

> I would be like a stranger. I came here when I was twenty-four years old.
> Here is where I know. My kids were all born here, raised here, got mar-
> ried and had kids here. It's too late. Maybe thirty years ago. Not now.

Nora says that they thought about it a few years ago. When she visits her
mother in Egypt, she loves it. But then she realized that she could not
leave her children and grandchildren, as her mother did. "Maybe I will
visit, but not to move. I have lived here more than I have lived in Egypt.
You can love both." Nora and Samia observe: "People buy land in
Egypt, some buy houses, but they never go back."

As the discussion winds down to undirected conversation, there is
talk of the delays in immigration processing and the severe treatment at
airports experienced by so many Arabs and Muslims. With regard to
immigration paperwork, the group speaks of days becoming months
and months becoming years. Airport stories turn to one about a two-
month-old baby being held up because his name was on a terrorist list,
or about not being allowed to participate in early check-in or to preprint
a boarding pass. Samia says that she has never faced any problems at the
airport, despite her Islamic dress. But she notes that others singled out
for inspection have looked at her as if to say, "Why me? Why not you?"

The group concludes that 9/11 gave people who want to hate a
license to do so, but that not everybody is like that. Samia speaks of
her unremitting efforts to distance herself from stereotypes and to assert
her Americanness. "My opinions are always assumed to be a Muslim
opinion. Islam does not dictate everything in my life. I battle that on
an everyday basis." She ends by relating a recent experience at a large
grocery store in the northwest suburbs:

> A lady said to me, "How do you like it here?" I said, "Here in [name of
> suburb]?" And she said, "No, in America." I told her I was born in Park
> Ridge. Obviously, it is the hijab. It's an added thing. At some point you get
> sick of it. I reach my tolerance level, then it goes back down again. This is
> not a feeling of vulnerability. It's a feeling of not-fairness that I have to deal
> with this on a regular basis. I always have to assert my Americanness.

Hala Darwish

Hala Darwish was born in Chicago in the mid-1960s. Her parents had
immigrated to the United States from Palestine in the early 1950s. Her
father, Mahmoud, came first, by boat; his point of debarkation was New
York City, where relatives already living in the United States received
him. Mahmoud, who was about eighteen at the time, was quickly given
housing and set up as a linen peddler—an occupation somewhat common among Levantine Arab immigrants linked by networks to New
York wholesalers—and started night classes to learn English. After a few

years, he returned to Palestine to bring his wife, Hanaan, to live with him. Accompanied by Mahmoud's brother and his wife, Mahmoud and Hanaan moved to the south side of Chicago, where Mahmoud continued to work as a linen peddler. A few years later, both families moved to the north side of the city. Mahmoud eventually bought a linen store in the Chicago Loop, which he ran for ten years.

Mahmoud and Hanaan bore five children in Chicago. When the kids were still young, Mahmoud and Hanaan decided to move the family back to Palestine so the children could be raised in their preferred cultural environment; Hanaan would stay in Palestine with the children while Mahmoud continued to work in the United States. They sold everything they owned and moved back—in the post-1948 terminology—to their West Bank village. This arrangement lasted only a year because, according to Hala, Mahmoud missed his wife and children terribly. From then on, they returned to Palestine for visits only.

Hala lives in a modest, two-bedroom northwest side apartment with her second husband and their baby daughter. Although their neighborhood has some Arab American families, and her eight-unit building is owned by a relative, most of her neighbors are of European-white backgrounds; Hala has lived in this type of social context for most of her life. Looking back, she describes a very challenging childhood and young adulthood. There was not a large Arab American community in Chicago at the time, and certainly not on the north side of the city, where her parents chose to live. The children grew up largely isolated from other Arab American kids, except their cousins. According to Hala, the kids at school made it clear to them that they were different.

> I always looked different, I stood out; my hair was different. I was never in an in-crowd. I was overweight. I was called "camel jockey" a lot. It took people a while to catch up to me because I am fair-skinned, but once they saw the name, and we all went to the same school, then they all kind of knew. Then the racial jokes set in.

Hala went to three different high schools, not because the family moved but because her teenage years were filled with mischief and social difficulties. In public schools she got into trouble or ran with the "wrong kids." During her first run through a majority-white Catholic girls' high school, the teasing stopped, but she felt out of place during prayer, as well as socially excluded. She describes that feeling as a racial exclusion that a Latina at the same school also experienced. Hala sums up her high school years as a time when she was looking for attention and never fit in. "I never felt like I belonged anywhere. I was this lost soul."

Hala concedes that her experience might have been better if she had had Arab American friends. When she was sixteen, she started meeting other Arabs through her sister (who was attending a local college) at the southwest side Arab American Community Center (the *merkez*). She says that she also felt out of place there because most of the adult Arabs were immigrants who viewed her as culturally American. It was at the center that she met the man she secretly dated for seven years—not telling her parents—and who later became her first husband. He was from a refugee camp and conferred upon her the authenticity she had wanted. The marriage lasted five years. Looking back, Hala says she never really loved him. She found him attractive because he was a modern guy and she wanted freedom. His family was never crazy about her, she believes, because she was too American and knew too little about the Palestinian cause. Hala's father had one rule, says Hala, which was that you had to get your college education. Once you did this, you could choose your own career and marry who you wanted. During her marriage, Hala finished her bachelor's degree in nursing. After her divorce, she lived alone for ten years.

> There was not a day in those ten years my parents didn't fight with me about living alone. First of all, I got divorced without telling them. They found out accidentally. I pretty much wasted ten years of my life. I worked very hard and played a lot. The last two years of that period my mother got sick and that became my whole life.

Hala married for a second time five years ago. She met her husband, Yacoub, a Palestinian born in Amman, through informal matchmaking networks in the Arab American community. Yacoub's parents were visiting Chicago and put out the word that their son was looking for a wife; Hala's mother was informed by others who knew she wanted a husband for her daughter. Hala says she agreed to meet Yacoub because her mother was sick and she wanted to make her happy. When she first met him, she thought that he was not her type, but they were talking about religion, and he said it was not right the way parents force their kids to do things.

> Everything was *'ayb* (shameful) or *haraam* (forbidden) when I grew up. Because he said he did not agree with that, I gave him a second look. I started to talk to him, and I fell in love with him. I had been away from Arabs for so long. I married him within a month. Within two months, we applied for his legal papers, and my parents did not know about it. I married him in November, and in January my father found out.

Hala married Yacoub because she fell in love with him. Her father had been checking on his background and his family, but that process was not moving forward very quickly or smoothly. She did not want to wait. "I was living at home, and I told them I was working nights. I would then be able to spend time with my husband." When her father learned of their marriage, he made them wait eight months to publicly celebrate it. Although Yacoub has degrees in engineering and business, he spends fourteen hours a day, seven days a week, working in the grocery store they own on the west side of the city in "a crime- and drug-infested area." Hala says that Yacoub is "a hard worker. He'll work eighteen hours a day if he has to."

The birth of Hala and Yacoub's daughter in 2007 brought about a number of significant changes in their lives. Yacoub closes the store early on Sunday, working only eleven hours that day. Hala has stopped working outside the home, both at the store and as a nurse. During her pregnancy, Hala underwent a life-altering event. When she was five months pregnant, she started bleeding and had to be taken to the emergency room.

> At that point I was praying, but I wasn't covering. I had started praying during my mom's illness. That was very, very hard for me. I was sitting in the emergency room, and I asked God to please let me have this child. I said, "God, if you let me have a healthy child, I promise I will cover my head." I started wearing hijab from the day I had her. It has been a year and three months. I have been spit on, sworn at; some nasty guy came up to me [she acts out a person drawing up a large spit], spit at me, and said, "To you and Mohammed," like he knows who Mohammed is. This happened at Jewel, near here. I have always been tough. Since I started wearing hijab, people look at me like I am weak, including some Arab men. It has changed me so much. People look at me like I'm a weak dummy. When my mother stared wearing hijab, I remember I was embarrassed to stand next to her.

Hala says that the first year she wore hijab she was very angry.

> It was hard for me. I like my hair; I like makeup. I was angry. I felt trapped. I would say to myself, "You told God you would wear hijab if you had a healthy baby; you can take it off now." But then I thought maybe something will happen to my baby. "So I can't take it off because you gave me her." But something happened after the first year, something inside of me. I realized this is not what wearing hijab is about. Do it from your heart or don't do it. When I first put it on, I wondered how I was going to face anyone. It was very, very, very hard. I still cannot believe it sometimes.

Hala says daily life is hard. She has worked as a nurse, worked in the store, and now raises their daughter. "This job is the hardest of the three." She is tired all the time. She can't wait for her husband to come home. After he gets off work, he goes to a gym to work out. "I am okay with that because I know what it is like to be in a store. He needs to let the pressure out." The only time she has with him is from ten-thirty until eleven-thirty or twelve at night, with a few extra hours on Sunday.

His work is long hours; it is not safe, the store has been broken into. I cannot wait for him to get out of it. I worry that one day he'll go off. Recently he did, and the guy came back with a brick, put it through our door, and then five minutes later through our car window. What I learned, because I worked in these stores for five years with him, if you respect people and you don't mess with them, they'll respect you back. If you treat them badly, they'll give you the same thing. Arabs are murdered all the time in these stores.

I ask Hala about whether the 9/11 attacks and their aftermath affected her life. She remembers exactly where she was when it happened—in a patient's room.

I was shocked. I could not believe it. Then I started getting comments from coworkers about Arabs. People at work knew I was an Arab because I translated a lot. They would argue with me. I told them no one does such a thing in the name of Allah [God]. That's not right. Allah does not tell us to take a life. I remember riding to work and listening to us being torn apart on the radio, even on black radio stations. I was shocked, after what they have been through. I am very sorry for anyone who died. I have had death and dying around me all my life, as a nurse. But I could not understand why they could not see that people all around the world have experienced such violence repeatedly. It should not have to happen to anybody.

Hala says that because of her light features, before she wore hijab few strangers actually knew she was an Arab, so it was largely in the workplace where she faced problems.

Frankly, the major effect on my life came when I started wearing hijab. Before that, no one really knew where I was from, who I was. All of my relatives who wear hijab face abuse. I have been called a bitch and a whore since I began wearing hijab. My husband works on the west side. He does not have problems. He prays right in the store. In the black community they all understand and accept this.

Looking toward the future, Hala says that she is not sure she is going to stay in the United States. She would not wish her life on her daughter.

I don't think I want to stay here, because I had a terrible time growing up. My life is for my daughter now. She is why I stopped working. I want to protect her. I don't want her to go through what I went through. Maybe I will have to leave here. I don't want my daughter to experience what I do.

Layla

Layla, a Palestinian American attorney with her own law firm in the southwest suburbs of Chicago, was born on Chicago's south side, in the Hyde Park neighborhood. Along with other vanguard Palestinians (mostly young men) from the Jerusalem-Ramallah area, Layla's great-grandfather had immigrated to Chicago in the 1920s, earned a living in sales, and became an American citizen, returning to Palestine for his late years. Her great-uncle owned and ran a clothing store in Hyde Park from the 1940s through the 1960s. Layla's father emigrated from Palestine with his brother in 1954 and went directly to Chicago. In 1965 he returned to Palestine to marry and brought his wife back with him. Most of Layla's relatives—and there are many—emigrated from Palestine to Chicago; the men worked in the steel industry, manufacturing, and men's clothing, and many started as peddlers. She adds that quite a few of them served in the U.S. armed forces during the Korean and Vietnam Wars. Layla's father took a different occupational path. He had tried peddling door to door and did not like it. Instead, he took a job plating food at a well-known Chicago Loop restaurant while he completed high school. By the time he retired forty-three years later, he had become the executive chef of a renowned Chicago German restaurant.

In 1968 Layla's family left Hyde Park and moved to the predominantly Lithuanian southwest side neighborhood of Marquette Park, where there was a handful of other Arab American families. North of the park near Sixty-third Street was a growing Arab American enclave, populated mostly by Palestinians. Layla's family stayed for ten years in the Marquette Park area. Racial tension and riots, according to Layla, made the family's last years there contentious and difficult.

> I don't remember getting picked on. I don't recall any problems until the bussing started. Emotions were heightened. We Arab Americans were in the middle. Some of us looked white, some of us were olive-skinned, dark. There is one incident that sticks out in my mind that I will never forget. My sister and I were walking home from school with my cousins. My darker-skinned cousins were attacked, but not us. [*By whites or blacks?*] By blacks. It ended up being white versus black and black versus Arab. There always needs to be someone at the bottom, and we were it. I understood that I did not get beaten up because I was white and that my cousins got beat up because they were dark.

In 1978 Layla's family moved to the southwest suburb of Chicago Ridge, where they were the only Arab American family. She says that at first she was terrified because at least in Marquette Park there were other Arab families. She remembers that a girl who was popular at the school came to their home the day before school began to welcome them. When school started, she introduced them to other students. "We never had any racial issues there, and we did not change our names." At this time, her difference as an Arab and Muslim was also protective.

What helped me in high school was that my religion and my background were a shield against peer pressure. I could not go to parties or dances. We were not allowed after-school and weekend socializing. We were not outcast because kids said, well, they are Arab and Muslim, and they can't do it. Today it seems like the pressure is on everyone, the assimilation pressure. It protected us, but may not do so anymore.

Layla's aunt and her family moved to the suburbs within a couple of years, and over time many other Arab American families did the same, eventually rendering the Arab American presence in the southwest suburbs larger than that of the southwest side. Today all of Layla's immediate family and their children, along with thousands of other Arab Americans (still predominantly Palestinian), live in the southwest suburbs.

Layla finished her bachelor's degree at the University of Illinois at Chicago, which she describes as a "hidden gem" because of its scholastic quality, accessibility from all parts of the city, and diversity. "The Arab students had organizations, as did all the other groups, and everybody got along and had equal access to resources." She then entered DePaul Law School, which is where she first experienced the feeling of being treated as an outsider. A wave of anti-Arab sentiment accompanied U.S. government involvement in the first Gulf War, following the Iraqi invasion of Kuwait in 1990, and she was caught up in it, as was her family, who experienced phone threats.

It was around the time of the first Gulf War. There was nothing flagrant, just a different demeanor compared to my first year of law school. Conversation was more strained. I remember thinking I had gone through my entire life without feeling I was different. I always felt I was an Arab and an American, a meld of both cultures. I never felt like an outsider. And here I am at law school, learning about equality and justice, and I am getting these under-the-surface vibes. It was just a few people, not all of them. I also had some good experiences there. One woman came to me and said she had never in her life met or known a Palestinian or a Muslim, and she said she wanted to have lunch with me and pick my brain. I welcomed the opportunity. Overall, I had a good experience at law school. But during the Gulf War, that happened. And then at home we had hundreds of threats. They were going to bomb our house. They were going to set it on fire. They were going to kidnap the kids. We made police reports, and ultimately the FBI got involved. They determined three different people were responsible for the threats. They must have found our name in the phonebook. So we unlisted our number and haven't had any problems since.

During law school Layla clerked at a boutique Loop law firm specializing in business transactions and corporate litigation. The firm was predominantly Jewish, and she recalls that one of the hiring partners asked her during the interview whether she was sure she would be comfortable there since her résumé showed her as an Arab American activist. Her response was, "Of course." Layla is a strong believer that people getting to know each other is what breaks down barriers. She credits her parents with teaching her some important lessons in life about human relationships.

> My father and my mother had similar experiences with Jewish colleagues and Jewish friends, both in the United States and in Palestine. They always taught us not to label people, not to judge people based on stereo-types. It is one thing to be preached at and another to live it, as they did.

Over the years of her clerkship, Layla spoke with her colleagues about politics, and they debated "honestly, frankly, and respectfully." Upon her graduation from law school, the firm hired her as an associate. Some years later, Layla started her own law firm, equipped with the business transaction knowledge she had learned on the job. After a few years, she brought on a partner with the litigation skills she needed to balance her own strengths. They had met on opposite sides of a real estate transaction. He was Jewish.

> We speak openly and honestly about anything we want. We don't tiptoe around each other. It is so refreshing. When you know a person's heart and where they come from, you can say anything. If you don't, every-thing is kept bottled up. I think a lot of problems with Arab Americans is a result of that. It's a dual problem. There are Americans who don't know much about Middle East history, and it's a difficult history to follow. As a result, they don't know how to form opinions on those issues, so they follow the stereotypes promoted in the media. But Arab Americans also need to make a conscious effort to be involved in their communities, and I don't mean in the Arab American community, I mean in the communi-ties they live in, whether in Chicago or the suburbs. They need to get to know their neighbors and associate with them.
>
> If Arab Americans prior to 9/11 had made more of an effort to partic-ipate in their communities, things might have been a bit different. But they did what all new immigrants do—they sought each other out. They floated toward each other for safety and survival. Then there are lan-guage barriers if they don't speak English. There are also cultural issues; they think if they adopt American that their culture will be erased for their kids. They seem like selfish reasons, but I understand them.
>
> It seems like after the 1980s Arab immigrants, whether they immi-grated for education or to live here, were less likely to advance them-selves in American culture. What's great about my family and most of the people from my parents' village of origin is that they tried to balance both. Non-Arab friends came to our home, and this was the norm in the 1950s, '60s, and '70s. Today my niece has friends from all communities, but I see she gravitates more towards her own. Many of her friends are Arab Americans, both Christian and Muslim.

Layla is quick to point out that the "isolation" that has characterized Arab American communities is "not all their fault." Especially over the past decade, the mood in the southwest suburbs toward Arabs seems to be quite different from when she was growing up. Layla, engaging the language of "race," notes that wearing hijab is interpreted by "Americans" as a symbol of difference and a state of otherness.

> I was at the community pool last week, and there was a long line, and a family of about fifteen or twenty Arab Americans came. You knew they were Arab Americans because of their features and hijabs. Everyone stared at them. You should have seen the looks they got. I had no problem, but then I don't wear hijab and I blended right in. Orland Park has a huge Arab American community. The mayor there is great. We had a few issues with building the mosque, but the trustees voted the right way. Things are a lot more subtle out there. Along with Arabs, it has some Indians, Pakistanis, and Asians. People blend in because they are the same social class. But when you have easily identifiable features, such as the hijab, something that stands out and identifies you as being of a certain race, it just calls attention from Americans. I think it is not that they have anything against them; they just don't understand them. Why is she wearing that scarf and a long robe and coming to a pool? The realities of coexistence are not addressed.
>
> I grew up in these suburbs. What you notice a lot more today than ten and fifteen years ago is all the Middle Eastern stores, the Arabic handwriting on the signs. The landlords are not inhibiting this growth. I think things come down to one-on-one relationships. The same thing happened when our community tried to buy a church and make it a mosque [referring to a failed effort in the southwest suburbs in 2000]. Despite the number of Arab Americans who lived in Palos Heights, their neighbors voted against the mosque. It seems like, you can live here as long as you blend in with the rest of us, but if there is something that identifies you, it's a stigma, we don't want it here. I think most people are tolerant once they get to know you. But I hate the word "tolerance." That should not be our goal. It should be compassion and understanding. We need to go further.

In 2004 the Orland Park city council held hearings on annexing land to Orland Park that would be the site of a proposed mosque. Layla says that she was "completely dumbfounded" when she read newspaper articles about the controversy that had erupted. Referring to quotes appearing in all of the major local newspapers, she says, "The stereotypes were like those used for African Americans in the '60s."

> There were no issues of permission or zoning, the citizens were just all riled up. People did not want Muslims praying in their neighborhood. When I attended hearings, no substantive issues were raised. It was just a "we don't want these people here" attitude. "They will lower our property values." But the property around the Bridgeview mosque rose in

value after that mosque was built. The village trustees allowed every single person to speak. Approximately 85 percent were against the mosque and 15 percent were for. The seven trustees heard everyone, and I remember thinking that, because of the hatred and fear and impassioned pleas, they would vote with the majority. Instead, they voted unanimously that the mosque should go up because there was no legal reason to prevent it. [*How do you explain this given prior experiences?*] I happen to know the mayor, and he seems to be open-minded. I don't know. Perhaps the trustees anticipated this type of response and felt the proper thing to do was to provide everyone with a chance to speak and then vote based on the law. I don't know what was inside their heads.

Layla is civically active in a number of organizations. She counts as her top civic duty her fourteen years volunteering for St. Jude Children's Research Hospital in Memphis. Although her nephew's four liver transplants at the University of Chicago drove her initial interest, St. Jude's values and Arab American legacy wooed her commitment.

> I picked St. Jude because it is a global hospital; they treat children from all over the world, regardless of race or religion. Also, it was founded by Danny Thomas, an Arab American of Lebanese descent. I loved what it stood for. The bylaws state there shall be no discrimination based on race, nationality, or religion.

Layla is also an active member of the Amman-Chicago Sister Cities program, which she says is important because "it introduces Chicagoans, Americans, to Jordanians and Arab Americans." Volunteers for Sister Cities are ambassadors, and Layla says, "I have always felt in my adult life that I am an unofficial ambassador. I am always asked my opinion on Arab issues, Muslim issues, the Palestinian issue."

Layla derives satisfaction from knowing that her contacts with others have "enhanced understanding." She says that she has "seen transformations among people, their opinions and views. Including among some Jewish American friends." She speaks in detail about being on vacation with a Jewish friend and seeing *Schindler's List* together, after which both were very upset. Layla notes that before seeing the film she had not recognized the similarity between the social status of Jews prior to the Holocaust—the "ghettoization" and "demonization"—and the Palestinians under Israeli occupation.

> My friend said, "No way." I told her this was not something I had read. I knew it on a personal level. I had seen it. My own cousin was killed by Israelis. We were having a friendly argument, and the news came on that an Israeli man had entered a mosque in Hebron and murdered all the people inside praying. She was shocked. She said, "God just intervened to prove your point." That moment was transforming. She went home and

spoke to her parents separately. Her father agreed with me, and her mother disagreed. Now she is married to a son of Holocaust survivors. She keeps these issues alive in family discussions, but much of her family thinks it's all Palestinian propaganda. If I died today and that was the only thing I know for sure I accomplished, in terms of changing someone's opinions or at least acknowledging another side, I would feel blessed that I had that opportunity. That is what drives me. I am single, I have no kids, and much of my time is spent doing work or civic activity.

Also, for me, it's not so much about being an Arab and an American, and it is not about promoting Arab issues or wanting things just for the Arab American community. It really is about promoting America. I love what America stands for, and I love the opportunities we have. My mother and father lived the American dream, and they did it on a shoestring with no higher education. They love this country and have voted in every election. We have been taught to participate in our country. It does not mean we turn our backs on being Arab or Palestinian. But we embrace this country and what it has to offer. And we also don't turn our back on our culture. I love that America allows us to do that, and I love that Chicago is a place that embraces culture.

I ask Layla whether the events surrounding 9/11 changed her life in any way. She responds, "Definitely."

It was just so shocking and haunting. I really felt like a zombie for several weeks. I was in a state of extreme shock. And what happened to our community after that reinforced the need for Arab communities, organizations, and professionals to become more active in their non-Arab communities.

I remember I got a call from a friend who said, "Turn on the television," and I saw a tower fall and then saw a second tower fall. Then I remember I saw the clip of Palestinians celebrating, and I felt like I was punched in the stomach, because I hate to see anyone celebrate death. That was not the only reason. I was also upset because I understood their reaction. I don't feel they were celebrating the death of Americans, the carnage. It was almost like this vindication, like, it happens to us on a daily basis and no one cares. Now you know how we feel.

I expressed this thought to a couple of friends. A few months later, one of them said to me, "You agreed with 9/11," and I was in shock! Of course I don't agree! I don't agree with suicide bombings, with killing innocent civilians. I told her, "You know me. You know I am not like that." And I repeated my understanding of this event. But the subject was closed, and I was accused of changing my mind. This was a close friend of mine, and it really hurt. This is someone who really knows me. She did not focus on what I said. She focused on my response, "I understand."

I don't hide my true feelings. I have always been against suicide bombings. I speak about the Palestinian issue in truth. I think there is enough blame to go around. Because of 9/11, I have been so much more diligent in reading and rereading my history, so I try to convey the right facts, like an attorney on a case. I think one problem with Palestinian Americans and Arab Americans is that they convey superficial views of the conflict, so people ultimately do not understand. If we all know our history and the facts, I think we'd be able to garner a lot more support and understanding. It does not mean it is anti-Jewish or anti-Israeli or anti-American. We are asking people to form an opinion based on knowing all the facts involved.

I have been to the 9/11 site two times. It was a horrible, horrible event. If one good thing came out of it, it opened up a window for Muslims as well as Arab Americans to tell their story. And as much as a lot of groups have taken advantage of this opportunity, I think they have not done enough. There is a lot more to be done. They should participate in collaborative efforts with all different organizations and religions.

Layla was afraid that her firm's office might be attacked and vandalized, since it is clearly an Arab American business and many other such businesses in the southwest suburbs were targeted, but this did not happen. However, as a lawyer she has handled quite a few claims of discrimination.

I met women who wore hijab and were afraid to leave their homes. I met women fired from their jobs. One of my cousins was fired from his job. We settled a number of discrimination cases. I have a cousin who was hired and right before training was fired and told, "You can keep the job if you take off the hijab." No one tells Christians to take off their crosses or Jews to take off their yarmulke.

Ever optimistic, Layla finished our interview by noting that some positive things happened after 9/11.

I saw a lot of collaborative efforts. I saw the imam at the Bridgeview mosque initiate a prayer vigil and a blood drive. These were new things for them. They never participated in these types of activities on such a large scale. It was great to see the imam encourage the community to participate. The churches, synagogues, and mosques had prayer vigils. We did have a lot of positive things. In the end, things were not completely negative or positive, you saw things on both sides.

Usama Alshaibi

Usama Alshaibi was born in Baghdad, Iraq, in 1969 to an Iraqi father and a Palestinian mother. When he was less than five years old, the family moved to Iowa City so that his father could study for a doctorate in business administration at the University of Iowa. Usama has fond memories of those days: he attended school in Iowa City through the third grade and returned to Iraq for family visits during the summer. The summer visits, his name, and his looks all signified to Usama that he was different and that "we were from there."

> I had an idea . . . that I had family over there, and that we were from there, you know. My name was different. I looked different. I think there was one kid from Japan, another kid from Spain, not a lot of [others]. There were a few foreign kids because it was a university town, but it was predominantly white. There were good times. Those were nice memories around that time . . . the . . . early '70s.

By the time he was in fourth grade, Usama's family had moved back to Iraq, in a most unconventional way.

> Then we literally drove back to Iraq, if you can believe it. My father was in love with his Volvo station wagon, and he wanted to ship it. So we drove to New York, shipped it. Stayed in Germany for a while. Got the car. Drove through Europe into Baghdad. I had a very—from a child's point of view, I had a very pedestrian or sort of road trip adventure when it came to returning back.

Usama's elementary school experiences after that point were fairly tough, especially compared to his time in the Iowa City schools.

> My parents enrolled me in a public school, Baghdad public school. Like a Ba'athist school. That was a shock. I found the educational system harsh. It was almost brutal. Coming from an American system, where they were a lot more patient, and going to schools in Iowa, where they more patient and they took the time. Being thrown in this public school . . . I remember I was having trouble in one of the classes and to teach me a lesson my teacher made me stand up in front of everyone and escorted me to a grade lower than me, which my sister was in, and made me sit in the back of the class. Those kind of tactics.

Usama's father had "all sorts of trouble" with the government, which pressured him to join the Ba'ath Party. So they moved again.

> They wouldn't let him teach at the university unless he joined, and he didn't want to join. So we moved to the south of Iraq. We moved to Basra. And I continued going to school when I was in Basra, and the schools were a little better. So I was in fourth grade, eventually fifth grade.

Then the Iraq and Iran War started. Usama recalls being terrified and realizing that his parents were unable to protect him from injury, death, and his own fears.

> That was a pretty bad time. I think my parents really expected it to be done soon, that it was just this trivial thing that would be over. But I was

terrified. To me it was a very dark time in my childhood. Things that I remember, is like everything became militarized. In the United States I was a Cub Scout, and so they had something similar in Iraq. It was like Ba'athi Youth. You dress up in these uniforms, and you do marches and sing Saddam Hussein songs. I actually became a mini-Saddam follower, I had a poster in my bedroom. But that was just kind of propaganda, I really didn't know what it meant, who Saddam was. But I do remember my father saying, "Well, the United States is on our side," and that, in my child brain, I was like, "Oh, that's a good thing." And they were, they were supporting Iraq. But really, the thing I remember the most is the bombings and the sirens. And seeing houses destroyed. There was a mosque near our house, and I would always see women in their black *abayas* [cloaks] carrying the body wrapped in white. I'd see it daily, crying, you know. But every time those sirens would go on, I would just rush to the bathroom. . . . I realized at a young age that my parents can't protect me.

Usama's family left Iraq when his father took a job in Saudi Arabia. Experiencing another shift in pedagogy, this time Usama found himself in a school environment oriented toward religion and with a teaching style he once again found "brutal."

It was okay for a while. We moved to Riyadh, the capital of Saudi Arabia. I was enrolled again in a public school, but it was more . . . you know, Saudi Arabia, so it was all boys. It was divided: girls go to one side, boys go to another side. It was more religiously based. And that was also strange to me. I really did not have much experience with Islam or things like that. I also found their school methods quite brutal.

"Suddenly," when he was ten years old (in 1980), Usama's parents decided that his mother and the kids should go back to Iraq to sell their house. "They thought, 'Well, the war is going to die down.'" They stayed in Basra for a short period of time, where they found conditions "much, much worse."

It really bothered me that we went back. . . . Eventually we sold our house, and that was it. We only stayed there for a little while, and we left everything. I remember my mom asking what I wanted to take back with me, and I said, nothing. I didn't want anything. And that was the last time that I saw Iraq until 2004, when I went back again.

The family returned to Saudi Arabia. Usama went to an all-boys public school, where he made friends with some Saudi boys, many of whom saw him as American. He recalls the presence of American fast-food outlets and malls, which represented to him the America he missed. He also went through a period of heightened religiosity. But what Usama had discovered that he liked to do best, paint and draw, was not in the school curriculum and was looked down upon in Saudi Arabia, which was quite different from arts-promoting Iraq.

> We had science, math, things like that; art was looked down upon. That was my thing, I liked to paint and draw, and that was not really encouraged, like sports, engineering, and science. It was all right. It is strange, because Saudi Arabia had all of the . . . materials . . . the consumerism that I craved and missed of America. The Arby's, McDonald's, KFC, the malls . . . but in many ways it was more strict than Iraq. My mom and sisters had to cover up when they went out, women couldn't drive or vote. I found all of that very strange. But weirdly enough, I became very religious and would pray in mosques and things like that. I was really impressionable and, you know, got into and tried to be a good Muslim.

When he was in seventh grade, Usama's family moved back to Iowa City. And then, just as he was adapting to the cultural milieu of this small American university town, his family moved again, this time to Amman, Jordan, where his father got a new teaching job, Usama was enrolled in a private American school, and the family lived in the city's more flexible Arabic cultural environment.

> I'm in seventh grade at South East Junior High School, and everyone's concerned about dating and TV shows and lip gloss and bubble gum, you know, and that was okay. Every time I try to catch up and figure out where I'm at, it's like, oh, here we go again. So then we're back in the Middle East. My father got a job in Amman, Jordan. School got a little better; I was enrolled in an American private school. So that was a nicer cross between two worlds.

English was Usama's primary language, but he also spoke Arabic. At home it was "kind of a mixture."

> Weirdly enough, my parents spoke English to us. So it was mainly English. My father from time to time, actually in Amman, Jordan, was working with the United Nations, and the school I went to, a lot of the kids were from diplomats.

Usama's family moved again when he was in ninth grade. His father got a job in Abu Dhabi, the United Arab Emirates (UAE), as a professor of business administration. "Abu Dhabi was a nice place. More contemporary, so I was able to fit in as this internationally mixed kid. I met other kids like me." When he was in the middle of ninth grade, his parents decided that the kids and their mother should go back to the United States while his father worked in Abu Dhabi. They returned to Iowa City, where Usama finished high school. Usama has lived in the United States since that time. His parents eventually got divorced.

By the time I finished high school, my parents were on the way to getting a divorce. I've been here in the United States since then. My parents did get divorced. So I mean, that's my own Middle Eastern story. I mean, of course there [is] a lot of stuff in between that happened.

A "long struggle" began when Usama turned twenty-one in the United States and he was no longer covered by his mother's visa. Now he would need to apply on his own. The 1990 Gulf War had started, he was being drafted by the Iraqi government, and the American government had begun deportation proceedings against him.

I had lost my status under my mom's visa because I had turned twenty-one. And Saddam Hussein's government was drafting me. They were contacting my dad, saying, "We need your son." And then I was being . . . what do you call it when they are kicking people out? . . . deportation procedures . . . so they were kicking me out. So I had to plead my case. And I was actually seeking political asylum, which I received. And from the political asylum I was able to at least work and stay here until my citizenship in 2002.

Prior to this period, he had been compelled to take whatever job he could as a young man without a work permit.

Okay, so like, the period when I was seventeen, before I could legally work, I was doing a lot of these under-the-table jobs. You know, dishwashing and things like that. I didn't really pursue it too much because your position is really low. I worked. It was hard, because there were a lot of jobs I couldn't take, because of my status, that I was totally qualified for. So I took these jobs until I got my green card. I spent most of my earlier time in the United States working illegally. So I had a lot of jobs like washing dishes, janitor jobs, de-tassling corn, which is kind of like migrant labor.

A few years after being approved for political asylum, Usama obtained his permanent residency. After he became an American citizen in 2002, he was able to return to Iraq.

After being here for so long, that felt good. The only reason I went back to Iraq is because I have an American passport. Not that it would matter if I were kidnapped by insurgents, but I felt a little more secure with that than an expired Iraqi passport. It was a bittersweet moment because it was after 9/11.

Usama described becoming American at the same time that America had become highly anti-Arab as a "strange time." Shortly after 9/11, he received an anonymous death threat "from some fake e-mail address," and hate messages would appear while he was in the midst of online blog discussions.

Getting my citizenship after that happened was a strange time. I felt like there was a lot of anti-Arab hostility. Everything felt super-charged. You know . . . just saying you're Arab or Muslim or Iraqi or Palestinian. Also, the Internet was becoming bigger. One of the first e-mails I got after 9/11 said, "Be careful where you go, sand nigger. I'm gonna kill you. I'm gonna bury you, sand nigger." You know, these online communities at the time where you discuss politics, and suddenly you see something come up, someone saying, "I'm coming after you. You all deserve to be dead. You should all leave this country." Things like that.

At the time, Usama was living in Chicago, where he had settled after years of moving around. He finished a bachelor's degree at Chicago's Columbia College, which is known for its arts curriculum. Then he worked at the Chicago History Museum, a job that enabled him to collaborate with the Chicago author Studs Terkel and that gave him first-hand knowledge of Chicago history.

I was pretty transient throughout the 1990s, throughout my twenties. I lived all over: Madison, Wisconsin; Boulder, Colorado; Providence; and just traveled a lot just within the United States. I really had trouble finishing college. I just had trouble with it. I couldn't seem to finish school. It's strange, because I come from a very academic family. I just couldn't get it together. I was into art, photography, and filmmaking; it was to me a natural progression. So I went to Columbia College, and I finished there.

Since then, I worked briefly at the Chicago History Museum as a technical archivist. I worked closely with Studs Terkel, and I worked with various historians and filmmakers, like the group that did *The Weather Underground*. We had all of the WGN-TV news footage. I was sort of in charge of transferring it, cleaning it. I was in charge of transferring and digitizing Studs Terkel's interviews. So I got like a mini-education in Chicago history.

Usama began making films, some of which have played in various film festivals. His first feature film, made after 9/11, explores ideas about difference and being seen as the enemy.

Well, my first film that got a little bit of attention was called *Dance, Habibi, Dance,* and it was just a very colorful, psychedelic, sexual film with sort of a mutation of Eastern/Western visuals. I was just exploring that mutation in a very organic way. Without exploring it intellectually, it was more artistically and emotional[ly] . . . this is what I want to do. I was not seeking commercial success. I was looking at it in a more artistic angle . . . and continued making films after that and did okay.

It really wasn't until 9/11 that I made a feature film, called *Muhammed and Jane,* that talked and was more specific about the experience of coming from somewhere else or being seen as an enemy or being seen with suspicion, and [it] explored that idea. I was really disturbed by some of the

things I saw around me and made a film about it. And shortly after that I
. . . when the United States said they were going to invade Iraq, I decided
to go back to Iraq and make a documentary about that experience.

Usama married a woman from Kansas shortly before 9/11, and their
marriage started off "with a bang." In 2004, nine months into the war, he
returned with his wife to make a documentary film about Iraq.

I was married. I met her here in Chicago. I met her a little before 2001, so
our whole marriage started off literally with a bang. I was just like, Oh, my
God, and I have been consumed with it ever since. So my wife came with
me—she's from Merriam, Kansas—and we flew to Amman, Jordan, and
we drove into Baghdad. I spent three weeks there, and I went to the house
that I grew up in, and met my family that was still there . . . my uncle and
my aunt. I made a very personal kind of diary film about the experience,
and it's done well since then. It has opened up more doors for me.

Usama punctuates his discussion of filmmaking in Iraq with: "But we
had problems after 9/11."

Well, I was telling you about the Internet. It started to boom around that
time. There were a lot of online communities. My wife had an online
journal, and she was talking about racial profiling . . . that it just doesn't
work. Her argument is that no one is qualified . . . that it is poor policing
to look at someone [and] say, "That person is Arab, they look like a terrorist, we should stop them," when really that's just based on their own
limited experience with these things. I mean, racial profiling is just poor
policing, it just doesn't work, it doesn't help; it just distracts you from the
real problem. I mean, when the Oklahoma City bombing happened, they
detained a Jordanian doctor for twelve hours, and Timothy McVeigh
walked away because he was blond. It just doesn't work. So she said, "If
you're looking for an Arab, the next terrorist that is going to blow something up is going to be a white, blond woman. If their attention was
there." A few days later, two CIA agents—no, sorry, two FBI agents—
came to the door. They asked my wife about the journal entry, they
asked her if she had any intention of carrying out a terrorist attack
against the United States or Israel. And she said no.
    And then . . . they ask me a little bit. I was just there, they didn't say
they were interviewing me, just my wife. They asked her a few more
questions. They asked me a little bit about where I was from, and then
they said something like, my English was really good, which I found
funny. They were nice; they gave me their card and left.

Upon returning from Iraq, Usama was interviewed in Amsterdam by
a Dutch security agent.

When I went to Iraq and came back, I was at Amsterdam in the airport,
and I was interviewed thoroughly by someone there. She asked me

about my family, she asked if I was religious, what I was doing there. So I explained it was for a video for a film I was doing. And when I got back to the United States, they knew everything. It was the same questioning, but it was more relaxed. More like, How was Iraq? You are making a film, right? They had all of the information. Where I was from, where I had been. They even asked me how my trip was to Iraq. So they knew.

I asked Usama about his experiences with interpretations of his identity in the United States, where he spent half of his childhood as well as his teenage and young adult years. His reply covered a range of topics and responses.

It's been mixed. I've had Hassidic Jews come up to me and ask where the nearest kosher grocery store is. I've gotten Jewish, I've gotten Italian. I mean, most of my experience in the United States has been respectful, but of course you have jerks, you have people that have ridiculous ideas.

It seems like a lot of folks are misinformed, like that somehow Iraqis voted Saddam in, it's really horrible what we're doing to Saddam Hussein. I think whenever it comes to conflict it's never a simple answer. It's not just like, here are the good guys and here are the bad guys and they're [the U.S. government] doing something good. It was really sad going back to Iraq and seeing it so devastated. But, you know, I . . . I guess I try not to be so defensive anymore, just be more open about what people have to say, listen to them, and try to respond intelligently as much as I can, but things piss me off.

I saw America become hysterical. The medical students traveling in the South, you know, just hanging out, and some crazy woman calls up and [says], "You know they are planning something," I mean, what they did to them . . . not even a "Hey, what about her?" not even a question, not even a "Let's investigate her first before we go after these poor guys and ruin their lives." I mean, they were just treated like pieces of garbage, like they were the worst criminals ever. And they had done nothing, nothing. I think people hear what they want to hear and see what they want to see.

I don't know . . . I think in many ways that Americans are quick to react and not quick to learn. So that, in many ways, still pisses me off. And people would [get mixed] up and say, "So you are from Iran." No, big difference. But in many ways I also saw an interest in the Middle East and politics, so that was kind of nice. There were some folks that could actually talk about it. And weirdly enough, I met a lot of people in the military, and they were a little bit more reasonable to talk to. Some of the ones who had been there, or at least had come back and said, "I'm not going back." I met a few folks in the military that were okay; I made some friends.

I had read Studs Terkel's interview with Usama and thought it was interesting that Usama had told him that as soon as he got his American passport he was ready to leave. I asked Usama about his sense of identity. "What do you tell people when they ask, 'What are you?' "

I say, "I'm Usama Alshaibi." I have American citizenship. Any sort of nationalism . . . I don't take that stuff too seriously. I see it on both sides. I'm weary of anything tribal, my team, my people, my religion, my country, whatever it is. I just don't respond to it. I just don't care. [*Have you always felt like that?*] No, it's new. Well, there were moments when I'm like, "I'm Iraqi and I'm proud," there are moments when I'm just like, "I'm an American kid," there are moments when I'm a Muslim. There are moments when I was like this or that. I just don't want . . . when I was a teenager, I embraced punk rock and being more artistic and creative and hanging out with more open-minded people and people that explored sexuality and politics and their life . . . and seeking alternative forms of living that didn't rely on religion or nationalism, so I knew there were different ways of living. I was exposed to that at a young age. And I even knew that within the Arab world there were different people. It doesn't have to be one way or the other. It's not like all of the Arab world thinks or behaves in a certain way, and when you get down on the ground, you realize the gradations of how everyone is. I mean, my cousin calls himself a Muslim atheist, which . . . I like that idea and started to embrace [it]. You know, you can still be respectful of these cultural things that we grew up with, but you don't have to believe all of the nonsense if you don't want to, and you're not going to get your head cut off. It's fine, you know. I think it's fear that keeps people acting or saying certain things.

I feel that I have a healthy perspective on both ends. So when America is like, "Rah-rah-rah, America is number one," I'm like, "Oh, my God." And when the Arabs react to these Mohammed cartoons, I'm like, "Come on, people." All of that kind of hyper-defense of what people consider their people or religion or God, and I just feel a little more distant from it . . . I don't care. I don't associate myself with that, I don't feel that rage.

But I love my culture, I love where I'm from, I'm proud of where I'm from, I'm proud of who I am. There is no conflict in that. I don't have to be Muslim to be an Arab. I don't have to believe in God to be okay with who I am. That's been the newest thing. And I see my family and my siblings embracing it more. In some ways I think maybe that's an immigrant curse, that when you leave you want to hold on to it even more. But when you are there, you are like, hey, it's just who you are. It's no big deal. I don't have to wave an American flag to prove anything. I've never waved an American flag. Honestly, I've never waved it, and I don't plan on it. I don't want to wave any flag.

Usama now works at a new Chicago public radio station called Vocalo.

I was hired as a hosting producer about a year ago. Our goal is to give the little guy a voice. We are sort of a user-generated radio. That means anyone and everyone can upload their audio on our website, and we'll play it on the air. We're a little bit more . . . we are just kind of wild and spontaneous, and just a little different than regular public radio. It's a good home for me; everyone here is awesome. It's closer to what I do making film and media and art. So it's been good. I just feel like I can be myself here.

I asked Usama if he had met any of the Iraqi Shiites who went to Chicago in the 1990s as refugees.

> Not really. I met one guy who was a cabbie. I know there are not a lot. I was really surprised to have met him. We talked for a while, and he wouldn't accept my money. I've met a lot of Christian Iraqis, Palestinians, and some Iraqi Jews.

I asked Usama if our discussion had sufficiently covered his important life experiences and his post-9/11 experiences. With this opening, much more followed—about feeling watched, about hiding or being open about his Iraqi identity, and about having the name Usama.

> I did feel followed and watched. And I still do feel that. And I don't know if that will go away. I had two choices when 9/11 happened. I could keep it all in to myself and stay out of the way. Or—since I work in film and I'm on the Internet, I sort of have a very vocal presence, and I was doing things where I was having film screenings and people would ask me very pointed questions—I can just come out with it and just be like, this is who I am. How I feel about this stuff. Be more open about it. Just say it. Which is not the tradition I come from. My family is always, "Be quiet. If anyone asks you anything, say you are from Jordan, or Kuwait, somewhere benign. Don't even tell them you are from Iraq. Don't even tell them you are Arab."
>
> My mom even at one point asked me to change my name. Because Usama is the same Osama that is in bin Laden. And I was like, change my name? I'm not going to change my name! So I get that all of the time, I get shit for that. Oh . . . so I get people, like, "Not like bin Laden, not like Osama bin Laden, right?" No, like Osama bin Laden. Like having the same name is the worst crime you can have. But I stuck to my guns and kept my name. And now it's a humorous joke. They're like, "What's your name?" "My name is Usama." They're like, "What? Usama?" "Yeah, like bin Laden." They're like, "Oh! Ha, ha!" Now there is, "Ha, ha, ha."

When he spoke about the experiences of other members of his family, he mentioned the particular experiences of women wearing hijab.

> Things have happened to everyone in my family. My aunt who lives here, she wears a hijab. A brilliant woman, she actually helped the CIA with some of their computers that had to do directly with counterterrorism tactics. She was in the airport once, and they detained her and her daughter for almost twelve hours. They were treated very poorly here in the U.S. They made a big stink about it in the media. It was like three years ago.
>
> Some of my cousins, because they wear a hijab, just gave up. Stopped wearing it. It's too much . . . too much harassment.
>
> So maybe in a way I'm like, people don't know what I am. But I don't really hide it. I think Americans respond to language, like, if you sound like them. I don't really know. I've had so many problems in my family

growing up. But at the same time, it's balanced. . . . You know, I grew up in Iowa, I've traveled to these tiny little towns in Iowa, and it's been fine. I think most folks in the United States are good people, but I think they are afraid. What they don't understand . . . they may come after me.

Then Usama spoke of his younger brother, Samir, who was born in the United States.

Yeah, things have happened across the board in my family. I had a brother, a younger brother born here in the United States, the first one that was born here. And after my parents divorced, things became very hard for my family. My father . . . just disappeared. He wasn't . . . it's like he saw us as a unit and not as individuals and just stopped helping us for a while. The divorce was very messy between my parents, they both just got very vicious, and I think the kids, all of us dispersed, just felt ungrounded. And my younger brother Samir suffered. At fourteen, he ran away, got into drugs, was in prison. He was in prison here in Illinois during 9/11, and they threw him into solitary confinement for over two months in a maximum-security prison, no charges. Nothing. They transferred him. He was in a minimum-security prison, and they transferred him to a maximum-security prison where he was in a tiny room with no windows or light, and he was allowed out only one hour a day inside a little field. There were no charges pressed, just suspicions. They said they did it for his own protection.

He had been in prison for almost two years prior. And he has nothing . . . it's ridiculous . . . he's more interested in scoring heroin and drugs . . . but in prison he did become more religious. So he suddenly became religious. Got out of prison, he stayed with me for a little bit, he got married, and then he died from a drug overdose. He was twenty-eight.

Usama's mother, whom he calls "a tough lady," has remarried and lives in Colorado. His two sisters and another younger brother live in the United States. His father has remarried and has two sons from that marriage. Usama plans on staying in Chicago for a while, although he says his "restless father" put restlessness inside of him. Meanwhile, his father recently moved to Irbil, Iraq, from Jordan.

He really loves Iraq. He is a nationalist. He is someone that's in love with Iraq. His family is Shiite Muslim, which is one of the reasons he didn't want to join the Ba'ath party. He was really happy they got rid of Saddam.

Walid

Walid is from a mountaintop village named Yaffa in the former South Yemen, but he was born in 1958 in British-controlled Aden, where his father worked as a pharmacist for the British. At the age of one, upon his father's retirement, Walid returned with his family to Yaffa. He came back to Aden when he was seven years old to attend school; at that time in the early 1960s there were no schools in Yaffa.

> The English would not allow anyone from the villages to enter public school in Aden. Actually, to just enter Aden. The English took the city—which is beautiful, by the water—surrounded it, and called it the British Zone. To enter you have to come through a gate and have some paper stating why you are allowed to enter, for work or whatever. Anybody from the mountain areas or out of that area is not allowed to go to public school, period. I was lucky enough, because I was born in Aden. I have a birth certificate saying I am from Aden.

After the Yemeni revolution in 1967 the British left, and Yemen was split into two countries, the Republic in the North and Communist-ruled South Yemen. Walid left South Yemen as a teenager, in 1975 or 1976, for Abu Dhabi in the United Arab Emirates, "where there is opportunity for someone looking to better [themselves] and support their family, like most Yemenis." He stayed four years, working for the government and private companies, but wanted to continue his education. A friend from Washington, D.C. encouraged him to go to the United States to study, and in 1980, "before you know it, I am in Washington, D.C., studying in one of the city colleges." His days as a student did not last long because of financial issues. "Actually, it was really harsh on me because the only goal I came for was to continue studying." He had been promised support by a person at the UAE embassy, but it never came through.

> Before I left to [go to] America, I had to get my Yemeni passport, and I had to add the United States. I am from South Yemen, and we were falling under the Communists at that time. So I had to get my passport changed, even though I was holding a North Yemen passport. First to get out of Yemen, actually you had to run away from South Yemen to North Yemen and then make it out to Saudi Arabia or the Gulf, because you are not permitted to leave South Yemen under any circumstances. When we left Yemen, the passport did not permit you to go just anywhere, you have to write where you are going, certain countries. You could only travel to Arab ports. If you want to go somewhere else, you have to go [to] the Yemen embassy, and you have to get the country added, otherwise you are not allowed to go to that country.
>
> I went to the North Yemen embassy in Abu Dhabi, and the ambassador himself said that he would not add the United States. He did not want to add the United States for some reason, and when I insisted three times, he sat me down and told me stories. He told me stories of people who left before me and what happened to them. He asked me questions: "How much money do you have?" He said, "You know, it's not going to be an easy journey." He told me, "Most stories I heard about people similar to your situation, they would go, they may succeed, but a lot of them will end up in depression, a lot [of] them commit suicide, a lot of them, they really have, you know, very hard consequences." Finally he did,

you know, he said, "Under your responsibility, I just told you what you are going to be facing. If you don't have the financial support. . . . " But I was sure I was going to have support from the United Arab Emirates government because I worked for the military there.

After staying in Washington almost a year, Walid decided to move to Chicago because he had a friend who lived there and there were other Yemenis in Chicago.

Then I wasn't studying. My mind went to, how long can I survive? You know, I've got to just eat. I stayed for about two months with a friend of mine who had a place with some other Yemeni guys. Actually, they kind of accommodated me; I had very little money left. After that, I decided that I would go into business—just in my head, because I had no money.

So with a friend of mine, we decided we are going to do business, but we said, while we are looking for business, we have to look for the financial support. How are we going to do it? Also, we should go to improve our English, because when I was in Washington, D.C., even though I stayed about two semesters in school there, my English was not enough to understand. It was not enough to understand that I shouldn't get off at Detroit. When I came from Washington, D.C., to Chicago, the plane stopped at the Detroit airport. When the plane stopped, I saw people getting off, and I just got off. I did not know I was in Detroit. So that's how I knew my English is not enough.

So we contacted people back in Abu Dhabi, friends and families. For my part, I did at least contact friends and family, and I told them, I just have to go for business, I cannot study. It's very expensive, and I need your help. I need to borrow money from you so I can start a business. You know, whatever, it's something to live. Because at that time there were jobs, there were Yemeni workers in factories. There was at least one place on the north side of Chicago. There were about one-hundred-plus Yemenis, mostly singles, families abroad, and they all or most of them, the big majority, were working in industries. Actually, to be specific, they were working in steel-grinding houses, precision grinding operations in the steel industry, and this is what I'm doing now.

Walid explains that the first Yemenis came to Chicago in the late 1950s and early 1960s from Sheffield, England, where they had worked in the steel mills and learned grinding operations. When they went to Chicago, these skills were in high demand. He explains, "Basically, when you come to a small community of yours, the first thing you are going to do is see what they are doing. You probably are going to do the same thing. So that's what happened to every Yemeni that came after them." Walid, however, wanted to get some schooling and start a business, any business. His sister's husband in Abu Dhabi and some people with whom he had worked lent him money. He got "about twenty thousand dollars in total, which was a lot of money at that time." He enrolled in Truman College on the north side to study English and take GED courses.

Then I got my first business, which was a grocery store on the south side of Chicago, and that's how I started. I started the grocery store with two other partners. We gathered about fifty thousand dollars, sixty thousand dollars, and that was the first business I had. It was around Sixty-third and Wentworth on the south side of Chicago. And I was living in the Lawrence and Kedzie area, Albany Park. It was a convenience store, like a 7-Eleven. It's small, but it's a start. I guess I felt I have to do something. Even when I was in Abu Dhabi, I had the idea to do business. I almost did start over there doing business. But then came the school idea.

The warnings of the North Yemeni ambassador in Abu Dhabi proved prescient a year later.

A year later, I was in contact with the friend of mine who helped me get accepted in [a] Washington, D.C., college. He's Yemeni. Actually, he's Somali, but he's from Yemen, he was living in Yemen. I called him maybe every six months, we talked and everything. One time I called and I got his friend, and I asked for Yasid, can I talk to Yasid? He said, "I'm sorry," he said . . . [Walid begins to cry]. Every time I remember this it's kind of hard. Very hard. Because I always remember what the ambassador said, how real it was. Even though they let people go through it, it's very hard because . . . he told me Yasid had just hanged himself. So it was really depressing, because I just started a business. I wanted to know about America, it's the land of opportunity, even though growing up in a Communist country, we really didn't have a love for America, whether the country or the people. You know, in my childhood, in my elementary school, and after that growing up in a country where Communists were dominating everything. Even our religion was taken away, lots of things.

It was really hard for me to know that a friend [of] mine just hanged himself. Because whatever his reason, it has to be a financial reason or an emotional interruption, which I never knew. It did depress me, but also I had to really think more towards success. I have to make it. I'm not going to surrender to depression, I'm not going to surrender to failure. I just know in my heart I have to succeed, there is no other way. I borrowed money, I have to give it back. I guess I don't want to be a bad example for my family and my friends.

So even though I had a lack of experience, I had to manage the place. When we bought this established business, they had five or six employees, and they were all American. They were writing payroll, writing checks to employees. It's a lot of responsibility, so the manager of the place stayed with us for maybe a month to show me and explain to me how business works. I've never been [in] business in my life. And I'm in business. It's a tough neighborhood.

It was 1982. Walid describes that first year, when he was only twenty-four, as a "struggle." For example, he had no idea about inventory. The second year got better, and by the third year they were doing very well.

Actually, I forgot about school. Talking to the people and salesmen, my English got better. My mind just went to business. And I . . . maybe in the fifth or sixth year I started a branch. By the eighth year in the business I probably had six places, all with partners. I had one in Chicago downtown, I had one on Taylor Street, I had one near Albany Park. I had one on the east side of Chicago. They were all convenience stores, basically the same thing. I was managing more than anything else. I would run from place to place. I would do the buying, which is probably the most important thing in that business, in any business actually. I would do the buying, and I would oversee the operation. I would train the person sometimes to be manager in the store.

In 1986, when he was twenty-eight years old, Walid decided he was ready to get married. He went to Yemen, saw his father, and on his way back to the United States stopped in Sheffield, England, where Yemenis worked in the steel industry. He not only met his wife-to-be in Sheffield but got "the idea" that would seal his economic future.

I started looking. I went back to Yemen in 1985 for the first time, and I saw my father; my mother had died in 1973. On my way back, I went through Sheffield, England, because the steel industry is in Sheffield. I saw the mills, I saw a lot of Yemenis over there working in the steel industry. That's how the idea came to me. This is where the people in Chicago work, in the steel industry. The precision grinding, this is where they learn. When I was there, I had the chance to meet a family, and I had a chance to meet the woman who is my wife now. I stayed there for a couple of weeks, and a year later I went back and got married.

Walid's wife was born in Yemen but moved to England when she was four years old. She was from the same region of Yemen as Walid, so he felt a certain level of comfort with her family.

We are actually from almost the same village. I resided in the Aden area, but we are originally from the mountains, like one hundred kilometers from Aden. Her village and mine are ten minutes away driving. She is from the same area, and I felt comfortable talking to them.

My wife came to the U.S. in 1988 because, even though we got married, she couldn't come here because I had to file papers for her. At that time, while we were waiting for her visa, a law came to permit British citizens to enter the United States without a visa. So she did, although her visa was almost ready. She came, and she really helped me a lot.

In the early 1990s, Walid decided that he had had enough of the convenience store business. He had made a substantial amount of money and wanted to do something else. He had misgivings about profiting from the sale of alcohol, owing to its conflict with his religious beliefs. His thoughts turned back to Sheffield and the steel industry.

Since I visited Sheffield, it was in my head, you know, a connection between the Yemeni community in Chicago, even though very small. But it connected the percentage of Yemeni communities working in the steel industry. It's just something not normal. You know, when you say we have 150 Yemenis living in Chicago, and out of 150 there are probably 100 working in the steel industry. That is not normal. Something is there. It got [into] my head that I have to do something, you know.

I just connected this. I said, maybe this is best for me because it was like, it's probably more than anything else a religious reason. You know, because in some of the stores I had liquor. I just decided one day that I wanted to be out, I want to be out completely whether they have pork or alcohol or whatever. I just recognized it's probably not the right thing to be doing, which is true, it wasn't the right thing. So in about two years, almost three, I kind of sold all of my shares in those businesses, one after another. The last one I sold was the year I opened this place right here.

It was late 1994, I was looking for an empty place to rent. I said, I got Yemenis working in the steel industry for a reason. I have to think about this. You got Yemenis [who are] experts. They are experts in precision grinding. It's not easy to find a precision grinder, an expert. It takes years to learn, more than any other industry. But there are a lot of them. And they are all people I know. I'm talking to a friend of mine, and he said, "I'm sure you're not going to have any problem with finding the workers." I thought, you know, I will rent a place, I'll buy the machines that we are going to need.

By speaking with Yemeni grinders, Walid learned which machines to buy. He said when he told them he was planning to open a steel grinding business they would laugh. They were working for large companies, and they knew that it would take a substantial investment.

Some machines are $100,000 just for one machine. And I said, okay. I talked to a friend of mine: I will rent the place, I will get the workers, and then what? You are going to have to sell the product. You are going to have to have a salesman. And that's how I started. I started advertising for a salesman before I even got the place. I started advertising in the *Tribune*. I rented this place in late 1994. In 1995, by June, I decided to bring in machines. The first piece I bought was a forklift. I remember very well because my nephew was visiting from Texas. He was a pilot. I'm in my office trying to do the calling, trying to see what to buy, and he's outside driving the forklift. I remember we ran out of propane, it didn't start. I didn't even know we had to replace a propane tank. I started buying stuff, I advertised. I got a lot of applications back, but I didn't have the things ready. So I kept the applications with me.

The final piece of Walid's vision fell into place when he hired the perfect salesman.

I was looking for a salesman in the steel industry. I got a call from a head-hunter one day; he said, "You looking for a salesman?" and I said, "Yeah." He said, "I got a beautiful one, he's down at Ryerson Steel." When he said Ryerson, I already had a pile of companies I'm going to go after to get the grinding services, and Ryerson was one of the biggest ones. So when he said Ryerson, I said, "Send him in." So he sent me the salesman who was really very impressive, Italian guy. He's retired, in his early fifties, he's already retired from Ryerson, but he wasn't maybe the one I was looking for. I was looking for somebody who would sell a pre-cision grind bar or who would bring me services for grinding. That guy's job was . . . he was a buyer of the "hurro" for Ryerson Steel. That guy was traveling . . . he goes to Sheffield I don't know how many times a year. He came, and I see the guy, he looks beautiful. I don't know about steel much, but the personality of the person convinced me. I said fine. I took him in, and I paid at that time seven thousand dollars just for the head-hunter. I had to do something maybe. But you know, at the time that guy really helped me a lot. A lot. He had a personal relationship with the CEOs of the companies . . . I would say [in] most [of the] Midwest area. So within a year I'm already doing services. I got the people, I got the machines, I got the place, I got the salesman.

Walid went into extensive detail about the steel industry—how steel is processed from raw material to finished product—and then returned to what his company does, precision grinding and polishing. After a few years, he moved beyond the provision of precision parts to service centers and on to a new challenge: finding direct buyers for the company's products.

You have to find those guys, you know. Mostly we sell to Swiss screw machine houses or we sell to service centers. You know, those big ware-houses where they keep nominal sizes in stock. But we do special sizes also. I would say in about 1997 I was doing only service, where I take material and clean it up and send it back to the service centers. You need a lot of money to buy steel if you are going to produce the product itself. It takes a lot of capital. Now, in 2008, now I'm about 80 to 20: 80 percent product sales and 20 percent service.

Nonetheless, there were some very difficult years in between.

I bought machines that were made in Birmingham, England. I got them kind of less. I had to do some work, I had to bring in an electrician and do some work to them. But it was, it was for me a struggle. I sold all of the businesses I had before I got here. I spent all the money I earned on the grocery business within a year. Within a year, it was all evaporated. I started in late 1994. At the end of 1995, we just started producing. It's getting worse, because what's happening . . . now you got employees, you got electricity, you got oil, you got wood, you got so many things.

The biggest thing is payroll. And to make it even worse, now you have to wait. It is not cash money, like in a grocery store where you can sell it or buy it; you have to wait for your money a month, some companies sixty days. I'm carrying payroll, I'm carrying expense for this place, for insurance, and to make it worse, I'm carrying other companies' debt. So within a year it was really hard. I borrowed from some good friends. A lot of people I had good relationships with. A lot of money. Actually, I even borrowed from my wife's family, my uncle in Sheffield, and a friend of mine in Abu Dhabi. It was a disaster to me because of all of the years I worked, it's gonna be gone if it's closed, it's done. And I'm liable for the lease, it's so many things. I had no doubt in my heart I'm going to have to make it. I have no choice, I have to make it. I just cannot fail. Then things start getting better. It did get slowly better: 1996 was really bad, 1997 started getting better, by 1998 we are doing fine.

In 2000, Walid bought the building he had been renting and the building next to it. "So it got worse again for me a little bit. I have more space, I got more machines, I got more workers, I got more work. You start stocking inventory, you start stocking steel."

I wondered how Walid's company survived with the steel industry in decline in the United States. He noted that much business has shifted to China and India, but he was able to compensate for this loss because of the weakened dollar in the European market and the high level of American military activity.

The weakened dollar helped us a little bit, and the war helped us a little bit. One of our customers for the past fourteen years started exporting heavily to Europe. He's making, as he's telling me, he's making more profit, more money selling to Europe than selling here because of the euro and the dollar is weak. So, yes, and the war, we've been doing a job over and over. We are selling some forty-forty material, like a quarter-inch small round. And that's going to the military, the head of the bullet. Which I don't really feel good about. But it's a job I have to do sometime. It's very, very . . . it's . . . for now it's really . . . war is bad, but we are losing big jobs. We are losing bigger jobs to India and China. A lot. One big job we lost was for the fishery industry in Minnesota. They used to buy the steel from us. They are getting it from China at a fraction of the price. I would say 30 percent of the price or less. I would say there is . . . you cannot know what to do. We have been grinding for a couple of houses who contract with the military for the past fifteen years. Actually, our next goal here is to get approved by the military standards. So we may have a chance to do direct sales to the government, to the military. There is a good chance, but we have to be qualified, we have to go through all of the programs, maybe some training. We are looking into it.

In the mid-1990s, Walid and his family moved to a rented house in the southwest suburb of Bridgeview, closer to his business in a west-southwest suburb. Prior to that, they had been living on the north side of the city, making for a long commute. "I rented for a year to see the area. There is a mosque, two schools, two Muslim schools, which I really wanted my kids to go to. That's really what encouraged me to move, besides time saving."

In 1997 they built a house in Bridgeview on land they purchased near the mosque. He describes the area:

> The subdivision I live in has two schools, about fifteen hundred students, and a mosque. There are about five hundred families in that subdivision, probably 98 percent Muslim. Not necessarily Arab, but the majority are, and probably Palestinians are the majority. I'll give you an example. On my street the neighbor to my right is Syrian, the one after him is Algerian, the one after him is from Sudan, and there is a Jordanian; there is a Bangladeshi across the street, a Syrian next to the Bangladeshi, there's another Yemeni; people are from a variety of Muslim countries. Actually, it's a little village of Muslims because of the mosque and the school. When I moved in, in 1997, it was probably fifty-fifty. Half was still empty land, and maybe 50 percent were Muslim. The rest—you know, Americans, some Christian, some Jewish—but a lot of them sold their property, not because this is a Muslim area and they want to get away, no. They got a lot of money for their property. In five years' time, people doubled their money in that area because of demand.

Our conversation moved to 9/11. For Walid, getting a ticket on that day for not wearing a seat belt signaled to him that there were going to be "consequences."

> It started for me within hours, the . . . consequences. That day when it happened, it was like nine o'clock in the morning. I was astonished. I was just looking at the computer, looking at the Internet, at the news . . . just kind of not believing what's going on, you know. I went home at six o'clock that day. I'm driving in a normal way, and all of a sudden this cop is behind me. I'm thinking about what happened. I'm not really thinking about him driving behind me. I noticed when I drove close to Archer and he's still behind me, and he is McCook police and he shouldn't really go that far. [Archer is within Chicago city limits.] But then he tried to pass me. I slowed down to let him go, but he slows down, and he was looking at me. He was driving beside me for a few minutes. I don't know why. He saw my face, that's for sure. So I turn close to where you go [on] the highway, because it's safer if I don't take the highway. So he's behind me, then he passes me, and I slow down . . . I just want to let him go. I wasn't thinking about . . . I could've easily gotten my seat belt on. And then he pulled me over. I didn't know about seat belts at that time. He stopped me, got my driver's license, insurance, everything is fine. And he wrote me a ticket; I have no seat belt. I mean, yes, I had no seat belt, but usually this is not enforced unless you do something, then

you get the ticket for [the] seat belt. It was just kind of like he felt something, like he just wanted to give me a ticket, that's all. He drove behind
to see if I would do something wrong or whatever. He pulled me over,
my papers were fine, but he still gave me a ticket for [the] seat belt. So
this is one of the things that said to me, there is something wrong.

On September 12, Walid and his wife felt that the way people looked
at them at the Dominick's grocery store near their home was different
from before; people looked as if they were scared of them.

Then the second day, we go to Dominick's, close by the house on Harlem
Avenue and Eighty-seventh Street. Across from Dominick's there are
about nine hundred trailers. This is how beautiful Bridgeview is, we've got
a beautiful new industrial complex of about fifteen to twenty buildings,
which sits in the middle between the trailer park and our subdivision, with
houses selling for $500,000 to $1 million, in a town where the average
house is $130,000 to $150,000. That area is a mixture of doctors, lawyers,
businessmen. It's probably one of the highest profiles for Muslims. They
are very well educated in that area. That's diversity, you know.

We were going to Dominick's across the street, and I don't know, it's
just a different . . . it's like a different feeling I had. Me and my wife, my
wife wears a scarf, it is very noticeable that you're a Muslim. I saw people looking more at us than normal. We are normally there twice, three
times a week. I saw like a scary look. That's the look that I've seen, I can
remember it now like that day. It's not [that] they want to do something
to us. It's something like they're scared [of] us. And I said this to my wife,
and she agreed. It's not a hate look that I see. People are scared honestly.

Okay, this is the second day. By the end of the day, police are already
in the area. So there are probably a few things that happened; one lady
in Dominick's got into a fight with some ladies who tried to beat her up
because she had a scarf. So the animosity starts. A little bit of hate started
in that area. Maybe because it was populated with Muslims, and was
populated also with, I'm not going to say a low-class people, but uneducated people. There is a lot of uneducated people in that area.

By nighttime, the situation in the area near the mosque had escalated.
In Walid's view, the general mood went through a dramatic change—
from one of fear to hatred and revenge-seeking.

By the night there is a riot coming from Harlem Avenue. A lot of kids
and adults, and they're marching toward the mosque. I mean, it's just
obviously a situation of hate. They are marching against the mosque.
Police cannot contain them, there's so many of them. Already there was
a shooting at the mosque, somebody shot the door of the mosque. I don't
know when and how. Rocks were thrown from the back. In the back
where we live there's a train, and the last houses by the train got hit with
rocks. If you cross the train tracks, then there is an industrial area, then a
big vacant lot, and then those trailer houses. So assumingly, people came

in from the trailer houses to behind the train and threw rocks at the windows of the last houses. So it is coming from the back, it's coming from the front, and it's coming inside the mosque with the bullet. The police cannot contain them, the Bridgeview police force is not large enough. Then, by the end of the day, they contained it. I mean, the march, they stopped the march. They brought fire engines, ambulances. There's more police, the state got involved. They pushed them back from the neighborhood, they took them back to Harlem. They were still shouting hate slogans and everything, but they would not let them pass through Harlem to where we live.

If you want to contain the area, you can. We have a train from the west, Harlem Avenue from the east, and on the south we have the industrial area. Every time you want to leave that area you have to cross Harlem or you have to go through the industrial area—that's the only two places that you can leave the area. They were shouting, "Go back home," "Death to the Arabs." It's people with hate, I would say people with less education. Or people just being with the crowd . . . you know, just walking with the crowd.

By the end of the second day, only persons who could prove they lived in the neighborhood were allowed into the subdivision near the mosque.

By the end of the day, to come in and go out you have to have . . . it just reminded me of concentration camps, you know. Like we are really in a camp where you are going out and you're coming in, and I have to show my driver's license, which is protection for the people who live there. I give all of the credit to the Bridgeview police department and the mayor himself.

Still, Walid and his neighbors were apprehensive because attacks on the neighborhood had been coming from across the railroad tracks and from the industrial park.

I'm afraid somebody may throw something through the window, my kids might get hurt, somebody might shoot from a distance—these were the burning things in my head, what someone would try to do. I'm kind of like at the end of the houses. I'm across the street from the industrial area, so I'm exposed a little bit. Not like the people in the back by the train, they are exposed more. But I'm still exposed because I'm the first house facing the industrial area. Anything could happen . . . somebody could, you know, sneak from the industrial area very well. They could shoot, they could do anything. You never know what's going to happen. After I saw the fear look, I wasn't feeling comfortable at all.

Walid described the change he saw in the look on people's faces, from the fear he had observed the day after 9/11 to a look of revenge, and this look made him apprehensive.

The look two days later was a different look. It's like a look of revenge. In my own personal analyzing, I'm just analyzing how it looked. It varied so quickly. A couple of days, and it's a different look. Because if you watch the news and you see they're saying these people got knives and they did this and the plane and they get in their head this scary thing, it's scary people. In the second day and the third day, you are talking about the revenge. What we gonna do about it? This is exactly what we saw.

That night, under cover of darkness, Walid and his close neighbors met to figure out what they would do to prevent their homes from being attacked. They decided to take turns keeping watch. While walking back to his house at 2:00 A.M., Walid saw the mayor of Bridgeview walking through the neighborhood. Interpreting the mayor's presence as a statement of commitment to their protection, his fears were calmed.

So many things happened that you can only remember the thing that touches you. I was walking across the street in the dark after meeting with my neighbors, and I saw the mayor of Bridgeview walking through the neighborhood. It gave me a great feeling. It gave me back the thing that was taken away by some, I would say, illiterate people, people who don't have meaning in life. Those people who were shouting, the people that were throwing rocks, the people who were shooting at the mosque for no reason. And when I saw the mayor, I just felt like, okay, I'm safe now, I can go to sleep. Two o'clock in the morning, after all this disruption. I had just talked to my friend, telling him, "You have to watch, I'm going to sleep for a few hours, you have to sleep for a few hours, everybody has to watch." But then, as soon as I walked back to my house, the first thing I did, I picked up my phone and called my friend across the street. I told him, "Ali, you can go to sleep."

Walid said it took about "a week to go back to normal," after which time identification was no longer checked for entry into the area, although the police stayed in the neighborhood for about two weeks. "It took away something from me when I have to show my ID and everything, you know, I felt like I don't belong here, you know. But this is what I felt. I am not born here, I'm not raised here . . . what do my kids feel? That's what I was always thinking."

Walid's eight children range in age from five to nineteen. He says that some were probably too young to remember these days, but he is sure the older ones will. Right now, he says, the situation in Bridgeview has returned to normal.

They are beautiful . . . it's normal. At that time, I'm not going to say it was Bridgeview; it's not Bridgeview . . . it's a bunch of people with hate in their heart. Those people, you know . . . they put the flags on their car and think they are more American than anybody else. But in my opinion, my kids, they love this country more than me. I would say the number-one cause is a lack of education. On the north side, we haven't really noticed a lot [of] things, it's just in certain areas. It's probably the crowd, because there are so many Muslims and the mosque. Because they connected . . . you know, how the news goes. They say, you know, there is a connection . . . they are connected to that mosque; it was in the paper that it was in the southwest. Some people will believe that. Most of the people have a limited education. They just read and do.

Walid's wife and eight kids were in Yemen for the summer when I interviewed him. A few years earlier, the family of ten went for a visit. His wife was the one who wanted to go; she had not been in Yemen since she was four years old. Walid asked her why she wanted to go; he told her, "There is nothing to see there." Now, over the past five years, Walid and his wife have built a six-story apartment building in Aden, where a number of his siblings and their families now live, as well as a forty-bed hospital and pharmacy. Walid says his wife loves Yemen and would like to stay there. "She likes it there, surprisingly. She likes it very much." But the whole family was coming back in August so his two oldest daughters could begin studying at Loyola University in Chicago. Walid had just bought his daughters a lakeside condominium apartment on Sheridan Road so they could easily walk to classes a few blocks away.

These oral histories reveal that, seven years after the 9/11 attacks, the individual lives of the interviewees had returned to a mechanical normalcy but that their psychological states were different from before 9/11. Something had been taken away after 9/11; some might call it dignity, others might call it freedom or the feeling of living with ease in the United States. The interviewees had led lives that were socially and economically diverse, but the thread of homeland insecurity ran through all their stories, even if it was clearly substantially reduced in severity from the period 2001 to 2005, the subject of most of this book. Still, the pain and memories of that period had not yet fully receded. For these Arab American Muslims, life goes on with a taut rhythm that flows from being part of American society yet knowing that some people might seek to harm them if given the power to do so. This combination of security and insecurity will continue to shape the Arab and Muslim American experience for the foreseeable future. It is important to realize that this sense of a common fate arose not from an inherent sameness shared by all of these Arab American Muslims, but from the very real repercussions of being spoken about, represented, and acted upon *as if* they were all the same. The power of social action to shape the contours of people's lives is what gives meaning to the term "self-fulfilling prophecy." Chapter 3 examines the genesis of the social construction of the essential Arab/Muslim, the scaffolding upon which the collective experiences of Arab American Muslims after 9/11 was built.

Chapter 3

The Social Construction of the Arab (and Muslim) American

THE NEGATIVE post-9/11 experiences described by Arab Muslims in the research interviews as chilling, destabilizing, and even frightening were set in motion by social constructions of their relationship to the attacks, not by the attacks alone. When allegations (examples of which are provided in this book) were made inferring that Arabs and Muslims living in the United States were a potentially collaborative fifth-column population, many in the United States accepted such claims as credible because they were built on social constructions that were in place well before the events of 9/11 appeared to lend credence to them. Those who posited Arab/Muslim collective culpability for the attacks did not necessarily charge that all Arabs and Muslims in the United States could have or would have committed such a deadly attack on Americans, but they did assert that Arab/Muslim communities silently supported the attacks and willingly hid terrorist sleeper cells. Pre-9/11 social constructions that had proffered the existence of a collective value-set and orientation shared by Arabs and Muslims, including a propensity to violence, a disposition to terrorism, and an entrenched hatred of America, had set the stage for these propositions to gain wide public support. (Gendered aspects of this value-set are elaborated in chapter 7.) Arabs and Muslims in the United States thus had experiences that were similar in sequencing to those of Japanese Americans before and during World War II. In the Japanese American case, widely held negative social constructions of their treacherous "character" existed long before the 1941 Japanese government attack on Hawaii's Pearl Harbor and had led to restrictions on their immigration (1908) and their state-based rights to own land and work freely, as well as to discrimination based on a range of symbolic cues (Takaki 1989; Parrillo 1997).[1] It was these preexisting negative stereotypes of Japanese Americans that empowered assertions of their group danger and collective complicity after the attacks occurred, resulting in broad American governmental and popular support for their incarceration in internment camps during the war.

The crisis of 9/11 crystallized preexisting sentiments such that the host of negative traits imputed to Arabs and Muslims in the United States assumed master status (Hughes 1945), forming the main architecture of their ascribed social status for a significant segment of the American population, just as the status of blackness is assumed primary for black men walking through white neighborhoods (Anderson 1990). This master status was associated with a set of symbols that included a phenotype (the dark-skinned, dark-haired Arab/Muslim/Middle Easterner), mode of dress, written script, and type of name. These symbols provided the visual cues for assaults, verbal insults, property damage, and reports of suspicious activities, as well as random arrests. (Under the assumption that a turban symbolizes the Arab/Muslim/Middle Easterner, Sikhs were attacked and also murdered after 9/11.) One could argue that prior to the 9/11 attacks Arabs and Muslims had been racialized in American society: they were socially constructed as groups of people who were different from others in American society, and those differences were attached to culture and place of origin and understood by many as "racially" identifiable. Racialization is a concept used in the sociological and anthropological literature to describe the social processes by which groups of people are racially formed, that is, how they are constructed and understood collectively and positionally by the pairing of a set of imputed shared characteristics and associated phenotypic (or biological) traits (Omi and Winant 1994). Racialization processes have defined the contours of American social life since the country's founding, and they were the basis for social practices and legislation that accorded differential sets of rights to whites, Native Americans, African Americans, Asian Americans, and Latinos, which in turn reified notions about "race" and produced racialized outcomes. I draw on the racialization paradigm because it allows us to capture social practices and processes that occur over a period of time and thus gives us a perspective on how Arab Americans and Muslim Americans came to be seen by a large sector of the American public as people who were different, with a unique set of characteristically negative attributes. The processual aspect is particularly important in the case of Arab Americans because they have experienced a collective shift in their social status in American society that is only captured by examining their history over time. Arab Americans were once seen as white, although often marginally so, and as such they benefited from a range of rights that were available to whites and denied to members of groups ascribed as nonwhite; they later experienced a reversal of this status through processes highly similar to racial formation.

The work of David Roediger (1991) and Noel Ignatiev (1995) focuses on racial formation and highlights the socially constructed nature of "race" while demonstrating how persons perceived to lie on racial margins can produce and experience "racial" shifts. Racializing processes enabled groups once seen as nonwhite (such as the Irish) to become white and thus to claim a range of benefits accorded to whiteness. In this constructionist view, race is shown to be a fluid concept, not a static one based on immutable biological attributes; as such, the formation of racial groups and imputations of their primary traits can vary over time and place. Here I show that Arab Americans lost many of the benefits of whiteness over time—such as being perceived as unique individuals, being associated with positive attributes, and being protected from structural discrimination—so that when the 9/11 attacks occurred, they were positioned socially to be readily constructed as collectively culpable for the attacks and too politically weak to defend their rights without external institutional support.

The racial formation of Arab Americans as a people whose allegedly innate cultural traits made them different from the white majority occurred at a different historical time than that of the groups historically racialized as nonwhite (Native Americans, African Americans, Asian Americans, and Latinos), and its genesis and outcomes have a number of important differences from those of these groups. The racial formation of Arab Americans as non-white was not historically related to expansion of the American nation or its economic and labor needs, and its burgeoning during the civil rights era, when legal discrimination by race was considered illegitimate, meant that Arab Americans, who entered this racial-shifting period in relatively good socioeconomic position, experienced fewer legislative, residential, and economic barriers than historically racialized groups. Despite these differences, which are reflected in Arab American economic status and minimal residential segregation, Arab American experiences with stereotyping, media vilification, discrimination, government profiling, assertions of collective culpability, hate crimes, and political exclusion share enough in common with these negatively racialized groups to render the racialization paradigm useful. The fact is that while sociologists have a range of concepts to describe social processes that result in positive changes in group status—assimilation, integration, upward mobility—we have few that capture well the collective downfall of a group's social status. Racialization is thus a paradigmatic tool that explains better than any other paradigm or concept currently in use the social processes that transformed a group of individuals whose origins lie in a certain place into a unitary group that came to be understood by large sectors of the American public as different in values and orientation from others, in a way that was symbolically tied to skin color, hair type, mode of dress, script, and name.

The racial formation paradigm is imperfect, however, for a number of reasons. Many Arab Americans identify themselves as white, and quite a few Arab American organizations have taken on a "white ethnic" agenda (Shryock 2008). While the majority of Arab Muslims interviewed in this study said that Arabs were not white, for reasons explained later, this finding differs substantially from the contemporaneous Detroit Arab American Study (DAAS) (Baker et al. 2004), which found that 64 percent of the Arabs and Chaldeans surveyed identified as white.[2] I argue that part of the explanation for this difference is an artifact of methodology: in the DAAS study, respondents were asked to select from a choice of standard American race boxes for which Arab Americans have been socialized to check "white," whether they accept such a designation or not, whereas in my study the question allowed for open-ended responses.[3] I explore this phenomenon briefly in this chapter and in greater detail elsewhere (Cainkar 2008). I also argue here that, as a socially constructed concept, "race" as applied to Arab Americans has specific contextual meanings that vary across time and place and that demographic concentrations matter; understandings about the racial location of Arab Americans may also fluctuate as these variables intersect with skin color and social class. These divergences are matters that require comparative urban studies to determine the social factors at work. But as Andrew Shryock (2008, 99) points out, the racialization paradigm allows us to talk about "the growing rift between 'Arab' and 'white' identities," as well as the social processes that have caused this rift. It is a paradigm that locates a place for Arab Americans as socially constructed "others" within prevailing scholarship on American ethnic groups, while it simultaneously gives "Arabs and Muslims a more secure place within dominant structures of American identity politics" (Shryock 2008, 98). The racial formation paradigm is imperfect because Arab American historic experiences around the concept of race are messy, yet it is useful because it allows for analyses of the social processes that invented how Arab and Muslim Americans were to be seen by others. Racial formation helps to explain how Arabs and Muslims came to be viewed by a large proportion of the American public in a collective and largely negative way, and how these ascriptions were tied to origins in a specific geographic place, which was symbolized by skin color, hair type, written script, mode of dress, and name. This understanding is foundational to explaining Arab and Muslim American experiences after the 9/11 attacks (for a comprehensive discussion of race and Arab Americans, see Jamal and Naber 2008).

Racialization is only tenuously applied to the Muslim American experience, a group for whom there is a much more complex social history. Some have argued that social processes similar to those experienced by Arab Americans have been brought to bear on Muslim Americans, resulting in an understanding among many Americans that Muslims as a religious *group* share a plethora of undesirable characteristics, usually the same ones as Arabs are alleged to hold (Naber 2000; see also Jamal and Naber 2008). Indeed, it is difficult to untangle American stereotypes of Arabs from those applied to Muslims, and in this chapter I point out some of the specific historical reasons for this conflated packaging. The intertwining of caricatures of these two groups helps to explain, for example, why white middle-class opponents of a new southwest suburban Chicago mosque frequently referred to the Muslim "race,"[4] and why some Arab Christians try to disentangle the American understanding of race (Arab) and religion (Islam), leveraging their Christianity as a bridge to the cultural mainstream and to whiteness (Read 2008). In chapter 7, I compare the contemporary treatment of Islam and Muslims in the United States to that of the mid-nineteenth-century treatment of Catholicism and Catholics, leaving the racialization paradigm aside while maintaining the social construction perspective. Nonetheless, in this chapter I tackle some of the historic processes involved in the social construction of Muslims as a deviant group. Since the two terms are often conflated in American culture, there is reason to believe that their social constructions are related to each other.

American Views on Arabs and Muslims: Public Opinion Polls After 9/11

I argue (and demonstrate) that negative views on Arabs and Muslims were widely held before 9/11 and that these views were only solidified by the attacks. This solidification produced widespread public support for collective government policies aimed at them as groups (just as in the case of Japanese Americans) and also produced a wave of hate crimes. Collectivized and negative views on Arabs and Muslims were the subject matter of a number of published articles that appeared in the months after the 9/11 attacks. In his widely reprinted November op-ed piece "Anti-Terror Campaign Has Wide Support, Even at the Expense of Cherished Rights," the Harvard polling researcher Richard Sobel (2001) expressed concerns about the boundaries of the American government's domestic security policies after 9/11 within the context of widespread American public support for treating Arabs differently than other Americans. Citing surveys by the *Washington Post,* the *Wall Street Journal,* the Chicago Council on Foreign Relations, NBC and ABC News, *Newsweek,* the *Chicago Tribune,* and the *Los Angeles Times,* as well as the Gallup, Harris, and Pew organizations, Sobel wrote:

> Most of the public is prepared to endure long waits, searches and identification checks at airports, public buildings and events—68 percent sup-

port letting the police randomly stop people who might *fit a terrorist profile* [emphasis added]. But only 23 percent have said they favor random ID checks on streets and highways, and slightly more than half oppose monitoring calls and e-mail. Half support the right to protest the military action, though an equal group expects people to "rally" around country.

The majorities would, however, more carefully scrutinize Arabs and Arab-Americans, including "more intensive security checks" of Arab passengers on airplanes. As many as one-third feel Arab-Americans should be put under special surveillance. Nearly half approve having Arab-Americans carry special ID cards, and 29 percent even approve internment camps for *suspect groups* [emphasis added]. Classic studies of the 1950s anti-communist era by Robert McClosky found the public willing to give up rights while leaders were more respectful of basic freedoms. Previous egregious rights violations such as the internment of 100,000 Japanese-Americans during World War II have chastened citizens and leaders enough recently to provide compensation, but anti-terrorist sentiment may parallel anti-communist concerns in willingness to take even ineffective efforts to "protect" against an unseen enemy.

Who will stop either the government or the citizenry from going too far? Recognizable end points both for the war on terrorism and for restrictions on free society need to be identified and pursued.

Similar concerns were expressed in an October 2001 article for the *Weekly Defense Monitor* by Colonel Daniel Smith (ret.), chief of research for the Center for Defense Information, who cataloged indicators of the broad public support for government profiling of Arabs and Muslims as a group, noting that negative views of them predated the 9/11 attacks (although he also draws the time line on "traditionally" shorter than it should be).

Gallup News Service, in a review of historical polling data, noted that "Americans traditionally have not held very positive views of Arabs." A February 1991 ABC poll taken during Desert Shield found that 59 percent of Americans associated the term "terrorists" and 56 percent associated the phrase "religious fanatics" with Arabs. A 1993 Gallup survey taken after the World Trade Center bombing revealed that 32 percent of Americans had an "unfavorable" opinion of Arabs.

Since Sept. 11, the poll responses have turned even more negative. A Time/CNN interactive poll on September 13 registered 57 percent of respondents supporting the use of "profiling by age, race, and gender to identify *potentially suspicious* [airline] passengers" [emphasis added]. When asked how they "felt" about Muslims (not just Arabs) living abroad, 31% responded they were less favorably inclined. That number increased to 41 percent with respect to Palestinians and 51 percent with respect to Afghanis.

More disturbing are two polls that included questions directed to security issues in the United States. *Newsweek* found (Sept. 13–14) that

32 percent of Americans thought that Arabs residing in the United States should be under "special surveillance." Thirty-five percent of those questioned in a CNN/USA Today/Gallup survey on Sept. 14–15 said they have less trust in Arabs living in the United States following the attacks. And Gallup discovered (Sept. 14–15) that the general public is "evenly divided" over the question as to whether all Arabs—including U.S. citizens—should be required to have special identification with them at all times.

Perhaps most surprising of all are some journalists, most vehement about their rights and freedom of the press, who are on public record supporting the use of profiling "for awhile."

Such results suggest that the terrorists have shaken, if only temporarily (one can fervently hope), America's embrace of diversity, which is one of our nation's most cherished strengths. Special identity cards are too much like yellow stars of David (Nazi Germany) or badges identifying Hindus (Afghanistan under the Taliban). Special surveillance is reminiscent of procedures applied against Japanese-Americans following December 7, 1941; so far no prominent person has suggested incarcerating citizens of Arabian or "Middle East" heritage as was done in World War II.

Other post-9/11 polls found a majority of Americans in favor of profiling Arabs, including American citizens, and subjecting them to special security checks before boarding planes (*Chicago Sun-Times*, October 2, 2001), and a University of Illinois poll (reported in the *Waukegan News Sun*, December 20, 2001) found large support (nearly 70 percent of Illinois residents) for sacrificing civil rights to fight terrorism, but less support (about one-quarter) for Arab Americans surrendering more rights than others. Nearly one year after the attacks, an August 2002 Gallup poll found that a majority of respondents felt there were "too many" immigrants from Arab countries in the United States (Jones 2002). In his article, Colonel Smith argues that security is "a fundamental issue," but stresses that "it must be security for all; no one group of law-abiding citizens, whether ethnic, religious, or any other category, can be singled out if America is to beat terrorism." The analysis here of government policies implemented after 9/11 (see chapter 4), however, shows that Arabs and Muslims were indeed singled out by government policies, often as a composite group (see, for example, the discussion of special registration in chapter 4), with the stiffest of sanctions applied to those who had violated immigration policies. These strategies provided a perception of security to some Americans, but at the same time sacrificed that of Arabs and Muslims, leading to the sense of "homeland insecurity" articulated by study participants.

The spate of hate crimes that followed the attacks and the "compliance behaviors" (see chapter 5) of members of the American public are further indicators that a significant sector of the American public responded to the immediate implication of nineteen Arab Muslim visitors to the United States in the 9/11 attacks by veering strongly toward an assumption of collective culpability, which was informed by preexisting negative views of Arab and Muslim Americans. The stares, spitting, hate graffiti, finger signs, arsons, and assaults described in this book and documented by others were not aimed at particular individuals but at persons generally perceived to be members of a suspect group by their looks, names, or mode of dress. Similarly, the 96,000 anonymous tips received by the Department of Justice from members of the American public within a week of the 9/11 attacks (Ashcroft 2001a) exposed a correlation in much of the public's mind between a perception of guilt or suspicion and the presence of persons fitting the Arab/Muslim (or Middle Eastern) phenotype or embodying the associated symbols—mode of dress, name, or script. While President Bush made public statements condemning hate crimes and opposing profiling, members of his administration developed policies that relied on profiling and made frequent public statements that threw the light of suspicion on Arab and Muslim American communities (see chapter 4). Even after the National Commission on Terrorist Attacks Upon the United States (National Commission on Terrorist Attacks Upon the U.S. 2004) concluded that there was no evidence of American Arab or Muslim participation in or knowledge of the 9/11 attacks, such collective policies continued. In such a context, public support for special measures reserved for "suspect groups," the "potentially suspicious," or persons who "fit a terrorist profile" is ominous when one considers how broadly such categories were construed to encompass Arab and Muslim American communities across the country.

The supportive acts to defend Arabs and Muslims in the United States (chapters 4, 6, and 8) were likewise based in tacit rejections of racialized understandings of their collective guilt or malevolence. The ring of support around the Sixty-third Street mosque was a performance motivated by opposition to racializing and its propensity to impose collective guilt, and it stood in counterpoint to the angry siege of the Bridgeview mosque (chapter 6). The work of civil rights, immigration, and other nonprofit organizations to protect Arab and Muslim American rights from an overbearing government seeking to sweep them away was also grounded in a rejection of racialized constructions and policies. The Arab/Muslim accounts presented in chapter 2 relay both positive and negative experiences around such understandings, from the close friend who charged that Layla's explanatory statements amounted to support for the 9/11 attacks to Bridgeview's mayor, who walked at 2:00 A.M. through a predominantly Arab Muslim neighborhood under siege, providing a sense of comfort to its Arab and Muslim residents. The jokes of Samia's mother about concentration camps emerged from the fear that collectivization can bring about, while her daughter's bowling alley experience and Hala's hijab taunting show that negative and racialized perspectives on Arabs and Muslims remained years after the attacks. At the same time, the prompt increase in resources and tools made available to Arab and Muslim American organizations, the intensification of anti-racializing work within civil society organizations, and the American public's increased interest in learning more about Arabs and Muslims provided a majority of the Arab Muslims interviewed in this study with a degree of optimism for the future, even though many remained concerned because of the connection they saw between social constructions of Arabs/Muslims and American foreign policy (see chapter 8).

Arab Americans: A Brief History of Immigration and Racial Formation

I argue that Arab Americans had been racialized (Omi and Winant 1994) long before the 9/11 attacks as a unique set of persons from a specific place of origin who share a cluster of negative traits that promote violence and hatred. This racialization was mobilized by a range of parties to produce the social understanding after the attacks that Arab Americans were somehow culpable for them. Out of these racializing processes emerged an identifiable Arab/Muslim/Middle Eastern phenotype, which could be seen as the embodiment of these characteristics; a set of symbolic cues (mode of dress, script, and name) served as further indicators of group status. Although the racialization paradigm is more tenuously applied to Muslims and is sometimes described as a process of "othering" (Said 1978, 1997), Muslim American experiences bear many similarities to those of Arab Americans, and the stereotypes are nearly identical. Many aspects of the racial formation processes experienced by these groups were similar to those experienced by other subordinate groups in the United States, where multiple social institutions engage in imprinting selected traits—portrayed as inherent and unchangeable—on all group members.

It was midcourse in the more than one hundred years they have been in the United States that the social status of Arab Americans changed from one characterized largely by socioeconomic and political inclusion to that of social pariah and political outcast. Just as one can document and measure the process of becoming white (Roediger 1991; Ignatiev 1995), a downgrading of the social status of Arab Americans, accomplished through processes of social construction and racial formation, is measurable by a range of indicators of their social exclusion and by their powerlessness to halt their demonization. A wide range of social institutions—the media, the arts, the news industry, pedagogy, academia, civil society, political organizations, public policies, and popular culture—engaged in a plethora of "racial projects" in which social constructions of the essential differences of Arabs (and later of Muslims) were put forth so extensively as to be widely accepted as common sense and measurable by public opinion polls. The subordinate status of Arab Americans that emerged shared many features with the experiences of people of color: negative mainstream representations, profiling, discrimination, political exclusion, and, after 9/11, observation of and controls over movement and, for immigrants, informal barriers to naturalization.

As Arab Americans *as a group* experienced a major shift in their treatment in American society, a corollary shift occurred in the subjective understanding of many (but by no means all) Arab Americans of their racial position in American society. One need only view dominant representations of Arabs, consult public opinion polls, or spend time among Arab Americans, who strive to lead normal lives in the context of ever-present stereotypic and hostile images, to establish their current subaltern position. Negative representations of Arabs have been a constituent part of American culture for the past three decades and led to the understanding of their collective culpability after the 9/11 attacks. There was a time in Arab American history, however, prior to the unfolding of these processes, when Arab Americans held a social structural position as whites. For example, Arabs were purposely excluded from immigration legislation that established the racial barrier of the Asia Barred Zone (see next section).[5] Although marginal whites, and sometimes contested whites, Arab Americans were largely embraced by the structural perquisites of whiteness, which included understandings of individual uniqueness and personal (not collective) culpability. By September 11, 2001, however, that privileged status was long gone.

Arab Americans in the Early Period: 1900 to the Early 1960s

The overall Arab American experience in the first five decades of the twentieth century differs remarkably from that which followed. Arab Americans spent this early period as a comparatively advantaged group and were afforded many of the protections and benefits of whiteness, which mattered significantly at the time because whiteness made them eligible for homestead lands, unionized jobs, better housing, full legal and voting rights, upward mobility, and access to political office. Between 1880 and 1924, some 95,000 Arabs are estimated to have migrated to the United States from "Greater Syria" (present-day Syria, Lebanon, Jordan, and Palestine/Israel), with additional smaller numbers from Yemen, Iraq, Morocco, and Egypt (Cainkar 1988).[6] While initially males dominated the Arab migration, by 1920 there were more adult female immigrants than adult males (Cainkar 1988). The majority of Arab immigrants had little formal education, were from peasant origins, and were Christian by religion. The published literature on Arab American communities of this period shows that they held structural positions and faced barriers of prejudice and discrimination similar to those of white ethnics, especially Italians (Boosahda 2003; Bragdon 1989; Elkholy 1966; Gualtieri 2004; Hooglund 1987; Naff 1985; Orfalea 1988; Samhan 1999; Zogby 1984). Using as primary indicators of their social status at the time their legal rights to property ownership, voting, and immigration and naturalization and their patterns of residential settlement, intermarriage, and employment, early Arab immigrants and their American-born children—numbering some 100,000 persons by 1924 (Hitti 1924)—largely fit into a marginal white category, similar to the one occupied by Italians, Poles, Slavs, Jews, and Greeks. Although Arabs were barred from a broad range of institutions run by dominant white groups and faced discrimination, they settled without documented restrictions in urban and rural areas, ran businesses and traveled freely about the country as traders, worked as unionized laborers in manufacturing, built community institutions, flourished as writers, and held offices in state and local governments. They achieved a degree of economic success, experienced upward social mobility, and led social lives that were intertwined with members of white ethnic groups, often resulting in intermarriage.

Of course, there are meaningful exceptions to this broadly simplified history, and there were specific localities where, for example, the right of Arabs to become naturalized U.S. citizens was challenged on the basis of race, especially during the era of widespread nativism that characterized the nation between 1910 and 1924. During those times, Arab whiteness was contested in specific localities, such as Detroit, Buffalo, Cincinnati, St. Louis, and parts of Georgia and South Carolina, by particular court clerks and judges seeking to block their naturalization, such as in the emblematic Dow case (Smith 2002). In the words of the historian Helen Hatab Samhan (1999), in these places Arabs were "not quite white." Disparate experiences around racial status showed that Arabs sat in an ambiguous position at the margins of whiteness; indeed, Nadine Naber (2000) refers to Arab Americans as "ambiguous insiders." Arab American marginality is graphically illustrated in the boundaries of the Asia Barred Zone, created by Congress in 1917 legislation to denote geographic barriers to immigration: some parts of the Arab world, specifically parts of modern-day Yemen, Saudi Arabia, and Somalia, were included, while others were excluded (see map 3.1).[7] These boundaries were quite arbitrary at the edges because they were crafted using rough measures of latitude and longitude, but the inclusion of parts of Yemen in the zone provided ammunition for those who opposed Yemeni naturalization on the basis of race.[8]

These negative experiences around race, however, were neither universal nor representative of the early Arab American experience and are counterposed, for example, by the widely documented, largely unfettered

Map 3.1   Asia Barred Zone, 1917

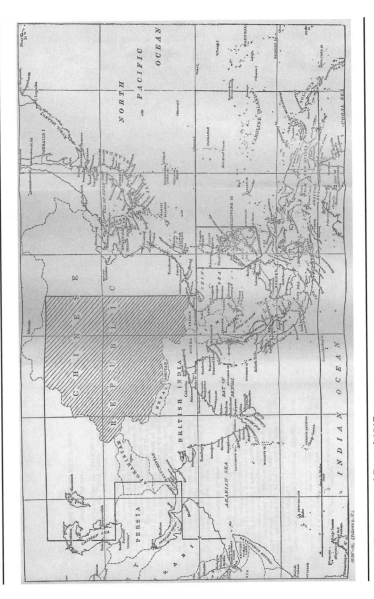

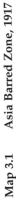

Source: Congressional Record 1917.

Note: Section indicated by diagonal lines covered by treaty and laws relating to Chinese. The Philippine Islands are United States possessions and therefore not included in barred zone.

freedom of movement experienced by Arabs—whether Christian, Muslim, or Druze—engaged in commerce (Hooglund 1987; Naff 1985; Orfalea 1988; Zogby 1984). The variations in early Arab American experiences around racial status highlight that racial projects are given meaning as they are embedded in local social relationships (Omi and Winant 1994; Gualtieri 2004). Locally embedded meanings as applied to Arab Americans and race would emerge again to produce variations in Arab American experiences after 9/11, as illustrated in chapter 6. Overall, in the early part of the twentieth century, Arab Americans experienced levels of social and political inclusion and economic mobility largely reserved for whites and denied to negatively racialized groups (African Americans, Asian Americans, Native Americans, and Latinos). The migration of Arabs to the United States was significantly reduced in the 1920s owing to quotas based on their small numbers in the 1910 and 1890 censuses (Cainkar 1988) and to ideas about racial hierarchy among groups now considered white.[9]

Orientalist ideas about Arab culture that constructed a place where the mystical, exotic, sexualized, and barbaric played out as primary modes of daily life were present in American culture during the first half of the twentieth century; such ideas were represented at world's fairs (Little Cairo), in films (*The Sheikh*), and in dance productions (Salomé's "Dance of the Seven Veils"), while associated arabesque shapes and styles could be found on theater marquees (the Oriental) and in commercial advertising (Shohat and Stam 1994; Salem 1999; McAlister 2005; Little 2002). The following quote invoking sexualized imagery, *Arabian Nights,* and harems, reported by Ray Hanania (2005, 13), is from the book *Chicago Confidential* (Lait and Mortimer 1950, 71). It describes the "Sons of the Prophet" as follows:

> You won't find any camels at 18th and Michigan. Chicago's small Arabic quarter is surrounded by Automobile Row. If you can digest such, there are several native restaurants serving Near Eastern delicacies which you are supposed to eat with your hands. Arabs sell tapestry and rugs, wholesale and retail. Many merchants who say they are Arabs (because business is business) are not. You will find no orgies out of the Arabian Nights here. Chicago's Arabs don't keep harems and if they did you wouldn't care to look twice at their women. They wouldn't be to your taste. The chief past time is drinking thick, black coffee and playing cards.

While these images and descriptions expressed notions of the Eastern, Arab, and Muslim other, who was not only different from the white American but culturally inferior, little evidence has been presented to date that these ideas were imprinted on Arab Americans to justify discrimination against them or to argue for their social and political exclusion. It was only later that such Orientalist ideas would provide a ready-made tool kit for vilifying Arab Americans.

Arab Immigration and Race

Contested cases around Arab immigrants, race, and immigration benefits were put to rest in 1943 when the Immigration and Naturalization Service (INS) took a stronger hand in clarifying its policies, asserting control over the discretion of local clerks and judges in ambiguous cases. The INS view was that Arabs were white and fully eligible for immigration and naturalization benefits (unlike most Asians at the time), and it issued an "instruction" on the matter for INS offices across the nation. The INS used an argument prepared for a government brief in the historic 1923 *United States v. Thind* case to support its assertion that Arabs were white because of the "shared civilization" between the Near East and the West (U.S. Department of Justice 1943).[10] Marian Smith (2002), who studied the history of U.S. immigration policy and race as applied to Arabs, describes the case of Majid Ramsay Sharif (Shariph) as emblematic of INS views on the racial status of Arabs in the early 1940s. Sharif, an Arab, had applied for an immigration visa in 1941, but was denied as an alien racially ineligible for citizenship. Because Sharif's case was not a petition for naturalization, the question went not to a court clerk or judge but to the Board of Immigration Appeals (BIA). According to Smith (2002):

> In Sharif's case involving the eligibility of an Arab, the Board, like the courts, relied on the *Thind* decision. Unlike the courts, the BIA was persuaded by a brief for the U.S. government in the *Thind* case that argued that "whiteness," for lack of a better term, is associated with Western civilization, and Western civilization includes "so much of the Near East as contributed to, and was assimilable with, the development of Western Civilization of Greece and Rome."[11] Having recalled the cultural link between the ancient and modern western worlds, the Board concluded "that it was not intended, either in 1790 at the time of the first enactment of the governing statute or certainly in 1940 at the time of its last enactment, that Arabians be excluded from the group of 'white persons.' "

Although Orientalist tropes about Arabs as culturally different and inferior had already been invented and were circulating widely in Europe (Said 1978; Mitchell 1988), which administered quite a few Arab colonies at the time, and these tropes were widely evident in American popular culture, they were not universally mobilized in this period to argue for special policies based on inherent civilizational differences between Arab Americans and the rest of American society. As these cases show, although the "color" of Arabs brought about challenges to their rights in some places, a competing discourse of shared civilizations affirmed their qualification for the rights associated with whiteness.

In comparison, around the same historical time Japanese American citizens and noncitizens living in the western United States were being forcibly relocated and interned by the U.S. government. These government policies were backed by the Roberts Commission Report of January 1942,[12] which argued that an alleged Japanese American espionage network was complicit in the Pearl Harbor attack. The following month, President Franklin D. Roosevelt issued Executive Order 9066 authorizing internment. The U.S. Supreme Court upheld the legality of internment in its 1944 *Korematsu* decision when the majority of justices found that military interests prevailed over the presumption against racial discrimination.[13] These events showed what could be done by government in times of national crisis to a sector of the American population that had been racialized as inherently different, with the kind of popular consent that Smith (2001) and Sobel (2001) noted with reference to Arabs and Muslims in the United States in 2001. Some forty years later, the U.S. Commission on Wartime Relocation issued "Personal Justice Denied," a report that concluded that Japanese internment was not justified by military necessity and that the policy was the outcome of racial prejudice, war hysteria, and a failure of political leadership (U.S. Commission on Wartime Relocation 1983).

Mass-mediated discourses during the World War II era spoke of Hitler, Mussolini, and the "Japs."[14] Hitler and Mussolini, as whites, were represented, not as symbolic of European, white, or Christian culture, but as deviants and outliers to those cultures. Modernity, rationality, peacefulness, and individuality had been established in the dominant American culture as primary correlates of whiteness, so that reprehensible acts committed by whites would be constructed as matters of individual culpability bearing no reflection on the group. The Japanese, on the other hand, were represented as both monolithic and culturally flawed, so the negative actions of any Japanese were symbolic of the potential actions of all. These notions of cultural culpability gave support to the designation of Japanese Americans as fifth columnists and their subsequent internment, an outcome neither German Americans nor Italian Americans experienced en masse. The Japanese American experience with internment was a historical event of the first half of the twentieth century that would become highly meaningful sixty years later for Arab and Muslim Americans as it emerged as one of their most haunting fears. It was also the core reason for quick Japanese American mobilization in support of Arab and Muslim American civil rights after 9/11.

The Post–World War II Period

Internal pressures to end the racial exclusions that were core to U.S. immigration policies intensified after World War II, from which the United States emerged as a new global power. Racial exclusions were increasingly seen as impractical in a context in which the U.S. government sought to enhance its power and influence through global alliances, including alliances with nations whose people were barred from immigrating to the United States. The emerging American empire amended its immigration policies to fit the battle against world communism, trading racial bars for ideological bars. The Alien Registration Act (also known as the Smith Act), passed by Congress in 1940 as an anti-Communist measure, made it illegal for anyone in the United States to advocate, abet, or teach the desirability of overthrowing the government and required alien residents over fourteen years of age to register with the government. The Chinese Exclusion Act (dating from 1882) was repealed in 1943 in recognition of China's partnership in World War II, and Chinese immigrants finally became eligible for naturalized U.S. citizenship. In 1946, Filipinos, persons of Filipino descent, and persons of the "races" indigenous to India became eligible for naturalization. The Immigration and Nationality Act of 1952, also known as the McCarran-Walter Act, among other things, finally removed all racial bars to naturalization, eliminated the Asia Barred Zone, and established immigration preferences for certain occupations. In place of race, membership in Communist or other "subversive" organizations became a cause for exclusion from the United States.

In one of its first implementations of a specific refugee policy, the U.S. Congress passed two refugee relief acts for Palestinian refugees, one in 1953 and another in 1957, necessitated when more than 770,000 Palestinian Arabs became de facto permanently expelled from Western Palestine upon the creation of the state of Israel in 1948 (Abu-Lughod 1986) and the U.S. government found it to be in its strategic interest to maintain good relations with Arabs and Muslims. The Palestinian refugees, as they came to be known, fled to neighboring Arab countries and to parts of Palestine still under Arab control, including East Jerusalem and the areas now referred to as the West Bank and Gaza. A total of 1,939 Palestinian refugees entered the United States between 1954 and 1958 under the 1953 act, and an additional 985 Palestinian refugees entered between 1958 and 1963 under the 1957 expansion.

When President Truman voted in 1948 in favor of the partition of Palestine into Jewish and Arab states, his letter of transmittal and the U.S. Department of State (1950) document to which it was attached strongly supported generous American aid to the Palestinian refugees because it was good for American foreign policy interests in the Near East:

> The security and prosperity of the Western World, and its relations to other parts of the world, are closely linked with the fate of the Near Eastern countries. . . . Together these countries comprise an area of great strategic importance in world affairs. . . . It is estimated that the Near East, including the whole Arabian peninsula and Iran, contains about

50% of the potential oil supply of the world. . . . The Near East is the center of the Moslem religion, which is of great influence in the area stretching from Africa on the Atlantic and Mediterranean to Indonesia and the Philippines in the Pacific. If the Near East were dominated by powers hostile to the United States, those powers would be in a position to extend cultural and political penetration to the remainder of the vast Moslem area, now generally friendly to us. . . . From these contacts [a reference to the contributions of American missionaries and schools in the area] from which both Americans and Arabs have gained, there have arisen firm bonds of sympathy and cooperation. This reservoir of good will is a valuable asset to this country and is well worth preserving. All of these interests have been threatened by developments in Palestine, over the last few years. The fate of the Arab refugees from Palestine, numbering some three quarters of a million people, destitute, disillusioned, underfed, ill-housed, and idle, is a matter of deep concern to those countries bordering on Israel who now give them sanctuary, as well as to other nations throughout the world who are seeking peace and lasting security. Humanitarian considerations deeply affect our attitude toward these people; the American people also have reason for concern on grounds of self-interest.

Truman's statement offers a humanized and sympathetic view of the Palestinians, documents the goodwill between the Arab people and the United States and friendly American relations with the "vast Moslem area," and notes the importance of transportation routes and oil to American interests. But in a turn of political history that would presage dramatic changes in the Arab American experience, scholars mark 1956 and the U.S. government's handling of the Suez Crisis as a turning point in the American role in the Arab world and as the last time U.S. policies in the area were even-handed. According to the historian Rashid Khalidi (1993, 536):

It is acknowledged by virtually all students of Suez, of the policies of the superpowers in the Middle East, and of the Arab-Israeli conflict, that Suez marked some sort of turning point. . . . Thus, the United States emerges from the Suez crisis in most accounts as the dominant Western power in the region, having benefited from the disaster of the Anglo-French-Israeli aggression on Egypt, to replace Britain and France, and soon to inherit Israel from Britain and France as a privileged regional client and ally.

From that time on, American foreign policies for the region focused on building allies and thwarting enemies in the Cold War, gaining and maintaining unfettered access to oil, and supporting Israel's stated interests. These strategic objectives led to a more corporate definition of American foreign policy interests that would nudge humanitarian concerns and goodwill to the background.

These post–World War II domestic and global policy changes had qualitative impacts on the composition of Arab American communities. By 1936, Palestinians had surpassed Syrians and Lebanese as the largest Arab immigrant group to the United States (Cainkar 1988). Slowed down by the war, levels of Palestinian Arab immigration rose after 1945, according to INS data, with spouses and children of U.S. citizens constituting one-quarter to one-third of the Palestine-born immigrants from 1947 to 1950. According to Abdul Jalil al-Tahir (1952), after World War II, Arab Muslim American men who had previously lived separately from their wives and children began bringing them to the United States. In addition, male Arab immigrants who fought with the U.S. military in World War II brought their families to the United States under provisions of the War Brides Act of 1945 (Cainkar 1988). Changes in immigration policies brought about by the McCarran-Walter Act inaugurated the migration of a tier of middle-class, educated Arabs, from a wider range of countries, who came to the United States for study and professional work, many bringing with them vibrant pan-Arabist political ideas. Beginning in the 1950s, Arab immigrants included highly educated Egyptians and Iraqis, predominantly entrepreneurial Jordanians and laboring Yemenis, as well as Lebanese, Syrian, and Palestinian family chain migrants and new groups from advantaged backgrounds. Newly permitted migrations from Asia, averaging some fifteen thousand persons per year in the 1950s, started the trend toward an increasingly diverse immigrant population whose religious affiliations—Hindu, Buddhist, and Muslim—varied from the American norm.

In general, the period of the 1940s through the early 1960s is one of the least explored in Arab American history. Like that of many other groups limited by quotas, immigration from the Arab world was relatively low throughout this period. New immigrants were relatives of earlier immigrants or part of the new Arab brain drain, augmented by a few thousand Palestinian refugees. The impacts of the pan-Arabist political views brought by new immigrants and the growing Palestinian diaspora on Arab American organizing have yet to be fully explored, with a few exceptions (see Zaghel 1977). Some scholars have argued that pan-Arab organizing existed in the United States during this early period; they point out that throughout the period from the 1920s to the 1940s Arab Americans had attempted to lobby members of the American government to oppose the partition of Palestine, but found their efforts dwarfed by larger and well-organized Jewish efforts supporting its partition (Davidson 1999; Bawardi 2007). Arab Americans were active labor organizers in cities where Arab Americans were core industrial laborers (Suleiman 1999; Georgakas 1975; Ahmed 1975). Although relatively unknown to other Arabs, thousands of Yemeni immigrants toiled as farmworkers in California (Bisharat 1975; Friedlander 1988).[15] In Chicago,

Palestinian Muslims had ongoing relationships with African American Muslims, and a few taught in Nation of Islam (NOI) schools. This relationship was severed after teacher Jamil Diab rejected the religious legitimacy of the NOI in a 1959 article published in the prominent African American newspaper, the *Chicago Defender* (Curtis 2002, 81).

As the narrative is now written, from the 1940s through the mid-1960s, Arab American demography was dominantly second- and third-generation; these groups intermarried extensively with whites (especially Irish Americans), lost the use of the Arabic language, and participated in organizations based on religious affiliations and local places of origin, although some organizations built more broadly on national origins did exist (Orfalea 2006). Michael Suleiman (1999b, 10) provides a profile of new Arab immigrants anxious to be engaged actors in American society:

> Immigrants who arrived after World War II came with a well-defined view of democracy and the role of citizens within it. . . . Their higher level of education and social status gave them greater confidence about participating in American politics as soon as they arrived in their new country. Even when they thought about returning to their Arab homeland, they were anxious to live full and productive lives in the United States or Canada for themselves or their children.

Although further research is needed to complicate this profile of the 1940s through early 1960s, the dominant Arab American story of the first half of the twentieth century is one of economic success and upward mobility, relatively unhindered by barriers of race or religion as compared to historically racialized groups.

Arab Migration to the United States After 1965

The overhaul in U.S. immigration policy codified in the 1965 Immigration Act—the removal of country quotas, introduction of family reunification preferences, and expansion of immigrant visas for persons with skills needed in the United States—brought about major changes in the character of migration to the United States. The majority of new immigrants were no longer from Europe but from Latin America, Asia, and Africa. Although Arabs were not a new immigrant group, their numbers increased markedly after these changes. Between 1965 and 2000, more than 630,000 Arabs immigrated to the United States, mostly under family reunification preferences, although a significant proportion of some groups, particularly Egyptians, came on professional visas. In the 1990s and early in the twenty-first century, large numbers of Iraqis (including Assyrians), Somalis, and Sudanese came to the United States as refugees. Palestinians, the largest refugee population in the world for much of the second half of the twentieth century, became ineligible as a group for U.S. refugee status after the early 1960s (Cainkar 1988). There were also short periods during which small numbers of Libyans were admitted as refugees and asylees and during which Lebanese and Palestinians from Kuwait received temporary protected status. Overall, family migration has been the dominant pattern among Arab immigrants, who migrate seeking personal safety, political stability, better work and educational opportunities, a better life for their children, and the capacity to generate enough capital to support family left back home. Global economic policies and external demands for restructuring, relatively low local salaries, and slow economic development have made life more and more economically difficult for greater shares of the population in much of the Arab world; in addition to war and military occupation, these conditions impel people to emigrate (see chapter 1 for more data on Arab immigration to the United States).

In 2000 the U.S. Census Bureau counted about one and a half million persons of Arab ancestry in the United States, although the Arab American Institute argues that the correct number is closer to three and a half million. The Institute's census information center (CIC) notes, "Like other ethnic, minority, and immigrant populations, Arab Americans are undercounted in the U.S. census. Some simply do not understand the relevance of the census, its confidentiality, or did not respond to the question on the sample 'long form' that measures ethnic ancestry."[16] In chapter 1, I mentioned other problems with census data collection among Arabs, in particular the fear factor. According to data from the 2000 census, Arab Americans boast a range of income, education, and skill levels whose medians place them above the American norm. Their median household income at the national level was $47,000, higher than that of the overall American population ($42,000).[17] A greater proportion of Arab Americans have a bachelor's degree or higher than does the U.S. population as a whole (40 percent versus 24 percent) and 17 percent of persons of Arab ancestry in the United States have a postgraduate degree, compared to 9 percent of the overall American population. The Arab American rate of 85 percent holding a high school diploma parallels the overall U.S. rate, as does the Arab American labor force participation rate (64 percent). Although Arab Americans are widely dispersed in the United States, their largest numbers are in California, Michigan, Illinois, Ohio, New York, Texas, and Florida. The largest municipal concentration of Arab Americans is in Dearborn, Michigan.

In an analysis of 1990 census data, Jen'nan Ghazal Read (2004) finds that Arab American women had lower rates of labor force participation (60 percent) than Anglo (73 percent), black (73 percent), Asian (70 percent), and Hispanic (66 percent) women, and that much of this difference is explained by the low rates posted by immigrant Arab women (45 percent versus 72 percent for U.S.-born Arab women). Read's survey of Arab American women found a high degree of intragroup diversity in ethnic identity, cultural beliefs, and religiosity, high rates of educational achievement and English-language proficiency, a propensity to work in professional and managerial occupations, and a "model minority" profile. A transnational study of Palestinian and Jordanian immigrants living in Chicago and "returnees" living in Amman, Jordan, found that many families with the resources to do so migrated back to their countries of origin only to return later, migrating and returning in circular patterns at different stages of the life cycle (Cainkar, Abunimah, and Raei 2004). These immigrants varied in their opinions as to whether life in the United States was qualitatively better than life in their home countries, but most agreed that it was economically better and offered more employment and educational opportunities.

Arab American Experiences: The Late 1960s to the Present

Scholars of Arab Americans and Arab American activists mark the onset of changes in the social status and identities of Arab Americans as June 1967 (see, for example, Terry 1999; Suleiman 1999; Naber 2008; Shryock 2008). The social context was the Israeli-Arab War. More precisely, it was American government support for Israel and its occupation of East Jerusalem, the West Bank, Gaza, and parts of Egypt (Sinai) and Syria (Golan Heights), as well as American media coverage of the war, which, according to Arab Americans, almost unanimously celebrated Israel's conquest, relying on tropes that denigrated Arabs to do so. As noted earlier, strong American government alliances with Israel were one of the foreign policy outcomes of the 1956 Suez Crisis, when Britain, France, and Israel attacked Egypt (see Khalidi 1993). According to Gary Awad (1981, 31), "The shock for Arab Americans was not so much the defeat . . . but the way it was received in the West and especially the United States, where strong derogatory racial overtones in the media toward the Arab contributed significantly, for the first time, to a growing political and ethnic awareness in the Arab American community." Referring to 1967 as a "watershed" in Arab American history, Suleiman (1999b, 10) reports that older and newer Arab Americans were "shocked and traumatized by the 1967 war," in particular by "how greatly one-sided and pro-Israeli the American communications media were in reporting on the Middle East." The 1967 Arab-Israeli War ignited an "Arab American awakening," reports Naber (2008, 33). Arab Americans reported stingingly negative portrayals of Arabs as backward, defeated, and primitive in newspapers and on television sets across the nation, both during the course of the war and persistently thereafter.[18] As a result, "Arab Americans were forced to rethink their identities in response to U.S. government policies and American media representations. The latter were negative, biased against Arabs and Muslims, and profoundly alienating," reports Shryock (2008, 94).

Although there are two narratives about who started the 1967 war—the dominant Western version places the Arabs as aggressors, and the alternative narrative places Israel in that role—facts are not particularly relevant to racial formation, which relies on notions of innate cultural attributes and inevitable fates. The war's outcome was the Israeli military occupation of parts of three Arab countries (Egypt, Syria, and Jordan) and its military absorption of the rest of Palestine, including East Jerusalem. While this outcome was celebrated by many Israelis, it was a devastating blow to Palestinians, for whom it marked yet another forced migration, a bureaucratic revocation of residency rights, more land confiscations, and presaged decades of living under an oppressive military regime. The American media overwhelmingly portrayed the outcome of the 1967 war as a victory that Americans should identify with and be elated about. This sense of shared triumph was accomplished through the use of an "us-and-them" dichotomy: Americans and Israelis stood together on one side representing power, success, and another step forward for civilized humanity; on the other side were the Arabs, who were weak, incompetent, backward, and morally undeserving of controlling their own destiny. The political scientist Amaney Jamal (2008, 119) links these oppositional discourses, which have been used fairly consistently in the American media ever since, to the racialization of Arabs and Muslims in the United States. She argues that "the racialization of Muslims and Arabs stems from the consistent deployment of an 'us' versus 'them' mentality, excessively propped up for the justification of military campaigns in the Arab world."

By 1967, the United States had reached superpower status and was competing for global hegemony with the Soviet Union. Its foreign policies and foreign aid were dominated by three major concerns: anticommunism, maintaining open access to oil resources, and support for the state of Israel.[19] Its immigration policy mirrored these political objectives: Communist ideology remained a bar to immigration, and U.S. refugee policy prioritized persons fleeing Communist governments. The idea behind this particular refugee policy was that the Communist enemy was an ideology and form of political rule from which people could be, and should be, saved. But because Arabs were increasingly represented as a *people* who were dangerous (as opposed to an ideology), there was little space to develop popular compassion for them, including those who were refugees. How can an Arab flee his or her own essence? If communism was the Cold War enemy of the United States, *Arabness* was portrayed as the enemy of American interests in the Middle East. In this construction, Arabs become refugees when they are fleeing political rule that is portrayed as *characteristically* Arab: oppressive, dictatorial, and irrational. This construction cleverly reaffirms the stereotype of the Arab while allowing that Arabs who reject Arabness can be saved; at the same time, it explains the popularity of books in the American corporate press by Arabs (and others) that are exposés of Arabs (and others) escaping the alleged unvarying inflexibility and constriction of Arab societies—augmented later by the genre of Muslims fleeing Muslim-majority societies.

Erecting negative constructions of the Arab in American popular culture and in political discourses did not require major work or innovation. Deprecating Orientalist tropes developed in Europe during the Middle Ages and expanded during the centuries of European empire were readily available for use (Said 1978). These tropes could be mobilized to explain the actions of Arabs (and later Muslims) "as congenital, not as having any foundation in grievances, prior violence, or continuing conflicts," as Edward Said argued in the debate sponsored by the Middle East Studies Association (MESA) that featured Said, Bernard Lewis, Christopher Hitchens, and Leon Wieseltier (MESA 1987). Arab grievances with American, Israeli, or other externally generated policies would be described with reference to supposedly unchanging seventh-century modes of life and to tribes, feuds, and emotionalism. They were therein transformed into predicaments that defied rational solution. Arab responses to these policies were framed as irrational, self-defeating, and reflecting an inherent brutality, and notions such as "Arabs know only violence" became cultural givens (MESA 1987). The Arab world would be persistently described in the mainstream American media as a cauldron, chaotic and unstable, containing cities teeming with people driven by emotions. Americans largely came to assume that, like nowhere else in the world, all of the twenty-two widely varying Arab countries were largely the same, united in their inherent cultural dispositions and hatred of Americans and the West.

The use of Orientalist tropes in the American mass media to garner public support for American foreign policies has been well documented by scholars of literature, culture, and the media (see, for example, Said 1978; Abu-Laban and Suleiman 1989; Karim 2000; MESA 1987). While this foreign policy role has often been discussed, the underpinning role of Orientalist tropes in evolving perceptions of Arab Americans has received much less attention. Nonetheless, Mary Ann Fay (1984, 22) noted that "the source of today's defamation of Arab-Americans might be described as the domestic counterpart of the Arab-Israeli conflict." James Zogby (1984, 21) wrote in the same American-Arab Anti-Discrimination Committee (ADC) report that domestic "images of greedy oil sheiks and bloodthirsty terrorists" were tied to political and economic events in the Middle East. Also highlighting the foreign policy connection, Baha Abu-Laban and Michael Suleiman (1989, 5) have noted that the source of bias against Arabs in the United States relates "more to the original homeland and peoples than to the Arab-American community."

Although perhaps unintended, the domestic social by-product of the widespread use of Orientalist stereotypes to garner support for U.S. foreign policies was the racialization of Arab Americans, who came to be seen by many Americans as a unique group of people sharing an inherent set of negative traits. Since the alleged negative traits of Arabs were portrayed as innate, it is no surprise that their persistent highlighting in the context of ongoing world events (in which the United States was an interested party) would lead many Americans over time to view Arab Americans in the same light. Although Arabs in the United States were not the specific subjects of these stereotypes and caricatures spreading through American popular culture, little could block the eventual imprinting of these stigmata on Arab Americans. The specific meaning of innate traits as interpreted in an American social context would produce their racializing impacts. Explaining his use of the term "anti-Arab racism" instead of Orientalism, Stephen Salaita (2006, 14) points out that the Arab American experience must be located in the specific context of American traditions:

> Orientalism is not entirely appropriate when we consider the effects of stereotyping and bigotry on Arab Americans, who . . . need to be located in a particular tradition of which they have been a partial inheritor. That tradition, uniquely American, includes the internment of Japanese Americans during WWII, institutionalized anti-Semitism until the 1960s, and a peculiarly durable xenophobia spanning decades.

Arab American intellectuals were stunned by the way in which Arabs were portrayed in the American media during the 1967 war and immediately mobilized to provide the American public with an alternative discourse on the war and its outcome. Shortly thereafter, they established the Association of Arab-American University Graduates (AAUG), whose mission was "to develop, foster, and promote educational and cultural information and activities on the Arab World and the Arab-American community." In its introductory statement, the AAUG noted that "the June 1967 war changed the Arab-American community by jolting many . . . second- and third-generation Arab-Americans and causing a highly hostile attitude toward Arab-origin individuals in the U.S. and Canada."[20] Cultural constructs about the core of being Arab were undergoing transformation in American society, and Arab Americans found that they ceased to be embraced by the protections of whiteness, in particular its corollary of individual culpability. From then on, acts constructed as negative that were committed by Arabs anywhere in the world were easily imprinted on all Arabs, and stories of Arab violence and brutality were destined to become the primary theme of films, television shows, books, and cartoons, reinforcing notions of the collective sameness and cultural inferiority of Arabs. Stories of everyday Arab life revolving around birth, death, love, marriage, family, health, work, sports, or leisure would become unmarketable in the United States, unless they could be used to demonstrate the theme of Arab difference.

Arab Americans identified little with the images of cruelty and irrationality, and many raised in the West went on life-shaping journeys to discover firsthand a reality that they knew was different from these images, but Arab Americans were nonetheless increasingly identified with these images by others. Some forty years after its inception, the efforts of the AAUG and countless others to humanize the construction of the Arab in the United States had made little headway. They were up against a mighty industry that produced Halloween masks, video games, films, television series, talk shows, musical lyrics, and school curricula that leveraged Orientalist stereotypes of Arabs for fun, profit, or political gain, establishing these ideas as part and parcel of American popular culture. Despite persistent documentation of the proliferation of these dehumanizing images and repeated formal appeals to put a stop to them, Arab Americans found little external support for their claims.[21] A complex set of factors produced this lack of support, including the absence of Arab Americans at the table of the historically racialized groups who were institutionalized as the only legitimate claimants to charges of racism.

Pollsters discovered that American attitudes toward Arabs were becoming "close to racist" by the mid-1970s. Seymour Martin Lipset and William Schneider (1977, 22) reported:

> If large numbers of Americans feel warmly toward Israel, there is some evidence to suggest that a significant minority has negative, close to racist, attitudes toward the Arabs. This conclusion is suggested in the results of a poll taken by Pat Caddell's Cambridge Survey Research organization in the summer of 1975. Caddell gave respondents a list of images and asked them: "Does each word apply more to the Arabs or more to the Israelis?" Nearly half or more said that the terms "greedy," "arrogant," and "barbaric" apply to the Arabs; relatively few described the Arabs as "peaceful," as "honest," as "friendly," or as "like Americans," while a majority used these terms to describe the Israelis.

In 1981 a public opinion poll conducted by Shelley Slade showed that large percentages of Americans used the adjectives "barbaric," "cruel," "treacherous," "warlike," and "bloodthirsty" to describe Arabs. She concluded that "Arabs remain one of the few ethnic groups that can still be slandered with impunity in America" (Slade 1981, 143). Research on Arab Americans after the late 1960s emphasized the significant roles of prejudice, discrimination, stereotyping, political and social exclusion, and government profiling on the Arab American experience (Abraham and Abraham 1983; Abu-Laban 1989; Aswad 1974; Bassiouni 1974; Cainkar 1988; McCarus 1994; Shaheen 1984, 2001; Suleiman 1999; Zogby 1984). The American mainstream media and popular culture representations were consistently charged with producing and reproducing anti-Arab sentiments. Jack Shaheen's (1984) first analysis of portrayals of Arabs on American television examined more than one hundred television shows featuring an Arab character that appeared in 1975–1976 and in 1983–1984. He found pervasive and persistent negative stereotypes of Arabs, including in children's educational programming. According to Shaheen, the depiction of Arabs on American television relied on what he called "four basic myths": Arabs are "fabulously wealthy"; Arabs are "barbaric and uncultured"; Arabs are "sex maniacs with a penchant for white slavery"; and Arabs "revel in acts of terrorism." In his subsequent study of portrayals of Arabs in American comic books, Shaheen (1991, 8–9) made the following discoveries:

> Out of 218 Arab types appearing in 215 comic books, this author found 149 characters portrayed as "evil," 30 characters portrayed as "good," and 39 characters portrayed as "common people." Hence, the comic book reader sees three villainous Arabs to every heroic one. Not a flattering ratio. In reality, the imbalance is much greater. How so? The thirty Arab types the author has classified as "good" are almost without exception passive and play minor roles. They are not actively good in the same way nearly all 149 villains are actively evil.

Ronald Stockton's (1994, 138) analysis of the caricatures appearing on newsprint editorial pages, in cartoon strips, and in comic books shows their similarity to past images that portrayed blacks as inferior and subjectable, Japanese as savage and subhuman, and Jews as socially hostile with "thought processes alien to normal humans." Laurence Michalak (1983) finds negative representations of Arabs located across a broad spectrum of American popular culture: songs, jokes, television, cartoons, comics, and films. In American cinema, he finds "overwhelming and undeniable evidence that there exists a harshly pejorative stereotype of Arabs" (30). Comparing films of the 1920s to those of the 1960s, Michalak concludes that (1) "the Arab world had changed but the Arab stereotype had not," (2) that "Hollywood's Middle East has become a more sinister place," and (3) that there had been a "change toward more explicitly anti-Arab movie genres (30)." Films themed around the Arab-Israeli conflict portrayed Arabs and Jews in ways characteristic of American cowboy and Indian films—one group always good, the other always bad. Michalak notes that Israeli films on this topic were far more complex than the simplistic American fare of good and evil. According to Shaheen and other analysts (Ghareeb 1983), American films produced in the 1970s and 1980s cemented the cognitive association between terrorism and Arabs; the images in turn associated a particular phenotype, gender, and mode of dress to the terrorist profile: males with swarthy complexions, dark hair, and hook noses, wearing turbans and scarves and carrying swords reminiscent of eras long past but ever-present to the unchanging Arab.

Dismantling these popular understandings of an innate and barbaric Arab personality and reversing the conditions of discrimination that emerged from them were the primary organizational objectives of the most important pan-Arab American organizations founded since the 1960s—the Association of Arab-American University Graduates (AAUG), the American-Arab Anti-Discrimination Committee (ADC), the Arab American Institute (AAI), and the National Association of Arab Americans (NAAA). One of the first studies of early Arab American communities commissioned by an Arab American organization (the ADC) noted:

> At a time when the United States is more receptive to cultural pluralism, and ethnicity is no longer socially unacceptable, Arab Americans remain primary targets of defamatory attacks on their cultural and personal character. Thus, much of the activity of the Arab-American community has been directed at correcting the stereotypes that threaten to produce a new wave of anti-Arab racism in the United States and endanger the civil and human rights of the Arab-American community. (Zogby 1984, 21)

Not only did these images affect Arab American identities and social relationships, but they produced waves of hate crimes against persons perceived to be Arab each time a crisis unfolded in the Arab world where an Arab protagonist acted against Americans or American interests, or when American military action was taken against an Arab country. Cataloging a long list of assaults, murders, bombings, arsons, attacks on property, and telephone threats against Arab Americans that occurred in the 1980s, the anthropologist Nabeel Abraham (1994, 162) wrote in the mid-1990s that "a pattern is nonetheless discernable—terrorist incidents and other events occurring in the Middle East, especially those involving U.S. citizens and played up by the administration and the press, could trigger threats and violence against Middle Easterners anywhere in the country." Abraham further pointed out that most of these incidents went unmentioned in major reports on hate violence in the United States, a pattern that "extends to the scholarly literature as well" (178). In a postscript added after the 1990 Gulf War, Abraham wrote: "Prior to the (U.S.) invasion of Kuwait on August 2, 1990 the ADC had recorded only five anti-Arab hate crimes for 1990. After the invasion, the ADC recorded eighty-six incidents between August 2 and February 2, 1991" (204). While 56 percent of the reported incidents were directed at "Arab-American organizations, political activists, and others who publicly dissented from official U.S. policy," Abraham found it to be "most revealing" that 42 percent of the attacks were "directed against ordinary persons who fit the Arab stereotype (204)." Arab Americans feared for their safety during the Gulf War, reported Abraham, and many received harassing phone calls, had their homes egged, or had their car tires slashed. He argued that the tone for these hostile actions was set by the statements of government officials, demonizations in the press, and derogatory references to Arabs expressed on "radio talk shows, bumper stickers, T-shirts, pins, and posters" (205). Patterns of hate violence against Arab (and Muslim) Americans continued throughout the 1990s, according to reports of the ADC Research Institute. Discussing anti-Arab violence in the United States, the Arab American writer Lisa Suhair Majaj (1999, 323) concluded that, "in contrast to white ethnic Americans," who enjoy "ethnic options" (Waters 1990), "Arab Americans experience their identity not as a choice but as a fact from which they cannot escape."

The historically belated (relative to other racialized groups) emergence of racialized understandings of Arab Americans in the midst of the era of civil rights mobilization and legislative remedies was a paradox that had negative consequences for Arab Americans. Its timing coincided with a dominant understanding that race was an objective phenomenon, that no new groups could be "racialized," and that racial prejudice was linked specifically to domestic structural inequality and not global affairs. Arab Americans, although present as activists in the 1960s civil rights movement, did not issue civil rights claims or make organized demands for redress on their group's behalf because they were not yet experiencing *systematic* defamation or discrimination and were economically advantaged. (There were also no national "Arab American" organizations in the early 1960s, but this is secondary to the facts of Arab American social status at the time.) When the categories of disadvantaged racial and ethnic minority groups were officially created in 1977—through Office of Management and Budget (OMB) Directive 15—Arab Americans were not included among them. Although official government recognition of racial discrimination inaugurated many positive changes in American society, it also set in motion an organizational stasis. There was no room at the table for new "racial" claimants;[22] Arab Americans were largely excluded from organized discussions of racism and discrimination, from multicultural education, and from textbook treatments of American racial and ethnic groups; and Arab American experiences would not be monitored for discrimination except by Arab American organizations. The Arab American scholar Therese Saliba (1999) argues that while Arab Americans were the victims of racist policies, their experiences were rendered "invisible" by the dominant discourses about race. Their legal classification as Caucasian, moreover, placed a cover "over discriminatory and racist practices" and disempowered them (309). Arabs remained officially white at the very same time as narratives about their essential difference from other human groups were increasingly saturating American culture. They thus experienced the double burden of being excluded from the benefits of whiteness *and* the recognition accruing to the experiences of people of color (Samhan 1999). These structural conditions (which have changed in the post-9/11 era) permitted the dehumanization and stereotyping of Arabs in American culture to continue largely unfettered. In other words, assumptions about race and the timing of the racialized plummet of Arab Americans effectively averted the gaze of millions of Americans to what was transpiring for Arabs in American society.

Arab American Social and Political Exclusion

Racial discrimination and subordination in American society are historically tied to a host of domestic laws, policies, and practices that created and reproduced social, economic, and political exclusion. Arab American racialization occurred outside of this historical trajectory: its historical timing and raison d'être were quite different, and it had few legislative corollaries until after the 9/11 attacks (see chapter 4). Its close association with American foreign policy objectives instead of domestic economics and expansion ensured that its structural outcomes would be quite different from those of historically racialized groups. Its impact is not well measured by indices of income, occupation, education, or segregation, which are traditionally associated with racial status in American society. Because these racializing processes intervened in the ongoing trajectories of historically successful Arab American communities, Arab Americans have maintained their overall profile of economic success. Not only were Arab Americans negatively racialized *after* accruing the economic resources and mobility that was possible for whites, but a large percentage of post–World War II Arab immigrants have come to the United States with significant amounts of human capital, contributing to the group's elevated socioeconomic status. Furthermore, Arab Americans tend to concentrate in professional and entrepreneurial occupations, areas largely peripheral to the corporate mainstream and locations of power where we would expect some protection from discriminatory impacts. Furthermore, as many scholars of Arab America have noted, quite a few Arab Americans appear to be white, are able to accrue the benefits of whiteness, and prefer to see themselves as white, while others do not see themselves this way. From a certain perspective, then, some Arab Americans may be able to escape discrimination generated by phenotype (though not necessarily by associations tied to names or countries of origin), but in a multiplicity of other ways, as Majaj (1999) argues, Arab Americans have been compelled to face social reactions and identity issues from which they cannot escape. Steven Salaita (2006, 1–2) reports that he learned at a young age through films, television, and the news that everyone in his family was "afflicted with innately violent tendencies." He describes growing up as a first-generation Arab American who hated "the essence of my very existence." Summarizing his own history of anti-Arab racist experiences (Salaita is a Christian

Arab), he asserts that recipients of racism understand something that whites often do not, that "identity does matter, and matters deeply" (13).

Although at the social structural level Arab Americans are generally economically successful, they have experienced extensive political exclusion. In particular, Arab Americans argue that their political claims vis-à-vis American foreign policies have been largely ignored, dismissed, or silenced in mainstream circles. In the past few decades, there has rarely been a conference or panel on Arab American political activism that did not stress the ways in which Arab Americans were treated as pariahs by mainstream political and civic organizations. Arab American speakers are often asked to keep silent about foreign policy issues related to Israel and the Palestinians. Organizational leaders may not have personally opposed such discussions, but they considered them potentially frustrating to other organizational objectives, such as fund-raising and coalition-building. Similarly, open debates or educational panels about the Palestinian-Israeli issue have frequently been kept off the table at public meetings and conferences in the United States, relegated to more limited venues that could absorb the political and economic repercussions. Defenders of various Arab American positions on these issues have also been visibly absent from popular television news and talk shows. The result as experienced by Arab Americans has been political exclusion and a sense of voicelessness in American society. This exclusion has been even more salient when prominent candidates for political office openly return Arab American campaign donations in an effort to avoid charges of being "tainted" by Arab money, a pattern that continued into the 2008 election cycle (Abraham 1994; Akram and Johnson 2004). Arab American feminists have described similar "silencing" in American feminist forums, as "Arab American" and "feminist" are often viewed through the lens of stereotypes as oxymorons (see chapter 7; see also Jarmakani 2005).[23]

These social and political exclusions have been complemented by a law enforcement approach to Arab American civic activism at the federal level. In the early 1970s, Arab American activists were the targets of an intensive surveillance program called Operation Boulder (Bassiouni 1974; Akram and Johnson 2004). Attorney Abdeen Jabara won a civil rights lawsuit filed in 1972 that charged the U.S. government with tapping his telephone, intercepting his mail, and monitoring his bank accounts, writing, and speeches.[24] In 1974, the DePaul University law professor M. Cherif Bassiouni published a monograph entitled *The Civil Rights of Arab-Americans: "The Special Measures,"* which documented the government harassment and wiretapping of Arab American activists who were seeking to engage members of the American public in dialogues about U.S. policies toward the Palestinians. Palestinian American activism stepped up in the 1980s as the number of Palestinians who migrated to the United States for a university education rose.[25] During that period, the INS repeatedly tried to deport Palestinian activists who were U.S. permanent residents (Cainkar 1988; Akram and Johnson 2004). In 1987 the Justice Department used the ideological bars of the 1952 McCarran-Walter Act in its unsuccessful but persistent attempt to deport a group of Palestinian activists for whom it had no evidence of subversive activities, despite years of wiretapping and covert filming (Akram and Johnson 2004). When the Communist exclusion clause of the 1952 act was repealed at the end of the Cold War in 1990, it was replaced by one referencing "terrorist activity"; the government altered its charges in the Palestinian case to match the new terminology.[26] The case, known as the L.A. Eight (seven Palestinians and one Kenyan arrested in the Los Angeles area), was finally dropped in 2007, some twenty years later. These government measures sent a strong message to those who might consider hearing Palestinian claims: engaging the issue meant entering a zone of potential danger.

These measures that acted out an exclusion of Arab Americans in certain social and political arenas merit more extensive treatment than I have given them here because they are important to Arab American history; although I only touch on them here, I do so for two primary reasons. First, organizational exclusion and a criminalizing approach to their activism left Arab Americans with few powerful allies from the 1960s onward (although they had measurable local successes); their challenges to hostile media representations, textbook biases, and selective policy enforcement could therefore be ignored by mainstream antidiscrimination groups, and their vilification could persist, with few social or political repercussions. The institutional invisibility of prejudice and discrimination against Arab Americans exploded out into the open after the 9/11 attacks and is no longer invisible. But perhaps some of the worst negative impacts of 9/11 on Arab (and Muslim) Americans could have been avoided if steps had been taken earlier by a wide range of American institutions to mitigate the stereotyping and demonizing of Arabs and to punish instigators of hate crimes against them. Second, the U.S. government's law enforcement focus on nonviolent political organizing, especially organizing in support of the Palestinian cause, diverted and diluted the attention its agencies could pay to situations that might actually pose a threat to the United States. Over time, chief policy architects in Washington were either unable or unwilling to distinguish between persons engaged in healthy political debate about American foreign policies in the Middle East and "potential terrorists"—that is, between lawful political discourse and actual threat. After the 9/11 attacks, federal law enforcement officials and the Justice Department acknowledged that they knew very little about Arab and Muslim American communities and that they had no relationships with them, a condition that was of their own creation. After the 9/11 attacks, their limited knowledge and capacity to discern lent support for the use of dragnet policies ("targeting the haystack," as the Nixon Center policy analyst Robert Leiken [2004] advocated) and the use of the fear-evoking language of "fifth columns" and "sleeper cells" (see chapter 4)—which, despite these policies and claims, were never located.

Arab Americans and Race: Study Data

As noted earlier, Arab Americans vary in their understandings around their racial status in American society. Scholars do not yet have a firm grasp on what this variation is correlated with—experiences, social class, religion, skin color, political alliances? Read's (2008) survey research comparing members of a mosque and a church in central Texas found that Muslim Arab Americans were more likely to define and perceive themselves as a minority group than Christian Arab Americans.[27] The Detroit Arab American Study (Baker et al. 2004, 15–16) found that Arab Christians (73 percent) were more likely than Arab Muslims (50 percent) to identify as white, even though many Muslims checked the "white" box while many Christians did not, and that 31 percent overall (45 percent inside the Dearborn enclave and 25 percent outside it) said that no existing census category represented them. The DAAS suggested that residence inside or outside the Arab American enclave of Dearborn (covarying with religious affiliation and social class) affected racial identity. Community organizing and political alliances shaped by racial politics at the local level may be affecting Arab American racial identities, a hypothesis suggested by some scholars of Arab America but yet to be tested by systematic comparative study. Furthermore, Arab American racial self-identification may not be a static phenomenon; it may vary situationally or change over the course of a person's lifetime owing to life experiences and aspirations. Arab Americans may have racial identification options— a modification of Waters's (1990) concept of "ethnic options"—that members of other groups historically racialized as nonwhite do not possess, even if they do not have ethnic options as Majaj has suggested. Racial identity formation is probably best seen as unfolding and ongoing for Arab Americans at this point in time, and as a process that should be considered in its domestic and international context.[28]

Data from interviews conducted for this study provide insight into how Arab Muslims living in metropolitan Chicago viewed their place in the American racial structure. Study participants were asked: "There have been discussions about whether Arabs are white or not, with different points of view; do you think Arabs are white, not white, or what?" Sixty-three percent of respondents said Arabs were not white; 20 percent said they were white, while another 17 percent gave equivocal responses. (Note that the question is not strictly framed as one of self-identification, although the impact of this question wording on responses, as compared to self-identification, is unknown.) Neither reported social class nor residential location—suburban versus urban, inside or outside an Arab American enclave—correlated with response patterns, suggesting other variables were at work. Individuals who said Arabs are not white explained this assessment on the basis of (in order of frequency) their treatment in American society, skin color and other phenotypic criteria, the fact that Arabs are multiracial, cultural and historical differences from white Europeans, and Arab distinctiveness ("Arabs are Arabs").[29]

The largest response category among the 63 percent of persons who said Arabs are not white (36 percent) revolved around how Arabs are treated in American society. They saw their racial place as nonwhite because they said that Arabs do not benefit from the perquisites, assumptions, and rewards that accrue to whiteness. Instead, they spoke of political exclusion and discriminatory treatment in schools and in public spaces. The overwhelming majority of interviewees who gave this type of response were born in the United States, suggesting that deep understanding of a relationship between inequality of experience and race is particularly American, formed as part of an American socialization and upbringing.[30] Their responses, some of which are provided here, invoke issues that existed before 9/11 and support the thesis that a racializing project vis-à-vis Arab Americans was in place long before 9/11.

> Arabs are definitely not white. That categorization comes from the treatment of a community by the institutions of American society. Arabs in the schools face the same institutional racism as other students of color.

> The issue is, are you part of a privileged group of people that can dominate others, and I do not think we are part of that. Arabs are not part of the white or European ruling structure. We are politically excluded.

> You understand that there is racism even if it is not personally inflicted on you. Being a first-generation Egyptian American and Muslim is a difficult thing—to form an identity of your own and feel like an American and that you fit into this country when you feel you really don't anyway. So, there's always been this sort of racism . . . that outlook was always there, it was just exaggerated [after 9/11], making you feel like the enemy.

One interviewee saw Arabs claiming whiteness as a survival mechanism developed in an earlier era, but one that is no longer effective in today's cities and suburbs, where Arab Americans face oppression from members of the dominant white culture.

> There is a great proportion who are going to say "white" because when the court allowed them [Arabs] to come into this country, one of the most racialized societies in the world where there is a white-black dichotomy, identifying with white was a way of surviving. But as kids grow up in urban areas and in the suburbs, I think they reject whiteness as oppres-

sion. Many are gravitating toward the black experience and black culture as something closer to their experience. Young Arab kids growing up here definitely do not see themselves as white.

The second most common response type (28 percent) among persons who said Arabs were not white revolved around skin color and other phenotypic features. Both U.S.- and non-U.S.-born respondents gave these responses, although immigrants frequently mentioned that they learned about social systems organized around skin color only after arriving in the United States.

> This country is very race-conscious—color-conscious I mean. My sister married a very dark man, and when you look at him you would say he is black. We never thought that was unusual. . . . I complained about my hair once at school, and they said, "Oh, yeah, you have that Semitic hair." I never thought of my hair being Semitic. Sometimes the girls would say to me, "Well, you are olive-skinned." I don't see myself that way. So I think in their minds they have a perception of gradations of color, and I don't have that.

> People look at me and they don't know what I am. They know I am not white or black. People think I am Hispanic. Brown is in the middle.

> Clinically, Arabs have dispersed around the world enough to fall into both categories. Clinically, they are a people of color.

Arab Americans who said that Arabs are not phenotypically white pointed out that more than skin color enters into the equation; as the person just quoted observed, Arab American hair textures and facial features are often distinguished as different from those of whites.

> We don't look white. What matters in the U.S. is not Caucasian blood but skin color. This has a huge impact on us. And you see nappy hair, even with blue eyes and light skin.

> In this suburb it is lily white. We don't belong here. I am very aware of my skin color and looks.

Many respondents were extremely uncomfortable with the very concept of race and color. After stating that Arabs are not white, some respondents explained that they found the very idea of race useless or offensive, and quite a few noted that racism is abhorred in Islam.

> You are not the color of your skin. It is ridiculous to try and categorize everybody into certain groups of skin color. You are who you are because of what sits in your heart and the experiences you have encountered in your life.

> I don't feel comfortable classifying people by color anyway. It is against
> my ideology, my thinking, and my religion.

The third most common response type (24 percent) among persons
who said Arabs are not white was that Arabs cannot be a racial group
because the Arab world encompasses many geographic regions and skin
colors. As such, it is not possible to assign a color to Arabs.

> I think Arabs should have a different category until things change. . . . If
> you look on the map, Arab countries cover two continents, and the white
> white and dark black. If this is my cousin and he's dark, and he's from
> Africa, are you going to call him white?

> Arabs are distinct upon themselves, and the Arab world encompasses
> both black and white.

> Arabs are a race of colors, many colors.

The fourth most common response type (20 percent) among persons
who said Arabs are not white engaged notions of culture and heritage. To
these Arab Americans, being white means being Caucasian and European,
and Arabs are neither.

> If white means European, then being white for an Arab means denying
> your own culture and heritage, and allowing your history to be sub-
> sumed into that of Europe.

> Their history and culture is quite separate from Europe's. I find it a
> disgrace that the Arab people should be so blatantly insulted by the
> disregard of their history.

Seventeen percent of respondents gave what may be considered equivocal responses to the race question, marking the difficulty they had with
the very idea of race and of pigeonholing Arabs into a racial category. The
following quote expresses this ambiguity as it reveals the socially constructed nature of the way Arabs respond to the formulaic race question.

> I don't really know. I think, for me, it's always been white because of what
> I look like. I consider myself white. That's probably a personal reflection
> because my skin color is white. I've always thought all Arabs were white.
> I've never really thought of them as being nonwhite. But, again, why do
> we say we're white, because we're not white? Like people say, "You put
> 'white,' " and I think that it just doesn't make sense. I don't know what
> white means in terms of technical definition. Is it people who live north
> of the equator? I don't know how the experts have defined it. If you ask
> anybody, they say to put 'white' as a race. Do I think we're white? I don't
> think so.

A majority of persons who said Arabs are white (and about one-third of persons who said Arabs are not white) moved immediately into an unprovoked discourse about forms—especially census forms and job and school applications. In other words, the discussion of race became a discussion of categories and boxes, their views on these boxes, and the way American society groups people by color. Arabs know that they are supposed to check the "white" box on forms, and a majority of interviewees said that they do so, even if they had serious problems with the concept and if they believed Arabs are not white.

> This confuses me every time I fill out an application. We are not white, black, Hispanic, or Asian. We are Arab. I put "white." If there is an "other," sometimes I put that. But I put "white" because I know we are not "other."

A majority of interviewees made a distinction between what they write on forms and what they see as their reality. In other words, Arab American responses on forms are social constructions in themselves, as much the products of social context as statements of racial identity, if not more. This man spoke about writing "white" while knowing it is not "true."

> We used to report quarterly on affirmative action, and I always asked my boss, "What should I do? Should I put myself as a minority or not?" He did not know either, so we called the company headquarters, and they said, "You will be considered white." But of course, in real life, we are not. As far as statistics go, that's what they say, legally.

Still, some Arab Americans insist on checking the "other" box. Surely, few who do this know that persons who check "other" and can be determined to be Arab, or who write in "Arab," are recoded as "white" by the Census Bureau. "I always choose 'other,' " one respondent explained. "I'm not white and I'm not going to check white."

Many interviewees who said Arabs are white said they knew this because they had been told it was the case.

> I was really surprised when I learned that we were Caucasian.

> Geographically, Egypt is in Africa, but they classify all the Arabs as white, so I write "white."

Many respondents saw being required to participate in a sociopolitical project that denies their realities and refuses them minority benefits as yet another layer of discrimination.

> I am resentful that I have to put down "white." I don't look white. I am not treated as white.

> Sometimes you put "other," but what is "other"? "Other" could be anything. You feel like inferior, you know. Like the minority of the minorities. We're not defined. . . . Officially we are white, but we're not white. Somebody can say, "I don't have to hire you because you are white and I have a lot of white people here." But you're not white!

Some respondents said that placement in the white category effectively hides the discrimination that Arab Americans face by removing them as subjects in the study of social inequalities.

> If we were recognized as a minority, it would be acknowledged that oppression and discrimination occur. Socially we are not accepted in white circles.

Even though the race question in this study did not employ standard racial response boxes and was not formulated as a discussion of forms and categories, responses nearly always invoked them, signaling a learned relationship between racial identification and state categories as well as a deep tension between the Arab experience in the United States and the phenomenon of racial categorization. Nonetheless, when asked whether racial identification matters, 30 percent of the persons interviewed said that racial position is important in American society, whether they like the concept or not, because it is used to determine one's benefits. As neither de facto white nor de jure nonwhite, Arab Americans in this study complained that they accrue neither the benefits of whiteness nor the protections of minority affirmative action. They felt that this exclusion is unfair and further indicates their subordinate status. While many respondents said that Arabs should have their own category, like Hispanics, since they do not fit into any existing categories, many others thought that the whole discussion about race was absurd, except that American institutions are required to work on these premises. It should be noted that Arab American requests for a special category have been declined by the Census Bureau. This is a complex matter, but one part of the problem is that the term "Arab" does not incorporate other groups that are officially white but that may be viewed similarly and report experiencing similar treatment in American society, such as Iranians, Assyrians, Armenians, Chaldeans, Kurds, and Afghanis—in other words, the iconic "Middle Easterner."

These study data show that a majority of Arab Muslims in metropolitan Chicago viewed their social position in American society as subordinate and translated that status into a nonwhite racial position in a race-based societal hierarchy. It is notable that religion and religious discrimination were rarely invoked in responses to this question, except in statements that Islam does not condone racial distinctions. The following comments from a young man living in a middle-class, southwest suburb of Chicago reveal how Arab is counterposed to Caucasian/white/ American on the ground, and how racialized antagonisms take shape differently depending on whether Arabs are a numerically large or small group in an area. The quote also indicates something long observed by Arab American parents: that racialized enmities become concretized in public schools.

> I was with a group of friends. These Americans, Caucasians, drove past us and yelled out remarks—racial remarks. They turned around, and they ran at us, and we started to fight. In Chicago Ridge everyone was Arabic mostly, our whole neighborhood was Arabic, so no white person or American would say something about us unless it was in school, but in Orland it's a little different. Arabic are like, they are not the minorities over there.

Centering the Muslim Sidebar: Social Constructions Embracing Muslim Americans

Arab American experiences with the social constructions, hate violence, and political exclusion attendant to their racialization intersected historically with three other highly significant processes toward the end of the twentieth century: (1) increasing levels of Arab immigration to the United States within which a larger proportion of immigrants were Muslim as compared to Christian, a reversal of early patterns; (2) the growth of Muslim American institutions, related to increases in the population of immigrant and native-born Muslims; and (3) the global spread of Islamic revival, which produced increased religiosity among Muslims, including Muslim Americans, and the concordant rise of Islamist political movements, many of which opposed U.S. foreign policy interests and some of which engaged in armed violence to express that opposition. The convergence of these historic trends that rendered Muslims increasingly visible, with interpretations increasingly openly proffered by some American political actors, commentators, and religious leaders (some of whom were close advisers to the George W. Bush administration) that Islam itself was intrinsically faulty and promoted violence, produced an understanding among many in American society that Muslims pose a number of threats to Americans, both at home and abroad. The tropes and allegations these spokespersons used to describe Muslims were so similar to those used for Arabs that many Americans could not distinguish between them, and so, for example, Christian and Muslim Arab Americans experienced hate crimes during the Iranian hostage-taking crisis (1979 to 1980), although Iranians are Muslims but not Arabs. As a result of conflations and confusions, the expanded social construction emerged of the Arab/

Muslim/Middle Easterner, who had the same phenotypic traits, modes of dress, scripts, and types of names as those with which the Arab had been understood.

Growth in Muslim American Communities

"The religion of Islam is now an American phenomenon." So opened the 1987 report *Islamic Values in the United States* by the religion scholars Yvonne Yazbeck Haddad and Adair Lummis (1987, 3). At that time, the authors enumerated 598 mosques and Islamic centers in the United States and estimated that between 2 million and 3 million Muslims resided in the United States, the majority of whom were "unmosqued." They predicted that Islam would be the second-largest religion in the United States by the first decade of the twenty-first century, propelled by natural increase, conversion, and the migration of "some 25–35,000 Muslims a year" (3). Haddad and Lummis's predictions appear to have been borne out. Ihsan Bagby, Paul Perl, and Bryan Froehle (2001) counted 1,209 mosques in the United States in 2000, 30 percent of which were established in the 1990s. By 2005, there were between 6 million and 7 million Muslim Americans—although this estimate is disputed, with other estimates putting the figure as low as 1.88 million and others as high as 11 million[31]— the majority of whom lived in medium- to large-sized American cities and were born outside the United States. By racial and ethnic composition, Haddad (2004) estimates that 30 percent of American Muslims are African American, 33 percent South Asian, 25 percent Arab, 4 percent each sub-Saharan African, other Asian, and converts, and 3 percent European. For the purposes of a survey sample, Zahid Bukhari (2003) sets the African American allocation at 20 percent, the South Asian at 32 percent, and the Arab at 26 percent. Jane Smith (1999), on the other hand, estimates that 40 percent of American Muslims are African American. Geographically, the Association of Religion Data Archives places the largest American Muslim populations in California, Illinois, Michigan, New York, New Jersey, Maryland, and Connecticut.[32] While difficult to measure except by extrapolating from U.S. census country-of-origin and ancestry data, the American population identifiable by these specific indicators as having historic ties to Muslim-majority countries posted rates of educational attainment and median family income that exceeded those of the U.S. population as a whole in 2000.[33]

The history and growth of Islam in the United States is often described by scholars of religion using a dichotomy that distinguishes between "indigenous Muslims" (meaning African American Muslims and some seventy-five thousand U.S.-born converts) and "immigrant Muslims" (including their second- and third-generation descendents), a distinction reflecting complex doctrinal and social realities related to Islam in the American context.[34] Africans brought forcibly to the North American continent as slaves were the first large group of Muslims in the United States, but most were compelled to convert to Christianity. Islam made an epochal reemergence in the United States during the first decades of the twentieth century because of a combination of African American conversions and Muslim migration, mostly Arab (Curtis 2002; Smith 1999). It is widely believed that "Chicago had more Muslims than any other American city in the early 1900s," according to Jane Smith (1999, 57), reflecting the convergence in place of the headquarters of the Nation of Islam (led by African American Elijah Muhammad from 1934 to 1975) and a few hundred Arab and Ahmadiyya Muslim immigrants. African Americans and Arab Americans constituted the overwhelming majority of American Muslims throughout the first half of the twentieth century, a demographic profile that would only begin to change when the immigration-related Asia Barred Zone was removed in 1952 and U.S. immigration law was overhauled in 1965, both of which changes spurred a new immigration from Asia, including a large number of Muslims. By the turn of the twenty-first century, the number of Muslims of South Asian origin or descent in the United States (including immigrants and their American-born children) exceeded that of Arabs and approached or exceeded that of African Americans (see Haddad 2004; Bukhari 2003). Muslim immigrants from India, Pakistan, and Bangladesh were particularly well educated and financially resourced and quickly became institution builders. They constructed mosques and Islamic schools at a much faster pace than African American and Arab American Muslims and founded a number of important national American Muslim institutions (Leonard 2003).

While unsatisfying for cross-generational sociological study, the indigenous-versus-immigrant dichotomy does capture some of the doctrinal and social variation under which American Islam grew: racial segregation imposed on African Americans, the American immigrant trend of establishing religious institutions along ethnic lines, and differences of theology and religious practice between immigrant and African American Muslims. All of these began to converge after the civil rights movement ended de jure segregation and Imam Warith Deen Mohammed, the Honorable Elijah Muhammad's son, led the Nation of Islam to mainstream Sunni Islam. Imam W. D. Mohammed eventually dropped the NOI appellation altogether, but it was later (1981) taken up by the Reverend Louis Farrakhan, whose congregations' membership in the community of Muslims has been often contested by mainstream Islamic authorities and institutions (Smith 1999).

The racially and ethnically distinct congregational patterns that characterize Islam in American society are rooted in a racially and ethnically stratified American society and run counter to the pluralistic and egalitarian message of Islam, posing a challenge that many American Muslims are working to overcome. Michael Fuquay (2001) has observed: "In his sermons, Martin Luther King Jr. was fond of quipping that 'eleven o'clock Sunday morning is the most segregated hour and Sunday school is still the most segregated school of the week.' . . . Forty years later, Jim Crow segregation is a memory, and racism has become America's most popular metaphor for evil. Yet King's description of Sunday services remains largely unaltered." In a country in which the prayer hour is the "most segregated hour of the week," however, American Muslims appear to be achieving a greater degree of racial integration than any other American religious group.[35] Invoking the immigrant-versus-indigenous dichotomy, Ihsan Bagby (2005, 19), a scholar of American mosques, reports that although "the two groups have distinct histories which were largely separate until the 1990s, this is changing rapidly. . . . One sign of change is that only 7 percent of all mosques are attended by only one ethnic group" and that "over 90 percent are attended by some African Americans and some Arabs or South Asians." New social processes have become evident in Muslim American communities over the past twenty years. Second- and third-generation children of Muslim immigrants and African American Muslims are beginning to converge socially, igniting a process of discerning between cultural patterns and religious practices (Cainkar 2004d; Haddad 2004), a process that the sociologists Fenggang Yang and Helen Rose Ebaugh (2001) find to be characteristic of the children of immigrants in the United States, who seek to shed their parents' cultural twists on religious practice. Further complexity has been added to this process of discernment by a global Islamic revival that became evident as a major force of religious renewal in the United States in the 1990s, especially among immigrant Muslims and their American-born children (Cainkar 2004d).

Islamic Revival and the Rise of Political Islam

Real-world events in the latter decades of the twentieth century and the relationship of these events to American interests played a major role in the social construction of Muslims in the United States. Islamic revival, which brought about a return to religious practice for many Muslims, and the mobilization of Islam as a major political force were chief among them. Islamic revival, a movement whose birth in 1920s Egypt and resurgence in the 1950s called upon Muslims to return to religiosity as their guide to daily life, to adhere to Islamic dogma, and to publicly engage in religious practice, resonated with many Muslims who had a very grounded sense that something was wrong in their societies and in the world in general. It received a substantial boost after the 1979 political victory of the Iranian Islamists who overthrew the Shah of Iran. As a religious and cultural force, Islamic revival brought about a wide range of social changes in Muslim-majority countries that varied significantly from place to place but were most evident in places where public expression of Islamic practices had been most extensively weakened by secularism and modernization, such as Palestine, Turkey, Egypt, Iran, and Jordan. Political Islam, one segment of this movement, was characterized by a range of political platforms articulated by Islamist activists, who called for social and political changes that would create a milieu more amenable to Islamic practice (Kurzman 2002). Some of these groups believed in, and waged, armed struggle to achieve these and other objectives, while others did not. For the most part, state leaders viewed organized political Islam as a domestic threat and responded to it in a range of ways, from execution or imprisonment of its leadership to legalization and enfranchisement of Islamic parties. Popular support for these parties also varied from state to state, depending on the urgency with which the need for change was shared by specific segments of the population and the political group's ability to organize and mobilize, which was easier in some places than others. Islamic revival and political Islam evolved as distinct and complex but interrelated historical processes, both driven by ideologies that found receptive audiences because of real-world conditions of injustice and inequality on the ground. While religious revival claimed broad appeal among Muslims, political Islam has received much less public support (Roy 1994; Kurzman 2002).

The U.S. government was entangled in social and political changes in Muslim-majority countries in a plethora of ways, and whether it supported or opposed Islamist groups depended on which alliance U.S. policymakers saw as best suited for American interests. For example, after the Iranian Islamic revolution, which was openly anti–U.S. government, the American government embraced the mobilization of men in Afghanistan fighting under the banner of Islam to expel its Communist Soviet occupiers. According to the Columbia University anthropologist Mahmoud Mamdani (2002):

> The grand plan of the Reagan administration was two-pronged. First, it drooled at the prospect of uniting a billion Muslims around a holy war, a Crusade, against the evil empire. I use the word Crusade, not Jihad, because only the notion of Crusade can accurately convey the frame of mind in which this initiative was taken. Second, the Reagan administration hoped to turn a religious schism inside Islam, between minority Shia and majority Sunni, into a political schism. Thereby, it hoped to contain the influence of the Iranian Revolution as a minority Shia affair. This is the context in which an American/Saudi/Pakistani alliance was forged, and religious *madresas* turned into political schools for training cadres. The Islamic world had not seen an armed Jihad for centuries. But now the CIA was determined to create one.

In the interest of its Cold War strategy, the U.S. government provided substantial logistical, financial, and military support and training to the largest transnational in-gathering of men ready to take up armed struggle in the name of Islam, an effort co-organized and co-financed by, among others, the wealthy Saudi businessman Osama bin Laden. When President Reagan introduced the Afghani leaders of the mujaheddin (from jihad) on the White House lawn in 1985, he called them "the moral equivalents of America's founding fathers" (Mamdani 2002). Following the Soviet Union's ouster from Afghanistan, this U.S. government strategy—which can be viewed as shortsighted—had negative consequences for the people of Afghanistan when the Taliban took over, and drastic consequences for the United States and for Muslims in general because the planning for the 9/11 attacks emerged, according to American officials, from bases in Afghanistan.

With the fall of the Soviet Union in 1990, the Cold War ended. U.S. policymakers increasingly perceived Islamic revival and Islamist political mobilizations as an expanding monolithic enemy that threatened its extensive and multifaceted interests in the Middle East (however that geographic space is defined). Islamic revival meant change, and change had the potential—and in a few places the capacity—to upset the web of political and strategic alliances that the U.S. government had built to protect its interests in oil, anticommunism, and support for Israel. Because of the political role of Islamist movements vis-à-vis American interests, Islam as a religion was placed before the American public as the enemy of the United States by a wide range of anti-Muslim activists of secular and religious persuasion, particularly neoconservatives and evangelical Christian groups. Following an analysis of the mainstream American media and its treatment of Islam, Karim Karim (2000, 11) argues that, "prior to the collapse of the USSR, the confrontations of Western Powers with state and non-state Muslim actors seemed to prepare the way for 'Islam' to become a post Cold War 'Other.' " Regardless of "the specific historical, economic, and political factors" involved in a wide range of events—such as various Middle Eastern wars and regional conflicts, "the OPEC crisis," the Iranian and Lebanese hostage situations, and "the Rushdie Affair"—their reportage implicitly or explicitly attributed blame to a monolithic Islam. The American public's knowledge and understanding of a wide range of developments was increasingly filtered as the prerogatives of U.S. foreign policy objectives came to be reflected in the types of programs, experts, and information to which the public was given wide access (MESA 1987; Said 1997). Some Orientalist scholars supported these notions of Islam's inherent opposition to the West and argued, by condensing all Muslims into a single group opposed to Western civilization, that a clash of civilizations was at hand (Huntington 1996). These contributions to the American public's understanding of Islam were strengthened when some Muslims used religious dogma and slogans to justify their violence (especially suicide bombings), adding fuel to the social construction of Islam as intrinsically evil. The real world of Muslims was thus simplified, flattened, and distorted; the diversity in practices and beliefs of the world's 1.6 billion Muslims were homogenized into a simple picture of violent American-haters who shared one essential feature: Islam.

Following the pattern documented earlier for representations of Arabs in American culture, Muslims who opposed or threatened American interests received substantial press, film, and literary coverage, while all else related to Muslims became somewhat invisible, a phenomenon that the literary scholar Edward Said (1997) referred to as "covering Islam." There were few portrayals of Muslim birth, life, sorrow, work, culture, music, adolescence, creativity, sportsmanship, or scholarship. This loss of a sense of the complexity and diversity of Muslims thus supported by default the premise of Islam's inherent violence. The perception of the Middle East (itself a social construction) that came to dominate in the minds of Americans was that of a place fraught with danger, inhabited by Arab and Muslim peoples who do not operate according to accepted rules of human behavior—a place where parents do not hug their children and mothers send them to die, and where the civilized peoples of the world, such as Israelis and Americans, can expect constant, unexplainable danger.

Highly visible domestic changes in the religious practices of Muslims, combined with their increasing immigration and institution building, intersected historically with these events and representations. By the 1990s, the spread of Islamic revival as a religious force was evident in the United States and was especially observable in heightened levels of religiosity and religious practice among formerly secularized immigrant Muslims and Muslim American youth. Many American-born children of Muslim immigrants became more deeply steeped in religious practice than their parents, as evidenced by American-born Muslim women choosing to wear hijab when their mothers had not (Cainkar 2004d). Muslims who had immigrated during more secular times revived their religious practices, including adopting Islamic modes of dress, praying five times a day, and fasting during Ramadan (although fasting was one practice that had seemed to persist during secularized periods). The institutional outcome of growing numbers of American Muslims and Islamic religious revival was evident in increases in the numbers of mosques and Islamic schools, the sizes of mosque congregations, and the number of commercial enterprises supporting a Muslim lifestyle, such as *Halal* meat markets, Muslim women's clothing stores, and Islamic books and artifacts. All of these trends increased the visibility of American Muslims in the public sphere.

Community-wide transformations from secular to religious in ethos, practice, and organization were highly visible among Arab American Muslims in metropolitan Chicago during the 1990s (Cainkar 2004d). As mode of dress made them appear increasingly different from those around them, social distances between Muslim Americans and their non-Muslim neighbors increased as well and were exacerbated by media messages of violence and terror associated with Islam. Some people began to refer to Muslims as a "race."[36] American groups with specific political interests leveraged these co-incidents to identify American Muslims as a growing threat to the security of the United States and to the American way of life. As happens with all stereotypes, real-world events provided support for these claims: the 1993 parking garage bombing at the World Trade Center in New York by a group of Arab Muslims provided such a domestic incident. The conflated Arab/Muslim (sometimes referred to as a Middle Easterner) was the first to be blamed in the 1995 Oklahoma City federal building bombing, especially after the "terrorism expert" Steven Emerson proclaimed on national television (CBS News) that the attacks had a "Middle Eastern trait" and CNN reported that specific Arab/Muslim suspects were being sought; both reports helped fuel a spate of hate crimes against American Arabs and Muslims (Fuchs 1995).[37]

In a dialectic common to groups experiencing institutional discrimination, as Islam and Muslims were increasingly denigrated, Muslims increasingly identified with, found self-respect in, and publicly embodied their religious beliefs (Cainkar 2004d). Religious faith offered a set of valuable resources to Arab American Muslims: a source of hope, a way of life based on belief in God, and social relationships that offered dignity, inspiration, and strength. While the capacity of religion to provide "refuge, respectability, and resources" is well recognized (Hirschman 2003), interested parties openly suggested that the social phenomenon of Islamic revival in the United States was a growing threat to the country and its way of life. In one of the few public opinion polls to survey American attitudes toward Muslim Americans prior to 9/11, the Pew Research Center found in March 2001 that less than half of Americans polled (45 percent) reported a favorable view of American Muslims (Keeter and Kohut 2003).

Conclusion

The U.S. Immigration and Naturalization Service, in describing Arabs in 1943 as persons who "shared in the development of our civilization," affirmed their whiteness and eligibility for all immigration benefits, including naturalization (U.S. Department of Justice 1943). Yet in the latter half of the twentieth century, as Arabs were increasingly represented and popularly understood as a monolithic group with negative traits, including an alleged inherent proclivity to violence, some would frame them as members of a distinctly different (and clashing) civilization. As negative representations increased and proliferated throughout American popular culture, views of Arab Americans sank, and one could argue, in the discourse of anthropology and sociology, that they had been racialized. Repercussions of these harmful social constructions were documented by the mid-1970s and continued through the end of the twentieth century: pollsters found that American attitudes toward Arabs were "close to racist" (Lipset and Schneider 1977, 22), Arab Americans repeatedly experienced hate crimes, Arab denigration was used to sell films, video games and Halloween costumes, and Arab American attempts to engage in political discourse were frustrated by claims that their views were illegitimate because they were based in hatred and violence. When similar social constructions about an inherent tendency to violence were nearly seamlessly extended to Muslims, Arabs and Muslims came to be viewed by many Americans in an undifferentiated way (often under the rubric "Middle Easterners") that was associated with a certain phenotype, mode of dress, written script, type of name, set of religious beliefs and attitudes toward women, and specific countries of origin. These would be the symbols that Americans, both the public and the government, acted on after the 9/11 attacks, in ways both positive and negative in outcome for Arabs and Muslims in the United States. The actionable but sloppy category "Arabs, Muslims, and persons assumed to be Arabs and Muslims" became terms without which no analyst could accurately describe the targets of hate crimes, verbal assaults, and mass arrest in the United States after the 9/11 attacks.

Because of social changes that materialized in response to this collective backlash (see chapter 8), the social and political exclusion of Arab and Muslim Americans was reduced—but by no means ended. By 2005, the proportion of Americans who said that Islam is more likely than other religions to encourage violence had fallen from 44 percent in 2003 to 36 percent, despite what many would describe as worsening objective conditions, such as the wars in Iraq and Afghanistan and the Madrid and London bombings.[38] This attitudinal change, measured in the immediate wake of the London subway bombings, further supports the social construction argument: behaviors that held Arabs and Muslims collectively responsible for the 9/11 attacks were driven by *social constructions and perceptions* as they were used to interpret real-world events. Positive changes in attitudes, however, were not to occur until after efforts to change them were mobilized by a range of American civil society organizations that increasingly embraced Arab and Muslim Americans, no longer standing alone. Those efforts, in turn, emerged in response to the enormous wave of hatred and profiling that followed the 9/11 attacks, the topics of the next four chapters.

Chapter 4

Whose Homeland Security?

On September 11, the wheel of history turned and the world will never be the same.... The attacks of September 11 were acts of terrorism against America orchestrated and carried out by individuals living within our borders. Today's terrorists enjoy the benefits of our free society even as they commit themselves to our destruction. They live in our communities—plotting, planning and waiting to kill Americans again.

—Attorney General John Ashcroft (2001b)

ATTORNEY GENERAL John Ashcroft's declaration that "the world will never be the same" was a prescient script for the American government's actions after the 9/11 attacks, whether in the United States, the Arab and Muslim worlds, or other outposts of the global "war on terror." In the United States, the notion that terrorists were hiding in American communities just waiting to attack, living undercover lives that had public veneers of normalcy, provoked fear in the hearts of Americans and cast an air of suspicion on Arab and Muslim Americans. Government statements were clear in their directives: "The federal government cannot fight this reign of terror alone. Every American must help us defend our nation against this enemy" (Ashcroft 2001b). Since terrorists were alleged to be inconspicuously residing in "our communities," the message was apparent: Arabs and Muslims in the United States should be closely observed and their seemingly normal activities should be treated as suspect. Arabs and Muslims, who understood their position as subjects of watchdogs in a panoptical world, were to be placed under a microscope by their non-Arab or non-Muslim neighbors. Study data show that social relationships between themselves, their neighbors, and strangers were commonly perceived by Arab Muslims to have changed into a new set of roles: one party was looking out for danger, while the other was behaving in ways that would demonstrate innocence.

The government's statements and pleas for help thus socially constructed Arabs and Muslims living in the United States as persons who were likely to be connected to the 9/11 attacks and other future acts of terrorism. They were people who, if not terrorists themselves, might be hiding terrorists or covering up their knowledge of brewing terrorist plots. So constructed, Arabs and Muslims in the United States were symbolically reconstituted as people who were not really part of the American nation; they were the "them," and thus not fully eligible for the nation's package of civil and constitutional rights. In fact, they were often described as persons whose presence in the United States was to take advantage of these very rights in order to plot destruction, as in the Ashcroft statement opening this chapter. As a result of the way they were now publicly perceived, many of the persons interviewed for this study were visited by law enforcement authorities because a neighbor or coworker had reported them as acting in a suspicious manner—whether because they made overseas phone calls, because they opened their trunk frequently, or because of the way they were dressed. Others reported being removed from airplanes or denied boarding; some lost their jobs, and some simply reported that life in the United States was no longer the same. These and other aspects of the post-9/11 Arab and Muslim experience, as discussed in this and subsequent chapters, all contributed to a sense of "homeland insecurity." This feeling abated over time, but never really went away during the period of this study.

This chapter focuses on federal government statements and policies implemented after the 9/11 attacks. At the same time as it asked the American public to watch out for suspicious behavior, the government crafted an extensive set of policies aimed at "trimming the haystack" to find the needle that "resists discovery" (Leiken 2004, 136). These measures included mass arrests, preventive detentions, FBI interviews, registration and fingerprinting of tens of thousands of male foreign nationals, widespread wiretapping, secret hearings, closures of charities, criminal indictments, and reviews of private Internet, telecommunication, and financial records, which were secured through more than thirty thousand national security letters issued annually to American businesses after the passage of the USA PATRIOT Act (Cole 2006). These measures were directed almost solely against persons of Arab ethnicity or the Muslim faith. Their ongoing reportage effectively sent a message to the American people that ethnic and religious profiling was acceptable, even necessary, so long as it was directed at these groups.

In the end, few terrorists posing a threat to the United States were actually uncovered by these extraordinary efforts of the American government. Not a single person was convicted of a terrorist crime after eighty thousand domestic special registrations, five thousand preventive detentions, and tens of thousands of FBI interviews, activities referred to by the

Georgetown law professor David Cole as the "most aggressive national campaign of ethnic profiling since World War II" (Cole 2006, 17). The U.S. government claimed to have broken up domestic terrorist cells in Buffalo (Lackawanna), Detroit, Portland, Seattle, and northern Virginia, but none of these groups was proven to have plans to inflict damage on the United States. Only one of the groups, the Lackawanna Six, had an Al-Qaeda connection. This group of young Yemeni American men was not new to the government. They had been reported to the FBI months before the 9/11 attacks by an Arab Muslim neighbor, who learned of their plans to join an Al-Qaeda training camp in Afghanistan in the spring of 2001. Shortly after arriving at the camp, some of the boys fled in fear, wanting nothing to do with what was going on there, while others finished training and later returned home (Purdy and Bergman 2003). They resumed their lives in Lackawanna and were under FBI observation and wiretapping. Although there was no evidence that they ever had plans to stage an attack, they were arrested in September 2002 and heralded with much publicity as the government's key homegrown terrorist find.

Criminal indictments in "terrorism-related" cases fared slightly better than the outcomes of interviews, mass registrations, charity closures, and detentions without charge: more than four hundred post-9/11 indictments produced some two hundred convictions, very few of which, however, were for terrorism (Eggen and Tate 2005). In fact, only thirty-nine of these "terrorism-related" cases ended in convictions on terrorism charges, and the majority of these convictions were for "support" (encompassing a wide range of noncriminal activities) of a terrorist group, not for actual terrorist activities. The Syracuse-based Transactional Records Access Clearinghouse (TRAC 2003) found that the median sentence handed down in cases the Justice Department identified as "terrorism-related" was fourteen days. New York University's Center on Law and Security (NYU 2005) found upon review of "terror-related" cases that there were "almost no convictions on charges reflecting dangerous crimes" (1). According to Cole (2006, 18), "several of the government's most prominent 'terrorist' cases have disintegrated under close scrutiny." While some have argued that the government's dragnet antiterror tactics had deterrent value, such value is as immeasurable as the claimed deterrent value of the death penalty.

The government's highly rhetorical public statements, its claims concerning its arrests and roundups that would never be substantiated, and the sensationalized media coverage that accompanied each government action, all led the public to believe that the government was acting intelligently while it was actually producing undue punitive outcomes for many Americans. The government's actions stoked public fears, while granting it the leeway it wanted to sidestep the rule of law, and appeared to confirm the notion that Arabs and Muslims living in the United States were posing a collective danger to other Americans, thus encouraging hatemongers anxious to retaliate against any perceived group member. Although the 9/11 Commission (National Commission on Terrorist Attacks Upon the U.S. 2004) found no evidence of Arab American or Muslim American knowledge of, participation in, or support for the 9/11 attacks, its conclusion was never really given much play in the American media or by the Bush administration. The commission found that the persons held responsible for the 9/11 attacks were visitors to the United States who were on a deadly mission and took pains to stay separate from Arab and Muslim American communities, but federal law enforcement authorities appear to have acted on a wholly different set of premises. After "about half a million interviews," according to one former FBI special agent in charge of counterterrorism, some in government concluded that there was no one "who had they stepped forward could have provided a clue to help us get out in front of this."[1] The FBI interviews in particular stigmatized Arab and Muslim Americans in the presence of onlookers, who were likely to presume that the visit had been spurred by something serious—something more than a name or a look, a suspicious neighbor, an overseas phone call, or a way of dressing.

Many policy analysts (and many Arab and Muslim Americans) were arguing at the time that Arab and Muslim American communities should be among the government's primary allies in its domestic antiterrorism work (see, for example, Chishti et al. 2003). Such a strategy would have required a very different perspective, one that viewed Arab and Muslim Americans in an individuated, knowledge-based manner, contained a kernel of trust, and conveyed, instead of a view of collective suspicion built on stereotypes, an understanding that Arab and Muslim Americans also cared about the lives of others. By the fall of 2008, however, academics with direct access to Homeland Security secretary Michael Chertoff were still advising him about the potential usefulness of these types of cooperative efforts.[2] In other words, seven years after the 9/11 attacks, top-level Bush administration officials were still not convinced of the value of the non-coercive domestic security strategies that were being pursued at the local level in various cities across the nation—a lack of support that produced frustration on the ground.[3]

Instead, Human Rights Watch (2002) found that Arabs and Muslims who volunteered to help the federal authorities sometimes ended up in indefinite, incommunicado detention. Such arrests were based not on data, but on presumptions of suspicion, grounded in the notion that persons of the Muslim faith or of Arab origins could not be trusted. Human Rights Watch (2005, 6) concluded in "Witness to Abuse" that needless incarcerations "aggravated distrust towards the government in Muslim communities in the United States that have been repeatedly targeted by sweeping, ill-advised, and at times illegal post–September 11 investigation,

arrest, and detention policies." If it had been true that terrorists were lurking inside Arab and Muslim American communities, the government's
strategies were counterproductive to finding them because its policies
instilled a deep fear of government agents (Cainkar 2004c). In sum, despite
nearly unrestricted power, dragnet policies, a cooperative citizenry, and
the evidentiary leeway permitted by secret evidence and secret hearings,
the government's allegation that Arab and Muslim terrorists were lurking in Arab and Muslim American communities, "plotting, planning and
waiting to kill Americans," as Attorney General Ashcroft told the U.S.
Mayors Conference in October 2001, was never proven correct. Yet it was
the nearly 100 percent rate of false positives during this entire domestic
security roundup period that created extensive anxiety among Arabs
and Muslims in the United States, producing an understanding that
really anything goes. The fundamental human right to personal security
was sacrificed, and each person knew it on an individual level.

"Homeland Insecurity"

> Let the terrorists among us be warned: If you overstay your visa—even
> by one day—we will arrest you. If you violate a local law, you will be put
> in jail and kept in custody as long as possible. We will use every avail-
> able statute. We will seek every prosecutorial advantage. We will use all
> our weapons within the law and under the Constitution to protect life
> and enhance security for America. . . . Some will ask whether a civilized
> nation—a nation of law and not of men—can use the law to defend itself
> from barbarians and remain civilized. Our answer, unequivocally, is
> "yes." Yes, we will defend civilization.
>   —Attorney General John Ashcroft (2001b)

Substituting "Arab and Muslim men" for the word "terrorists" in this
statement by Attorney General Ashcroft provides a proximate rendering
of the U.S. government's antiterrorism policies in the aftermath of the
9/11 attacks, and certainly reflects the way those policies were perceived
by Arab and Muslim men. In this statement invoking the language of the
clash of civilizations, where terrorists, barbarians, visa violators, and local
lawbreakers are defined in relationship to each other, the missing link is
supplied by Arab and Muslim male noncitizens, the suspects and primary
subjects of these particular government strategies. A close reading of John
Ashcroft's language in his October 25, 2001, speech shows how Arab and
Muslim men who were at most visa violators were transformed into terrorist suspects. The trick is located in the vague definition of "the law," the
positioning of the word "or," and the linkage of this blurred language to
terrorists:

> In the "war on terror," this Department of Justice will arrest and detain
> any suspected terrorist who has violated *the law*. Our single objective is

to prevent terrorist attacks by taking *suspected terrorists* off the street. If suspects are found not to have links to terrorism *or* not to have violated the law, they are released. But *terrorists who are in violation of the law* will be convicted, in some cases deported, and in all cases prevented from doing further harm to Americans. [emphasis added]

In the subsequent paragraph of this statement, Ashcroft is able to leverage this vague language to claim that nearly one thousand terrorist arrests had been made:

Within days of the September 11 attacks, we launched this antiterrorism offensive to prevent new attacks on our homeland. To date, our anti-terrorism offensive has arrested or detained *nearly 1,000 individuals* as part of the September 11 terrorism investigation. Those *who violated the law* remain in custody. Taking *suspected terrorists in violation of the law* off the streets and keeping them locked up is our clear strategy to prevent terrorism within our borders. [emphasis added]

In fact, these detainees were overwhelmingly Arab and Muslim men who were arrested on the basis of their looks, or on reports of suspicion, and who could not prove *at that moment* that their presence in the United States was legal. They were then largely unable to obtain release from prison until a host of government agencies proved that they were *not* terrorists—a very lengthy process, only after which visa violators were deported and others were released (Human Rights Watch 2002, 2005). In the end, *none* of these post-9/11 detainees were found to have terrorist connections (Cole 2003; Human Rights Watch 2002, 2005). Yet these statements by government officials offered the American public a grossly exaggerated sense of government accomplishment, as well as of domestic threat. A distinction between terrorists and Arab and Muslim men living in "American communities" was effectively blurred, a technique that should be credited for its efficiency because it flowed easily from prevalent social understandings that Arabs and Muslims were monolithic and inherently violent; government spokespersons simply latched on to these popular stereotypes in existence long before 9/11 and put them to work.

That these ideas were already in place in the American public's mind is evidenced in Attorney General Ashcroft's (2001a) statement at a press briefing on September 18, 2001, only seven days after the attacks:

To date the FBI has received more than 96,000 tips and potential leads: more than 54,000 on the website, nearly 9,000 on the hot line, the toll-free WATTS line, and more than 33,000 leads that were generated in the FBI field offices.

These tips and leads singled out Arab and Muslim Americans—citizens, permanent residents, and visitors alike—and eventually led nowhere. Persons who experienced law enforcement visits based on these tips reported that their allegedly suspicious actions pertained to normal activities interpreted by onlookers as suspicious—for example, unpacking the trunk of the car or opening the mail. The award-winning documentary *Brothers and Others* reported on a man arrested because a postcard of the World Trade Center was taped to his deli counter *and* he was Arab,[4] while Human Rights Watch (2002) reported the arrest of a man who, with his family, was taking tourist photos, among many other arrests based on profiling alone. Despite President Bush's (2001) statement on September 20 that "no one should be singled out for unfair treatment or unkind words because of their ethnic background or religious faith," the U.S. government was engaging in precisely such actions, lending strength to public suspicion of Arab and Muslim Americans. While Ashcroft asserted that the rule of law and the Constitution would be respected, the constitutionality of many post-9/11 government strategies has been legally challenged (Cole 2006; Chang and Kabat 2004).

This study found that fear of government far outweighed any other post-9/11 fears among Arab Muslim Americans. Their sense of "homeland insecurity" was driven less by the public's behavior than by the government's.[5] During the period of research, a substantial number of Arab Muslim Americans expressed worry that they might be rounded up and sent to internment camps by agents of the American government—especially if another attack occurred, an event over which they would have no control—and believed that the American government had the power and mass media influence to auger popular support for such an action. From their perspective, "democracy" and "the rule of law" had become hollow phrases that government spokespersons used to defend targeting Arab and Muslim communities. These respondents perceived that the rule of law did not apply to them and that the government could do what it wished to them, with widespread popular approval. Their citizenship, it seemed, had been rendered meaningless. This perspective, and the distinction between the government and the American public, is expressed in the following quote from an interview with an Arab American woman:

> I lost trust in American values, to put it very simply. I no longer have the serene sense that I will always be safe here. I feel that being an American citizen is meaningless. That it doesn't really protect you in any way. It's an immense sense of danger, and I've never gotten over it. I did not lose faith in Americans. I think my friends are the same. My relationships with my students haven't suffered. It's the same. On that level, I don't think I suffered, but I think the way I approach things made me less sure-footed, less confident even about the future of our family here. Can you believe it? I came home and told my husband, shouldn't we be putting our money in banks overseas? Maybe one of these days we'll end up being in concentration camps.

An Arab American man articulates the sense of arbitrariness that characterized what he calls the American "police state" as he reflects on the possibility that Arab Americans would find themselves repeating the Japanese American experience with camps.

> I suffered, physically no, but mentally and psychologically yes. And I would say, not because I'm Palestinian-born. Primarily because I'm an American citizen—i.e., this is the land of the free, rule of the law, democracy, etc.—and suddenly it became a police state. Human rights, laws, protection against individual [individual protections], and so on, are out of the window. Everybody becomes a target, for whatever reason the government decides. It doesn't have to be just violations. An edict by somebody in an office makes your life in jeopardy. It did affect me as a Palestinian in that the police state that prevailed after 9/11 reminded me of what happened to the Japanese in this country.

Few persons interviewed in this study said that their lives were unchanged after 9/11. A majority reported a sense of living on the edge in the United States, with lingering fears of government policies that might force their expulsion or internment. At the same time, there was broad recognition that the climate for their treatment as enemies of the United States had been established long before 9/11; as this Arab American woman notes, even American-born Arabs were viewed as foreigners:

> The attitude and outlook was always there, it was just exaggerated, making you feel like you're the enemy, that you're the bad one, and you're definitely a foreigner and do not belong in this country, when I was born and raised in this country, and I'm just as much an American as anyone else. I feel like maybe I need to get the hell out of this country because something bad is going to happen to our people here. It's a horrible feeling.

Many interviewees said that this sense of uncertainty led them to take steps to protect themselves and their families; some sent their college-bound children to schools outside of the United States, for instance, and some accelerated their efforts to build a home overseas. Indeed, a November 2002 survey by the Chicago-based Muslim Civil Rights Center found that 25 percent of immigrant respondents reported seriously considering moving to their country of origin because of the post-9/11 climate.[6] Some Arab and Muslim American families did choose to leave the United States, while others were forced to leave by the government policies enumerated in this chapter. Most, however, decided to wait and see what the American experience had in store for them.

> I don't feel this is a safe place. I don't know if I will be here in ten years, whereas at the beginning I had established that I was going to be here in this country, that I had given up on Europe, Lebanon is a bit too hectic. I

> don't know what I'm going to do, because this is the country where I
> thought I would stay and that my daughter will grow up here. I don't
> know where we're going to be.
>
> I sent my daughter to college in Canada. I do not know what will happen
> to us here. Who knows what will happen to us here? I want her to be safe.

These findings about fear of the government and the abrogation of the
rule of law have been replicated in other studies. The Vera Institute of
Justice's national study of Arab Americans finds that community members "expressed greater concern about being victimized by federal policies and practices than by individual acts of harassment" (Henderson
et al. 2006, 184). Sally Howell and Andrew Shryock (2003, 449) report that
government policies created "a climate in which Middle Easterners and
South Asians in the U.S. can be treated as a special population to whom
certain legal protections and civil rights no longer apply." Under such
conditions, the homeland, whether adopted or by birth, is perceived to be
a very insecure place to live.

Government Domestic Security Policies After 9/11

The rest of this chapter offers an inventory of some of the American government's known domestic security policies following the 9/11 attacks.
It points out the methods by which these policies were used to target
Arab and Muslim American communities. It looks most intensively at
the government policy that was visibly the broadest in scope—"special
registration"—which brought in for government questioning, fingerprinting, and photographing more than eighty thousand male foreign nationals from Arab and Muslim-majority countries who were living in the
United States. By exposing the legal precedents on which this policy
rested, we gain insight into the strategic thinking of the government during this time of national crisis. After examining these policies, we look
at some of the social-psychological outcomes of the government's secret
surveillance on Arab and Muslim Americans. The chapter concludes
with a review of some of the active defense that was mobilized on behalf
of Arabs and Muslims in the United States. Although the government's
exaggerated claims bought popular support for its policies, Arabs and
Muslims in the United States did not stand alone in their opposition to
them. Finally, to highlight the crucial role that civic inclusion and social
relationships with people of influence play in fair treatment and the protection of civil rights (justice), we move to the individual level to look at
two very different outcomes of government attempts to define someone
as a terrorist—one in which the subject was socially embedded in a white
middle-class community and one in which the subject was not so embed-

ded. In the former case, public doubts about the government's allegations of threat were able to significantly challenge the government's attempts to whisk the person away; in the latter case, a Muslim employee of the U.S. military found few allies to contest his incommunicado detention.

Most of the government's post-9/11 national security policies were designed and carried out by the executive branch of government and were subjected to little or no a priori public discussion or debate. Twenty-five of the thirty-seven known U.S. government security initiatives implemented in the first two years after the September 11 attacks either explicitly or implicitly targeted Arabs and Muslims living in the United States, who were singled out by the government as one conflated *group* (Tsao and Gutierrez 2003). These measures included mass arrests, secret and indefinite detentions, prolonged detention of "material witnesses," closed hearings and the use of secret evidence, government eavesdropping on attorney-client conversations, FBI home and work visits, wiretapping, seizures of property, removals of aliens with technical visa violations, freezing the assets of charities, and mandatory special registration. I have argued conservatively that at least 100,000 Arabs and Muslims living in the United States directly experienced one of these measures; others, including the FBI agent quoted earlier, have cited much larger figures.[7] The most severe measures were taken against noncitizens, who were accorded a lesser set of rights than Arab and Muslim American citizens and permanent residents, whose treatment, in turn, fell below the standard most would consider acceptable for U.S. citizens.

Mass Arrests

The first to be caught in the post-9/11 "investigation dragnet" were some 1,200 Arab or Muslim males (presumably noncitizens) who were arrested shortly after the attacks and detained under high security conditions.[8] The exact identities and individual fates of these detainees are not known because the federal government has to this date refused to release specific information about them. The government denied a Freedom of Information Act request filed by dozens of organizations and appealed a District Court judge's order to release the names; the U.S. Court of Appeals for the D.C. circuit supported the government's secrecy (Chang and Kabat 2004). Males who matched an Arab/Muslim phenotype and were determined for any reason (or no reason) to be suspicious were the first to be locked up, after which the government looked for violations with which to charge them (Cole 2003). Being unable to prove legal residence in the United States at the moment of contact was a sufficient condition. Arab and Muslim men seen in rental cars or observed taking photos of buildings or tourist sites were arrested by government agents and eventually jailed for months as "persons of interest"—that is, as potential security threats. Detainees could not be released (or deported) until they were cleared of terrorist connections, a process that took many months. Attorney General Ashcroft announced the rule change on September 18, 2001, that gave government largely unlimited time to find and press charges on persons it had detained by expanding "the twenty-four-hour time period to forty-eight hours, or to an additional reasonable time if necessary under an emergency or in other extraordinary circumstances" (Ashcroft 2001a). On September 21, 2001, in a document known as the Creppy memo, Ashcroft ordered that every immigration hearing designated "of special interest" be held in secret (Cole 2003). By 2003, it was assumed that most of these early detainees had been released and that at least five hundred had been deported. Deportations were based on violations of immigration law, and one had to be *cleared* of terrorist connections to be deported. At least one man, Benatta Benamar, was held in U.S. custody for nearly five years despite being cleared of terrorist involvement in 2001, in a case riddled with abuse, government misconduct, cover-ups, and collusion between the FBI, INS, and government prosecutors (Chang and Kabat 2004, 7). The government netted not a single terrorist suspect from this dragnet operation.

Human Rights Watch (2002, 2005) issued two major investigative reports concerning these post-9/11 arrests. In its first report, "Presumption of Guilt" (Human Rights Watch 2002, 12), it found that government agents used stereotypes to determine who to arrest: "being a male Muslim non-citizen from certain countries became a proxy for suspicious behavior." Some men were incarcerated "simply because spouses, neighbors, or members of the public said they were 'suspicious' or accused them without any credible basis of being terrorists" (12). The Human Rights Watch report concluded: "Operating behind a wall of secrecy, the U.S. Department of Justice thrust scores of Muslim men living in the United States into a Kafkaesque world of indefinite detention without charges and baseless accusations of terrorist links."[9] Human Rights Watch's investigation found that fundamental legal protections were skirted as government officials abused material witness rules based on prejudice and "false, flimsy and irrelevant evidence" (12).

Human Rights Watch's (2005) second report, "Witness to Abuse," co-authored by the American Civil Liberties Union (ACLU), reported on its investigation of the cases of seventy persons it was able to locate who were picked up during this period and held on "material witness" charges. Its interviews uncovered aggressive armed arrests and denials of due process rights, as described by Tarek Omar, arrested as a material witness in October 2001:

> They treated us like professional terrorists. They put us in cars and had big guns—as if they were going to shoot people, as if we were Osama bin Laden. They didn't let us speak; they didn't let us ask why we were in

detention. I never knew for how long we would stay in jail. It felt like we would stay forever. I didn't even know why I was in jail.[10]

Interviews also uncovered repeated verbal abuse and physical deprivation during extensive periods of incarceration and frequent use of leg chains, solitary confinement, and banging on cells all night. Some detainees reported recurring strip searches and intentional physical cruelty. These abuses were also investigated by the Justice Department's Office of the Inspector General (2003), which found that intense psychological pressure was used on suspects to extract confessions. In one notable case, government agents claimed that the Egyptian student Abdallah Higazy, who was staying at the Millennium Hilton across from the World Trade Center on September 11, had "confessed" during a polygraph test to owning the radio transceiver found in his room. It later turned out that the radio had been found in another room, that it belonged to an airline pilot, and that the person who turned it over to government agents had lied about its location (Chang and Kabat 2004, 90). The Office of the Inspector General's (2003, 45) investigation of the treatment of post-9/11 detainees at the Metropolitan Detention Center in Brooklyn found a pattern of "unnecessary" body searches that appeared "intended to punish"; they were conducted in the presence of women and filmed in their entirety.

We found evidence indicating that many of the strip searches conducted on the ADMAX SHU (Special Housing Unit) were filmed in their entirety and frequently showed the detainees naked. The strip searches also did not afford the detainees much privacy, leaving them exposed to female officers who were in the vicinity. In addition, the policy for strip searching detainees on the ADMAX SHU was applied inconsistently, many of the strip searches appeared to be unnecessary, and a few appeared to be intended to punish the detainees. For example, many detainees were strip searched after attorney and social visits, even though these visits were in no-contact rooms separated by thick glass, the detainees were restrained, and the visits were filmed. We believe that the BOP (Bureau of Prisons) should develop a national policy regarding the videotaping of strip searches. We also believe MDC management should provide inmates with some degree of privacy when conducting these strip searches, to the extent that security is not compromised. . . . Because a strip search involves three or four officers, the BOP should review its policies of requiring strip searches for circumstances where it would be impossible for an inmate to have obtained contraband, such as after no-contact attorney or social visits, unless the specific circumstances warrant suspicion.

These types of repeated, invasive strip searches were not serving security purposes; rather, they played a symbolic role as degradation ceremonies intended to emasculate. Their repeated use on Arab and

Muslim men in American custody became somewhat characteristic of the post-9/11 world, whether in New York, Abu Ghraib, Iraq, Guantánamo, or elsewhere. The additional features of female onlookers and filming suggest that extra efforts were made to intensify the humiliation based on shared understandings of Arab/Muslim culture: that these aspects would increase the detainee's pain by adding public shame.

Once released from jail, many of these so-called "persons of interest" found that they had been imprinted with a terrorist stigma, which made putting their lives back together extremely difficult. Among those who remained in the United States, follow-up investigative reports indicated that former detainees were shunned by clients, customers, coworkers, and fellow community members. Arab and Muslim Americans feared that the ink of the terrorist stamp that was already tainting them might spill fully onto them and that a simple contact with a former suspect might render them the next person to disappear indefinitely in the hands of the American government and its web of prisons. Under the USA PATRIOT Act, and in consort with aggressive federal agents and prosecutors, "contact" has been used as evidence of aiding and abetting terrorism. Some former detainees intending to stay eventually left the United States because they could not reconstruct their lives—as in the case of the sensationally covered but wrongfully arrested Evansville Eight.[11] Human Rights Watch (2005, 98) provides the following account of Tarek Albasti, an Egyptian national arrested as a material witness in October 2001 as one of the Eight, a group that eventually received a government apology for the wrongful arrests:

> After we were released we were in hell, you tell yourself, okay, well they released us so everyone should understand we are innocent, but that was not the case. Because I mean there are some people who support you and stuff like this but everyone is curious: did you snitch on somebody else, or did you make a deal with the government, or why were you released, or did you really do something or not. It's just like all this doubt in people's mind. At the time we lost about 30 to 40 percent of our business and then it kept getting worse and worse. And even when we got the apology and the newspaper wrote about it we thought we were going to be slammed because it's an apology on the first page of the newspaper. And [business] is slow. But people remember we were caught and this kind of thing and [business got even] slower. . . . Most of the response from people was, yes, they had enough, okay, they are innocent, [but] let's go back to our life, if they don't like it let's tell them to go back to their home, we are trying to make the country safer.

These arbitrary arrests—simply matching a phenotype seemed to be the first step toward landing in abusive, incommunicado incarceration for months—signaled early on to Arab and Muslim Americans (both citizens and noncitizens) that American legal protections were easily circumvented and did not apply to them. In fact, it was the very secrecy and lack of transparency in these arrests that sparked fear in members of these communities. This fear was augmented by the statements of government officials: by referring to detainees as "terrorists," "suspected terrorists," and "barbarians," they seemed to ensure that there would be little public outcry over any action the government took. Taken together, these measures produced a very frightening world for Arab and Muslim Americans.

The USA PATRIOT Act

On October 24, 2001, the U.S. Congress passed the executive branch–crafted USA PATRIOT (Uniting and Strengthening America by Providing Appropriate Tools Required to Intercept and Obstruct Terrorism) Act of 2001; President Bush signed it into law two days later (P.L. 107-56). Under intense pressure from Attorney General Ashcroft, who used the rhetoric of fear in his speech to Congress, the act was quickly passed through the circumvention of normal congressional procedures; only a few congresspeople had read the act in its entirety (Cole and Dempsey 2002). Wisconsin Senator Russ Feingold was the act's sole opponent in the Senate, while some sixty members of the House voted against it. Among a host of other provisions, the USA PATRIOT Act expanded the power of the U.S. government to use surveillance and wiretapping without first showing probable cause, permitted secret searches and access to private records by government agents without oversight, authorized the detention of immigrants on alleged suspicions and the denial of admission to the United States based on a person's speech, and expanded the concept of guilt by association. From its passage through 2008, the provisions of the PATRIOT Act have been principally used on Arabs and Muslims in the United States and on their community institutions, charities, and businesses. While the act abrogates the fundamental rights of everyone in the United States, it was passed and has been renewed without much public protest. Indeed, these policies seemed to give much of the American public a sense of safety and well-being, partly because they believed that such policies were meant for the country's Arabs and Muslims and would not be applied to them.

Legal challenges have been brought against sections of the PATRIOT Act. The *Humanitarian Law Project II, et al. v. Ashcroft, et al.* suit filed by the Center for Constitutional Rights challenges the expansion of the definition of criminal material support (to designated foreign terrorist organizations) to include providing "expert advice and assistance," arguing that the vagueness of this clause could render providing human rights training or expert medical advice criminal acts in support of terrorism (Chang and Kabat 2004). In January 2004, the U.S. District Court in Los Angeles ruled in favor of the plaintiffs, agreeing that this clause was void for vagueness under the First Amendment. Congress amended sections of the material support statute pertaining to "expert advice and assistance" as well as "services" and "training" in December 2005, but the amendments were struck down by the District Court in 2006. As of the summer of 2007, a government appeal was pending. The *Muslim Community Association of Ann Arbor, et al. v. Ashcroft and Mueller* lawsuit challenged section 215 of the act, which permits the FBI to "obtain in total secrecy 'any tangible things,' including 'books, records, papers, documents, and other items,' whether they are in a person's home or in the possession of a third party." Under section 215, the government does not need to show probable cause for its actions and imposes a gag order on the parties served with a section 215 order, barring them from informing anyone of the government's actions or the gag order. An FOIA request for information on the government's use of this and other surveillance tools authorized by the USA PATRIOT Act, filed by the ACLU, was denied by the government, an action upheld by Judge Ellen Segal Huvelle of the U.S. District Court for the District of Columbia (Chang and Kabat 2004). In a second case, however, the same judge rejected the government's attempt to delay disclosure of section 215 records and ruled that the ACLU was entitled to expedited processing of the request. Judge Huvelle agreed with the ACLU that the information "unquestionably implicates important individual liberties and privacy concerns" given "the ongoing debate regarding the renewal and/or amendment of the Patriot Act."[12]

These PATRIOT Act surveillance provisions sent a major chill through American Arab and Muslim communities and were another feature of the social context that caused many interviewees to feel unsafe in the United States. We return to this impact later in the chapter when discussing how these laws in combination with the feeling of being watched produced in many Arab and Muslim Americans a type of double-consciousness (Du Bois 1995 [1903]; Fanon 1961 [1953])—a state in which they were watching themselves being watched by others.

Visa Holds

In an effort to gain control over the types of persons entering the United States from Arab and Muslim-majority countries, the State Department issued a classified cable in October 2001 imposing a mandatory twenty-day hold on all non-immigrant visa applications submitted by men age eighteen to forty-five from twenty-six countries, subjecting them to special security clearance. Over time their applications required approval in Washington, with no time limit imposed on the response. The impact of this policy was extensive and received substantial media attention. Foreign students were unable to return to school in the United States; professors, researchers, and Fulbright Scholars requiring non-immigrant visas missed one to two semesters of university work; medical and chemotherapy patients being treated at facilities like the Mayo and Cleveland Clinics were forced out of their treatment cycles; and artists, musicians, and businessmen were forced to break contracts they had signed. In fiscal year 2002 (October 1, 2001, to September 30, 2002), substantially fewer visitor visas (in all categories) were awarded to persons from the Arab and Muslim-majority countries that would be selected for special registration, except for Eritrea, than in fiscal year 2001, with an overall 39 percent decrease (see table 4.1). These decreases reflect not only increased denials and longer waiting periods, but presumably also diminished interest in visiting the United States given the conditions at the time for Arabs and Muslims in the United States. Decreases also characterized other parts of the world, but to a lesser extent: Europeans experienced a 15 percent decrease, Asians (excluding special registration countries) experienced a 24 percent decrease, and Africans a 23 percent decrease.[13]

FBI Interviews

In November 2001, the Justice Department announced its intention to interview some five thousand individuals who had come to the United States from Arab and Muslim-majority countries since January 1, 2000, on non-immigrant visas. It later announced a second round of interviews with an additional three thousand persons, and then a third round with thousands of Iraqis living in the United States, including persons to whom it had granted refugee status. The actual number of domestic security interviews that were conducted with U.S. citizens and noncitizens is unknown. John Tirman (2005), director of the Center for International Studies at MIT, estimated in April 2005 that the FBI had conducted at least two hundred thousand interviews. Retired FBI agent Rolince quoted earlier spoke of some half a million interviews. One study participant spoke about the disruptions and apprehension caused by the FBI interviews, as well as about what was perceived as the FBI's unprofessional ways of getting information—offering to pay people to spy on others or blackmailing them into cooperating.

> FBI investigations into Muslims, particularly those from the Middle East, have caused strains and hardships for families. Some have been targeted again and again. Some have been interviewed by the FBI six times, and asked the same questions that were asked the previous five times; some get visited at their home at 2:00 A.M. Some get visited at their parents' house instead of being contacted directly. The interviews of hundreds of Iraqis were not about national security—they were to get information to invade Iraq. Some are visited at work. Some are visited because the neighbor or the plumber called. They cause problems for people at the airport; people's homes are bugged. Some are being blackmailed to be informants for the FBI. Others are offered money to inform. We are ready to cooperate as partners, not to be bought out in secret. They need smarter, better-trained officers who can really help. The stories don't make you feel safe; everyone is suspect. You don't know who's going to knock at your door.

Table 4.1   Percentage Change and Visitor Visas Approved Fiscal Year 2001 and Fiscal Year 2002

Rank by Number of Visas FY2002	Country	FY 2001	FY2002	Percentage Decrease	Rank by Percentage Decrease	Special Registration Group
9	Iran	20,268	12,284	39%	12	1
18	Iraq	3,071	1,837	40	11	1
24	Libya	449	343	24	19	1
17	Sudan	4,576	2,258	51	7	1
11	Syria	14,399	8,529	41	10	1
22	Afghanistan	1,983	1,178	41	10	2
13	Algeria	7,516	5,084	32	16	2
16	Bahrain	4,671	2,279	51	7	2
20	Eritrea	1,590	1,574	1	21	2
6	Lebanon	32,321	21,741	33	15	2
4	Morocco	26,159	22,775	13	20	2
15	Oman	3,963	2,312	42	9	3
19	Qatar	3,769	1,826	52	6	3
23	Somalia	1,003	429	57	3	3
14	Tunisia	9,161	4,269	53	5	3
12	United Arab Emirates	17,247	6,090	65	2	3
21	Yemen	2,875	1,304	55	4	3
2	Pakistan	95,595	61,538	36	14	4
5	Saudi Arabia	66,721	22,245	67	1	4
8	Bangladesh	21,107	15,556	26	18	5
3	Egypt	61,828	37,381	40	11	5
1	Indonesia	96,961	68,478	29	17	5
7	Jordan	33,548	21,043	37	13	5
10	Kuwait	19,756	11,242	43	8	5
Total		550,537	333,595	39	—	—
—	North and South Korea[a]	841,863	802,552	—	—	2

Source: Author's calculations based on Immigration and Naturalization Service raw data.

[a]North Koreans were subject to special registration (group 2) although North Korea is not a Muslim majority country. Data provided by the INS combined North and South Korea.

Many interviewees stressed that if they had learned of anything harmful to the United States, they would have been willing informants, because this was their country too. Their lack of any such reporting was interpreted by the government, however, as indicating not an absence of terrorist plots, but community complicity in them.

The Absconders Initiative

In January 2002, the Immigration and Naturalization Service launched the "absconders initiative" to track down and deport 6,000 noncitizen males from (unnamed) "Middle Eastern" countries who had been ordered deported (usually for overstaying a visa) by an immigration judge but had never left the United States. At the time there were an estimated 314,000 so-called absconders in the United States, the vast majority from Latin America. Although fewer than 2 percent were Middle Eastern, the government's ethnic profiling targeted this group. By May of the same year, the Justice Department reported that 585 Middle Eastern absconders had been caught, and a year later it reported that 1,100 persons had been detained under this initiative (Cole 2003). In a meeting with members of Chicago's Arab American community at which I was present, top regional federal government officials (such as the U.S. attorney and INS leadership) argued that this initiative did not signal racial profiling because other communities would be approached next. As of 2008, that has not happened.

The Enhanced Border Security and Visa Entry Reform Act and Other Border and Domestic Immigration Control Procedures

On May 14, 2002, Congress passed the Enhanced Border Security and Visa Entry Reform Act. Among the many provisions of this act—which calls for the integration of INS databases, the development of machine-readable visas, the requirement that all airlines submit to U.S. authorities a list of passengers who have boarded any plane bound for the United States, and stricter monitoring of foreign students—is a restriction on non-immigrant visas for individuals from countries identified by the State Department as state sponsors of terrorism. In late June 2002, the Department of Justice issued an internal memo to the INS and to U.S. Customs requesting that these two agencies seek out and search all Yemenis, including American citizens, entering the United States. Reports circulated that Yemeni Americans were being removed from planes and boarding lines and having to wait hours for security clearances. On July 14, 2002, the INS announced that it would begin enforcing section 265(a) of the Immigration and Nationality Act, which requires all aliens to register changes of address within ten days of moving. According to a participant in a National Immigration Forum conference call of August 15,

2002, one regional INS official openly stated that this rule would not be enforced on everyone. Shortly thereafter, a Palestinian legal immigrant in North Carolina who was stopped for driving four miles over the speed limit was detained for two months and then charged with a misdemeanor for failing to report his address change. The INS was seeking his deportation, but a local immigration judge ruled on August 5 that he could not be deported for this infraction because he did not willfully break this law. The policy change concerning enforcement of section 265(a) ultimately led to the special registration program for Arab and Muslim men.

The Special Registration Program

On September 11, 2002, the Immigration and Naturalization Service implemented the "special registration" program, which required "*certain non-immigrant aliens*" (hereafter referred to as "visitors") to register with the U.S. immigration authorities, be fingerprinted and photographed, respond to questioning, and submit to routine reporting.[14] The special registration program had a massive impact on Arab and Muslim American communities. According to the Department of Homeland Security, between September 11, 2002, and June 1, 2003, 127,694 Arab and Muslim men were initially registered at their U.S. port of entry, and another 82,880 were registered in domestic call-in registration.[15] Removal (deportation) orders were issued for 13,434 of the latter group who had visa irregularities, although all were cleared of connections to terrorism. The number of Arabs, Muslims, and others from Muslim-majority countries eventually deported from the nearly 13,500 ordered deported under this program is not known, nor do we know the number of family members they took with them, because persons with a pending application for adjustment of status were permitted to present a case for staying in the United States. Even prior to special registration, more Arabs and Muslims (none accused of terrorist connections) had been removed from the United States since the September 11 attacks than the number of foreign nationals deported for their political beliefs following the infamous 1919 Palmer Raids (Gourevitch 2003).[16] The potential of an additional 13,000 deportees rounded up for visa violations through the special registration program— a highly select group amounting to less than 1 percent of the 3.2 million to 3.6 million persons living in the United States while "out of status" and the 8 million to 12 million undocumented—has few historic precedents, except for perhaps Operation Wetback of the 1950s.[17] Removal data for nationals from countries selected for special registration show significant increases beginning in DHS fiscal year 2002, as seen in figure 4.1 and table 4.2.

In May 2003, after gaining Arab and Muslim American cooperation with the program through community public forums in which they stated that they were not targeting Arabs and Muslims because the pro-

Figure 4.1   All Removals: Countries Selected for Special Registration

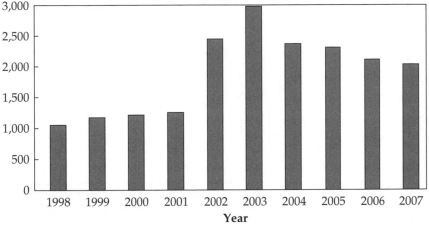

Source: Author's compilation based on U.S. Department of Homeland Security. Deportable Alien Control System (DACS), July 2008, Enforcement Case Tracking System (ENFORCE), October 2007.

Note: Data do not include North Korea. Totals include criminal and non-criminal causes for removal, although the largest number in all cases is non-criminal. Increases in removals were also evident after FY 2001 for some non-special registration countries.

gram would be expanded to all visiting aliens, government officials announced the phasing out of the program. During the program's tenure, its scope was never expanded beyond males age sixteen and over from twenty-three Muslim-majority countries, plus heavily Muslim Eritrea and North Korea. Pressed for the criteria behind its selection of countries, government officials stated at times that the countries (whose citizens and nationals were required to register) were selected because of Al-Qaeda presence, although some countries with no proven Al-Qaeda presence were included and some countries with known Al-Qaeda presence, such as Germany and England, were excluded. In a May 19 press statement, the Department of Homeland Security, which had taken over immigration functions from the INS, referred to special registration (eventually renamed NSEERS, for National Security Entry and Exit Registry System) as a "pilot project focusing on a smaller segment of the nonimmigrant alien population deemed to be of risk to national security."[18] Explicit in this statement was the notion that Arab and Muslim males born in Asia, the Middle East, and North Africa posed a security risk to the United States.

Although the exact number is unknown, thousands of Arab and Muslim families with a member whose immigration status was irregular

Table 4.2   **Number of Aliens Removed from Countries of Nationality Subject to Special Registration, 1998 to 2007**

Fiscal Year	Number Removed from Selected Countries of Nationality
1998	1,056
1999	1,169
2000	1,215
2001	1,262
2002	2,444
2003	2,990
2004	2,361
2005	2,316
2006	2,113
2007	2,032

Source: Author's compilation based on U.S. Department of Homeland Security. Deportable Alien Control System (DACS), July 2008, Enforcement Case Tracking System (ENFORCE), October 2007.

Note: Data do not include North Korea. Totals include criminal and non-criminal causes for removal, although the largest number in all cases is non-criminal. Increases in removals were also evident after FY 2001 for some non-special registration countries.

left the country permanently rather than be subjected to registration, a pattern that particularly characterized the Pakistani American community. While the INS had estimated that fifteen thousand Pakistanis would be subject to call-in registration, the Pakistani embassy estimated the number at sixty-five thousand.[19] In 2002 and 2003, FOR SALE signs were widely evident in Chicago's Pakistani neighborhoods, and many families were reported to have sold their homes at great financial loss. One Chicago attorney with Pakistani clients told me in March 2003: "I advise my clients who have no hope to adjust their status to leave with dignity before the registration program ends. They can't imagine that Americans would want to deport them. The dream of America is over for them. The only other option is to live as a psychological fugitive." Some families— again, largely Pakistani—fled to the Canadian border seeking asylum and were hosted by local churches (see, for example, Saytanides 2003). When the surge became so great at the Lacolle-Champlain port of entry (north of Plattsburg, New York), the INS used police roadblocks and rigid outbound checks to prevent anyone from going north. According to reports posted on a list-serve created just to bring clarity to the special registration process (and mainly used by attorneys), individuals who registered at that border and were found to be out of status were placed immediately in deportation proceedings. All Pakistani men were detained, as well as others on a case-by-case basis.[20]

Special registration had two components: port-of-entry registration and domestic call-in registration. Port-of-entry registration required visitors from specific countries designated by the attorney general, as well as others who fit certain discretionary "criteria" and "reasons," to: (1) be fingerprinted and photographed and to "provide information required" by the INS at their U.S. port of entry; (2) report in person to the INS within ten days after staying in the United States for thirty days and to provide "additional documentation confirming compliance" with visa requirements, such as proof of residence, employment, or study, and any "additional information" required by the INS; (3) report annually, in person, to the INS within ten days of the anniversary of entry to the United States with any documentation and additional information required; (4) notify the INS, by mail or other means decided by the attorney general, within ten days of any change of address, job, or school, using a special form for registrants; and (5) report to an INS inspecting officer upon departure and to leave the United States from a port specified by the INS and published in the Federal Register.[21] The first list of acceptable ports was published on September 30, 2002, and registrants seeking to travel internationally were not free to choose any airport of departure from the United States. Registrants were given "fingerprint identification numbers," which were written in their passports (sometimes on their I-94).

The attorney general gave INS inspecting officers the discretion to order port-of-entry special registration for visitors of any nationality if the inspecting officer had reason to believe that the person met certain criteria. Some of these criteria were contained in an undated "limited official use" INS memo that became publicly available. They included: unexplained trips to Iran, Iraq, Libya, Sudan, Syria, North Korea, Cuba, Saudi Arabia, Afghanistan, Yemen, Egypt, Somalia, Pakistan, Indonesia, or Malaysia; travel not well explained by the alien; previous overstays; meeting a characterization established by intelligence agencies; identified as requiring monitoring by local, state, or federal law enforcement; the alien's behavior, demeanor, or answers; or information provided by the alien. Because of this extension, the INS was able to claim: "To date, individuals from well over 100 countries have been registered," which it offered as proof that the program was not targeting Muslims and Arabs.[22]

One impact of the "persons believed to be such" clause was the requirement that dual nationals register, such as persons who were Canadian and Syrian citizens, or Swiss and Iranian citizens. In other words, a man could be a Canadian citizen, but if agents of the U.S. government believed that he originated from any of the targeted countries, he would be subjected to special rules. The Canadian government issued a travel warning for its citizens traveling to the United States shortly after the program began, when Canadians of Arab and Asian descent reported harassment at U.S. borders and after the U.S. government detained and then deported to Syria a returning Canadian citizen in transit at JFK Airport. Canadian citizen Mahar Arar was held in coercive, incommunicado American custody for nearly two weeks and then chained, shackled, and deported to Syria, where he was imprisoned for about a year and tortured. Arar and the U.S. Center for Constitutional Rights filed a lawsuit against the U.S. government after his return to Canada in 2003. The Canadian government established a Commission of Inquiry into the Actions of Canadian Officials in Relation to Maher Arar, which in 2006 cleared Arar of all terrorism allegations; the commission found that there was no evidence to indicate he had committed any offense or constituted a threat to the security of Canada.[23] The commission also found that the actions of Canadian officials very likely led to his ordeal. Arar's case would become one of many extraordinary renditions conducted by the U.S. government: persons taken into U.S. custody being extrajudicially transferred to third countries for coercive treatment. Research published by *Mother Jones* (Bergen and Tiedemann 2008) documented sixty-seven known cases of extraordinary rendition by the United States government since 1995.

The First Group Required to Register   Visiting citizens and nationals of Iran, Iraq, Libya, Syria, and the Sudan were the first groups required to comply with port-of-entry special registration on its effective date of September 11, 2002. The process of designating countries whose citizens and nationals were required to specially register upon entry to the United States required that the attorney general confer with the secretary of State and then publish the countries' names in a Federal Register notice. This quick and simple formula for designating countries was instituted in 1993 under former attorney general Janet Reno, who published a Federal Register notice requiring "certain non-immigrants from Iraq and the Sudan" to register; in 1996 she added non-immigrants with Iranian and Libyan travel documents.[24] Former attorney general Dick Thornburg of the Bush Sr. administration was the first to require port-of-entry registration, in 1991, when visitors "bearing Iraqi and Kuwaiti travel documents" were required to do so.[25] Ashcroft added Syria to this list on September 6, 2002, and declared that citizens and nationals of these five countries, as well as *persons believed to be such,* were subject to the new, expanded special registration.

"Hey, Arab and Muslim Man: This Notice Is for You"   Domestic "call-in" registration for non-immigrants who were already in the United States was implemented on November 6, 2002, when Attorney General Ashcroft published a call-in notice in the Federal Register for "certain visiting citizens and nationals" of Iran, Iraq, Libya, Syria, and the Sudan who had entered the United States and been inspected by the INS prior to September 11, 2002.[26] Providing the ten-day notice required by law, these persons were ordered to report to specified INS offices between November 15 and December 16, 2002, unless they were leaving the United States prior to the latter date.[27] Call-in special registration was

limited to males age sixteen and older, was based on "intelligence information" and "administrative feasibility," and excluded applicants for
asylum. Although U.S. permanent residents and citizens were excluded
from special registration, applicants for adjustment of status (to permanent resident) were required to register. Since the Federal Register is not
a commonly read publication, the INS produced flyers to advertise the
call-in program with THIS NOTICE IS FOR YOU splayed across the top, eerily
reminiscent of the notices posted for Japanese living in the western
United States during World War II. The INS also enlisted the cooperation of community and ethnic organizations to publicize the program.
Placed in a position similar to Japanese American organizations during
the period of Japanese registry prior to internment, community organizations had to promote the program despite their dissent. A *San Jose
Mercury News* article (Mangaliman 2003) entitled "Role in Registration
Worries Ethnic Media" cited an Iranian magazine editor in California
who felt "used by the government" when his publication of the notice
contributed to the arrest of hundreds of Iranians.

Upon appearing at an INS office, persons who reported for call-in special registration were required to: answer questions under oath before an
immigration officer, who recorded them; present all travel documents,
passports, and an I-94; present all government-issued identification; present proof of residence, including land title, lease, or rental agreement;
present proof of matriculation at an educational institution or proof of
employment, as required by the visa; and provide "such other information as is requested by the immigration officer." They were also subject
to all of the other special registration requirements listed earlier for port-
of-entry registration, such as reporting in person annually, reporting
changes of address within ten days, and undergoing exit registry upon
departure. Willful noncompliers were subject to criminal charges, fines,
and removal.

Attorney General Ashcroft amended the Code of Federal Regulations
(CFR) to declare the willful failure to register and provide full and
truthful disclosure of information a failure to maintain non-immigrant
status—a deportable offense.[28] He also amended the CFR by declaring
that failure to register upon departure from the United States was an
unlawful activity, making one presumed to be inadmissible to the United
States because one "can reasonably be seen as attempting to reenter for
purpose of engaging in an unlawful activity."[29] Ashcroft thus made
noncompliance with special registration a bar to immigration, although
only Congress has the right to establish such categories of inadmissibility. Conceivably, then, noncompliance with special registration could be
used to deny benefits in a future amnesty or legalization program to
Arabs and Muslims who entered with inspection but did not specially
register, in the absence of challenges to the legality of Ashcroft's bar.

The arrest and detention of hundreds of registrants, mostly Iranians, in southern California during this first period of special registration sparked nationwide protest as persons voluntarily acting in compliance with the new rules were handcuffed and led off to jail for visa violations. Some reported sleeping on concrete floors in rooms holding up to fifty prisoners. Others reported verbal abuse and body cavity searches. One Iranian-born database manager was handcuffed, leg-shackled, and flown to a grim prison near San Diego, forced to sleep on a cement floor, and awakened at fifteen-minute intervals for five days by guards shouting questions at him. He had registered two days late because he was not sure the program applied to him as a Canadian citizen.[30] Most of the detainees were working taxpayers with families who had lived law-abiding lives in the United States for decades, and quite a few had pending applications for permanent residency (Serjeant, Jill. 2002. "Hundreds of Muslim Immigrants Rounded Up in California." Reuters, December 19, 2002). The Iranian American Bar Association issued a request that persons with firsthand knowledge of the detentions and alleged misconduct perpetrated against Iranian nationals call a toll-free number and share their information. The association sought "to ensure transparency and accountability in government" and to analyze whether the detentions or mistreatment by INS officials violated any U.S. laws. Most of the detainees were eventually released on bail, with removal proceedings started by the INS at the same time.

The director of the southern California chapter of the ACLU said the arrests were "reminiscent of the internment of Japanese Americans during world War II" (BBC News Online 2002). As a result of protests surrounding INS handling of this group, Attorney General Ashcroft's Valentine's Day press release stated that "prosecutorial discretion" would be considered if a registrant had a current application for change of status (to permanent residency), the applicant appeared eligible, and no adverse information was revealed from "indices, checks, or other sources." In other words, individuals would be handled on a case-by-case basis, and some who were out of status would be allowed to post bond and appear before an immigration judge. Meanwhile, removal proceedings would be started against them. Stories of shackling, detention, and being shuffled from one detention center to another continued to be reported throughout this round of registration. At the end of January, the INS announced that it had begun deportation proceedings against 2,477 men (McDonnell, Patrick J. 2003. "Registration of foreign men has wide effect." Los Angeles Times, January 19, 2003)—about 10 percent of the 25,000 persons (Mangaliman 2003) who had registered at that point.

The Second Group Required to Register   On November 22, thirteen more countries were added to the special registration domestic call-in list:

Afghanistan, Algeria, Bahrain, Eritrea, Lebanon, Morocco, North Korea, Oman, Qatar, Somalia, Tunisia, United Arab Emirates, and Yemen. Visiting male citizens and nationals of these countries age sixteen and over who entered the United States with inspection prior to October 1, 2002, were required to report to designated INS offices for special registration between December 2, 2002, and January 10, 2003, unless they left the country by the latter date. The addition of North Korea captured "six of the seven designated state sponsors of terror," excluding only the Cubans, and was the only country covered by special registration that was not predominantly Muslim.[31] The INS extended the call-in period for "Groups 1 and 2" through February 7, 2003, in response to protests from community and national organizations across the country. In mid-December, the American-Arab Anti-Discrimination Committee, the Alliance of Iranian Americans, the Council on American Islamic Relations, and the National Council of Pakistani Americans filed a class action lawsuit against the government seeking an injunction against arrests of persons registering without federal warrants and an order preventing deportations without due process. On December 12, Senators Russ Feingold and Edward Kennedy and Representative John Conyers sent a letter to Attorney General Ashcroft requesting suspension of the registration process. The three congressmen demanded that the Department of Justice release information about what it was doing, "to allow Congress and the American people to decide whether the Department has acted appropriately and consistent with the Constitution" (Letter to John Ashcroft, December 12, 2002). But the program forged ahead because, as an executive branch project, there was little recourse available to stop it. Special registration was yet another component of what the journalist Nat Hentoff (2002a) called the Bush administration's "parallel legal system" in which aliens had different rights than citizens, and some citizens had different rights than other citizens.

The Third Group Required to Register   Pakistanis and Saudis were added to the call-in registry on December 16, 2002, and were given from January 13 through February 21 (later extended to March 21) to register, unless they departed the United States by the latter date.[32] The demeaning treatment of a young Pakistani man in Chicago seeking to register made the cover of *Chicago Reader* (Sula 2003). The young man was married to an American citizen and looking for work on the "optional practical training" extension of his F-1 student visa, which he received after completing his master's in electrical engineering. Upon voluntarily arriving for registry at 9:30 A.M. on February 6, he was interviewed, arrested, handcuffed to a Syrian doctor, and then transferred with a dozen other men to a different INS office. His offense was looking for work instead of working. His passport, driver's license, and work permit were taken from him. After being fingerprinted and photographed and undergoing a second round of interviews, he was permitted release after payment of a $7,500 bond. He was then relieved of his watch and keys, transported with other men to an INS detention facility in the Chicago suburbs, and issued a green jumpsuit with "INS" on the back. Now visibly a "national security" prisoner, he was taken at around midnight with other men to another jail in DuPage County, and then at around 4:00 A.M. taken back to the suburban jail and placed in a locked room. Meanwhile, his father-in-law had posted bond but was being sent from place to place looking for his son-in-law. If this young man had been less eager to comply and had waited only four more days to register, he might not have experienced such demeaning treatment: four days after his release from custody, he received his green card application.

The Fourth Group Required to Register   The last group to be called in, on January 16, 2003, was male visitors who were citizens and nationals of Jordan, Kuwait, Bangladesh, Egypt, and Indonesia. These individuals were required to register between February 24 and March 28, 2003 (extended to April 25).[33] This round of registration had the greatest impact on Chicago's Arab American community, since Palestinians, most of whom carry Jordanian passports, and Egyptians are the dominant groups in the Chicago metropolitan area. Initially, it was unclear whether Palestinians who carried Jordanian passports but were not full Jordanian citizens (West Bank Palestinians) were required to register. A few community organizations asked the INS for an official opinion on this matter and were told that only Jordanian citizens with a Jordanian identification number and family book (depending on when they received these documents) were required to register. As the final days to register approached, the Arab American Action Network put out a call "to all those interested in advocating for civil liberties and immigrants rights."

Posted 4/20/03 RE: INS' "SPECIAL REGISTRATION" POLICIES
Activists from all over the city will be volunteering to advise and support the nationals of BANGLADESH, EGYPT, INDONESIA, JORDAN, or KUWAIT, who MUST register with the INS by April 25th.

Considering the mass detentions that were implemented by INS authorities in Los Angeles on December 16th of last year, there are worries that the same type of policy may be used here in Chicago on April 25th. Some of the Middle Eastern men, mostly Iranian, detained in Los Angeles were photographed, fingerprinted, interrogated, and strip searched. Some are still in detention, and others have been deported.

To protect the Chicagoans who must register, a team of volunteers will attempt to gather contact information from these immigrants BEFORE they proceed into the Federal Building (where the INS has moved its "special registration" offices) for the registration. The information will be used to advocate for and help provide legal assistance in the event that these immigrants are detained by the INS.

We need people from 8 AM–5 PM from Monday, April 21st through Friday, April 25th, at the Federal Plaza (200 S. Dearborn). Please mention which shift you would be able to cover (morning, afternoon, early evening), how many hours you will be available to help, and whether or not you speak Arabic, Bangla, Bahasa, Malay, or Javanese.[34]

Banners reading STOP THE DEPORTATIONS and WHAT'S NEXT? CONCENTRATION CAMPS? were held by dissenters standing outside the federal building during this final week of special registration.

Confusion, Arbitrariness, Uncertainty, and Fear   One indicator of the type of impact that special registration had on Arab and Muslim communities is the confusion it created even among attorneys, who throughout the special registration program's existence were baffled as to who was covered by it and who was not. Stories of chaos, inconsistency, and arbitrary decisions were circulated among immigration lawyers on a special registration list-serve created by attorneys to help them advise their clients about the process. The rule that "citizens and nationals" of designated countries had to register provoked questions such as: How are citizens and nationals defined? Does it vary by country, and whose rules apply? Does one ever cease to be a citizen of the place in which one was born? Must a dual-citizen register? (Yes, unless one is a U.S. citizen or permanent resident.) Does the type of document with which one entered the United States matter? (In some cases.) What happens to persons who entered on visa waivers or are applicants for adjustment under 245(i)? What about someone who entered the United States as a visitor but has since become a permanent resident? What about travel documents that are not passports?

Immigration attorneys and specialists found it difficult to advise their clients, who faced the possibility of very serious negative consequences (deportation) in the event of bad advice. No one could predict whether someone who appeared for registry and was out of status would be held in detention or released on bond, even if they had a pending application for immigration benefits. There was considerable variation in treatment from case to case and region to region. Bonds for persons considered out of status were set at widely varying levels, ranging from $1,000 to $10,000 in cases that otherwise appeared quite similar. While attorneys were legally permitted to be present at the questioning of clients, often they were prevented from doing so.

Questions also surrounded the "additional information" that INS and other agents took from persons who registered. There were reports of agents photocopying credit cards, airline frequent flyer cards, ATM cards, and video rental cards. Some said that every document in their wallets and on their persons was copied. Some were asked by INS agents about their friends, the organizations they belonged to, and their political beliefs. Information was taken under oath so that if at some future date the U.S. government wanted to deport someone, it would only need to allege that a statement given during registration was false to start the removal process.[35] Individuals released on bond usually did not get their travel documents, driver's licenses, work permits, or other forms of identification back. One registrant's post to the list-serve imparts the anxiety induced by the registration process, even among persons with no INS-determined irregularities:

> During special registration we gave the INS our information like addresses, employer/school info, credit/debit card numbers, telephone numbers etc., etc. If any of this information changes (like address, employer/school, telephone #) we have to inform the INS using AR-11 form. But what about the rest of the information (which we gave them during registration) like credit/bank card numbers, relative/friends contacts ("who can be contacted if INS cannot reach us"—this explanation was given by the officer who did my registration)? Does INS have some other form for these details or ????

Another post on the same list-serve underscores the arbitrariness and secrecy of the conduct of the government:

> I have a colleague at my work who is from Afghanistan. His brother came to the U.S. a month ago from Pakistan to interview with a few hospitals in the U.S. for a residency program. He went on Monday to get an extension on his visa until March, since the match results will not be out before then. When he was at the INS in Des Moines, they took his passport and told him you have to leave the country right away. He came back to Iowa City and changed the ticket that he already had to go back to Pakistan on Wednesday. The FBI came yesterday to his house and took him away. No one knows where he is and they can't contact him. Only he can call them. They told him yesterday that they will keep him till Wednesday and they will take him to the airport. But he (my colleague) got a call from his brother today that they are not letting him go and they are moving him to another facility. Do you know of any organization or someone that can help him. At least to know where his brother is and what are they planning on doing?

The following post by an attorney shows that a now-super-empowered immigration service was able to pick up and detain American citizens without recourse, as long as they fit the "terrorist" phenotype:

> Dear Colleagues, My client is a U.S. Citizen of Jordanian origin. Three weeks ago he was picked up by INS and held for 14 days until he was released 2 days before a scheduled appearance before an Immigration Judge. INS kept his naturalization certificate and social security card. He is not politically active and he sells ice-cream on an ice-cream truck. Are there grounds for suing INS? How do we retrieve his naturalization certificate and social security card? Thanks in advance, [attorney's name removed][36]

In the end, special registration was nothing short of a massive roundup of male Arab and Asian foreign nationals from predominantly Muslim countries. While it launched the potential removal of some 13,400 Arab and Muslim men from the United States—the 16 percent of registrants who *may* have been out of legal immigration status, many of whom were placed in detention—it produced no terrorists. Indeed, it revealed an incredibly law-abiding population in which fewer than 1 percent of eighty thousand registered men could be tarred with any record of predatory criminal activity.

Special Registration in History

An examination of the historical precedents upon which the Bush administration crafted the special registration program provides clues to the strategic thinking behind it. Attorney General Ashcroft cited legislative authority for the special registration program that encompasses a history going back to the 1798 Alien and Sedition Acts, which were primarily aimed at restraining and deporting aliens living in the United States who were considered subversive. Ashcroft specifically cited as his authority the 1940 Smith Act, formally known as the 1940 Alien Registration Act, which was passed to strengthen national defense in response to fears of Communist and anarchist influences in the United States. It required that all aliens over the age of thirteen be fingerprinted and registered, and it required parents and legal guardians to register those thirteen years of age and younger. In turn, the registrants received a numbered alien registration receipt card from the DOJ/INS proving registry, and they were required to carry this card with them at all times.[37] The Smith Act was built on 1919 legislation making past and present membership in "proscribed organizations and subversive classes" grounds for exclusion and deportation, and that act was built on the Alien and Sedition Acts of 1798. The Smith Act was not only aimed at foreigners but also prohibited American citizens from advocating or belonging to a group that advocated or taught the "duty, necessity, desirability, or propriety" of overthrowing any level of government by "force or violence." The first peacetime federal sedition law since 1798, the Smith Act was the basis of later prosecutions of persons alleged to be members of Communist and Socialist parties. The special registration program thus lies within the family of policies permitting the government to monitor, restrain, and remove persons whose political beliefs and ideologies it perceives as a threat.

The 1950 Internal Security Act (section 265) added the requirements for all aliens of annual registration and ten-day notification of change of address, as well as quarterly registration for temporary aliens. It also made present or former membership in the Communist Party or any other totalitarian party a ground for inadmissibility. It allowed the attorney general to deport aliens without a hearing if their presence was prejudicial to the public interest. The 1952 Immigration and Nationality Act (also known as the McCarran-Walter Act) brought all prior laws concerning aliens into one comprehensive statute, retaining the registry, reporting, and address notification features.[38] In addition to exclusions for the sick, insane, criminal, likely public charges, and anarchists from earlier laws, the 1952 law contains ten provisions for excluding aliens based on their political beliefs, especially communism, anarchy, and any other belief that advocates the overthrow of the U.S. government by unconstitutional means.[39] Based on this legal history, we might conclude that being Arab or Muslim was interpreted as a potential ideological threat to the United States, like communism or anarchism, but in this case the threat was measured not by organizational activity but by blood (ethnicity) or religion.

On the other hand, because the special registration program identified persons who had to comply based on their country of birth (citizens and nationals), not their beliefs, it shared features of the family of U.S. policies based on ideas of racial exclusion (beginning with slavery, abolished in 1865, and Indian removal), such as the 1790 Naturalization Law denying naturalized citizenship to nonwhites (repealed in 1952); the 1882 Chinese Exclusion Act (repealed in 1943); the Asia Barred Zone (repealed over time); and immigration quotas, which were enacted in 1921, revised in 1924 and 1952, and finally abolished in 1965, signaling the end of an era in which U.S. immigration policies were based principally on race. After this time, it was considered racist and against liberal democratic principles to blatantly discriminate against persons because of their country of birth. However, in 1981, the potential for the regulation of persons from certain "foreign states" reemerged in immigration legislation. Although they eliminated many reporting requirements for aliens, the 1981 amendments to immigration law permitted the attorney general to give ten-day notice to "natives of any one or more foreign states, or any class or group thereof" and to require them to provide the government with address and other information. Interestingly, the Iran Crisis of 1980 was specifically mentioned in the House Judiciary Committee report submitted for the 1981 law, which noted that "immediate access to records of nonimmigrants may be vital to our nation's security."[40] Attorney General Ashcroft used this law to authorize the call-in component of special registration.[41]

Country of birth emerged again in 1991 during the presidency of George H. W. Bush, when Attorney General Dick Thornburg implemented the special registration of persons holding Iraqi and Kuwaiti passports and travel documents, citing the 1940 Smith Act that permitted the registration and fingerprinting of classes of aliens who were permanent residents in the United States.[42] Thornburg constructed Kuwaitis and Iraqis as a "class" of people.[43] From that point on, special registration policies based on country of birth or nationality were applied solely to Arab and Muslim-majority countries, until North Korea was added in November 2002. While it is evident from this history that Arabs and a broad range of Muslims have been the subjects of place-based discriminatory immigration policies, the question remains: Are these policies about ideology (which includes cultural and religious beliefs) or about national origin and race? This analysis suggests that some members of the American government constructed a connection between "race," religion, and subversive ideology that was little different from earlier immigration formulas connecting national origin and race with cultural inferiority.

Policies Guided by Stereotypes, Not Knowledge

Homeland security policies cast a net so broadly and indiscriminately over Arab and Muslim men as to suggest that they were guided by stereotypes rather than concrete information. Our rendering of the history of the Arab American experience (chapter 3) lends additional support to such a conclusion by indicating that the nation prior to 9/11 was already riddled by pervasive negative stereotypes of Arabs and Muslims. Over a period of decades, Arabs and Muslims had been rendered homogeneous in American culture as their breadth of difference became less interesting than the acts of violence that negatively affected American allies and interests, which were perpetrated by a minuscule proportion of their hundreds of millions worldwide (in the case of Muslims, 1.2 billion). By commission and omission, interested parties, the mainstream media, and government officials helped to produce a common American understanding that Arabs, and later Muslims, were mostly, and almost innately, about violence and hatred of Americans. "Arabness" as an essence had been put forth as a collectively shared cultural system that stood in opposition to American values and interests, nearly genetic in its individual insurmountability. Scores of scholars and pundits weighed in on this story with their own evidence of the existence of a generic Arab and Muslim "rage" (Said 1997). Criticism of American foreign policies in the Arab world became equated with support for terrorism.

These ideas continue to be invoked in the twenty-first century. Somewhat backhandedly appealing to the notion of genetic predispositions, the neoconservative Gary Schmitt (2003) of the Project for a New American Century has written: "However the early signs suggest that the president is right to believe that the instinct for liberty is not missing from Middle East *genes*" (emphasis added). Nonetheless, Schmitt argues, "American power is key" to maintaining peace and order and to hunting down "Islamic terrorists." The difficulty in finding Arabs and Muslims who agree with American foreign policies vis-à-vis the Arab and Muslim world is often translated into proof of this insuperable condition and reinterpreted as support for terrorism—to wit, either you are with us or you support terrorism, a simplistic binary construction that equates policy disagreements with willingness to kill. Steven Salaita (2006, 82) refers to this syndrome that transforms dissenting Arab and Muslim Americans into terrorists or their supporters as "imperative patriotism." Attorney General John Ashcroft revealed the shallowness of his actual knowledge of Islam, while holding one of the highest public offices in the United States, when he described Islam as "a religion in which God requires you to send your son to die for him" (Hentoff 2002b). Indeed, a *St. Louis Post-Dispatch* editorial of February 13, 2002 (Editorial. 2002. "On the Record." p. B6.), observed that the attorney general's prejudices might lead to unfair targeting and misguided efforts:

> Mr. Ashcroft is overseeing the investigation of terrorist activity in the United States, which inevitably involves many Islamic men of Middle Eastern descent. If Mr. Ashcroft believes—on a deeply personal, and usually safely hidden level—that all Muslims practice the kind of radicalism that Al-Qaida and the September 11 hijackers embrace, he could not only unfairly target hosts of innocent people, he could also steer the hunt for terrorists in thousands of wrong directions.

There are many indications that prejudices such as these headed the American government in the wrong direction for a long time before 9/11, and that its perspectives on Arab and Muslim American communities prior to the 9/11 attacks contributed to its own intelligence failures. Since the late 1960s, American government resources vis-à-vis these communities were used largely to silence their dissent. Law-abiding community members who criticized American foreign policies were criminalized. American government agencies focused their time and resources on wiretapping, interviewing, spying, banning, charging, and trying to deport Arab and Muslim Americans who were engaged in building nonviolent opposition to American foreign policies (Bassiouni 1974, 1991; Butterfield 1999; Akram and Johnson 2004). These activities and the rhetoric behind them seem to have made it impossible for government agents to distinguish between law-abiding Arabs and Muslims and persons who might actually pose a threat to the United States. Arab and Muslim American exclusion from civic institutions and foreign policy debates lent a confirming air to these sweeping notions. After the 9/11 attacks, the American government admitted that it knew almost nothing about Arab and Muslim American communities or about where to look for potential terrorists, and so, armed only with stereotypes, it engaged in dragnet behavior. The words of Attorney General Ashcroft at the U.S. Conference of Mayors on October 25, 2001, are instructive as he compares Robert Kennedy's intimate *knowledge* of organized crime to the Bush administration's "growing knowledge" of its subject.

> An observer of Robert Kennedy wrote that RFK brought these assets to his successful campaign against organized crime: "A constructive anger.

An intimate knowledge of his subject. A talented team of prosecutors. And, finally, a partner in the White House." Today, as we embark on this campaign against terrorism, we are blessed with a similar set of advantages. Our anger, too, is constructive. *Our knowledge is growing.* Our team is talented. And our leadership in the White House is unparalleled. [emphasis added]

At the intersection of the government's ignorance of the real lives of Arab and Muslim Americans and the availability of a handy toolbox of stereotypes that seemed to endorse the appropriateness of racial and religious profiling, a relationship between the 9/11 attackers and Arab and Muslim Americans was constructed and acted upon. It was these racialized notions, not knowledge, that guided the government's post-9/11 homeland security policies. Only after the most comprehensive and visible of the post-9/11 policies had run their course would government agencies commence with a new approach, one of community engagement, although many at the top in Washington were never particularly convinced of its value. Throughout these periods, however, silent spotlights focused on members of these communities remained in place.

The Deceptive Calm of Surveillance

By late 2003, high-profile government activity in Arab and Muslim American communities appeared to slow down. Mass arrests and special registration had ended, and thousands of visa violators had been expelled from or left the United States (often accompanied by their U.S. citizen family members). In January 2003, FBI director Robert Mueller ordered his field offices to construct their wiretapping and undercover activity goals according to the number of mosques in the field area, thus shining hidden (and not so hidden, according to community members) spotlights on geographic areas with concentrations of Muslims (Isikoff 2003). There were still sensationalized arrests that more often than not fizzled into nonterrorism cases (Chang and Kabat 2004), closures of Muslim charitable institutions, and documented patterns of delays in immigration and naturalization processing (CAIR-Chicago 2007). In his State of the Union address, President Bush (2003) had spoken of *suspected* terrorists around the world meeting with arrest or other unspecified fates—"Let's put it this way: They are no longer a problem to the United States and our friends and allies"—leaving little doubt that the rule of law was still elusive. The everyday concerns of Arab Americans turned to more subtle government security measures, like being watched, secretly wiretapped, or clandestinely searched. An Arab American woman describes this state of deceptive calm:

> Yeah. I mean, after September 11, I don't think anybody felt safe, not anyone in general. Nobody felt safe, but Muslims definitely did not feel safe. It's been a couple of years now, so people feel less of the fear and

the shock than they did afterwards. I don't feel that somebody's going to physically hurt me. As far as infringing on my privacy, that's a different story. It's pretty much given that all our phone calls are tapped and our e-mails are read and all that stuff. Who knows if people watch us or not? We don't even know exactly what's happening, but we're very much aware that tabs are being kept on us to make sure that we're not doing anything anti-American.

Similarly, an Arab American man describes his compromised sense of safety as a loss of personal privacy:

I guess I feel safe. Anyone could be at the house, you know. Anybody could get the key from the manager and get in my house if they want to check sometime in the house. I'm not talking about stealing, you know. The Patriot Act allows it, so I don't know if they were there or not. They can come even if I don't know it. They have the ability to come. It doesn't matter, because I have nothing to hide.

Arab Muslims described conducting routine activities, such as loading their car trunks or checking their mail, with the sense that they might be watched. This double-consciousness (Du Bois 1995 [1903]) is qualitatively different from the certainty of being watched. W. E. B. Du Bois expressed it as "this sense of always looking at one's self through the eyes of others" (45). Nadine Naber (2006) describes this phenomenon as "internment of the psyche" as the disciplinary effects of the state penetrate everyday actions. Hatem Bazian (2004) has argued that internment camps are unnecessary when people can be virtually interned, their every movement watched, their every sentence recorded, their every transaction noted by hidden cameras, microphones, Internet tapping, and compilation of phone, bank, credit card, and library records. The government's power and secrecy, and its call for citizens to be watching their Arab and Muslim neighbors, had great capacity to produce a psychological state in which few ever felt fully safe or secure. As study participants describe it, double-consciousness brings about its own particular type of damage, often articulated as a loss of self-confidence. The following quotes from two Arab American women refer to connections and disconnections–being connected to terrorism and disconnected from the community around them, and being forced to take the role of the vigilant "other" when looking at themselves.

I think it affected the quality of my personal life and in terms being connected to the broader community (other than Arab). Because I feel that the Arabs became labeled and I feel that it put us kind of on the defensive mode in trying to explain ourselves that we're not "The Them," whatever "Them" was. I feel that has an impact on the quality of life, so the kids, when they go to school, the issues they had to deal with in terms of how Arabs were and are stereotyped and perceived. I live in a basically middle-class European American community, and until 9/11 I don't think who we were made a lot of difference to our neighbors. I think they were more troubled when our African American friends came over to our home, but after 9/11 they questioned us in terms of "who are we, where are we from, where are our relatives?" They came and asked me. I didn't feel in the beginning that it was very friendly. I felt like it was "you people" like, "who are you people?" It was like, we'd be standing out there to get the mail, you know, it was kind of like, "look what you people did to us." Then it's part of the disconnectedness and that's part of making you feel uncomfortable in terms of quality of life I think. You lose your self-confidence.

I feel like there's this big burden that I'm carrying around. You know that book *Black Man's Burden?* I don't know who wrote it, but it's kind of like this big burden that you carry around with you wherever you go— that you are an Arab—and they connect you with the Twin Towers and the Pentagon, and they connect you with terrorism. . . . I think that's very difficult. I think people monitor themselves much closer because there's an issue going on presently in terms of who is a terrorist. Those are the issues that as Arabs we feel a lot of pressure.

The loss of confidence among Arab Americans stemmed from a sense that people who already knew them to some degree started looking at them in a new way. Who they were was transformed by images that were not about them; distrust now seemed to define people's approach to them. They had to be conscious of every word and move, and it seemed to them that everything they did was subject to mis- or reinterpretation. Round-the-clock double-consciousness constructs a psychological jail.

You begin to realize that maybe people now are viewing you differently. That's what takes away self-confidence. I mean, I used to be as self-confident as anything, thinking that I don't care what people think of me and I can do anything I want here. I don't have that sense anymore. When I introduce myself to people and I tell them my name, I sort of wait to see what sort of reaction they have on their faces. I really feel that people don't like Arabs and Muslims anymore. They view us with suspicion. I have no direct experience of that . . . nobody rejected my friendship on that level, but I feel that really secretly that's how they view us now.

In May 2004, Attorney General Ashcroft and FBI Director Mueller announced an intensification of domestic antiterrorism activity, although they said they had no new intelligence concerning a threat and were not raising the nation's terror threat level. Another round of FBI interviews was announced, references were made to the upcoming 2004 elections, and the American public was kept on fear-alert and asked to be "extra vigilant about their surroundings, neighbors, and any suspicious activity."[44] This initiative, later revealed as Operation Front Line, a multi-agency effort spearheaded by Immigration and Customs Enforcement (ICE) that used the new NSEERS, SEIS (Student and Exchange Information System), and US-VISIT databases to identify targets, led to 2,556 investigations and 504 arrests of persons largely from Arab- and Muslim-majority countries; none were charged with a terrorism-related crime (Lichtblau 2008; Yale Law School/ADC 2008).

Organized Responses to Government Policies

The public opinion data presented in chapter 3 showed fairly widespread public support for domestic security policies that focused on Arabs and Muslims even when they entailed civil liberties losses, including significant support (nearly 50 percent) for more severe tactics, such as issuing members of these groups special identity cards. In addition, a majority of Americans said that they were willing to sacrifice their own civil liberties to fight the "war on terror." The poll data also indicated that not everyone held the same views; indeed, there was organized opposition to the government's methods from the very beginning of its domestic antiterrorism campaign. The Japanese American Citizens League (JACL) was among the first to step forward and issue a statement opposing the secret arrests, reminding Americans of the shame of Japanese internment.[45] While most of the public and government agencies were reeling from the shock of the attacks and were focused on what could be done to prevent another attack, Arab and Muslim Americans took heart from these dissenting voices, which indicated to them that others were watching what the government was doing. The organized momentum of opposition reached its highest level of coordination (locally and nationally) late in 2002, after the passing of the most intense period of mass arrests, secret detentions, detentions of "material witnesses," FBI home and work visits, visa denials and delays, and removals of Arabs and Muslims from airplanes (which were often private initiatives) and after passage of the USA PATRIOT Act. It developed around the government's domestic special registration program and massive call-in of male visitors over age sixteen from Arab and Muslim-majority countries (and North Korea).

The special registration program began in September 2002 and took place over an eight-month period of time. It required voluntary accession to the mandatory program and technical legal advice, embraced a wide range of immigrant and ethnic communities, including Iranians, Syrians, Pakistanis, Sudanese, Afghanis, Eritreans, Somalis, and Indonesians, and was "open" and observable until registrants entered an INS office; at that point, its workings became hidden. Arab American, Asian American Muslim, and certain sub-Saharan African Muslim communities may not have worked together before, but special registration forged a new sense of commonality of status among them, and they worked collaboratively to develop resources and hold community meetings to clarify and advise about special registration. Muslims were not the only religious group affected by this program—based as it was on country of citizenship and nationality, it also called in Christians, Jews, and Baha'is—but it nonetheless gathered together Muslims living in the United States with roots from across the globe and gave a boost to the collective sense of Muslim *umma* (the single community of Muslims) among American Muslims. In Chicago, the Mayor's Advisory Council on Arab Affairs (established under Mayor Harold Washington) of the Chicago Commission on Human Relations actively embraced the civil rights concerns of South Asians, largely because South Asians and Asian Muslims lacked meaningful representation on the Mayor's Council on Asian Affairs.[46] Muslim American women rose to prominent and visible roles as community organizers, speakers at community events, advisory attorneys, and civil rights activists. Mobilizations expanded to other communities when the special registration program was interpreted in the historical context of Japanese internment, profiling of racialized groups, and collective policies based on race or religion. Members of groups not personally affected by these measures—such as African Americans, Jewish Americans, and Euro-Americans—were increasingly mobilized and vocal in opposition to the government's domestic security policies. The fact that another terrorist attack did not occur certainly lent credibility to this opposition, and one can only speculate what would have happened in that event.

Civil rights and legal advocacy organizations from within and outside the Arab, Asian, African, and Muslim American communities began tracking the experiences of persons subjected to special registration after learning of the humiliating treatment of Iranians in California, who were largely upper-middle-class professionals, a proportion of whom were Jewish. Immigration attorneys joined in advisory and advocacy efforts, especially members of the National Lawyers Guild. The American Immigration Law Association, the National Immigration Forum, the American-Arab Anti-Discrimination Committee, and the American Immigration Law Foundation teamed up to develop a web-based special registration questionnaire to document these experiences. The American Civil Liberties Union took a prominent stance opposing special registration and calling for an end to its arbitrary abuses.

At the local level, members of local coalitions handed out flyers at INS offices asking registrants to call and report on their experiences. In some locations, local branches of the Council on American-Islamic Relations (CAIR) assembled support teams that offered preregistration check-in, free legal advice, and refreshments. CAIR–New York was part of the Coalition Against Special Registration, which established an emergency family fund to assist families of "uncharged" detainees and included an extensive range of participants from faith-based, labor, ethnic, civil rights, African American, and green organizations.[47] The Muslim Public Affairs Council (MPAC) in southern California trained human rights monitors and positioned them near INS offices. During the final period of call-in registration, the Arab American Action Network in Chicago assembled teams of multiethnic, religiously diverse volunteers to advise and support registrants on their way to registry. All of these on-site preregistration activities were necessitated by the fact that registrants frequently and arbitrarily disappeared after entering INS offices, entering a limbo world of movement from one detention facility to another.

Domestic special registration was called to an end in May 2003. By that time, Senator Edward Kennedy's office was coordinating with a coalition of national organizations—including the American Immigration Law Association, the Arab-American Anti-Discrimination Committee, the Council on American-Islamic Relations, the American Civil Liberties Union, the National Immigration Project of the National Lawyers Guild, and Hate Free Zone—on the Post-9/11 Public Forum. The coalition sought testimonies from members of affected communities who had "suffered under any of the following Post 9-11 measures":

> Special Registration; Iraqi surveillance and interviews; Arab/Muslim men interviews (the first and second round of a couple thousand "voluntary" interviews); Secret Detentions; Local law enforcement and deputization of police by INS; **Airport raid issues; and Watch lists of any kind (travel, money transfer, etc.). (Siskind 2003)

These activities attested to a vibrant civil society ready to mobilize in opposition to government policies perceived as unjust, but they also drained the financial and human resources of the Arab American, Asian American, and Muslim American institutions so engaged. In Chicago (and probably elsewhere as well), the mainstream and progressive philanthropic organizations stepped in to provide emergency resources for these mobilizations, although secular ethnic organizations found these funds easier to obtain than faith-based Muslim organizations. Local funders such as the Crossroads Fund, the Field Foundation, and Woods Fund, as well as the national Tides Foundation and Four Freedoms Fund, provided emergency money. After the offices of the Arab American Action Network were struck by arson, additional in-kind donations were made by nearby offices of Metropolitan Family Services (formerly United Charities of Chicago) and the Southwest Youth Collaborative. Muslim organizations, especially mosques, were strained as they took on new community action roles that went well beyond their religiously specific ones (Cainkar 2003a, 2004c). Mosques across the nation began holding open houses in an effort to reduce the air of mystery that surrounded them.

The government's actions in the post-9/11 period thus produced a civil society response that ushered in and helped to finance an intensified civic integration of Arab and Muslim American organizations to a degree not witnessed before (at least not outside of Dearborn, Michigan), a topic we return to later in this book. This heightened civic integration took place in a social context that was still characterized by strong negative public attitudes toward Arabs, Muslims, and Islam (the last being subject to the most negative views), hate crimes and harassment, media treatment that ranged from vilification to exploration of Islam, a policy of regional law enforcement engagement of local Arab and Muslim communities in dialogue (supported little by top DHS officials), and FBI announcements of an increasing focus on mosques. These were complex, energetic, and at the same time frightening times when active explorations for new allies occurred in the ever-vigilant framework required by double-consciousness.

On Being "Known": Connected and Disconnected Insiders and Outsiders

In 2004, while driving through southwest Michigan, I was struck by the preponderance of posters prominently displayed on people's lawns and in front of businesses calling to Free Ibrahim. At a time when names like Ibrahim carried great negative stigma, and public support in defense of Muslims was active but certainly not widespread, these posters indicated to me that something different was occurring here. After investigating this story, I came to understand that the effective criminalization of Arab and Muslim Americans following the 9/11 attacks was made possible not only because of widely held stereotypes but also because they were "outsiders" in many places. It would have been much harder for the government to convince the public that mass arrests were required and that the people it had picked up were terrorists if those individuals were well known by people outside of their own communities, especially known by others with a significant degree of social capital. There are a number of post-9/11 "terrorism" cases that can be examined in this light to highlight the social factors that come into play to cast doubt on or empower the government in its charges. Here I briefly summarize two cases that, with similar charges but vastly different processes and outcomes, provide striking examples of the difference that social capital can make.

Ibrahim Parlak was a Turkish Kurd and Muslim who had been granted asylum in the United States in 1992. He owned a popular restaurant in Harbert, Michigan, named Café Gulistan, which served the Lake Michigan beach communities heavily populated by white, upper-middle-class Chicagoans (and former Chicagoans). In July 2004, when Ibrahim Parlak filed for his U.S. citizenship, he was arrested by immigration authorities (from the Department of Homeland Security) and jailed pending deportation as a terrorist. Prior to coming to the United States, Parlak had been active with the PKK, a Kurdish organization in Turkey that the U.S. government designated as a foreign terrorist organization after 9/11. Parlak's acknowledged membership in the PKK was the basis of his claim for asylum in the United States. In other words, the U.S. government knew he had been an active member of the PKK because it had awarded him political asylum on the basis of his documentation of imprisonment and charge of torture in Turkey for his activities with this group. Neighbors and restaurant patrons, however, knew Parlak well and did not accept the terrorist designation. They trusted that these government allegations were not the truth. They waged an intense campaign to free him, fueled by potlucks and fund-raisers, and created the Free Ibrahim signs that were posted across southwest Michigan. Parlak spent ten months in federal custody in Calhoun County Jail in Battle Creek, Michigan, and was released from jail in June 2005. He returned to run his popular Michigan restaurant, was required to report periodically to the DHS authorities in Detroit, and had to wage a legal defense of his case. Rich in social and cultural capital and financial resources, the Free Ibrahim campaign gained thousands of supporters, raised the capital needed for his legal case, and convinced Michigan Senator Jack Levin to introduce a bill in Congress to grant Parlak citizenship. In 2007 Parlak's case was pending with the Board of Immigration Appeals while the Levin-sponsored bill authorizing his citizenship was pending in Congress.[48] While attending one of the Free Ibrahim fund-raisers—a high-end art auction—during field research, I was surprised to find that Ibrahim's supporters did not see his case as having any relationship to post-9/11 events or the string of terrorist cases launched across the United States. In their view, his case was unique and quite separate from what was happening to other Muslims. I realized that, for them, not only was Ibrahim not a terrorist, but he was an individual, which symbolically disconnected him from the collectivity known as Muslims.

Trust and individuation were not the experience of the American-born Muslim military chaplain James Yee, whom the government, in a charge that received extensive media attention, falsely accused of espionage in the fall of 2003 in an arrest that occurred while he was en route for a home visit. Fellow Guantánamo Bay military officers fingered Yee and a few other Muslim officers for suspicious behaviors based mainly on the fact that they tended to socialize only with each other. Yee claims that, because they were Muslim, their military comrades at the Guantánamo prison camp never accepted them into their social sphere (Yee and Malloy 2005). Yee spent seventy-six days in solitary confinement and extreme deprivation at a Navy brig in Charleston, South Carolina. He eventually learned that he was jailed next to the two highest-charged security detainees within the

United States, Jose Padilla and Zacharias Moussaoui, both of whom report-edly were psychologically damaged by their confinement (Yee and Malloy 2005). Although the military eventually dropped all charges against Yee, he spent years touring the country raising money to pay for his defense, appearing mostly in Muslim contexts. After being fully cleared of all charges, Yee anxiously returned to military service, but resigned shortly thereafter because he was shunned by his military colleagues. Despite vin-dication, Yee was completely unable to remove the terrorist stigma (which happened, as noted earlier, to many other released detainees). Yee, the Muslim son of Chinese immigrants, was never able to forge a disconnec-tion between himself and the notion that Muslims have a propensity to ter-rorism because he lacked the social and cultural capital to do so.

These cases give meaning to the remarks of study interviewees about being "connected" (to terrorism) and "disconnected" (from broader com-munities). While the connections to terrorism were socially constructed, the disconnections were much more complicated. Many communities of Arab and Muslim Americans composed significantly of recent immi-grants were socially and civically excluded before 9/11 because they arrived during the period of demonization (described in chapter 3) and because they clustered in ethnic communities that lacked political clout and were not socially integrated with the larger community, conditions evolving from a combination of choice and barriers erected by others. Socially and politically excluded communities, whether resulting from choice or force, can do little to mitigate stereotypes, and their social sep-arateness over time nourishes stereotypes, which encourages further self-protection and closure. Internal community initiatives, in turn, can stress connection to others or difference—the former aiming for broader bases of solidarity while the latter aims for internal solidarity. Chapter 6 shows some of the differential outcomes of social inclusion versus social exclu-sion at the local neighborhood level for Arab Muslims in metropolitan Chicago, where inclusion produced safety and solidarity and exclusion provided fertile ground for hate crimes under the right conditions.

I argue strongly that local conditions of safety and empowerment for Arab and Muslim Americans may have been (and still are) quite differ-ent depending on a range of historic local-level variables, and that such conditions may vary between city and suburb. For example, an examina-tion of Chicago, Detroit, Los Angeles, New York, Cleveland, and Tucson and their surrounding suburbs may reveal varying patterns of social and political inclusion, support, hostility, and power. While many of the anti-Arab and anti-Muslim messages were broadcast nationwide, their mean-ing was subject to interpretation at the individual and local levels. On a national level, however, Arab and Muslim Americans have faced much larger hurdles to social and political inclusion than locally, although this is beginning to change. I argued in chapter 3 that exclusion at the national level has been particularly connected to their positioning in foreign policy debates. Connecting the local to the national to the global, I argue that in the end, from a sociological perspective, thousands of Arabs and Muslims living in the United States were jailed, interviewed, registered, watched, or deported, not because they were terrorists, but because they were socially positioned to be unable to contest these claims.

Conclusion

National narratives of the tragedy of 9/11 speak to the grave injury that these violent attacks and the thousands of deaths caused by them delivered to the American nation and people, but these narratives largely exclude the related experiences of millions of Arab and Muslim Americans (who, according to some sources, died in disproportionate numbers on 9/11). Their experiences are instead found in a second body of literature: the reports of civil liberties defenders, hate crimes reporters, attorneys, activists, and scholars who have documented the rights violations, assaults, and harassments they endured in the wake of the 9/11 attacks.[49] These two separate narratives about the impact of 9/11 on American society seem to mirror the American government's concept of homeland security after the attacks: there was a de facto and often de jure dichotomy between persons who symbolically lay within "the homeland" and whose safety and rights were being protected, and another group excluded from "the homeland" whose safety and rights were revocable. Arab and Muslim Americans and the immigrants within their communities perceived that they were symbolically placed outside the nation's protective boundaries, that their rights and security were sacrificed so the rest of the nation could feel safer. This effective dichotomization of the American population also gave a green light to the violent expressions of bigots, who signaled this understanding of ingroups and outgroups by the flag-waving that so commonly accompanied harassments of Arab and Muslim Americans after 9/11. This examination of the activities undertaken by the U.S. Departments of Justice and Homeland Security and other federal agencies to preserve "our freedoms" in the years following the 9/11 attacks does provoke questions about whose freedoms and whose homeland were being protected, and whether the rights of one set of Americans can be rightly sacrificed for another set of Americans.[50] These questions will be addressed by a wider segment of the American population when the two widely different American narratives of 9/11 are merged into one.

Chapter 5

The Security Spotlight and the Conduct of Everyday Life

THE GOVERNMENT'S measures directed at Arab and Muslim American communities were conducted with widespread public acquiescence, if not approval, according to the opinion poll data cited in previous chapters, although in the context of organized dissent. Public consent was built to a significant degree on fears that another attack might occur, perpetrated by terrorist sleeper cells hiding within Arab and Muslim American communities. This narrative was articulated more than once by U.S. government officials, who actually knew very little about who and what they were dealing with. Popular consent for aggressive collective policies was also built on the successful leveraging of widely held public understandings that Arabs and Muslims have some kind of inherent leaning toward violence and terrorism and that those who do not actively engage in violence probably silently support it. This interpretation of reality was constructed at the convergence of awareness of the increasing number of objective acts of violence occurring outside the United States (focused on those perpetrated by a small minority of Arabs and Muslims) and the meaning that was ascribed to these acts by journalists, "experts," policy analysts, talk-show hosts, pundits, Muslim haters, and others who by design or default portrayed these acts as irrational yet characteristic of Arab culture and the Muslim religion. Notions such as these had been graphically reinforced in the American media and popular culture through images that represented Arab and Muslim life principally through portrayals of evil men and mob scenes contextualized by themes of anger, violence, and rote behavior (Joseph 1999). Such scenes conveyed the idea that Arab and Muslim societies lack the capacity for individuality, diversity, rational thought, or choice and instead are characterized by widespread organic solidarity and collective unanimity. A complementary schemata was that Arabs and Muslims lack the very human values and feelings shared by other groups, for example, that they feel joy upon death. In other words, they are not like "us." These types of ideas were bolstered by the near-absence of images of Arabs or Muslims expressing grief over something for which "we" would be sad or happiness over something for which "we" would be happy—a birth, a wedding, or a victory in a football match. The arguments of persons such as Harold Bloom (1989, 30), who claimed in an *Omni* magazine article that Arab culture produces terrorists because Arabs do not hold their children or show them affection (quite the opposite of common observations)—"Could the denial of warmth lie behind Arab brutality?" Bloom asks—can only appear credible, and be publishable, under conditions of selective representation, when others hold the power to define who you are.

Discursive Rivalries

Using terms from Gary Fine's (1996) model of discursive rivalry, preexisting discursive and representational framing of Arabs and Muslims empowered the post-9/11 narratives that cast suspicion on Arab and Muslim American communities at large. Public figures from Arab American, Muslim American, and other communities who tried to offer counternarratives, especially about Islam as a religious faith, were impugned by groups that had greater resources and power and that labeled them terrorist supporters who were not credible.[1] The time period immediately after the attacks was one in which many respected mainstream voices were apprehensive about standing up in support of counterinterpretations because the stigma and political costs attached to such an action were high. President Bush's (2001) September 20 statement to Congress, in which he directed his words to the world's Muslims— "We respect your faith. It's practiced freely by many millions of Americans, and by millions more in countries that America counts as friends. Its teachings are good and peaceful, and those who commit evil in the name of Allah blaspheme the name of Allah"—was an important act of leadership, but his expressions of such sentiments were often drowned out by his far more emotive appeals to anger and fear. Bush's subsequent statements invoking the theme "why do they hate us?" seemed to carry much more media traction. Under these discursive conditions, the stereotype (so named because it assigns to all group members complicity in the acts of a few) was positioned well to drive social action after 9/11. Arabs and Muslims in the United States became spotlighted stereotypic subjects, and it could be claimed by those holding power that they were really a group of people whose intentions were "unknown."

The government's aggressive policies and practices were by its own admission built on lack of knowledge, which some might say was the cost to be paid in a free society. But there are less invasive and less coercive strategies than mass arrest, incarceration, and eavesdropping.

Over time, local committees and "roundtables" were formed in many American cities convening representatives of Arab and Muslim American communities, local police chiefs and sheriffs, and regional representatives of federal law enforcement agencies such as the Department of Homeland Security, the FBI, and the attorney general so that these groups could get to know each other. These gatherings often faced problems of trust, as some government agents asserted that local community members were holding back, evidenced by the fact that they were not turning in potential terrorists, which community members asserted as proof that their communities were not hiding terrorists.[2] In addition, federal law enforcement agents working at the local level often felt that the policies and practices emerging out of Washington were undermining their relationship-building work in Arab and Muslim communities.[3] Mistrust of the federal government was intensified within Arab and Muslim American communities by a series of weak federal government cases alleging terrorist connections that were built on interpretations of conversations and texts rather than on unambiguous evidence and that sometimes involved undercover entrapment or the use of information gained from overseas torture (Shane and Bergman 2006).

Acknowledging that media discourses about them were not good to begin with, Arab and Muslim Americans perceived that those discourses took a decisive turn for the worse after 9/11. In the words of one interviewee, "Genuine bigots now have access to media outlets and are getting credibility." Another said that media characterizations of Arabs and Muslims, when combined with their exclusion from national discourse except as villains, reinforced the notion that "you don't belong here, go back to your country." Across the nation, false rumors of Arab and Muslim American joy over the attacks circulated on talk radio (Fine and Khawaja 2005). Narratives claiming that American Arabs and Muslims were unknown entities, positioning them as foreigners at best and fifth columns at worse, drove public discourses. This one-sided jingoism and stereotyping eventually produced its own dialectical antithesis as some Americans realized that they knew very little about Arabs and Muslims and that they were not going to find answers to their questions on television shows, talk radio, or the nightly news.

The ensuing pedagogical shake-up erupted from the thirst for knowledge on the part of millions of Americans who recognized that their own knowledge base was weak. By 2002, new opportunities to learn about Arabs and Islam emerged in the United States, including in some elementary, secondary, and postsecondary schools and in publicly convened forums (CCFR 2002). These changes in awareness and knowledge-building among a significant sector of the American public eventually produced changes in the broader field of discursive rivalry. In the same way that the civic embrace of Arab and Muslim Americans began in response to the government's heavy-handed policies, the public demand for knowledge created favorable social conditions for offering credible alternative narratives on Arab culture, Muslim values, and Islam. Sensing a new market, or seeking to enrich it, newspapers, magazines, and television shows began reporting on a broader range of aspects of Arab culture, Islam, and Muslims. As these narratives increased in frequency, however, the producers of counterdiscourses often referred to as "Islamophobia" stepped up their work. The field of discursive rivalries was mixed, neither all good nor all bad: it encompassed more voices than it had prior to the 9/11 attacks and in the year that followed them, but the bigots seemed to be getting louder.

The events of 9/11 awakened a thirst for knowledge not only among non-Arab and non-Muslim segments of the American population but also among Arab and Muslim Americans. Many Arab Muslims interviewed in this study reported embarking on a quest for knowledge after the 9/11 attacks because they could not understand how their religion could be used to defend acts of violence and because defending their religion required a deeper understanding of it. They also understood that knowledge alone was not enough and that they had to force their presence into the sphere of civic action.

> I feel like I have to explain more about who I am and what I believe in, and I almost feel like there is a higher burden to overcome and explain that Islam is not the violent religion and Muslims are not the violent people that you think they are. Even though that idea did exist before 9/11, I think it's been exacerbated a lot after 9/11. . . . There are also various TV shows, 24 on Fox, and there's movies that play on that. While I understand their desire to create movies and TV shows that are based on recent events, their interpretations act to further solidify the stereotypes in the minds of most Americans. We have to be more vocal and involved. We cannot afford to be quiet and uninvolved. I would be more willing to go to a protest or rally. We need to say what we need to say. We don't have the luxury to be quiet anymore. More political participation is needed.

Shared Everyday Experiences

The security spotlight, notions that Arabs and Muslims were "unknown" and foreign, and narratives that asserted that *threat lay hidden* within Arab and Muslim American communities produced a number of patterned experiences for Arab Muslims in the post-9/11 period. Some of these experiences were highly gendered, while others tended to be correlated with certain spatial locations, and these are discussed in subsequent chapters. In this chapter, I present the post-9/11 experiences reported in the study that crossed lines of gender, social class, and geography. While the overwhelming majority of Arab Muslims interviewed in this study did not report an experience of physical violence or property vandalism after 9/11, 46 percent reported verbal harassment, and nearly all reported living in what might be called a "climate of harassment." It was largely due to this climate that few said that their daily lives had not changed in some way after 9/11 as they made psychological, physical, social, and other adjustments to social conditions on the ground. One respondent describes the climate as "something in the air" that made it permissible to say or do anything to Arab and Muslim Americans.

> It seems like there was something in the air that it was okay to do that, it was justified, and then, of course, you have the media bombarding the Arabs and Arab culture and religion. Before you saw it in the movies, and here and there, but it seems like it's out in the open. Like things below the skin were now above the skin. You feel like you're walking around either being watched because of experiences other people had with getting on a plane, getting kicked off the plane, being afraid to go to the store, not wearing the hijab over their head. These things just psychologically had an effect.

Fifty-three percent of Arab Muslims interviewed in the study said that they experienced discrimination; the largest proportion (39 percent) spoke of workforce discrimination. According to interviewees, the word was out that it was "not safe to change jobs at this time," so most of those who had negative on-the-job experiences searched for new ways to manage their work environment. As shown later in this chapter, however, discrimination was technically and narrowly defined as being denied something or treated differently than others because of being Arab and/or Muslim. Definitions of discrimination did not include, for example, being spit at, followed, or physically or verbally assaulted. Definitions of discrimination also did not include actions that I categorize as consulting the Arab/Muslim mind, knowledge tales, gestures of contempt, and compliance behaviors; these types of behaviors were repeatedly experienced by Arabs/Muslims, yet seemed to have no name. The psychological state induced by this overall climate in the context of the sensational statements that accompanied reports of government arrests was one of fear, informed by Naber's (2006) concept of "internment of the psyche." Arab Muslims reported changing their routine behaviors to suit this climate. This chapter looks at some of them: changes in travel patterns, remittances, charitable giving, and religious practice. Study participants also reported two positive social changes after 9/11: a thirst for knowledge among a significant share of the American public and a "wake-up call" for Arab and Muslim Americans. We discuss these at the end of the chapter. First, we look at components of the climate of harassment.

The Climate of Harassment

The climate of harassment was something an Arab Muslim understood from direct experience and from having knowledge of the experiences of others. While most of this chapter describes personal encounters, many Arab Muslims altered their own behaviors after they learned about incidents that had happened to like others. For example, while a small minority of Arab and Muslim Americans (and persons perceived to be, such as Sikhs) were attacked physically in the United States, most Arab and Muslim Americans felt a heightened sense of danger and vulnerability each time they learned of such an attack. They would attempt to identify aspects of the situation that brought about the attack to determine whether and how one could take action to protect oneself. In what type of place did the incident occur? Did the victim have darker or lighter skin? How was she or he dressed? Was the woman wearing a hijab? Did the man have a beard? The outcome of such queries often left limited options: women could stop wearing head scarves (which some did); both men and women could stop patronizing shopping malls and megastores; they could heighten their awareness when passing through majority-white residential areas; and they could keep their children out of public schools. Otherwise, they could continue in these behaviors but remain in a state of high vigilance. These are the phenomena missed by hate crime statistics: the anxiety and behavioral change such crimes produce among the countless others who experience collateral damage. Stories about Arabs and Muslims being harassed at airports and pulled off airplanes, which were quite common from 2002 to 2004, left only one preventive option—to stop traveling by air, a choice exercised by many persons interviewed in this study.

Likewise, when one mosque was placed under siege or vandalized, there was a sense that all Muslim institutions and the persons inside of them were vulnerable. Mosque boards of directors approved the installation of security systems, but little else could be done to avert the perceived danger. Thirty-one percent of interviewees named mosques and areas heavily populated by Arabs as places where they felt least safe. These locations were perceived as easy targets for persons seeking to take violent revenge on Arab and Muslim Americans for the 9/11 attacks. As we will see in chapter 6, such fears often stood on real data. Basing her fear of being at the mosque on a prior siege of it (presented in detail in chapter 6), an Arab American woman says:

> I feel safe because it's God's home, but at the same time, anything could happen, and that would be a prime target, and it has been. Our mosque in Bridgeview has been targeted. We had to have police get involved. Glass was shattered. There were mile-long protests with people from Oak Lawn walking over to Bridgeview with pickets coming towards the

mosque saying, "We don't want terrorists here." They broke lights on cars, windshields, and just created a climate of fear within the community when people were just coming to the mosque to pray. I feel safest in my parents' home with my family. The least safe would be at the mosque, especially on a crowded day like the holidays, just because I think those would be prime targets and prime events for anything to happen, because there's a large crowd of innocent people.

Similar fears were held about being in areas of high Arab residential concentration, as expressed by this Arab American man:

I don't feel safe in Arabic areas because I'm thinking some kind of nut is going to come in and do something. They know Arabs live around there, you know.

Although it should be acknowledged that most Americans did not act in violent ways toward Arabs and Muslims, that most Arabs and Muslims were not attacked, and that many Americans responded to them with compassion and gestures of support, it should also be understood that the statistical probability of an attack had limited immediate relevance to people who feared what *could* happen next. If a siege on a mosque later produced a wave of support, the perspective of the leery potential victim considering going to the mosque was nevertheless focused on the vulnerability such an act might produce; only later, while resting in the safety of one's home, can one consider the actions of support by others. This moment-to-moment interpretation of reality is a consequence of where one stands in relation to meaningful events—analyses of statistical patterns of human behavior are the luxury of the bystander and the spectator.

A nearly equal proportion of Arab Muslims, however, said mosques and areas of high Arab concentration were places they felt most safe. Their potential as sites of danger was outweighed by the qualities they possessed that no other place could offer: their high concentration of Arabs and Muslims made them zones of comfort. There one could escape the looks of disdain and the gestures of contempt. In conversation, one could be free from the discursive knowledge tales and talk instead about daily life, family, recent events, or the latest chapter of multifaceted Arab and Muslim American life under a microscope after 9/11. No one would expect an explanation of the behavior of the nineteen hijackers or demand, "Where is Osama bin Laden?" Here was a place—one of the few places—where one could be treated as a unique individual.

Consulting the Collective Arab/Muslim Mind

The accuracy of prominent media images of Arab culture and Muslim societies, in their displays of angry mobs, can be compared to exhibitions of women in American domestic violence shelters as symbols of American culture. The images are real, and they represent a slice of reality, but they neither qualify as snapshots of an entire society's daily life nor represent its fundamental ethos or moral order. More than thirty years ago, the legal scholar M. Cherif Bassiouni (1974, viii) observed that in American society, "almost all means of mass communication" were "saturating public opinion with an invidious portrayal of Arabs," such that "treachery, violence, and other odious characteristics became associated with all Arabs." Bassiouni tied the dissemination of these images to efforts in American civil society to curtail critical analyses of U.S. foreign policies in the Middle East. At the time Bassiouni wrote his report, the Nixon administration was engaged in its "special measures": a set of FBI, CIA, and INS monitoring and intervention strategies aimed at Arab Americans (and Arabs overseas), African Americans, intellectuals, leftists, and organizations engaged in peaceful political activities around U.S. foreign policies. These measures were aimed at "chilling" freedom of expression in the United States, according to Bassiouni, by invoking fear among activists. The negative media images and discourses about Arabs and the intimidation of persons and groups with counternarratives and dissenting viewpoints had the combined effect of limiting the knowledge set available to the American public.

Edward Said's subsequent explorations of the inventory of knowledge that constituted the Western world's understanding of the Middle East and Islam further supported Bassiouni's claims of bias (Said 1978, 1997). In great detail, Said itemized how popular understanding of Arab and Muslim societies was distorted by images and discourses that posed as scholarly, producing among those exposed to them an extremely limited understanding of societies that were incredibly diverse and complex. As shown in chapter 3, in the twenty-seven years between Bassiouni's report and the 9/11 attacks, there was little significant change in representations of Arabs in American popular culture and in pedagogy, beyond their expansion to Muslims and the vigorous return of formerly discredited Orientalist canons. This limited knowledge set informed the actions taken by much of the American public after 9/11; while many came to realize that their knowledge was shallow and incomplete, others accepted the notion that Arabs and Muslims are monolithic in thought and belief. They thus "consulted the Arab/Muslim mind" for an understanding of the reasons behind the attacks. For example, an Arab American police officer and Vietnam War veteran was asked by fellow officers at his university police department to explain the attacks.

> There were arguments with some of the coworkers I have. Some were heated arguments after 9/11. They implied that somehow, you know, my background, they just came out and said some things. One coworker asked me, "What's up with those people?" looking at me, things like that. How

do I know what's up with Osama bin Laden? People were trying to justify that it was okay for Arab Americans to be stopped for no reason because somehow they might have done something or they're up to something, or involved in something. People were actually trying to justify that it was okay.... They asked me about September 11, how it happened. People weren't thinking logically, and a lot of it was just ignorance, you know.

Although he says, "People weren't thinking logically," such thinking might have been quite logical given the knowledge base from which it was drawn.

Arab American students at some local high schools reported being asked by their teachers to explain why the attacks occurred, according to the Arab American director of a community organization. Young and lacking the insight that they might pay a price for responding to questions that had hidden assumptions of collective guilt, they obeyed their teachers.

> Kids in the schools around here experienced verbal attacks by fellow students, faculty, and the administration. In current events discussions, some of the kids from our programs were asked and tried to offer an analysis. They were attacked immediately as sympathetic to terrorists and persons who want to see Americans killed.[4]

An Arab American student at a community college reported a similar experience:

> On 9/11, I was the only Arab in the class. We were watching TV, and the teacher's way of dealing with me changed. He showed pictures of Osama bin Laden and said, "Ask *him* if you have any questions."

A female Arab American teacher reported being searched on the day of the attacks at a Chicago public school. While the search might be considered an example of "compliance behavior" (as discussed later in the chapter), it reflects the way Arab Americans are imagined more than it represents compliance with government edicts, since the action occurred within minutes of the attacks. Here the notion of collective guilt is played out and extended to collective danger.

> During 9/11, I was traumatized as an American and the fact that I'm an Arab. I was teaching that day, and about fifteen minutes after we found out what happened, the tragedy in New York, two security guards stormed into my classroom and told me to get out, to open my purse, and they searched me, which really shocked me. It really did! I jumped up, and I said, "Excuse me. Do you do this to everybody, or because I'm an Arab American?" They said, "Oh, no, ma'am. We're doing it to everybody." Well, I discovered later when I asked other people that I was the only one.

Other interviewees reported similar assumptions of group-think while in the company of the highly educated upper-middle class. The following quote from an Arab American woman notes the polite manner in which such speech was conducted and halted in a group setting. It also reveals that these assumptions carried into a professional work environment and included allegations of cultural complicity in events far beyond the 9/11 attacks:

> We heard comments. Like, people would be talking, and my husband comes into the room, and they would say, "We should stop talking about this. We don't want to offend you. We're talking about Osama bin Laden, and we know you like Osama bin Laden." They would ask us, "Do you feel that what's going on right now is okay?" I'll give you an example, the decapitation of Daniel Pearl. I was asked by a colleague, "Is the community going to come out with a statement denouncing it?" I thought that was very offensive because we have to keep trying to prove our humanity and trying to prove that we are as appalled as other people are.

An Arab American teacher working in a middle-class suburban school spoke about listening to offensive lunchroom discussions among fellow teachers that left her too traumatized to say anything. Neither consulted for the monolithic Arab/Muslim view nor asked for her opinion on the topic being discussed, she was perplexed that these comments were made in her presence. Did they not understand that as an Egyptian she was an Arab, or that she was Muslim even though she did not wear hijab, or did they not care? Her encounter reveals the performance of a requisite component in confirming the Arab/Muslim mind: rendering invisible persons who might disrupt the stereotype. It also highlights a relationship between everyday actions and the work of state actors seeking to quash dissent, what Bassiouni describes as "chilling." Most painful to this interviewee was the betrayal of friendship that emerged from associating her with the cluster of attributes associated with the Arab/Muslim—the stereotype trumped intimate knowledge of the other.

> The next day I had experiences with people at work that made comments that hurt me. But I was also in shock, so I did not deal with it. It caused me to reflect on who I was and how to deal with that feeling. I had never felt like people feared me. I feel I am more American than Egyptian, but I do not feel welcome here even though I spent my entire life here. The day after 9/11, I was in the lunchroom with colleagues, and one of my colleagues said he was at the grocery store and saw a veiled woman, "a woman with that thing on her head." He said he was so angry he wanted to hit her. Someone at the table said, "That would be stupid, they did not do it." Then another person said, "How do you know that? Those people who did it were living here." I did not say anything. I got up and left. I was angry and, at the same time, angry at myself for not having the guts to say anything. I was scared. They know I'm Egyptian, but maybe they did not make the connection, or they think I'm different from those types. After that, I was confiding in one of my friends what I felt, and she said, "If someone like you sat on a plane next to me, I'd get nervous."

Some interviewees described encounters in which their identity as an Arab or Muslim was not known, in which case the discourse lacked restraint, as this Sudanese Arab graduate student relates:

> I moved to a new dorm on August 23, 2001, a few days before the event. My neighbor in the dorm who was not aware of the fact that I am Muslim said, "Why don't we kill all the f——ing Muslims," while watching the news in my room.

Knowledge Tales

Knowledge tales are discourses in which the speaker asserts informed knowledge about Arabs and/or Muslims using information gleaned from American popular culture (the same source of knowledge that informs other harmful behaviors discussed in this chapter), claims to have better knowledge than Arabs and Muslims themselves or than scholars of Arabs and Muslims, and self-righteously defends this knowledge if challenged. I have had a wealth of personal experience with knowledge tales that may help to explicate the concept. For example, after returning from spending two years in Jordan as a Fulbright Scholar, I took part in many discussions in which other persons told me that I was wrong about what I had experienced there. In fact, this was the flavor of a majority of conversations I had, whether with university colleagues or strangers. Because my accounts of positive experiences threatened to disrupt their pre-ordained views, maintaining the stereotype required silencing my speech. Furthermore, the overwhelming majority of people with whom I spoke about my Jordanian experience were systematically interested in the answers to only three questions: Did I feel safe? Could I drive? And did I cover my hair? The assumption was of a world looming with danger and overwhelmed by female oppression. Little else was interesting or mattered: the cuisine, the landscape, or the complex features of daily social life in Jordan—it was as if these things were meaningless in such an odious context. This is the nature of stereotypes: they resist information to the contrary.

Arab American feminists have written at length about how such knowledge tales, and the certainty with which they are held, have been used to silence Arab women in feminist contexts (Abdulhadi, Naber, and Alsultany 2005). Once silenced, Arab women's energies must be redirected; their analyses and contributions to the discussion are subverted as they are forced to become "absorbed in the task of addressing and correcting this misinformation," in the words of the scholar Amira Jarmakani (2005, 132). Jarmakani relates a coffee shop encounter that mirrors this treatment at the level of everyday experience:

> A few years ago, I walked into a coffee house in Atlanta, Georgia, ordered a drink, and laid the book I was reading, *Opening the Gates: A Century of*

Arab Feminist Writing, down on the counter in order to pay for my drink. "Arab feminism," the coffee barista exclaimed, "that's just an oxymoron to me!" Her comment, cloaked as it was in certainty and self-assurance, solidified my understanding of the way in which Arab American feminism is, in some ways, forced to construct itself negatively. That is, Arab American feminists must necessarily respond to the stereotypical images by which they are largely understood in a U.S. context and are, therefore, put in a position of first correcting common misconceptions before creating a defining discourse (130).

An Arab American woman interviewed in this study observed how conversations framed by the limited knowledge set possessed by many Americans curtailed her efforts to expand understanding beyond the stereotype. If you do not fit the Muslim woman stereotype, then you are rendered a non-Muslim, instead of being viewed as one of the diverse range of Muslim women.

> Most people have no concept, I mean, educated people that you work with day in and day out, have no idea of what it is to be a Muslim. They consider Islam to be this horrible religion that degrades women and that if you're a Muslim woman that's in the workforce, or is not covered, or if you're outspoken, or if you drink, or if you do any of the things that don't fit in that box, they consider you to be a non-Muslim. Everybody identifies their religion as just part of who you are, I mean, it's not necessarily something you just choose, it's what you're born into. So I've had plenty of problems with that image because people would ask me stupid questions, like, "Does your husband tell you what to do and where to go and who to be friends with?" and stuff. And I say, "No, does yours?" Then they ask, "Why don't you cover?" I say, "For the same reason that some Catholic women use birth control . . . because I choose not to." They think it's a forced thing. That kind of ignorant stuff. It could be harmless, but it's really ignorant. They don't consider the religion a religion that people choose, especially women. They consider it a religion that's forced on women and that is horrible for women.

Arab Muslims interviewed in this study reported confronting knowledge tales in two main locations—on the job and in schools. These were the spaces in which they most commonly engaged in discussions with non-Arab Muslims—outside, that is, of meetings organized around civil rights and safety. The school encounters were on campuses or among fellow teachers, and some were not discussions at all but teachers' lectures as reported by students to their parents. Over the course of my own research career, Arab Americans have asserted during interviews that school-based pedagogy is dehumanizing to Arabs and Muslims. Such claims were not local; projects to systematically evaluate and then alter these biased conditions have been pursued across the United States over the past thirty years (Aswad 1993; Barlow 1994; Al-Qazzaz 1975;

Woods 1996; Suleiman 1988). These efforts to improve school-based ped-agogy about Arabs and Muslims, often based in university Middle East studies centers, had made little headway up to the 9/11 attacks. Indeed, if these efforts had been successful, the social construction theory of this book would be wrong. A 2002 study commissioned by the Chicago Council on Foreign Relations (now the Chicago Council on Global Affairs) found that teachers who sought to impart accurate information about Arabs and Islam to their students after the 9/11 attacks had difficulty locating pedagogical resources. It concluded that a primary source of the pedagogical problem lay in the university education of teachers, which had delivered to them little to no accurate knowledge about either Arabs or Islam (CCFR 2002). Teachers lacking independent scholarly knowledge are more likely to accept stereotypes and to teach with these premises in mind, even if they do not intend to do so.

An Arab American woman reported taking action after her son told her of his teacher's lecture about Islam and jihad. Her intervention to prevent further school-based knowledge tales was successful, and the elite private school agreed to a series of teacher workshops about Islam and the Arabs.

> On a personal level, my family was not harassed but kidded around a lot in school. Like, "You are an Arab and therefore you must go to prison now," "Camel jockey, go home," and this sort of verbal harassment. As well, the teachers, one of the teachers at [the] school, right after 9/11 said something to the effect of, the Muslims, their religion, allows them to become terrorists. This is part of what they believe, it is jihad. Of course my son was extremely humiliated by such a statement and was not able to respond because it was a figure of, you know, a teacher and educator. But he told me about it, and I verified it from another Muslim student in the same class.

Problems with the schools were not only about pedagogy, nor did they arise solely with teachers. Arab American women living on the southwest side and in the southwest suburbs of Chicago routinely reported to me in my pre-9/11 field research that they were poorly treated by public school staff, who they believed interacted with them in a demeaning manner. Many reported parent-teacher conferences in which teachers conveyed the assumption that the mother was weak and powerless. The following quote from an Arab American teacher in the post-9/11 study reveals that stereotypic ideas about Muslims may also be held at the top of a school's administrative hierarchy:

> I remember specifically one of the top administrators . . . we were doing a reenactment in case anything ever happened at the school like a terror-ist attack. The public schools had to have some type of a plan, and one of the administrators said, "Well, if a terrorist comes in, don't argue with

that person about your religious ideology." Kind of insinuating there would be a Muslim as a terrorist. I kind of thought that was a bit of a discriminating remark, because you wouldn't have someone say . . . if you were contemplating that it was a racial issue, don't stand and discuss your race with that person, insinuating there would be a black American. So I was a bit offended by that. So remarks like that, I think, are, you know, I would define as discrimination.

While Arab and Muslim American students suffered humiliation in classrooms when their culture and religion were demeaned, they could do little to change these circumstances without adult intervention. But oddly enough, it was as young adults at the university level that they found themselves most powerless to contest textbooks and articles that argued a causal relationship between Islam and terrorism, because in that location such claims were protected, that is, considered academic freedom.

Knowledge tales pose different problems in the context of the workplace. Arab and Muslim Americans must ask themselves, do we challenge our colleagues and risk losing our jobs, or do we silently bear it? An Arab Muslim American woman working at a telecommunications company says that the quality of her work environment declined seriously after 9/11; she was shunned by colleagues who preferred to listen to "self-proclaimed and hateful experts on Islam." She found herself shut out of everyday conversations with colleagues, even though, as she states, normally they did not discuss religion or politics. It should be noted that despite this experience and others like it, this interviewee said that she did not experience discrimination at work.

> My work experience deteriorated after 9/11. It depressed me a bit that people were more willing to openly say things about my religion and not be challenged. Hateful people came out of the woodwork; they were the experts. People were more willing to agree with them. People who know me, some would ask me what's true. But others I work with who normally were polite or indifferent started shying away from me. I never know why that happened, because we don't talk about politics or religion at work.

A significant number of interviewees, particularly those employed in the corporate sector, in schools, and in small non-ethnic businesses, reported similar encounters with coworkers and their knowledge tales. The problem was that, since the word was out not to change jobs because of widespread post-9/11 discrimination, they had to devise other ways to cope; that often required shrinking their circle of workplace friends and eating lunch alone. These adjustments of social patterns only enhanced the silencing effect of stereotypes and aided in their reproduction, because encounters between those who held them and those who could challenge them were curtailed. There were reports in the communities that many Muslim professionals with the right types of skills—such as accounting, legal, computer- and medical-related—decided to leave corporate work to start their own independent businesses. Knowledge tales and consulting the Arab/Muslim mind played meaningful roles in these decisions. In my research career, I have observed that protection from knowledge tales is one of the hidden wage benefits accruing to Arab and Muslim Americans who operate independent small businesses.

Gestures of Contempt

Belief in notions of the essential sameness of Arabs and Muslims and their collective responsibility for the 9/11 attacks was often communicated nonverbally. In chapters 6 and 7, we examine some of the more aggressive nonverbal expressions of contempt, but this chapter would be incomplete without mention of the "looks" so many interviewees reported. Some interpreted them as looks of suspicion, others as looks of hatred. One man said that they "fix their eyes on me as if to say, 'We despise you.' " The looks occurred during focused and unfocused interactions, with strangers and with persons known, and they were given in response to the individual's master status as Arab or Muslim, a status that overrode all others in these social encounters (Hughes 1945). In his study of street interactions in an area of demographic change, Elijah Anderson (1990, 167) found that "the master status assigned to black males undermines their ability to be taken for granted as law-abiding and civil participants in public places: young black males, particularly those who don the urban uniform . . . may be taken as the embodiment of the predator." So too did the power of the master status assigned to Arabs and Muslims undermine the public's ability see them as individuals, while it constructed them as the embodiment of the enemy. The signifiers of this status were the phenotype associated with Arabs and Muslims (often called "race," this phenotype produces many false positives in its messiness) and mode of dress—the clothing associated with Arabs or Muslims replacing Anderson's "urban uniform." The age-old association between Arabs, Ali Baba, and flying carpets led to hundreds of attacks on turban-wearing Sikhs, including the first murder victim of 9/11 backlash, Bablir Singh Sodhi of Arizona. If these signifiers were absent, master status could be assigned based on proximity to Arabic script or to a name. Seeking to divert electoral support from presidential candidate Barack Obama, some attempted to confer such status on him simply by highlighting his middle name: Hussein. As this Palestinian taxi driver notes, a name change could remove the master status stigma.

> I can feel too much discrimination in people's eyes when they gaze or stare at me after realizing I'm Arabian. Actually, my appearance is kind of tricky. I'm very white, so at the first glance people would think I'm American, or belong to some other nationality, therefore they treat me nicely. But when I tell them I'm Arabian, their looks would change suddenly. . . . In the past,

> I gave my business card to customers to call me whenever they need a ride, but they never did. It is only after I changed my Arabian name to be American that I have started to receive many calls from my customers.

Women wearing clothing that identified them as Muslims also experienced such looks, and some, such as this Arab American woman, believed that the master status stigma brought on further humiliating treatment.

> Shopping—people give an attitude, a look everywhere. Once I was with a friend at Kohl's. I bought a lot of stuff. Expensive. The lady said after I paid for everything, she wants to check my stuff. She thought I stole. It was so embarrassing. I said, "Bring your supervisor." She thought I'm afraid, that I don't speak the language. She started screaming at me. She called the supervisor. She checked. Everything was right. She asked the cashier to apologize, and she would not. I feel pressure is too high. I was so embarrassed.

An Arab American woman described the different treatment she began receiving at local businesses, highlighted by the look: "Of course we feel different. We are not like before. We feel lonely. I have a good friend who works in Hollywood Video, she was so nice to me, and I was so nice to her. But after 9/11, she looked at me in a different way."

An Arab artist who came to the United States as a refugee in the 1990s also spoke of the looks. He found that wearing a *kuffiya* (the checkered Arab scarf traditionally worn by males, usually peasants) brought on not just looks but an association with Osama bin Laden. He decided to decline the stereotype and confront its agent.

> The way people look at me is harder than their words or acts. The look of suspicion made it harder to be here in the city. And then, of course, what affected me a great deal was the aftermath of 9/11 used as an excuse to attack Iraq. I have lost two family members thus far because of the war in Iraq, which is a consequence of the 9/11 attack. . . . There was a guy where I used to come to school, he said something. I was wearing a kuffiya. He called me Osama bin Laden. I decided to go up to him. I said, "I am a very peaceful person. I could report you to the police. I could shout back at you. Instead, I will talk to you." I told him that I and my community repudiated those attacks and did not condone 9/11. You know, because I was a nice person, I told him I was letting it go. But if it was someone else and it happened again, it might not turn out the same way. He would say hi after that. I think he thought about it more.

There was broad recognition among study interviewees that their post-9/11 experiences represented a dramatic exacerbation of a negative climate that existed long before the 9/11 attacks. They were transformed from others into enemy aliens, as this Arab American woman notes:

> The attitude and outlook that was always there, it was just exaggerated, making you feel like you're the enemy. That you're the bad one, and you're definitely a foreigner and do not belong in this country, when I was born and raised in this country and I'm just as much an American as anyone else. I feel like maybe I need to get the hell out of this country because something bad is going to happen to our people here. It's a horrible feeling.

Living in Fear

FBI Interviews and Wiretapping

After special registration ended in the summer of 2002, the government shifted to reliance on more subtle national security programs, such as spying, eavesdropping, and monitoring communications and finances. Since the government was permitted to maintain secrecy around these operations and did not have to show probable cause to launch an investigation, conduct an interview, secure a wiretap, or scrutinize private records, the subjects of these interventions could be anyone. This state of affairs effectively put everyone in the Arab American and Muslim American communities on alert, especially because they perceived that the government was operating on limited knowledge and biased arguments that turned ambiguous actions into support for terrorism. Some believed that putting everyone in these communities on edge was a strategic element of the government's terrorism prevention. In chapter 4, we noted the statement by a former FBI official that as many as half a million persons were interviewed in the four years following the 9/11 attacks and David Cole's report that some thirty thousand national security letters had been sent each year by the government to businesses in order to monitor private information.

Whether conveyed through personal contact, at community forums, or in press reports, it was commonly understood by Arab and Muslim Americans that intensive monitoring was occurring. Such monitoring provoked fear among community members, not because they were associated with terrorists, but because they believed that, although they were innocent, the government could reinterpret data as it saw fit, substantial time and money would be required to secure release from government custody and endure a trial, they probably would not be able to see the evidence against them and launch an effective defense, and in the meantime their reputations would be tarred by stigma. If they were not U.S. citizens, they knew they might be deemed disentitled to a trial and easily deported. Citizen or not, it would be extremely difficult to move with ease inside their communities and clear up a spoiled identity (Goffman 1986). A prominent Arab American businessman comments on this fear and its intensified level among immigrants:

> I mean, it's no secret that there's tremendous fear in the community about there being a knock on the door, being interviewed, being interrogated, etc., and it's the community that's come from regions where this knock on the door means major trouble, so they're very apprehensive about it. It's not unusual. Take a look at the [*Chicago*] *Tribune*. It had an article about eighty-three thousand interviewed, fourteen thousand detained, zero convicted. All of those fourteen thousand have been cleared of terrorism, and of the eighty-three thousand, none had connections to terrorism. But that puts fear in the community.

At a certain point, it came to be understood in Arab and Muslim American communities that most of the "terrorist cases" the government was pursuing, although commenced with much media fanfare, had little terrorist substance. This information was gleaned from a range of competent sources, but not normally from the mainstream media, since case outcomes that were not sensational were buried in the back of newspapers and unreported on television. These failed investigations and trials (from the perspective of obtaining convictions) had the effect of *increasing* fear among law-abiding Arab and Muslim Americans because they highlighted the fact that everyone was vulnerable. When alleged terrorists were finally convicted for signing leases on behalf of undocumented immigrants, writing bad checks, or cheating on English language tests, or when the charges against them were changed from espionage to adultery (James Yee), no one could feel truly safe. The legal changes brought about by the USA PATRIOT Act that permitted ex post facto indictments had many people worried: could a check they had written to a Muslim charity in the 1990s land them in jail, or force their denaturalization or deportation, in 2005?

Some interviewees spoke of being visited by the FBI and of knowing quite a few others who were also visited. The visits were usually at home, but sometimes they occurred at work, in which case they brought substantial humiliation on their subjects, who reported feeling the stigma of suspicion imprinted on them in front of their coworkers. Few interviewees wanted to say much about the FBI visits, and I felt it was inappropriate to push on this sensitive matter. One young man did give this account of his parents' visit by the FBI:

> My father and mother told me maybe four or five months ago that, six months before, an FBI agent came over to the house and asked us questions like where my parents were born, who's their father and mother, connections with 9/11, do they hate America, what their opinions are on

America—stuff like that. Where they work, what do they do for a living, who do they work for, work with, questions like that.

Compliance Behaviors

The generalized air of suspicion cast on Arab and Muslim Americans, despite or because of the government's inability to locate terrorists, was reinforced by messages from government officials that the American public should be watchful of those around them and report suspicious activities. Public compliance with government security programs was encouraged and the chill was on; during the first few years after 9/11, few Arab and Muslim Americans could feel truly safe or unmonitored, especially if they had ties to immigrants. "There's a spotlight on us," said one interviewee; another described the atmosphere as a "nebulous cloud that hangs over us." An Arab American woman living in a high-income suburban development, who migrated to the United States as a young child, remarked: "That was the first time I felt like I did not belong. I felt people were watching me."

The American public was asked to help the government in its efforts to secure the homeland, and many felt the need to comply, as evidenced by the ninety-six thousand suspicious tips delivered to government agencies in the first week after the attacks, a pattern that continued over the years, although on a smaller scale. In chapter 4, I noted the double-consciousness that emerges when one feels watched by neighbors while performing routine daily behaviors. Naber (2006, 254) uses the term "internment of the psyche" to describe the state of mind that ensues from feeling watched, citing Michel Foucault's (1979, 201) panopticonism, or the state's capacity to induce within individuals "a state of consciousness that assures the automatic functioning of power." Naber's study, conducted in the San Francisco area during a period similar to this one, cites the reports of mental health workers and community leaders that Arabs and Muslims in the Tenderloin District had "an intensified sense that one is always under the scrutiny of others—strangers, hidden cameras, wire-taps, and other surveillance of the security state" (254). Naber's finding is replicated in this study: Arab Muslims from all social classes described consciousness of state surveillance and the watchful eyes of members of the American public who were complying with the state's call for security assistance. Respondents reported having these panopticonic experiences during everyday conversations and in institutional contexts, such as in bookstores, schools, workplaces, and mosques.

And I have to also admit, when I go to the bookstores, I'm really conscious now. Are they watching what I'm reading? What I'm buying and what I'm not? Is it my Internet that is slow now, slower, or is somebody really monitoring what I'm reading and what I'm not? I think I feel I'm more conscious. I've never felt this way in America, never before. I would buy anything I wanted, I'd go to the library and take any books I wanted, or read anything I wanted, or discuss anything . . . I would say what's on my mind. After September 11, I'm really weighing my words before I talk . . . whom I'm talking to, and what forum I'm in.

This Arab American health care professional describes feeling unsafe in his own home, vulnerable to the suspicious or retributive reports of others:

No, I don't feel 100 percent safe at home. The reason for that is, after 9/11, there were people just calling the FBI or other agencies or maybe local police, and all they have to do is say, "I think this guy is . . ." and because of what they say about Arabs, some people want to just make a phone call and say, "I saw something. I think they're up to something." That created paranoia in some people. The government's attitude is, let's go find out what this guy is up to. Just that feeling itself, that somebody can just . . . because they hate Arabs or they're just suspicious of them, you know, those few words can mean a lot. I know I'm not involved in anything, and they can tell what I do for a living. I'm not somehow secretly here for bad intents. I came here when I was little, and this country is all I know, basically, and this is it for me. I'm not having some kind of plans or anything, you know, it's just . . . I know I'm clear myself. But I don't have the choice. It could be little things. With these new laws that came out after 9/11 with the federal government, it was like, gee, you can hang somebody for no reason.

He continues by articulating another aspect of the post-9/11 context: that constitutional rights appeared to have been suspended for Arabs and Muslims living in the United States, including American citizens: "Some of the things I've seen are like, wait a minute, this is something I learned in grammar school about the Constitution, and then people say it's okay, because it doesn't apply to them."

An Arab American civil servant born in the United States describes his range of emotions: anger and sadness over the 9/11 attacks, then severe frustration with being held under a microscope as if he were responsible for them:

I don't know how to explain it. You feel, like, a variety of emotions . . . angry, sad, the ignorance in how this thing happened, how it affected people, the way they treat Arabs, and the logic behind it, like, I mean, I had nothing to do with it! My family and friends didn't have nothing to do with this thing!

Compliance behaviors were usually connected to neighbors or strangers, but occasionally they occurred in the workplace. A Euro-American woman who began wearing hijab after converting to Islam around the same time as the 9/11 attacks underwent FBI questioning twice because of suspicions reported by her coworkers. Her Sudanese husband begins to tell the story, noting how the timing of her conversion and, perhaps more importantly, wearing hijab made her suspicious:

> I think if 9/11 did not happen, no one would pay attention to the fact that she became a Muslim. I mean, the normal people will notice because she is wearing hijab, and we live in this big community, so some people accepted it and most did not, but to attract FBI attention, that is weird, especially that she is living a normal life with no special activities.

His wife then intervenes to tell the story of a work supervisor taking her to the FBI office:

> When I came back [from Canada], no one said anything to me directly of their suspicions. After two days, someone must have called the FBI about me. I was asked by "Tom," the marketing director, an ex-cop who hung with me sometimes, to go with him. I immediately thought he was going to show me something for the project I was doing. Then, as we left our office on the fourth floor and were going to the elevator, I asked him, "Where are you taking me?" I was thinking about lunch. He said, "Well, people have been worried about your activity in this last week." [She describes in detail the journey to and the setting at the FBI office.] Agent Bill stepped through the door by the window, and told "Tom" that it'd be a while, to have a seat; I was to come with him. He took me to an interrogation room, armed, with him was his pistol and a yellow legal pad. I explained where I went, what interstates I took, where [my husband] and I stopped, and why we went. He seemed satisfied after about an hour or so, no clock on the wall. I left, and "Tom" was still waiting.

She quit that job because she no longer felt safe or comfortable with her coworkers, who appeared to hold her in a suspicious light. Indeed, she described developing "paranoia" about her every move being monitored by coworkers, her conversations tapped. But at her next job, she was reported to the FBI again, allegedly because of a coworker's eavesdropping:

> The second time, again, a coworker from my present job had made a call to the FBI in December 2002. . . . He asked me about smuggling Saudi and Sudanese nationals into the country. I said, "What?" I replied, I have no idea about that. He said the complaint was made in December from a person at the medical center, the hospital in which I work, and then it dawned on me. My sister-in-law wanted to bring her son to the U.S. for medical care; she's Sudanese, but lives in Saudi Arabia. I must have been saying to a friend that she's trying to get approved for a visitor visa. Someone must have eavesdropped and only caught a few words of what I was saying and decided to call it in. I haven't heard from the FBI since, nor do I want to.

Discrimination

Prejudice, discrimination, and a compromised sense of safety are historically correlated with group subordination in the United States. Sixty-two percent of study respondents said that after 9/11 there were places in American society where they felt unsafe. Since these responses exhibited spatial and gendered patterns, they are discussed in more detail in chapters 6 and 7. Study participants were asked if they had experienced discrimination since 9/11: 53 percent said yes and 47 percent said no. Among those who responded yes, specific instances of discrimination were reported in the following sectors: employment (39 percent), public spaces (22 percent), schools (11 percent), law enforcement (11 percent), commercial transactions (9 percent), government offices (9 percent), airports or airplanes (7 percent), and civil society institutions (6 percent). It is important to note that these responses are related to a very specific interpretation of the meaning of the term "discrimination": to be denied something or treated in a different way than others. The following quote offers a sharp example of this understanding: after the speaker says he has not experienced discrimination, he then describes some of the measures he has taken to "protect" himself:

> [*Have you experienced what you would consider discrimination?*] No. I have not done anything to trigger it. I have not flown on a plane or applied for a job, where someone could say I couldn't. I have done things to protect me. I got tired of these things. I served in the military. People question your loyalty. I got veteran's plates from the state. I thought it would make a difference if someone sees me, or the police, or going somewhere, they would know that there is such a thing as the Arab face and serving in the military.

Indeed, reading full interview transcripts rather than focusing on responses to the discrimination question makes it clear that most respondents did not interpret hate speech or being spit on as discrimination. Nor did they categorize as discriminatory the behaviors described earlier, such as encounters with those consulting the Arab/Muslim mind, spreading knowledge tales, or giving looks of contempt. The same applies to having a general sense of precarious grounding in the United States; fearing arrest, internment, or removal from the country; or needing to change one's name to avoid prejudice—all topics that came up in many of the interviews. While the policies and attitudes that provoked such experiences may be legitimately labeled discriminatory, Arab Muslims did not so label them.

Verbal Harassment

Forty-six percent of study interviewees reported being verbally harassed in public after 9/11, although they did not always call this discrimination. Since this kind of behavior was most likely to occur in certain geographic areas and was often gendered, I introduce it here and discuss it in more detail in chapters 6 and 7. Harassment took different forms depending on the context in which it occurred and its subject. Public streets and shopping malls were primary sites of abusive behavior, and many incidents occurred while respondents were driving or stopped at a traffic signal. Verbal abuse was sometimes accompanied by spitting. An Arab American man reports:

> Once, we were in our car, and because my wife wore the veil, some people spitted on us, swore, and insulted us. Many times while walking down the street we found ourselves subject to many insults, such as turning someone's face, spitting, and using rude expressions that we didn't understand.

Both of the following incidents were reported by women, occurred while they were driving in the southwest suburbs, and happened when at least one of them was wearing hijab. The symbolic revocation of citizenship (whether by birth or naturalization) in the second quote was commonly reported; the woman who was told to go back to her country was born in Chicago.

> One lady said to me, "If I had a gun, I would shoot you."

> We were driving, and some teenagers shouted to us, "Go back to your country. We need to get rid of you guys, kill you off."

Workplace Experiences

Thirty-nine percent of interviewees who said they experienced discrimination reported discriminatory workplace and labor force experiences (but recall that interviewees did not label the demeaning behaviors described earlier in this chapter as discriminatory). Interviewees clearly labeled as discriminatory the perception of being denied a job because of their looks or name, being denied an expected promotion, and on-the-job encounters with hate speech. Open hate speech encounters were multisectoral—not specific to certain industries—and occurred even in arenas where Arab Muslims held high-status positions. For example, an Arab American physician reports, "I have heard 'We should kill all Arabs and Muslims' from the people at work." The U.S. Equal Employment Opportunity Commission (EEOC 2002) received 488 complaints of 9/11-related employment discrimination (so named partly because Arabs are not codified as minorities) from Arabs and Muslims in the first eight months after the attacks; 301 involved persons who were fired from their jobs. A study by Neeraj Kaushal, Robert Kaestner, and Cordelia Reimers (2007, 276) suggests that 9 to 11 percent of Arab and Muslim men (first- and second-generation) made changes in their industries of employment, from higher-paying to lower-paying industries, owing to post-9/11 job discrimination, which resulted in decreases in their "relative wages and weekly earnings" after September 11. The study also found that

> the earnings decline was broad based and of the same general magnitude for those with different education levels, nativity status, and residential location (i.e., ethnic enclave). However, earnings decreases were larger in areas with more reported hate crime related to religious, ethnic or country of origin bias. Finally, we find some evidence that September 11th was associated with a decrease in intrastate migration of Arab and Muslim men. (276)

These statistical findings are supported and to some degree explained by this study, by the widespread reports of workplace discrimination regardless of sector or position, and by the reports of professional movement from corporate to entrepreneurial work. Decreases in intrastate migration may be explained by the attitude prevalent at the time that making certain kinds of changes was highly risky in the unstable and unsafe post-9/11 environment and by a reluctance to go to places where one was not known (discussed later in this chapter and in chapter 7).

Employment discrimination came in many forms. An Arab American woman who migrated to the United States at the age of two reports discrimination in hiring because she wore a head scarf. In this case, prospective employers openly told her that her hijab conveyed the wrong image:

> Besides the physical and verbal abuse, I applied for a job, and it's not just that I'm imagining it. They said, "We don't know if we want someone who covers." Obviously, this is illegal, but this was when I was going to school and I was trying to get a job in retail. For example, "It's not part of the image we want to have, especially now being a negative connotation and with you covering and the whole post-9/11 thing." In that regard, I have absolutely been discriminated against. But I always have. That just goes with being covered—I was always discriminated against pre-9/11, but especially post-9/11. I went to talk to the corporate manager of that retail chain and said it was uncalled for. They basically apologized and offered me a job, but I didn't want to work there because of the bad experience I had, and because I would probably be working with other people who probably felt the same way.

An Arab American man who migrated to the United States at the age of one felt that he was denied a job because of his Arabic name:

> Actually, I face it personally—like when I go fill out applications or go fill out papers—because of my Arabic name. When you hear my name, you know I am 100 percent Arabic, of Arabic descent. When I write my name, it's like, I don't know, like, if they saw my name and some kid named Mike, they're going to pick the Mike kid instead of me. Well, I don't know for sure, but I know when I went to a place that has 110 percent hiring and

there was two kids with me—one of them Arabic and one of them white—and all three of us filled out the application and the white kid got the job.

The American-born daughter of Arab immigrants who worked as an underwriter in the private sector (she has since left for the nonprofit sector) describes the "bullshit comments" she had to listen to while working in that "don't have a clue" environment—that is, a climate in which people indiscriminately accepted the notion that Arab equals terrorist:

> Here in Chicago, I would say, not blatant, but right after 9/11 I took a job with a huge insurance brokerage firm, and I was an underwriter for them, and I basically assessed their risk for specific types of insurance coverages. And I had to deal a lot with the terrorism act that was made mandatory by Bush for all insurance policies. So when we were meeting about this and I was having to underwrite coverages and implement the terrorist act in there, there was . . . I dealt with a lot of bullshit comments from a lot of white people that were like, you know, "How . . . are we supposed to underwrite if Ahmed or Mohammad get crazy and decide to throw another plane into a building?" and I am just, like, I am sitting in this room, and I am trying to maintain my composure, and my managing director looks at me—she and I had a pretty good relationship, she was kind of like my mentor—she knows that I am just like brewing and steaming, and she's, like, "Well, first of all we shouldn't assume that it's going to be an Ahmed or a Mohammad," you know, and I quickly interjected it could be a Timothy McVeigh, you know, but either way you've got to underwrite it, figure out how to underwrite the risk that's involved. And everybody just kind of looked at me, and I was just, like, it's the truth. . . . So I didn't blatantly deal with discrimination on that level, but I had to hear it, you know what I mean? It just got really old. Especially in the corporate, just stale, white, "don't have a clue" kind of environment.

An Arab American health care professional's description of his workplace after 9/11 includes being denied a promotion, dealing with bomb threats (which he saw as an effort to get Arab employees fired), and the harassment of a Sikh coworker. He also describes the pain of being blamed for the 9/11 attacks and losing faith in the idea that the United States is a safe place for himself and his children.

> I was up for a big promotion, and unfortunately the events of September 11 happened and I was denied the promotion. Actually, the person who had proposed my name was already in the job and was told he either kept the job or the job would go to someone else. This is how I rank. The whole thing turned around, and that's why I say it. At work, we had quite a few verbal threats, you know, that they're going to bomb the place, kill and shoot. One of my colleagues was a Sikh, so he wore a turban and a

beard, so a lot of people mistook him for an Arab Muslim, so the poor guy had even more harassment than I did. The phone calls were because they just wanted to get rid of the Arabs. How can these Arabs work here? We should kick them out of here. They have no right to be here. That was shortly after September 11. . . . But I still felt at work that people somehow unconsciously were blaming me for it, and they didn't know how much I was hurting personally because I felt I had this big ocean between me and the Middle East, and this is a safe place for me to raise my child. I've seen enough war, enough killing in my childhood. I barely had any childhood, growing up in Jerusalem. Hopefully, things will just relax here, especially for my child. I don't want him to go to school and get picked at.

A significant number of Arab Muslim men in the workforce reported being subjected to jokes, such as, "Do you have a bomb in your briefcase?" or questioned about their whereabouts when 9/11 occurred. An Arab American network administrator says that he had more problems at work after the Oklahoma City bombings (perpetrated by an Irish American) than after 9/11. He feels that the presence of diverse nationalities at his workplace explains this difference.

I had more problems in my work after the Oklahoma City bombing than September 11. The Oklahoma City bombing wasn't Arab. I used to work in Ohio, and I remember what happened in Oklahoma City, and it happened about noontime, and I came back to the office, and the guards who worked with me, they were joking and they asked me, "Where you been? You been to Oklahoma?" They told me what happened, and they kind of put the finger on me, like, you guys did it, you know. I didn't feel comfortable, but the next day, when they found out who did it, things changed. I was working with another company two years after that, there was a guy who joked with me, I don't know if he was serious or if he was joking, he said, "If you want to bring a bomb here, just let me know, I'll leave the building before you come." I told him, "Listen, this is not a joke. Don't joke with me like that." This happened way after Oklahoma City and before September 11.

I think the difference is the kind of people I work here with is different. In Ohio, there's not international or foreign people a lot. Most of the companies I worked with, I was the only one who had an accent. I'm the only one who's not white, you know. I look different, and I have an accent and so on. Here in Chicago, it's different . . . different nationalities, different languages. A lot of people have accents, and people here, Americans and others, are used to that a lot.

A Chicago-born Arab American financial adviser says that prejudice in his workplace was lying under the surface, submerged because coworkers were aware that open statements would bring on legal trouble for the corporation. "Publicly no. But perhaps deep down, I know it's there. I work for a professional company, and people know one can sue."

Workplace issues were highly salient topics of conversation among Arab and Muslim Americans during the years after 9/11. Arab and Muslim men searching for work reported changing their names on applications and résumés. There were reports of professionals moving out of corporate work and into private practice. Interviewees in this study spoke of failed applications, contracts lost, public performances canceled, realty listings moved, and opportunities taken away. These negative outcomes in employment were minimally compensated by the increased readiness of nonprofit-sector employers to hire Arabs and Muslims, especially women. Data from this study provide qualitative insight into the workplace conditions that contributed to the findings of Kaushal, Kaestner, and Reimers (2007, 290), who concluded, "It is possible that greater prejudice reduced employment opportunities for Arab and Muslim men and forced them to make less desirable choices, resulting in earnings declines."

Immigration Revocations and Delays

Delays in and barriers to obtaining various types of visitor visas were reported in chapter 4. In a move criticized by the American Association of University Professors (AAUP), the Jewish Law Students Society at Notre Dame, and Chicago's Jewish Council on Urban Affairs, among many others, the prominent Swiss scholar Tariq Ramadan's visa to teach in an endowed chair at the University of Notre Dame's Joan B. Kroc Institute for International Peace Studies was revoked in September 2004 at the request of the Department of Homeland Security. No formal reason was given for the revocation, and charges by some in the public sphere that he had terrorist connections were never substantiated, leading to "protests that post–September 11 visa restrictions are being used to keep out an intellectual with unpopular ideas," according to an article published in the *Chronicle of Higher Education* (Bollag 2004). The American Academy of Religion and the Middle East Studies Association issued a statement arguing that in the absence of any explanation, "we fear pressures were applied to reverse the granting of a visa by people who disagree with Dr. Ramadan's views." The AAUP issued a statement calling this action one that was at odds with "our society's respect for academic freedom" (Bollag 2004, A8).

The policies that kept some people out of the United States for undisclosed reasons also kept many Arabs and Muslims already inside the United States from being able to access immigration benefits that not only were ones for which they were eligible, but that would have conferred on them a permanent right to stay in the country. Interviewees who were recently married (and one member of the couple was an American citizen) or who were waiting for adjustment of status to permanent resident or for naturalization papers for themselves or their spouses spoke of excessive delays in receiving their immigration paperwork. These delays caused heightened anxiety for Arabs and Muslims in the United States after 9/11 because one's immigration status determined what kind of due process rights one had, if any, during a period of widespread arrest and deportation. Arab and Muslim noncitizens (and some citizens) were also afraid to travel internationally after 9/11, for fear they would be prevented by the American government from returning to the United States. The case of Dr. Sabri Samirah from metropolitan Chicago, who had advance parole to permanent residency, sent chills through the Arab American community after his attempted January 2003 return from a visit abroad was halted by the U.S. government.[5] According to documents filed in his appeal, "on January 17, 2003, while petitioner was outside the United States, Brian R. Perryman, District Director of the INS Office in Chicago, Illinois, revoked petitioner's advance parole. The notice of revocation informed petitioner: 'The INS has received information indicating that you are a security risk to the United States and therefore, your advance parole authorization is hereby revoked.' "[6] Samirah was informed of this notice while en route to the United States on Royal Jordanian Airlines, at the INS pre-inspection station at Shannon Airport, Ireland, and subsequently returned to Jordan. With legal support provided by Chicago's nonprofit Heartland Alliance (formerly Travelers and Immigrants Aid), he lost all his appeals; Samirah's wife and American-born children subsequently moved to Jordan.

One interviewee said that he had been waiting three years (at that point) for his wife's permanent residency, an inordinate amount of time compared to the experience of his colleagues at work:

> The application for my wife at Immigration, I actually talked to the congresswoman twice, and she wrote them twice, and the first letter was nice. "We're waiting for authorities," and the second letter, "Due to the national emergency. . . ." They told the congresswoman to back off, even though they had told us, "You should hear from us in twenty months maximum." It turns out to be much more than that . . . it's been three years. They're not even apologetic about it. . . . When you work in a hospital, you have a lot of immigrants working with you who are naturalized citizens. Those who went outside, even after September 11, they applied, and roughly six months to a year, their wives got their green cards.

These delays continued for years after the 9/11 attacks. In 2005 the Chicago chapter of the Council on American Islamic Relations filed a class action complaint against the Department of Homeland Security, seeking a cap on the amount of time allotted to conduct the background checks necessary for acquiring citizenship and a prohibition on discrimination based on religion in applying for citizenship. In a June 2007 press release, CAIR-Chicago reported:

For the second year in a row, CAIR-Chicago's case totals rose 50 percent from the previous year. In 2006, 412 cases were reported to the Civil Rights Department. Of those cases, 66 percent were government, 14 percent were employment. The growth of the complaints involving government agencies rose nationally from 19.22 percent in 2005 to 36.32 percent in 2006. This is due largely to the number of cases regarding citizenship and green card delays. CAIR-Chicago spearheaded the citizenship delay project and was the first chapter in the nation to file a class action and individual complaints regarding citizenship delay cases. CAIR-Chicago reported the second largest number of total complaints among chapters in the nation, 13 percent of the number of national complaints, the highest per capita.[7]

Arguing that "many immigrants who have satisfied the requirements to become U.S. citizens are left in limbo for months or years due to slow processing of FBI name checks," the ACLU of Southern California, the National Immigration Law Center, the Asian Pacific American Legal Center, and the law firm of Munger, Tolles & Olson filed a class action lawsuit in federal court on December 4, 2007, seeking to enforce the time limits on name checks for people in the naturalization process.[8]

Changing Routine Behaviors

Short of leaving the United States—which many Arab Muslims said they had contemplated and some in fact did—Arab Muslims reported changing their normal life patterns in small and large ways to avoid placing themselves in situations where they expected danger or discrimination. Some changed their circle of friends, some their names, some the places they ate or prayed. One woman in hijab said that she stopped eating in restaurants while traveling for work; instead, she would buy food at drive-through windows and eat in the safety of her hotel room. The sense that watchful eyes, eavesdropping, and monitoring were pervasive caused interviewees to modify even the simplest of everyday routines. Here we focus on changes in travel patterns, which we return to in the chapter on gendered impacts.

Flying While Arab

An Arab American engineering professor argues that among the most affected by post-9/11 policies were foreign students, who could no longer return home for the summer for fear that leaving the country might put the completion of their degree at risk.

> I think students, if they want to go back home for a visit, they will find a lot of difficulties to come back, so now they prefer to stay until finishing, and then they go back for good. Of course, not seeing their family for these long periods affects them in a negative way.

Government policies affected more than the travel plans of immigrants. This U.S.-born Arab American sales representative says that she stopped traveling internationally after hearing about the case of Mahar Arar, the Canadian citizen deported to Syria by U.S. government officials (see chapter 4). The notion that she could be denied reentry to the United States, even though she is a native-born American citizen, highlights the precariousness that many Arab Muslims felt about their American citizenship.

> I go about my life as always. No, that's not true. I'm afraid to travel internationally. I am wary to do that. I am afraid they won't let me back. It may be an irrational fear. Domestically, I'm okay when I'm still in the U.S. I don't mind the security checks. But I fear that what happened to the Syrian-Canadian will happen to me.

Many interviewees said that airport profiling, known in the community as "flying while Arab," or "flying while brown," dampened their interest in traveling by air. This Arab American professional stopped flying after experiencing an airport search that made him feel he no longer had "control over his life":

> Me and my wife were carrying the baby, and the baby was sleeping, and they wanted us to be separated, and I wanted to help my wife because we were carrying all the stuff, and they wanted to search us and what have you. That's one moment I felt I was losing control over my personal life. When I told him I wanted to stay with my wife, he was really mean and he was really firm and said that these were the procedures now and everybody had to go through it. Ever since, I don't really think about it, but I really don't want to go to the airport.

Indeed, enough Arab and Muslim men were removed from airplanes in the three years following 9/11 to fuel a widespread fear of flying—a fear of humiliation more than of arrest. In addition, as the number of names on government "watch lists" and "no-fly" lists grew, the chance of having a matching name rose to the point that an increasing number of men decided to stop flying. It is, for example, easy to imagine that there are thousands of men with the name Mohammed Ahmed or Hussein Abdullah (because many Arabs are named after their grandfathers and fathers), one of whom is targeted by the watch list but all of whom will be stopped. Furthermore, each of these names can be transliterated in numerous ways, with a "u" in the place of an "o" or a single "s" instead of a double "ss"—for example, Hussein, Husein, Husayn, Hussain, Mohammed, Muhammed, Mohamed, and so on. The name of one person could appear as five or more different names, expanding exponentially the length of the watch list. In June 2007, a spokesman for the interagency National Counterterrorism Center (NCTC), which maintains the government's list of all suspected terrorists with links to international organizations, said it had 465,000 names covering 350,000 individuals. At the same time, the FBI's unclassified 2008 budget request referred to a watch list of "509,000 names" used by its Foreign Terrorist Tracking Task Force (Rood 2007).

While Arab and Muslim men have been the primary focus of U.S. government agencies and airport security staff, the following incident breaks with this gendered pattern. This Arab American woman (who does not wear hijab) describes being questioned at the Toronto airport, missing her flight, and later being forced to move out of first-class. Her case is an example of the problems that have emerged around government watch lists, including the difficulty in getting one's name removed from them.

> When I arrived [in Toronto], of course, customs asked me a million questions about why I was here, who I am, and just giving me a hard time. Finally, they let me through, and then when I went to take my plane from Toronto to Montreal, I guess my name was flagged in the computer to take me aside and check me, and so, when I was waiting for my flight, four FBI police came up to me and said, "Are you S——H——?" and I said, "Yes," and they said, "Come with us." They took me and they questioned me and wanted to see all my information, my passport, and all this stuff, and they said I was on the FBI suspect terrorist list. And I said that you and I both know that I'm not on this list. If I'm on this list, then I want to see my name. And they said, "Well, your name isn't necessarily on the list, but your name is similar to one that is on the list." I said then, "Why are you treating me like a criminal, when I'm not?" Finally, they let me go, but they watched me the whole time while I was waiting to get on my flight. . . .
>
> The same exact thing happened to me on my way back to Toronto, but this time they were very rude, and because I got very upset about it, they told me if I didn't calm down and stop making a scene in front of everybody, they were going to take me away, handcuff me and all this stuff. . . . They let everybody else on, and I didn't get on my plane, and I missed my connecting flight to Chicago, so I had to spend an extra night in Toronto.
>
> When I actually got on the plane, I asked them if I could upgrade, and they upgraded me to first-class. They gave me my seat—first-class, first row—and before the flight took off, I heard the flight attendants talking about me behind the curtain, saying, "I think we should move her." The other one said, "I don't want to be the one to do that. I don't know if I want to deal with that," and the other one said, "I don't care, I'll move her." So she came up to me and asked my name and said that I needed to move, and I asked, "Why?" and she said because I was wearing jeans. I said that was ridiculous, I was given this seat, I didn't pick it. And people in first-class do wear jeans, so that's not really a reason, so why are you telling me to move? She said, "You need to move!" She was really, really rude, and she didn't want to talk to me. At that point, I had been through so much, I was an emotional wreck . . . I knew I had to do what they wanted. . . . I just shut up and moved to the back of the plane until I finally got home.

Changes in Remittances and Charitable Giving

Traveling back to their country of birth for periodic family visits and sending remittances to help support family members are normative behaviors
for immigrants, but after 9/11 these activities became criminalized for
Arabs and Muslims. One Sudanese taxi driver told me:

> I started to have a hard time with the immigration office since I go to
> my country to visit my family every year, and I realized it started to be
> much more difficult for me to go and come back easy without trouble.
> I just came from there, and it is getting harder and harder, they are ask-
> ing a lot of questions. "Why do you go every year?" "From where you
> got all this money?" "Do you send money to your family?" "How
> much?" "Are you sure it is for your family?" and so on. . . . Someone I
> know was arrested twice over the money he sent to his family, and it
> cost him a lot to get out.

The U.S. Treasury Department closed six Muslim charities, froze their
assets, and made it a crime to engage in transactions with them shortly
after the 9/11 attacks. Of the six, criminal charges were brought and
then dropped against two, no charges were filed against three, and the
sixth, the Holy Land Foundation for Relief and Development, which the
government had been investigating for nine years, was charged with
financing terrorism—in particular, funding relief committees affiliated
with Hamas. Regardless of these differences in case status, the assets of
all were frozen. Under a Bush administration executive order, the government was not required to publicly produce evidence for these closures. As a result of these six closures, the charitable giving of American
Muslims, one of the requirements of their faith (*zaqat*), was largely cut
off from needy Muslim recipients across the globe. Persons who had
donated to these charities in the past feared government "list-making"
and prosecution, and the poor and needy in the Muslim world were de
facto abandoned by American Muslims. Repeated requests by American
Muslim and Arab leaders to the U.S. government to allow the transfer of
these charities' assets to agencies of which it approved were denied. In
October 2007, a mistrial was declared in the case against the Holy Land
Foundation for Relief and Development and its directors when the jury
could not agree on any of the 197 criminal violations related to funding
terrorism brought by the government (Cole 2007). A streamlined 2008
retrial resulted in guilty verdicts on 108 counts against the Holy Land
Foundation and five of its former organizers (Trahan and Eiser 2008).

In the meantime, however, fears were high in the Arab Muslim community concerning financial transactions, whether they were sending
remittances to family members back home or giving to charities. While

study respondents felt that these charity closures were unfounded and unjust, they spoke of a range of personal responses to the heightened scrutiny of financial transactions. Some said that their charitable giving patterns had not changed, others said that they now gave to non-Muslim charities, while others said that they gave to local Muslim institutions, but only in cash. Since, under the USA PATRIOT Act, charitable giving could now be prosecuted as support for terrorism (very broadly defined by the government) even if the donor was unaware of such support, and even if the organization was not labeled as terrorist by the government when the donation was made, quite a few Arab Muslims said that, as a matter of self-protection, they would not give to Muslim institutions without first seeing their financial statements. A Chicago-based Palestinian charity that was not closed, the United Holy Land Fund, reported receiving donations at one-fifth its pre-9/11 level. Decreases in support for U.S.-based Muslim institutions came at precisely the time when they were needed to support the mobilizations required to defend Arab and Muslim civil rights. Remittances to family members back home were now more likely to be sent in cash with persons traveling overseas, but this practice too was limited: U.S. customs officials and money-sniffing dogs were placed on outgoing airplane boarding ramps. Banks were asking their customers additional questions about overseas financial transactions, and there were many reports of banks arbitrarily closing the accounts of Arab and Muslim individuals and businesses or refusing to open new accounts. In some countries, financial institutions and money changers stopped accepting drafts drawn on U.S. banks. The remittance business was shifted to companies like MoneyGram, which maintained detailed records of senders and receivers.

Praying at the Mosque

In chapter 4, it was noted that the FBI announced that its field objectives were tied to the number of mosques in its field area. By also actively recruiting community members to spy on others at mosques, the agency changed the sacredness of mosque space.

> I think the most vulnerable are the people who are uneducated and the poor. Actually, my mechanic, who's an Arab and an American citizen too, and actually one of the police officers was on his case, an undercover police officer wanting him to go to the mosque to spy on people, and he's like, "I don't even pray, why do you want me to go to the mosque? If I wanted to work as a spy, I'd work as a spy in my country. I came here because I'm sick and tired of these people, who are doing crazy work. Why do you want me to go and spy on other people?"

An Arab American man said he stopped praying at the mosque because his sense of being watched there made it lose its "charm":

> My compatriots and I have noticed that there has been heightened scrutiny about our mosques. And in get-togethers, there is always a sense that there are those around watching and taking down our actions. Truthfully, going to the mosques does not hold the same charm as it did. Now the safest place I feel is at home.

The Kindness of Others and a Thirst for Knowledge

In the context of the government's dragnet policies and criminalizing statements, as well as verbal and sometimes physical attacks from multiple quarters—the media, coworkers, teachers, neighbors, and hatemongers—many interviewees reported being heartened by the concerned phone calls and offers of help they received from non-Arab, non-Muslim friends, neighbors, coworkers, and strangers. These encounters began almost immediately after the attacks, because it was very quickly clear that Arabs and Muslims in the United States were becoming the targets of backlash. Some said that neighbors who used to ignore them made efforts to build friendships, some offered protection, and others wanted to learn more about them. When asked if any good things happened after 9/11, an Arab American woman told me:

> Yes, for example, the dialogues and the friendships I've been able to have with my neighbors. People who used to be just acquaintances or just passersby have now become friends. It's interesting because we kind of found a common ground. You know, they don't realize that we have a lot more in common and that I'm not that different than you. Also, I've been more involved in interfaith dialogues between different places. There's been an interest between synagogues, churches, even among mosques. "Let's learn about each other. What do you stand for? What do you believe in?" Especially, they want to know more about our core beliefs and how this relates to suicide bombing and the jihad, and all this terminology that you hear about every day. There's a genuine interest in wanting to get to know more about each other. So I've been more involved in that, and that's been very positive.

An Arab American man who immigrated to the United States as an adult describes positive changes in his friendship networks, which he says reveal the "best of this country."

> Immediately after, I felt people were uneasy around me, which was understandable. What happened September 11 is something that is really huge and unforgivable. It's not a random act of violence with innocent bystanders. No, it was a deliberate mass kill crime, and these guys need to be punished and go to justice because, as a Palestinian, this is what

I've suffered all my life. . . . I have to admit, I have a lot of good American friends that I like and love. They were there for me. Especially some Jewish Americans have called to say that if I felt threatened or you don't feel safe and want to come and stay at our place, you're welcome. We're inviting them over or they're inviting me to their places. Before, we never used to go out. So maybe it's a blessing in disguise. So that's the other side of America too. It has brought the best out of this country in spite of some ugly, random acts.

Another Arab American man describes being personally touched by the concern others showed for his family's safety:

A lot of my friends or acquaintances went out of their way to call and check on us regularly and offer us refuge if things got too bad. Yes, it has brought a lot of good into our lives, and we feel touched by that.

An Arab American professor notes a major change in the American people's quest for knowledge.

Yes, a greater desire to be informed about the Middle East and Muslim affairs among the American people. There's definitely a change, a palpable change. Ordinary people want to know. My Middle East classes are full. People want to know about women. People want to know about Islam. There's a desire to know. Whether that desire is motivated by good intentions or by negative intentions, it provides an opening for us to speak out, and we are speaking out.

Another American-born Arab woman says:

More objective people have tried to find out about Islam and that truth and the difference between the people who did the bombing and most Muslims. The people who did 9/11 made life miserable for a lot of people. I have nothing but contempt for them.

An Arab American woman living in the southwest suburbs reports that relations with some of her neighbors improved after 9/11.

My relations with my neighbors have definitely changed. Before, they would say hi and bye. Now, after that, there were some very ignorant questions related to Osama bin Laden, or why do you cover. There's more interest in who I am, what I represent, and where I come from, as opposed to before. Those have become very good relationships. They are actually friends of ours now. I would encourage them to ask me questions, I would invite them over for dinner, and we would talk. The ones who would just say hi to me before, now there's no acknowledgment. If anything, I get dirty looks, rolling the eyes. I've had people who were neighbors of ours make comments like "I don't want people like you living next to us." You know, really ignorant comments.

While anti-Muslim and anti-Arab narratives were common to the American media in the years following the 9/11 attacks, and openly expressed hatred against Arabs and Muslims could be heard on certain television and radio programs and read on many websites, a space for counternarratives had been opened. This space opened because Arab-bashing and Muslim-bashing reached a level intolerable to many in American society and because American Arabs and Muslims rose to the occasion. An Arab American man describes what he saw as major changes in Arab and Muslim American communities, which were mobilized by the "wake-up call" that was delivered by the 9/11 attacks, and the public's and government's response to them, when it became clear that protection could not happen in isolation.

> I think because of the reaction to 9/11, there was kind of a wake-up call, not only for the country but also a wake-up call for Arabs and Muslims as well. From the Arab and Muslim side, I think a lot of the loose rhetoric has subsided quite a bit, which is a good thing. And reality kind of sunk in, and that everyone living in this society needs to look at the good as well as the negative of one's experiences. . . . Also, there is a larger number in the society at large who has knowledge of Arabs or Muslims, and they have done some homework on it, so it's not just what they see on TV. . . . I think that's been quite positive, and it brought out from the Muslim/Arab perspective a more proactive approach. Some of the older ones, as well as some of the younger generation, have become more aware of their own culture and their own religion and begun to speak out. So I think there has been a silver lining, and I think this is part of it. Another one is political activities. Whereas in the past the majority of the community—and you know this as well as I do and maybe even better—would say, "Why get involved? It doesn't make any difference. They're all the same. Our vote doesn't count. What's a few dollars going to do?" etc. Now we can marshal resources and get involved in political campaigns, both on the fundraising side as well as the voting side. I think these are all positive, and they also show a society and a group that's maturing. And I think that 9/11 helped them mature a lot quicker.

Another Arab American man describes his own change:

> I have to say that my community is getting more engaged politically, and on my personal level, I never before called the congressman's office. I was at the point of becoming so Americanized, I didn't even want to vote. I didn't even care who was in the White House. I believed that acting locally and helping locally was more important. But now I see it's very important to be very active in getting people registered to vote and making sure they go out and vote.

Conclusion

This chapter focused on a range of post-9/11 experiences that were shared by Arab Muslims across social classes, gender, and neighborhood contexts. The security spotlight that Arab Muslims felt shining on them created fear and insecurity, along with a plethora of altered daily life behaviors. Dominant discourses about an Arab/Muslim propensity to violence and terrorism and the government's call to be watchful of these groups informed a host of discriminatory behaviors aimed in their direction by members of the American public. Although most Americans were not physically violent, it appears that a much larger number behaved in objectionable ways, whether by looks, gestures, comments, or reports of suspicions, of which even the most seemingly subtle were experienced as palpably offensive and constitutive of a climate of harassment. Institutional discrimination carried the sense of pervasiveness as it was encountered in schools, workplaces, banks, and airports and perceived at libraries and stores; government watch lists and charity closures added another layer to the wall of barriers. It was the most extreme behaviors and discourses, however, that generated a new countervalence. The violence of some words and deeds moved many Americans to compassion and to stepped-up efforts to question what lay hidden behind simplistic stereotypic representations—leading to a widespread thirst for knowledge about Arabs and Muslims on the part of the American public.

The next chapter provides detailed accounts of some of the most violent public responses, as well as some of the most protective responses, experienced by Arab Muslims in metropolitan Chicago after 9/11. It demonstrates in yet another way a recurring theme in this book: that in a social context replete with stereotypes, negative representations, and the cultivation of hate, safety lies in being "known" and in having relationships with persons outside the group, while isolation brings on greater vulnerability. Groups that occupy the space of the "outsider" are in a space where others define them and where negative representations gain power to drive action (thus the power of segregation). Those who lobby for and support the maintenance of a group's outsider status know that changes in this status will disempower their own claims, and thus the most ardent of them are motivated to work harder when they perceive such changes are occurring. On the other hand, socially and politically integrated "insider" groups find the space to decline, interrupt, and reinterpret master narratives, to create a layer of noise between dominant and popular understandings, and to find power in solidarity.

Chapter 6

Hate Acts, Local Mobilizations, and the Crisis Point

Police turned back 300 marchers—some waving American flags and shouting "USA! USA!"—as they tried to march on a mosque in this Chicago suburb [Bridgeview] late Wednesday. . . . "I'm proud to be American and I hate Arabs and I always have," said 19-year-old Colin Zaremba who marched with the group from Oak Lawn.

> —Associated Press, "Arab Americans Attacked, Threatened,"
> September 13, 2001

A 39-year-old suburban man approached another young man who was working at a Palos Heights gas station. He asked the man what he was. The man said that he was "an American," but the offender wasn't satisfied. He said, "No, where are you from?" When the young worker said he was of Moroccan descent, the offender attacked him using a two-foot machete. The defendant later said he had been listening to the radio as he drove to the gas station. The news about the terrorist attack, he said, had upset him, and he lashed out at the first Arab-looking young man that he saw.

> —Cook County State's Attorney Richard Devine, in Illinois Advisory
> Committee to the U.S. Commission on Civil Rights (2003)[1]

Prosecutors said the 30-year-old Nix felt enormous hatred for Arab Americans after they started moving into south suburban Burbank where he lives and it was intensified after his van was towed and Salmi's was not.

> —Mike Robinson, "Illinois Man Who Wrecked Muslim Family's Van
> Going Back to Jail," Associated Press, August 22, 2006

I N GENERAL, the safety of Arabs and Muslims on the American street was fragile for a few years after the 9/11 attacks, although some persons were more vulnerable to hate encounters than others and some places presented more risk than others. Risk of death was highest in the first few weeks after the attacks, but over time hate actions directed

Map 6.1   Census 2000, Arab Ancestry Reported—Cook and Dupage Counties, Illinois

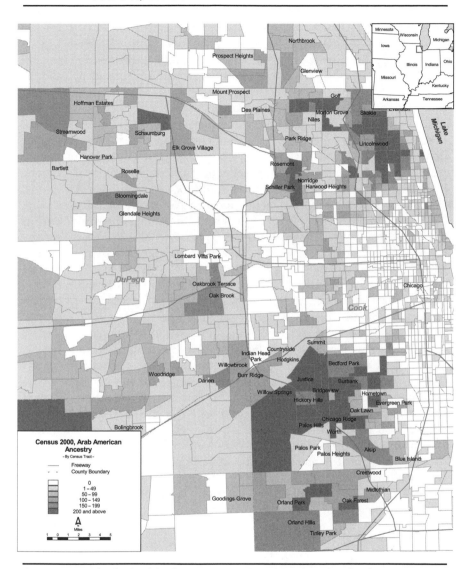

Source: Created for this book by the Arab American Institute, based on data from U.S. Census Bureau, 2000 Census of Population and Housing, Summary File 3: Technical Documentation, 2002 PCT018006 (PCT018007—PCT018015), 17, 81, 83 U.S. Geological Survey.

Note: The term "Arab" used here refers to three different ancestry groups as designated in Census 2000. The first are those of Arab ancestry including those from the following: Algeria, Egypt, Libya, Morocco, Tunisia or the western Asian countries of Bahrain, Iraq, Jordan, Kuwait, Lebanon, Oman, Palestine, Qatar, Saudi Arabia, Syria, United Arab Emirates, and Yemen. The second group is the Assyrian/Chaldean/Syriac. The third is those from the Sub-Saharan category: the Somalian and Sudanese.

against Arabs and Muslims were more likely to be minor assaults, verbal harassment, or vandalism. Although the statistical likelihood of being physically harmed or murdered was actually low, examined from a post facto perspective, an Arab/Muslim's personal assessment of risk at the time was another matter altogether. Aggression motivated by anger or hatred was often directed against persons wrongly perceived to be Arabs or Muslims, marking the strength of ideas that connected a "Middle Eastern" phenotype and a certain mode of dress to persons who were understood to be somehow complicit in the 9/11 attacks.

In the first nine weeks after the attacks, the American-Arab Anti-Discrimination Committee (ADC 2003, 7) reported "over 700 violent incidents targeting Arab Americans, or those perceived to be Arab Americans, Arabs, and Muslims," including several murders. Another 165 violent incidents occurred between January 1 and October 11, 2002, according to ADC civil rights reports. The Council on American-Islamic Relations (2002) reported 1,062 incidents of violence, threat, or harassment during the initial onslaught of the post-9/11 backlash. Full 2001 to 2002 reporting-year claims affected 2,242 victims, mostly in incidents of bias-motivated harassment and violence. In its 2004 report, CAIR reported a 121 percent rise in all anti-Muslim incidents and a 69 percent rise in reported hate crimes (2004). Overall, statistics show an initial surge in hate crimes against Arab and Muslim Americans in the first months after the 9/11 attacks, followed by a lower but persistent pattern of violence, bigotry, and discrimination across the nation. Whether hate crimes actually rose in 2004, or how much they rose, are other matters, because hate crime statistics measure both actual incidents and reporting behaviors. In light of the increased civic activism of Arab and Muslim Americans after 2001, we should expect that increases in reported hate crimes reflect to a certain degree "a successful outcome of social movement mobilization" (McVeigh, Welch, and Bjarnason 2003, 843). What we can say with certainty is that hate crimes against Arab and Muslim Americans did not end in 2001 and continued well into 2008.

Civil rights and advocacy organizations tend to place responsibility for the persistence of these attacks on mass-mediated radio and television programs, the print media, and the public statements of prominent personalities who dehumanize Arabs and Muslims as a monolithic collectivity. The ADC (2003, 9), for example, found that defamatory statements about Arabs and Muslims increased "in intensity and frequency" during the thirteen months following the attacks. As the source of these statements, it cited leaders of the evangelical Christian right, prominent public officials, members of Congress, and the mainstream media; in particular, it pointed to the media's increasing use of commentators "whose main aim is to promote fear and hatred of Arab Americans." The ADC cautioned that the behaviors of these spokespersons was laying "the groundwork for potential future waves of hate crimes." Others—

myself included—assigned a portion of the blame for stereotyping Arabs and Muslims on school textbooks and an American educational system that has treated Islam and Arabs in biased ways. To these social forces must be added the statements, policies, and actions of federal government agencies that imposed a criminalized stigma on Arab and Muslims in the United States and therefore did not work to dissipate hatred. As noted earlier in this book, Arab and Muslim Americans felt that there was "something in the air" that made attacks on them permissible.

> I saw how easily people resorted to stereotyping and hatred as a means of dealing with this tragedy. In the weeks after September 11, a man who identified himself by name and said he was one of my neighbors was among hundreds of people who sent e-mails threatening my life. What does it say about a society when someone can feel comfortable in their hatred with no fear of punishment? (Testimony of Arab American journalist Ray Hanania)[2]

Hate crimes reported for the Chicago metropolitan area mirrored national patterns, with an initial surge in violent incidents across the area, followed by a lower but persistent level of reports. The Illinois Advisory Committee to the U.S. Commission on Civil Rights (2003) reported 32 hate crimes perpetrated in Illinois against Arabs, Muslims, and people mistaken for Arabs and Muslims between September 11 and September 17, 2001, most occurring in the Chicago metropolitan area. These included violence against individuals, schools, and mosques; verbal harassment and threats; mob incidents; and anti-Arab protests. Illinois state police statistics showed 49 reported hate crimes against people of Arab descent in 2001 (up from 9 in 2000), while the city of Chicago reported 52 (up from 4 in 2000), 49 of which occurred on or after September 11 (see figure 6.1).

Over the years, reports of violent hate incidents at the local and national levels were outnumbered by claims of employment and government discrimination. CAIR-Chicago's civil rights coordinator, Christina Abraham, stated in June 2007 that of the 412 cases reported to CAIR's office in 2006, 80 percent were claims against the federal government or employers. In 2006, CAIR-Chicago's case totals rose 50 percent from the previous year for the second year in a row; this office, which did not commence operations until 2004, posted the highest number of claims per capita in the nation. It is difficult to sort out the extent to which these increases reflect CAIR-Chicago's increasing effectiveness as a professional organization (which is indeed the case) or the extent to which it measures an increasing and proportionately higher level of discrimination in the Chicago area. Across the nation, increased reporting is to some degree an artifact of increasing civic activism by American Muslims, while local-level reporting is influenced by the presence of an effective monitoring organization. These caveats make it difficult to draw concrete

Figure 6.1　　Hate Crime Reports: City of Chicago, 2001

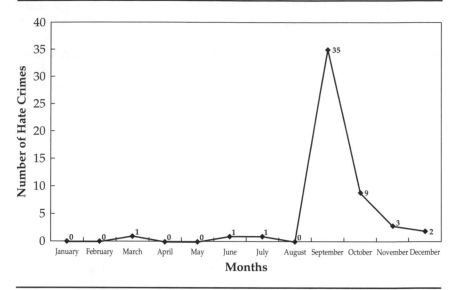

Source: Author's compilation based on data from the Chicago Police Department, Research and Development.

conclusions about increases or decreases in actual incidents across the nation or about variations from place to place.

There are many problems associated with hate crime statistics—such as not knowing the degree to which reports reflect actual incidence (not everyone reports hate crimes or incidents), geographic variation in the presence and quality of the advocacy groups taking reports, the extent to which data reflect social movement outcomes, the presence of official discretion in defining whether an act is a hate crime, variations in definitions of Arabs and Muslims, and variations in the specificity of the associated data collected (characteristics of the perpetrator, descriptions of the location and its demographic context). These problems make it difficult to move to a higher level of understanding about who is committing these acts, what is motivating them, and the social factors that mitigate or aggravate hate crimes (for a fuller discussion of the many pitfalls of hate crime data, see Green, McFalls, and Smith 2001). While a defamatory national context existed around Arabs and Muslims in general and Arab and Muslim Americans in particular after 9/11, not everyone accepted messages of collective responsibility, and among those who did, a much smaller number actually committed hate crimes, threw eggs at their neighbor's house, shouted, "I want to kill you," or spit on passersby. Notwithstanding social-psychological variations among people, identifying patterns of spatial and victim variation would help to deconstruct and place more specificity on what otherwise appears to be a national problem with violence and hatred toward Arabs and Muslims. This study was able to uncover two significant variations in hate encounters: one correlated with the gender of the victim and a second correlated with the geographic area of occurrence.[3] This chapter examines the latter, showing how race, place, and intergroup relationships intersected to produce quite different outcomes for Arab Muslims in metropolitan Chicago after 9/11, while chapter 7 looks at gendered patterns.

Hate Crimes and Hate Encounters Reported in the Study

Study statistics revealed that only a handful of persons said their lives went unchanged after 9/11; 62 percent said there were places where they continued to feel unsafe. Although the southwest suburbs ranked highest among places perceived to be unsafe, there were significant variations by gender in the range of places considered unsafe (discussed in chapter 7). Forty-six percent of study interviewees (47 out of 102 interviewees) reported personally experiencing a verbal assault after 9/11, and 10 percent (10 interviewees) said they were victims of hate crimes, half of which were property damage. When asked if they knew of others experiencing hate speech or hate crimes, these proportions rose. Fifty-seven percent (58 interviewees) knew of someone other than themselves who had experienced verbal assault, and 37 percent (39 interviewees) knew of someone other than themselves who had experienced a hate crime, largely minor physical assault or property damage. Sixty-nine percent of those who knew about a hate crime against someone other than themselves possessed detailed knowledge of the crime, while 31 percent were citing vague reports based on hearsay or press coverage of two events widely reported in the local media: the attack on an Arab gas station attendant in southwest suburban Palos Heights by a white man wielding a two-foot machete, and the detonation of explosives in an Arab American family's van parked in southwest suburban Burbank. Both of these offenders were charged with hate crimes. The most serious hate acts directly experienced by interviewees were a physical assault that was reported by a Sudanese man (and did not occur in Illinois), the attempted arson of a southwest suburban apartment building full of immigrant Palestinian families that was thwarted by watchful neighbors and the police, and a threatened vehicular assault reported by a Sudanese Muslim woman (reported in chapter 7).

Study statistics on verbal assault and hate crimes do not include, if there was no verbal or criminal component, reports of spitting, sneezing in the face, mocking, throwing eggs at cars, and "finger signals"; rude treatment from drivers, cashiers, teachers, and government employees; the looks of contempt that interviewees routinely spoke about (see chapter 5); or the mob siege on the Bridgeview mosque, since this was a collective experience. It is interesting from a sociological perspective that actions such as these, which constituted an overall "climate of harassment," are covered by neither definitions of discrimination nor definitions of hate crimes and verbal assault; their statistical computation thus falls into the proverbial black hole, were it not for ethnographic accounting. Many of these incidents are recounted in this book. Some additional incidents of hate crimes, vandalism, hate graffiti, and verbal harassment were not specifically mentioned by study participants but were reported in the local press, such as the September 18, 2001, beating of the taxi driver Mustapha Zemkour, presumed to be Arab, who was pursued into north suburban Evanston by his assailants (one a Cook County corrections officer), one of whom allegedly shouted, "This is what you get, you mass murderer," while pounding him with fists (Abowd 2002). An Assyrian church on the north side of the city was struck by arson on September 23, the same day a note was found at a different northwest suburban Assyrian church asking, "Are you with U.S. or with the enemy?" Local newspapers also reported on southwest suburban families sitting terrorized in their homes while vigilantes surrounded them shouting hate-filled messages, and traumatized children finding a sign that read WE ARE GOING TO KILL ARABS posted near their southwest suburban Burbank home (Franklin and Terry 2001). The two-day mob siege on the neighborhood surrounding the Bridgeview mosque received substantial press coverage and was reported by many interviewees as a terrifying event. The press also reported damage to institutional property in 2002 and 2003, when a Molotov cocktail was thrown at a southwest suburban Muslim school, hate graffiti was sprayed on a north suburban mosque, and a west suburban mosque window was attacked during prayer services by bat-wielding teens. This mosque was vandalized again in 2008.

There were some common patterns to the post-9/11 hate encounters reported by study participants. Across the metropolitan area, the greatest number of incidents occurred in the first few months after the attacks and were most likely to occur while people were driving; these incidents involved verbal "racial" slurs, death threats, or shouts to "go home" and were sometimes accompanied by items, such as bottles and garbage, being thrown at the car. Male taxi drivers and women wearing hijab were the most likely to describe such experiences. Some Arab Muslim women in hijab also reported being followed by strangers while driving; these incidents occurred in the northwest, western, and southwest suburbs. Many incidents of non-institutional property damage and vandalism were reported, such as tires being flattened on parked cars, store windows being smashed, eggs and firecrackers being thrown at homes, and hostile graffiti being painted on lawns, driveways, and mailboxes. These incidents occurred predominantly, and persistently, in the southwest suburbs. Graffiti messages tended to have an outcasting theme; for example, one Arab American woman reported that "go home" was spray-painted on the driveway of her large suburban home. Many women reported altercations at southwest suburban grocery stores, and a majority of study participants from the southwest suburbs reported experiencing harassment at the area's shopping malls. One Arab American man living in a southwest suburb describes the repeated assaults on his home and property:

> Well, my van in front of my house was covered with eggs several times, about one or two months ago. I didn't report it. I used to. . . . Also, some garbage was put in our mailbox, like ice cream cones and wrappers, stuff like that. Once we called the police because it wasn't just the cars but also the house! They pelted the door with eggs.

These acts of property damage, harassment, and intimidation in the southwest suburbs did not end after a few months but continued to occur for years after the 9/11 attacks.

Spatial Variations

This study found significant spatial variations in hate encounters. According to interview data, while hate encounters initially occurred across the metropolitan area, incidents tapered off in most areas within about six weeks and became concentrated in the southwest suburbs. Interviewees living in urban and suburban metropolitan areas other than the southwest suburbs reported either initially intense experiences with hate acts and harassment while in public spaces that subsided after a few months, or no experiences of hate encounters at all. Arab Muslims living in majority-white suburbs where relatively few other Arabs or Muslims lived reported proportionately few hate encounters, although some women wearing hijab reported being followed while driving shortly after the attacks. Persons from these areas also reported the discriminatory encounters described in chapter 5 at work and in schools, as well as negative experiences with the government (chapter 4), but the western, northern, and northwest suburban malls and neighborhoods were relatively quiet when it came to being able to use public space without facing aggression or being able to avoid vandalism to homes and businesses—the exception to this pattern being found in the vandalization of Muslim institutions and the Assyrian church. Most interviewees from suburbs other than the southwest nonetheless reported continued fear of using public space in areas with specific demographic features.

The southwest suburbs, an area of high Arab and Muslim residential and small business concentration, sat at the top of the list of places perceived as potentially unsafe by persons who did not live in them but who visited these areas to worship or do ethnic shopping. This designation of the southwest suburbs as a place of potential danger also held for

Arab Muslims from the southwest side of the city, another area of significant Arab residential and small business concentration. Arab Muslims who lived in the southwest suburbs, on the other hand, specified certain locations within these suburbs as places where they felt unsafe, such as shopping malls and areas where Arabs or Muslims are concentrated. Perceptions of a particularly heightened vulnerability in the southwest suburbs were built on personal experiences with harassment and on the reports of others. The sole exception to these spatially related perceptions of danger came from interviews with study participants who were Chicago taxi drivers (a large proportion of whom are Muslim), who reported continuing harassment across the city, although it was difficult for some of them to determine whether this harassment was post-9/11 backlash or routine xenophobia. Between 2001 and 2005, seven Chicago taxi drivers were murdered, and five of them were Muslim.

Unlike other study participants, interviewees from the southwest suburbs reported hate encounters that continued persistently throughout the entire period of the interview component of the study (2002 to 2004). This spatially related pattern continued into 2006, according to incident reports filed with the Chicago office of the Council on American-Islamic Relations, whose representative (Christina Abraham) told me in late 2006 that nearly all of the bias incidents reported to it in the 2004 to 2006 period, other than job discrimination and immigration delays, took place in the southwest suburbs. The reported incidents were direct encounters in public space and included a woman's hijab being pulled off at a McDonald's, verbal harassment in shopping malls, and multiple reports of hate crimes against Arab American students in southwest suburban schools, most of which occurred outside school property.[4] The most serious school-related case involved an Arab American boy who was beaten with a lead pipe while being called "camel jockey." This incident developed into a fight in which two parties participated, changing its character in the official interpretation of the event. CAIR-Chicago says that while police viewed the incident as a fight, they did not attend to the instigating hate incident or report it as a hate crime. (Despite attempting to do so, I could not locate official hate crime data for the southwest suburbs.)

In the city of Chicago, hate crimes tapered off substantially after an initial outburst, as noted in figure 6.1. First Deputy Kenneth Gunn of the Chicago Commission on Human Relations reported in 2003 that hate acts in the city of Chicago were initially citywide and perpetrated by persons from a range of racial and ethnic groups:[5]

> Up until 9/11 the city was seeing a relatively "good year" for hate crimes. . . . After 9/11, just everything totally fell apart. From September 11 through September 30, we have received 50 reported hate crimes. Of the 50, 41 were reported to be against Arabs and/or Muslims. The swelling numbers lasted probably for about three to four weeks, then the numbers

Table 6.1   Hate Crimes Against Persons of the "Arab Race" in the City of Chicago

	North Side	West Side	Loop	South Side	Southwest Side	Unknown
September 2001 T = 35	16	9	0	1	7	2
October 2001 T = 9	4[a]	1	0	0	3	1
November 2001 T = 4	3	0	0	1	0	0
December 2001 T = 2	0	0	0	1	1	0
Total	23	10	0	3	11	3

Source: Author's calculations based on data from the Chicago Police Department, Research and Development.

Note: Racial coding of Arabs is problematic, as discussed in chapter 3. Arabs are officially considered white, a categorization that may lead to reporting inconsistencies of the victim's "race." A majority of Arabs interviewed in this study said that in their view Arabs are not white. Human rights commissioner Sahar Mawlawi reported that Arabs were sometimes coded as Asians by Chicago police.

[a]Includes two in Logan Square, which is more accurately the near northwest side and could be arbitrarily added to west side totals.

> *tapered down significantly.* Unfortunately, we had all kinds of acts. We had people just harassed on the street. We had a major Arab center on the southwest side that became a victim of arson.[6] It was totally gutted. We had people in cars being stopped, and unfortunately it was throughout the city. Perpetrators were African Americans and white; there was no rhyme or reason to it. Anybody was involved. (Illinois Advisory Committee to the U.S. Commission on Civil Rights 2003, 12; emphasis added)

Mary Abowd (2002) reported that the largest number of urban hate crimes against Arabs occurred on the southwest side. A mapping of incidents between September and December 2001 that were reported to the Chicago police and recorded as hate crimes and in which the victim's race was coded as Arab (Arab as "race" was a new coding category) shows that a high concentration of hate crimes occurred on the southwest side, an area of significant Arab residential concentration, but that the largest number occurred on the much larger north side of the city, across a range of both ethnically diverse and dominantly white community areas (see table 6.1). Hate crime reports also show a concentration of incidents on the west side of the city; this pattern, along with the locations of some of the north side crimes, suggests that attacks were focused on Arab small retail business owners or their property, particularly in Latino and, to a significantly smaller extent, African American neighborhoods, both places where Arab American retail businesses tend to be located. These patterns match Gunn's testimony that perpetrators in the city could not be pinned to specific racial or ethnic groups. Data from the predominantly African American south side of the city stand out, however, as an exception to be explained. The south side hosts the largest number of Arab-owned small retail businesses in the city (Blackistone 1981; Cainkar 1998), but was the site of the lowest number of reported hate crimes, with the exception of downtown Chicago (the Loop).

Varying Social Contexts Across Space

Arab Americans live in substantial numbers in the southwest suburbs, so the probability that they would have hate encounters in those areas is higher simply because of their extensive presence. But numbers of Arabs/Muslims alone do not explain the incidence of hate encounters; for example, numbers cannot explain why such encounters occurred at disproportionately higher levels in the southwest suburbs than on the southwest side of the city, another area where Arab Americans live in large numbers. Nor do numbers explain the persistence of hate encounters in the southwest suburbs for years after the 9/11 attacks, long after the outbursts reported in Chicago and across other parts of the metropolitan area had receded. These two sites of Arab American residential concentration, the southwest side and the southwest suburbs, are adjacent to each other and tied to each other historically. Together they represent the initial reception areas and the southwesterly trajectory of Chicago's one-hundred-year-old Arab American community (see map 6.1 at the beginning of this chapter). Family networks stretch across both areas, as do Arab American businesses, creating in some subareas a nearly seamless web of Arab Americans, textured by socioeconomic differences and the physical separations marked by railroad tracks and industrial areas. The urban site hosts largely new immigrant and lower-income families, while the suburban site hosts families of all income levels and three immigrant generations, including recent immigrants. Both locations host a range of Arab American retail and service enterprises and social and religious organizations, and both have mosques. Arab American Christians attend churches in different suburban locations, including one in the southwest suburbs, according to their denomination. The southwest side and the southwest suburbs are places that are similarly linked for Euro-Americans, many of whom moved to the suburbs in the 1970s and 1980s from the newly desegregating southwest side, site of Marquette Park and Martin Luther King Jr.'s open housing marches of the 1960s.

Part of the explanation for differences in the patterns of hate encounters by place (propensity and duration) may be located in the demographic differences between the southwest side of the city and the southwest suburbs. The southwest side of the city, where Arab Americans are concentrated, includes a cluster of Chicago community areas that may in the aggregate be described as mixed multiethnic (Fasenfest, Booza, and Metzger 2004), within which are places of Latino, African American, and white numerical dominance. Arab American families are spread across this mosaic of laissez-faire diversity (Nyden, Maly, Lukehart 1997), with their densest census tract concentration standing at 4.5 percent in 2000 (without considering undercounting).[7] This southwest side area includes the communities of Gage Park, West Lawn, Chicago Lawn, West Elsdon, and parts of Ashburn and may be considered a "community" because its residents to a meaningful degree share social networks and local institutions (Hunter 1974) and each group's "ethnic shopping district" is woven into that of the others. Indeed, Arab Americans and Euro-Americans have always simply called it "the southwest side."

The southwest suburbs, on the other hand, are predominantly white in the aggregate, with variations by suburb in the proportion of Arab Americans and relatively small representation of other "racial" or "minority" groups. In the southwest suburbs, Arab Americans are understood to be *the* minority group, even if by official standards they are white (as are many Latinos). The suburbs in which Arab Americans constitute a significant demographic presence were reported as 87 to 93 percent white (recall that white includes Arabs) in the 2000 census (see table 6.2). Similar to the southwest side of the city, the southwest suburbs are linked to each other socially by families, commercial enterprises, high schools, and, for Arab Americans in particular, a mosque (two mosques in 2006) and a church; they are also linked symbolically in their role as zones of reception for former residents of the southwest side. When Arab Americans spoke in interviews about "the southwest suburbs"—or sometimes simply "the suburbs"—they were referring to these areas in the aggregate, specifically Alsip, Bridgeview, Burbank, Chicago Ridge, Oak Lawn, Hickory Hills, Orland Park, Palos Hills, Palos Heights, and Palos Park.

The designation of these suburbs as "predominantly white" is tricky, however, for a few reasons. For example, the Brookings Institution's Center on Urban and Metropolitan Policy "neighborhood integration typology" defines "predominantly white" as "at least 80 percent white, and no minority group represents more than ten percent of the population" (Fasenfest, Booza, and Metzger 2004, 5). In the southwest suburbs, Arab Americans are officially counted as white, enhancing the "white" portion of the equation, but in grounded reality they are a minority group. The second problem revolves around the proportion of the population that Arab Americans actually represent. Census 2000 data on persons of Arab descent, gathered from the long-form sample, place their proportions in these suburban areas in a range of 2 to 7 percent (table 6.2). In official

Table 6.2 Arabs in the Southwest Suburbs

Suburb	Total Population	Median Family Income	Percent Arab[a]	Percent Increase Arab 1990 to 2000	Percent White	Percent Asian	Percent Black	Percent Latino
Alsip	19,725	$54,846	2.0%	190%	81.6%	2.1%	10.1%	8.8%
Bridgeview	15,335	52,490	7.2	336	87.4	2.2	0.8	9.4
Burbank	27,902	56,279	4.6	33	90.7	1.8	0.3	11.1
Chicago Ridge	14,127	56,314	6.9	568	89.1	1.5	2.4	6.3
Hickory Hills	13,926	61,972	5.5	386	90.9	2.1	1.2	8.1
Oak Lawn	55,245	60,057	3.9	279	93.3	1.7	1.2	5.3
Orland Park	51,077	77,507	1.9	259	93.5	3.5	0.7	3.7
Palos Hills	17,665	61,764	3.3	83	87.2	2.7	5.5	4.8

Source: U.S. Bureau of the Census, 1990 and 2000.

[a]Based on ancestry data. Arabs are counted as white by race.

statistics on Arab Americans, however, they are significantly under-counted, according to both the Arab American Institute Foundation and my own research;[8] neither Arab Americans nor Euro-Americans from these communities accept these statistical proportions as accurate (and neither do I). They simply do not match the tangible and visible social reality of these areas. Consider the following perceptions as compared to official data on the size of the Arab American population in two southwest suburbs as reported in Chicago newspapers within days of the 9/11 attacks:

> "It's been brutal since Tuesday" with more than a dozen racial incidents in his town, Chicago Ridge Police Chief Tim Balderman said. . . . Balderman said Chicago Ridge has a population that is "about 30% Arab." (Newhart and Mendieta 2001)

> But in Bridgeview on Wednesday night the Elayyan family said they felt like foreigners. The Elayyans, like most of their Muslim neighbors, stayed off the streets, behind drawn drapes and bolted doors. The fear was still easy to find Thursday in Bridgeview, a suburb of 15,000 residents, about 30 percent of whom are Arab-Americans. (Terry and Ahmed-Ullah 2001)

The perception among Arab Americans and non-Arab Americans in the southwest suburbs is that Arab Americans constitute a substantial and increasing subpopulation of the area. The official census data used in table 6.2 clearly indicate large increases in the number of Arab Americans since 1990, averaging 226 percent across these suburbs, with a range of 33 to 568 percent. The Arab American presence in the south-west suburbs is significant enough to be on the Department of Homeland Security's radar. Southwest suburban Bridgeview, Burbank, and Oak Lawn appeared on the list produced for them by Census Bureau staff of zip code areas with large Arab populations, in addition to the cities of Chicago and Peoria in Illinois.[9] Here, then is an accurate description of the southwest suburbs: these suburbs have a majority Euro-white popu-lation with a demographically significant and growing Arab American population of at least 10 percent across the entire area, much higher in some suburbs than others; Arab Americans are highly visible as *the* dominant minority group in these suburbs; and the white population is culturally and politically hegemonic, with little Arab American (whether Muslim or Christian) civic or political representation.[10] Many Euro-white southwest suburbanites prefer to maintain their communi-ties as homogeneously white, a concept that in their understanding blends intersections of race and culture, and in this way they are quite similar to many whites in other predominantly white suburban areas. But because many southwest suburban families were part of the rapid white flight from the southwest side of Chicago during the 1970s and 1980s, when racialized attitudes were strong and became crystallized, their unfavorable attitudes toward people they perceive to be "racially" and culturally different run deep—as does their steadfast determination that they are not moving again.

The Crisis Point: Threat to Cultural Hegemony

Arab Muslims had their most serious and sustained hate encounters in the southwest suburbs, I argue, not because of the 9/11 attacks but because their rapid increase in settlement in these areas was perceived by some in the Euro-American (white) majority to have reached a point at which it threatened their communities and their way of life. The 9/11 attacks were important because they provided the trigger event for unconcealed expressions of disdain; for a short while, they seemed to legitimate the open demonstration of hate. Hateful actions continued to occur for years after the 9/11 attacks because these actions were about matters much larger than post-9/11 backlash—they were about cultural hegemony and the "moral order" of the neighborhood. Sociologists have found that normative understandings of a neighborhood's moral order are often built on who "we" are not, or on what "we" do not do (Suttles 1968; Rieder 1985), and in the case of the southwest suburbs, such under- standings for a segment of whites were built on excluding differences perceived as racially, culturally, and religiously at odds with theirs. Standing outside the boundaries of acceptability for those who shared this view were "Arabians" (locally shared nomenclature) of any religious faith and Muslims, who together were perceived and treated by many whites as community outsiders and racialized others.

Negative attitudes toward Arab Americans in these areas, shaped by the American media and education system, existed long before the 9/11 attacks; my field research shows that they had been a continuing source of conflict at local schools in the 1990s. Arab American Christians and Muslims were together seen by whites as a racialized group ("Arabians"), and there is no evidence of Euro-American efforts to distinguish between them, except for an understanding held by many that they had the power to block from their communities the institution that symbolized the increasing presence and embeddedness in the area of Arab Americans— the mosque.[11] The extensive civic and political opposition that arose to the establishment of a new mosque in southwest suburban Palos Heights the year before the 9/11 attacks highlighted local power to enforce Arab American social and political exclusion. The town's city council voted unanimously to approve the use of city funds to force a buyout of Muslim property owners in order to stop the mosque, an act stating loudly that the town's political elite supported boundary-setting and social exclusion. Although the town's mayor said that he found this legislative action reprehensible, the Muslims agreed not to establish the mosque, and eventually they lost a civil rights suit over the matter. In the pre-9/11 era, the social distance between Arab Americans and their non-Arab neighbors in the southwest suburbs was high, and both groups lived largely parallel social lives in a shared physical space. Anti-"Arabian" attitudes were prevalent prior to the 9/11 attacks, but they did not burst into protracted violence until after the attacks occurred.

In the absence of social inclusion, local community bridging organizations, or intergroup social networks offering an alternative model of neighborhood coexistence, persons vested in anti-"Arabian" and anti-Muslim (these were the same people to them) sentiments were mobilized when the 9/11 attacks occurred, their actions encouraged by the explosion of mass media messages promoting hatred and suspicion of Arabs/Muslims. Acting en masse for a brief period of time without contest, they gathered at a local community institution (a high school) and assumed that they had tacit popular and law enforcement support for their actions. Law enforcement entered the scene as a force of containment when the mob approached the Bridgeview mosque, and defense arrived within days in the form of a multiethnic, multireligious, and multiracial group of persons mobilized largely from the city of Chicago and other parts of the metropolitan area. Mass collective expressions of hatred were then quashed, but individuals and small groups carried on the mission of harassment to keep the message of social exclusion alive. In sum, the co-occurrence of increasing Arab American movement into the area and the 9/11 attacks set off an accumulated anger held by a segment of the white population toward Arab/Muslim Americans, because their growing presence was perceived to threaten Euro-American cultural hegemony in the area. After the massive assembly of hate was contained and restrained, hatemongers holding these views continued to harass Arab and Muslim Americans, but had to do so at lower levels of organization.

The Siege on the Southwest Suburban Mosque

The day after the 9/11 attacks, some three hundred young southwest suburban whites gathered at Oak Lawn High School and organized a protest march to the Mosque Foundation of Bridgeview about two miles away, a collective effort allegedly instigated by a talk radio personality.[12] The group drove in parade-like fashion to the area near the Bridgeview mosque, waving American flags and shouting, "Death to the Arabs," then exited their cars to lay siege to the mosque. The predominantly Arab American neighborhood hosting the mosque and two Muslim schools had limited points of entry: barriers of railroads, factories, and an interstate highway had closed off access on three sides (see map 6.2). When local police became aware of the mob's plan, they called in other police agencies

Map 6.2   The Neighborhood Surrounding the Bridgeview Mosque

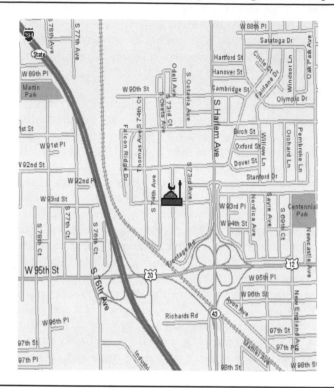

Source: © 2009 NAVTEQ. NAVTEQ is a registered trademark of NAVTEQ Corporation. NAVTEQ map content is used with permission.

to help, and more than one hundred suburban and state police officers armed in riot gear soon arrived on the scene. Police immediately sealed off the neighborhood around the mosque, an action facilitated by the preexisting barriers, and established entry checkpoints so that only persons who could prove they lived in the neighborhood could enter. The siege went on for two days, during which time Arabs and Muslims in the neighborhood lived in absolute fear.

An Arab American interviewee provides an extensive rendering of these events. His narrative reveals how the American flag was used by the mob of southwest suburban whites as a performance of outcasting, dramatizing their view of who is and who is not American.

> Late the next night, after my work was finished, I saw all the police cars coming down from Harlem Avenue with the sirens and lights. I thought there must be something wrong, something big. I was watching and

looking, and it seemed like it started by the mosque, the police cars. With all these police coming, it has to be something big, not a regular thing. I got worried and hoped nothing happened to the mosque, so I drove by and tried to see what was going on, and I tried to talk to a policeman, but he wouldn't talk. There was no smoke, nothing, so the mosque must have been safe, but I stayed there for a while.

I could see the kids, teenagers. They were saying to me, "Come on over, there's something here!" They were standing there with flags, and some were driving and honking, and there were some motorcycles coming too. Actually, when I was coming down, I turned on the news because I wanted to know what was going on, and they were talking about a demonstration in Oak Lawn by the Oak Lawn High School, which is near my house. So I was piecing it together. I tried to get permission from the police to go inside as an official of the Mosque Foundation, but they wouldn't let me in, which was fine, because I didn't care, as long I was sure everything was fine. I stood there for over an hour.

People were going back and forth with flags waving from the top of their cars or trucks. The people were not allowed in because they blocked it all the way to Ninety-first Street, because that's the only way you can get into this area. They blocked everything, from Ninetieth all the way to Ninety-fifth Street, so nobody could get in. It worked out good because there are natural borders like the train tracks. Of course, I was kind of worried because my colleagues were in the mosque. Some of them didn't know anything; some heard it on the news, but everybody was confused. It was kind of late at night, 11:00 P.M., and I stayed there until almost midnight.

For the record, I think the police did an excellent job. In a matter of minutes, they quarantined the whole area, and only people with an address there could go in. Nobody else could go in. They kept the mob, so to speak, outside.

The second day we tried to assess the damage and tried to find out what was going on, and we found out the story. This disk jockey called on people to go there. I think they sued the station's disk jockey for the costs, but I don't know what happened to that case. I never followed up on it.

Arabs and Muslims living in the neighborhood around the mosque told me that they were grateful for the police protection. Newspapers reported families "hiding behind closed curtains," not knowing how long it would be before it was safe to leave the house. Arab and Muslim American children were kept out of schools and women stayed at home; Arab and Muslim American men going to and from work was the only public movement in the neighborhood. Spending days in the neighborhood behind a wall of police with machine guns and passing through checkpoints in order to go home brought on a sense of social isolation. The police were legally required to protect the mosque and the neighborhood, but the mob embodied the loathing that Arab American and Muslim Americans had felt for years. An Arab American man explains his mixed feelings during the siege, when he felt simultaneously protected and isolated:

> You like to see the protection; at same time you feel isolated. It is a mixed feeling—am I under siege or under protection? Everyone was not feeling safe. Everyone was nervous. It was a horrible thing, 9/11. Hateful people took immediate action. People were marching on street. There was no clash, but some damage. I give credit to the mayor and entire police department for their swift action. It could have been much worse. If I think back about it, I think it was a good to close us off.

For some in this heavily ethnic Palestinian neighborhood, the checkpoints stirred memories of the Israeli checkpoints they had left behind in the occupied West Bank and Gaza. They felt as though their treatment as Israel's pariah had followed them even in exile.

> When the police closed off our neighborhood, it lasted almost one week. The schools did not open for days. They had to check our IDs to let us in. I thought I left checkpoints when I left the Middle East.

The Arab American man from this neighborhood whose life history interview is included in chapter 2 reported that rocks were thrown at the mosque and shots were fired at its back door prior to the mob's arrival. When the mob arrived, it was clear that the area had to be contained. He reported that he and his neighbors snuck quietly across the street in the middle of the night trying to figure out what to do. They had decided to take turns sleeping and keeping watch. Then he saw the mayor of Bridgeview, Steven Landek, walking through the neighborhood at two in the morning. "I picked up my phone and called my friend across the street, and I told him, 'Ali, you can go to sleep.' " The presence of the mayor signaled that the city of Bridgeview was not going to sacrifice its Arab and Muslim American community for hatemongers.

The earlier Mosque Foundation official's description of events in Bridgeview in the days following the 9/11 attacks continues with an acknowledgment of the support the community received from other sectors of the American public. Some citywide interfaith, ethnic, and civil rights organizations showed their disapproval of the mosque siege by offering protection to the mosque. This type of organizational support continued steadily after 9/11 and showed that not everyone accepted the idea that Arabs and Muslims should be held collectively to blame for the attacks. But as the following narrative indicates, most of this support was *not* from the "close neighborhood."

> On the second day, we decided that the [Muslim] schools should be closed until Friday to see what's going on. The whole community, especially the

women who wear the scarves or Islamic hijab, were discouraged to go out unless it was a necessity or if they were escorted by someone to protect them.

For the record, I think we had tremendous support from the community *at large.* When people got the news, we got a lot of calls coming into the mosque to support us. *Not necessarily from the close neighborhood, but the Chicago area . . .* tremendous support from the white community and condemnation of the acts of the protesters. A lot sent cards and flowers, and actually, we got more flowers than at a funeral. And of course a lot of them left messages. We also had a couple of bad ones, but the majority of calls were good.

We decided to hold a press conference at the mosque on Friday that week, and we invited some of the local politicians, and they were all supportive, and we had of course a lot of other civic organizations and churches calling us. They called to support any action and justice and asked what they could do for us. We were very thankful and grateful to the police for what they did. Some people were scared to come to Friday prayers, and we said we have to pray and we have to go on, and after that we met with the board of directors. We were scared to death, but we had to go out, that's life, you can't just sit inside, you know. You just have to be careful.

I personally suggested that some guys go and meet with those people. I said, "You're the same age. Those of us from the first generation should stay out of it. Ask them what they are protesting—the terrorist acts? We protest them too, so there's no difference. Why should we sit on the sidelines?" I encouraged them to go ahead and talk to them and let them know who you are. There's no harm in that. If things get bad, just withdraw from it and the police were there.

We received a lot of calls from people. Some people lost their jobs. Some were afraid to go to their jobs. It's almost three years later, and the effect is still going on. There were some arrests, especially some of those who did not have any papers for them to stay in the country. That was a problem. People were afraid to do business because there were some arrests by the police. In the suburbs here in this area, the police are generally good. They know the community very well, so they had no reason . . . some of them, when they got stopped for a ticket, were asked about what nationality they are, something like that. Of course, after that, when the new PATRIOT Act came out, that actually did more damage in the community, and the FBI was going around of course questioning people and talking to people about these things. And people got scared, no doubt about that. [emphasis added]

The narrative moves from the mosque siege to the ensuing problems faced by the Arab/Muslim community, all of which added up to a cycle of fear: issues around jobs, arrests, police stops, FBI monitoring, visas, traveling, and the vulnerabilities created by the PATRIOT Act. The siege on the mosque was followed by what felt like a full-circle siege on the community.

This narrative also reflects early recognition that Muslim women wearing hijab were likely to experience attacks, an estimation borne out in fact throughout the following years and discussed in further detail in chapter 7. Finally, it refers to a press conference at which local political officials were invited to speak. This event was an important step in the post-9/11 socially integrative civic activism of southwest suburban Arab and Muslim Americans, who were now able to get the attention of and engage the political establishment because of the social emergency that had been created. The crisis around the Bridgeview mosque brought many Arab and Muslim Americans to the realization that they needed to be part of local civic and political culture whether others wanted them to be or not—at a minimum for their protection, but also to assert their equal status as Americans, something both the flag wavers and the American government appeared to be determined to take away. In a decision mirrored across the nation, Arab and Muslim community leaders came to the conclusion that social apartheid at the local level and social and political exclusion at the national level had gone on long enough. They realized too that the burden of change largely fell upon them.

For at least the first week after the 9/11 attacks, Arab Muslims living in the southwest suburbs said they were afraid to leave their homes to shop, work, or pray. The Palos Heights machete attack, the smashing of windows of Arab American businesses, and the siege on the Bridgeview mosque, the only mosque serving the large Muslim community of the southwest suburbs until 2006, left members of the Arab American and American Muslim communities with a sense of trepidation. The mosque siege was particularly haunting, and some two years afterward this Arab Muslim man from the neighborhood around the mosque spoke of a continuing sense of danger.

> We all changed. I'm on the alert. We are all vulnerable. This is known to be an Arab neighborhood. If I was in a non-Arab neighborhood, I'd be afraid; in an Arab neighborhood, we are targeted. As neighbors, we were concerned especially when the mobs were here. We could not enter or leave without being stopped by police. We have a mosque here, and people have to come in. We get concerned.

In 2002 the Bridgeview Mosque Foundation began hosting open house *iftars* (the evening meal that breaks the daily fast) during Ramadan, to which local political officials, public servants, and schoolteachers, among others, were invited to learn about Islam and engage in one-on-one conversations with local Muslims. It is significant to note, however, for reasons explained later, that when Bridgeview's Universal School, a Muslim girls' high school, wanted to invite girls from another high school to visit as a gesture of outreach, they turned to Maria High School on the southwest side of the city instead of a suburban school.

Analysis of the Siege

The pattern of violence that erupted in the southwest suburbs after the 9/11 attacks conforms to what Jack Levin and Jack McDevitt (2002, 77) identify as defensive hate crimes: "In defensive hate crimes the hate-mongers seize on what they consider a precipitating or triggering event to serve as a catalyst for the expression of their anger." Perpetrators of this type of hate crime typically do not leave their own neighborhoods to look for victims, according to Levin and McDevitt. Instead, they attack persons whom they see as outsiders and intruders in their own neighborhoods and interpret their own actions as a moral crusade. Levin and McDevitt report that defensive hate crimes are most likely to occur after the in-migration of those perceived as outsiders has reached a *critical mass*: "In many previously all-White suburban communities, minorities have reached a critical mass, causing White residents to feel threatened by the influx of newcomers. This seems to be the point at which hate crimes escalate" (192). Donald Green, Dara Strolovitch, and Janelle Wong (1998) examined a number of large data sets to test a range of hypotheses about the causes of racially motivated hate crimes. After examining patterns of racially motivated crime in fifty-one New York City communities and comparing them to other case studies, they concluded that victimization tends to be higher in areas

> where whites have long been the predominant racial group, particularly when these areas experience significant growth in minority population. . . . This finding suggests a proposition with far-reaching social and theoretical implications: racially motivated crime stems not from economic frustration but from an exclusionary impulse on the part of whites defending what they perceive to be their territory. (373)

Green and his colleagues (1998, 393) also found that "fewer incidents are directed against a racial minority group when its numbers are large relative to the population," because at a certain point the symbolic attachment of whites to the area is undermined, as well as the networks and norms that facilitate attacks, causing the "most virulent opponents . . . to quit the community" (397). These theories help to explain why Arab Americans in Dearborn, Michigan, the Detroit suburb with the largest Arab American population in the country (comprising some 50 percent of the population), reported a relatively low rate of hate crimes after 9/11 (Baker et al. 2004). Green and his colleagues (1998) found that these hate crime patterns did not hold up when minority groups moved into neighborhoods dominated by other minority groups, which may partly explain why Arab Americans on the southwest side of Chicago did not experience the same protracted violence and harassment *as Arabs or Muslims* (as opposed to other types of violence common to the area) as did Arabs and Muslims in the southwest suburbs. Demography alone, however, should not be understood as the key explanatory variable; rather, it is the attitudes and social relationships that are intertwined with demography that explain human behavior.

Referring back to the quotes that open this chapter, I thus interpret the hatreds expressed in them as reflective of a built-up anger at the perceived Arab American threat to the neighborhood's moral order rather than as emotionally driven responses to a single catastrophic event. I assert that when Colin Zaremba said he "hated Arabs and always has" while en route to lay siege on the Bridgeview mosque, and when Eric Nix said in 2002 that it was his hatred for Arabs that propelled him to hurl explosives into his Arab American neighbor's van, they were talking about an anger developed over an extensive period of time that was grounded in the everyday life of the neighborhood. Similarly, when Robert Shereikis attacked the Arab gas station attendant with a machete after he thought the Arab man was mocking him by calling himself an American, he was acting on a long-held perspective that Arab Americans are outsiders, invaders of the area who do not qualify as Americans in the way he understood the meaning of the term.

The Texture of Urban Backlash

The same week as the siege on the Bridgeview mosque, Arab Americans on the southwest side of Chicago were experiencing the climate of harassment that largely characterized the metropolitan area and the nation immediately after the attacks. Someone broke a glass door on the Sixty-third Street storefront Al-Qassem mosque, women in hijab reported being taunted while walking or driving through the area, garbage was dumped on an Arab American family's lawn, and, as noted earlier, police recorded seven hate crimes on the southwest side of the city in the month of September. On October 3, 2001, a press report described the "Arab neighborhood" along Sixty-third Street as "returning to normal at varying paces." Muslim women in hijab had not returned to visibility, for instance, nor had the ethnic mix of people who normally patronized Arab businesses (Winograd 2001).

> Since Sept. 11, life has returned to normal at varying paces for those who live and work in Chicago's Arab neighborhoods—mostly along 63rd Street near Midway Airport. At the Nile Restaurant, 3259 63rd St., a waiter said white and Latino clients come in less frequently. At Rachid Bakery, a clerk said his female Muslim customers have disappeared. "The ones with veils are afraid of harassment," he said in reference to Muslim women who traditionally wear head coverings.

In most of the reported cases of harassment, the locations, perpetrators, and meanings of hostile acts were quite different from what occurred in the middle-class, majority-white suburbs. On the southwest side, the incidents tended to occur on the streets; in the suburbs, they occurred in stores and shopping malls. On the southwest side, most of the reported confrontations occurred among youth, whereas in the southwest suburbs they spanned the generations. In the urban neighborhoods, where violence, hate speech, and police harassment were common experiences for youth even before 9/11, ethnic insults had a different contextualized meaning than they had in the southwest suburbs.

> Things here and there were said in terms of, like, physical confrontation. Kids that we work with would come in and occasionally say that, you know, they were confronted, and in the process of being confronted, verbal insults were hurled at them, "Osama bin Laden" and things like that. But, again, I think this was an exacerbation of an already tense environment where there were already a lot of, you know, particularly among the kids we work with, a lot of street altercations, and they're not always along ethnic or racial lines. A lot of Arab kids are in gangs, and a lot of Latinos, and a lot of others, but I think after 9/11 it just became more of a convenient pretext for something with tensions that already existed.

Although there was an immediate backlash on the southwest side, local residents often chose to frame these incidents in the larger context of shared discrimination:

> They dumped garbage on one woman's yard, or the women here in the neighborhood, as they were walking down the street, people yelled at them and spit on them. You know, things like that. I don't think it's happening as much now, but it kind of comes with the territory. It's not as much, but you know that it is happening. I mean, there are so many things that happen every day to community members. We live in an environment where kids get shot. Many Arabs face discrimination, and then you have Latinos who face discrimination. It's like, there's so much going on in our community.

The connection that was being made in the media between Arabs, Muslims, and terrorism appears to have been more contested on the southwest side of the city, as it was interpreted in the context of shared experiences with institutional discrimination.

> Among the youth, they don't buy that crap in the first place. If there was anything, it became just another way for kids, who are sometimes really tough to one another, to talk with one another.... Why working-class kids? I mean, I've got to put it in context: "They want that nigger." They want him almost as much as they want one of ours now, and the idea of Osama bin Laden being the ultimate outlaw. Tupac Shakur had a group called the Outlaws where each one of them took on the names of nationally hated figures. Particularly among the working-class, disenfranchised

black community, they already come from a culture where they have become demonized and brutalized in that context. So while they may not articulate all of that, they are just inherently skeptical.

Now, for the older black community in this area, I think we have a tremendous amount of experience with just really brutal resistance to assimilation, and they've just responded to it. In fact, one of my neighbors heard one of the black neighbors [making comments about Arabs], and she got really upset by that and mobilized her whole block and got involved in trying to get to know the rest of the Arab community, and that's not uncommon.

Skepticism around mainstream media messages that connected Arabs and Muslims to terrorism and that incited suspicion of them may have been easier to produce in these areas, yet it could not be taken for granted. Some African Americans openly voiced their cynicism over the sudden concern of Arab and Muslim Americans with racial profiling. Local community activists—who had various missions but shared the common objectives of bridging ethnic and racial gaps and building a sense of shared community—mobilized, equipped with narratives of commonality, to convince local whites, African Americans, and Latinos (who have their own experiences with racism, stereotypes, stigma, and exclusion) to challenge the simplistic formulas emerging from the mainstream media. Community organizers worked to transform negative sentiments into collective efforts against racism. A local Arab American resident said she felt that this work, which had been started years before 9/11, had clearly paid off:

It's become better now with our neighbors, and now we're doing the best we can to make more good relationships between each other. Our neighbors are Middle Eastern, Hispanic, and African American. Also, at the churches, the nuns and priests took care to protect the mosque, and we have a connection now with all of them. We meet together all the time to discuss problems. In this neighborhood, the relationship between everybody is getting better. We have a beautiful community. Everybody gets along with each other. We respect each other. We built a bridge between our neighbors. Now people can understand more about the Middle Eastern and Muslim people. It's getting better, I think, in this community. Thirteen years of work!

Relations between members of the Arab American community and the local Chicago police district had been problematic for at least the past ten years, according to my earlier research. Arab Americans charged that police did not come to their aid when called and that they harassed and sometimes beat up Arab American youth, charges also made by black and Latino youth. The 9/11 attacks added a new pretext to the challenges faced by Arab American youth on the southwest side vis-à-vis the police. Yet at the same time, the outburst of hate crimes across the city forced Chicago police in districts with large Arab American populations to undergo sensitivity training. An Arab American man discusses his experience:

> After 9/11, there were comments that were hurled at kids while they [the police] were beating them up, calling them this and that. The only difference is not the cause of beating them up, but this time calling them "Osama bin Laden." It just became a pretext again for the hostility. I think young kids of color who are associated with drugs, and gang members, have grown to expect it. Though, having said that, I think the [police] district in the time period was sincerely interested in trying to deal with some concerns of the community. I personally spoke for the entire day in the district, and I saw a great difference between young cops of color and the old-timers in the way they responded to me when I was trying to talk to them.

The Arab Muslims interviewed in this study who lived on the southwest side said they felt safer there *as Arabs and Muslims* than in the southwest suburbs, an area they frequented to shop and worship. Women wearing hijab said that after the initial outburst of hostility ended, they walked more freely and felt much less hostility in urban public spaces, not only on the southwest side but in other urban places that were occupied by a diverse range of people and showed no visible white hegemony. This sense of safety from anti-Arab/Muslim attacks ended when they entered southwest suburban residential areas, public spaces, and shopping malls. Arab American men and women both commented on this difference. One Arab American man from the southwest side speaks about driving on Harlem Avenue in southwest suburban Bridgeview:

> If I'm driving out to Harlem after 9/11, driving out where it's a white majority, especially if they're working-class white folks, I'd think twice about being on the streets.

Another Arab American man compared the meaning of being called "Osama" in multiracial urban neighborhoods to the meaning of this act in the suburbs:

> For instance, when I got called once, "What's up with Osama bin Laden?" for me, I responded to that very differently than I would if I was out in the suburbs.

An Arab American woman compared the general level of urban violence that exists on the southwest side to the anti-Arab/Muslim hostility in the southwest suburbs:

> Here there is a cycle of violence so that in general you don't feel safe. But it's not because I'm Arab, and I don't dress in a traditional way also. So

when I go to the [suburban Arab strip] mall there, I really don't feel that comfortable, because it's all Arab and Muslim. Even when I go to the mosque, I don't feel safe. Even though you think you would feel safe because you're in a homogeneous community, I just feel like it's kind of hostile around us over there.

Rings of Protection Around the Southwest Side Mosque

Within days of the 9/11 attacks, plans were put in place at the Southwest Organizing Project (SWOP) to mobilize its member organizations to form a protective circle around the Sixty-third Street mosque whose door had been vandalized so that Muslims could safely attend Friday prayers. The head of the mosque, a SWOP member-institution, had contacted SWOP for support after the attack on its property. Aware of the siege under way at the Bridgeview mosque, local Arabs/Muslims were worried. SWOP's members included churches, mosques, and community organizations housed within the five Chicago southwest side community areas mentioned earlier. It was an outgrowth of the Southwest Cluster Project, an organizing effort affiliated with the Catholic archdiocese that was established in the 1980s to help stabilize the area during a period of rapid demographic change. To succeed in its mission, the Cluster Project reimagined the traditional Catholic concept of "community" to extend beyond the narrow definition of "parishioners" (Wedam 2005). So, for example, a Catholic parish would embrace not only the local Lithuanians and those who came in from the suburbs to attend Mass at their traditional parish church, but also the Latinos, African Americans, and Arab Americans who lived within parish boundaries but did not worship there. This inclusive vision was transferred to SWOP, which was formed in 1996 as a

> broad-based organization of churches, schools, mosques and other institutions in Southwest Chicago, which will enable families to exercise common values, determine their own future and connect with each other to improve life in their neighborhoods. SWOP's leaders are dedicated to building relationships across differences, and to bringing the common concerns of their institutions into the public life of the community as they act to "stand for the whole" in Southwest Chicago. (SWOP 2009)

Although SWOP needed no prompting to agree to form a "circle of peace" around the Sixty-third Street Al-Qassem mosque, events in Bridgeview reinforced its necessity. Sister Margaret Zalot, president of Maria High School, a Catholic girls' high school in the area and a SWOP member-institution, said that she planned to participate in the circle, but then she became even more passionate about the plan when she passed a large group of youth gathering at southwest suburban Oak Lawn High School while she was on her way home from a meeting. The scene reminded her of the racist white mobs she had observed on the southwest side of the city in the 1980s.

> On the way home, I took Ninety-fifth Street to Southwest Highway. That was where they were beginning to march against the Bridgeview mosque. Not knowing what was happening, I had to put on the radio. I was coming from an antiracism workshop, and here I was in the midst of it! When I figured out what was taking place, I decided I *really* needed to go on Friday. I was planning to go, but now I knew I really needed to go. . . . [*What did you see?*] I just remember driving through, and maybe they were just gathering together, and I remember it was a very scary thing. [*What did you see that made it "scary"?*] People were gathering where people don't usually gather. I don't know if it was the vans or the flags. It reminded me of this neighborhood in the 1980s.

On Friday, September 14, a "circle of peace" composed of local community members surrounded the Sixty-third Street Al-Qassem mosque. The gathering succeeded not only in protecting Muslims at prayer but in sending a message across the neighborhood that tolerance and mutual respect were integral components of the moral order of the neighborhood. Hatred and harassment of Arab and Muslim Americans were not welcome, and community institutions would actively defend against such actions. Police were not in the picture.

The following Friday, students at Maria High School sent handwritten notes of concern, compassion, and prayer to congregants at the Al-Qassem mosque. Sister Margaret handed them out to persons leaving the mosque, who, she said, "were crying" after reading them. The Friday circles continued and captured the attention of organizations across the city and the mainstream media, including a feature segment on *ABC World News*. The *Daily Northwestern* (Winograd 2001) reported these events as follows:

> On Friday, as Muslims prayed inside the mosque, community leaders gathered outside the once-broken doors to "physically and symbolically" protect those inside, event organizer Matt McDermott said. "We stand up for the Muslim community and they stand up for us," said McDermott, coordinator of the Southwest Organizing Project, a Chicago organization that includes 25 churches, schools and mosques. After the service, the crowd of more than 30 merged with those exiting the mosque to show their support. It was the third consecutive Friday—Islam's holy day—that non-Muslim Arabs, Jews, and Christians assembled for the event.

Less than a month after the 9/11 attacks, a Maria High School class spent the day at Universal School, a Muslim girls' high school next to the

Bridgeview mosque. The field trip was organized by an African American teacher, who felt the need to do something positive. She had asked Sister Margaret if she knew any Muslim schools or principals; through SWOP, Sister Margaret obtained contact names and numbers.

> They wanted to write letters. I got her a phone number. She called them, and they responded to her because they knew the work we do here. They weren't answering phone calls at the time. A school that was in the Bridgeview mosque's backyard asked: . . . "Yes, how do we connect with them [Maria High School]?"

The administrators of Universal School had wanted to invite in a class of peers to see the school and meet their students, but they wanted to invite persons with whom they could feel safe—not a foregone conclusion so shortly after the siege on their neighborhood. They trusted Maria High School because of its active participation in supporting the Sixty-third Street mosque.

In November 2001, United Power for Action and Justice and the Council of Islamic Organizations of Greater Chicago (a member of United Power) organized a citywide rally at Navy Pier; a Maria High School student spoke at the rally representing SWOP, which was affiliated with United Power.[13] The event, whose theme was "Chicagoans and Islam," was organized "in response to the tragic events of September 11 and the retaliatory backlash against Chicago-area Muslims" and was attended by some three thousand people.[14] The event was intended to send a message of unity across the Chicago area. Ten months later, on the first anniversary of the 9/11 attacks, Muslim girls from Bridgeview's Access and Universal Schools came to the southwest side to visit girls at Maria High School.

Temperatures Rise Again in the Southwest Suburbs

A few years later, in 2004, when St. Michael's Church in suburban Orland Park, some thirteen miles southwest of Sixty-third Street, wanted to invite speakers to a rally, the school principal and pastor turned to Maria High School on the southwest side of the city to find voices of youth espousing intergroup solidarity. Sister Zalot recalls thinking: " 'Don't they have young people out there who can do the same thing?' That's what I thought at the time. They called here to get somebody to go there. By that time our kids just knew a whole lot more because of their interactions." St. Michael's Church (a United Power member) was among the local community institutions that supported a group of Arab and Muslim Americans who sought a building permit for a new mosque just outside of southwest suburban Orland Park, an effort that was highly contested by organized members of the local community. The Orland Park city council was forced by strong community opposition to the mosque to hold three public hearings on the matter. Mosque opponents at the hearings often referred to characteristics of the "Muslim race" in their arguments, highlighting their racialized perspective on local Arab and Muslim Americans. The following statements from the final public hearing illustrate that the discourses used by opponents, which tied all Muslims to support for terrorism, in many ways echoed government statements that members of these communities might be dangerous and needed to be watched. One of the group's leaders, Baptist minister Reverend Lyons, said:

> Now, as a Christian, a Baptist, and an American, I'm a firm believer in religious liberty and favor any religious group buying property or erecting a house of worship, but liberty has limits! No group that jeopardizes our personal safety or our national security is deserving of our tolerance. . . . I think, at this point, it would be helpful, fair, and important to make a distinction between radical Muslims and moderate Muslims. The radical Muslim terrorists kill people every day. Moderate Muslims do not kill people. Moderate Muslims supply the cash to the militant Muslims [loud clapping].[15]

A local resident also connected Muslims to terrorism and, in a discursive exercise with twinges of American "no fear" bravado, asserted that a mosque would bring trouble to the neighborhood:

> We don't hate you. We have no ill feelings for you. I think what's happened today is because of what's going on in America and because our boys are losing their lives every day [loud clapping]. We care about America. We care about what's going on because we don't want to bring it here. We're not saying that you'll bring it, but you must understand, that because you're tied in with this religion and a possible mosque in Orland Park, it will come to our doorstep. We have a concern for this . . . not a fear, as was mentioned before. We fear nothing here in America [lots of cheering and clapping]. . . . If there is trouble in Orland Park, it will be our police force that will have to take the brunt of it. It'll be our fire department who will have to come in and take care of the problem. It will be our tax dollars that will have to take care of this problem.[16]

In the end, Muslims won unanimous city council support for the mosque, and its construction was completed in 2006.[17] This political victory was the outcome of a number of important social factors: the *long-established* presence of a *small* number of Arab American families in the upper-middle-class suburb (including a well-known, respected family who owned a major international media archive headquartered in the town), significant institutional support from some local churches, and a growing sense on the part of many Americans of the need for religious tolerance, an awareness brought about by the severe backlash and civil rights losses experienced by Arabs and Muslims after 9/11.

Although the conflict over the Orland Park mosque was resolved in favor of the Arab and Muslim community at an institutional level, this positive outcome was not necessarily mirrored in changes at the level of day-to-day neighborhood encounters, according to my 2006 survey of Bridgeview and Orland Park mosque congregants.[18] This survey showed that Muslims from Bridgeview (independent of the mosque at which they worshiped) felt less hostility in local neighborhood social encounters than Muslims living in Orland Park. In light of the siege of the Bridgeview mosque in 2001, this 2006 finding may indicate that changes had occurred in Bridgeview in the intervening years and reinforce the findings of Green and his colleagues (1998, 397) that at some point "the symbolic attachment of whites to the area is undermined" and the "most virulent opponents . . . quit the community." Once again we may be witnessing the dialectic at work: a siege of hatred and exclusion bringing about its opposite, social inclusion, through the counteractive work of others.

The negative attitudes of their neighbors exposed during the Orland Park mosque hearings were disconcerting to many Arab Muslims. An Arab American doctor pointed out at the hearing that it was he who mosque opponents trusted to treat family members at the local hospital emergency room.

> They said they don't want people "like that" in our area, although we are their neighbors. They said, "We don't want more terrorism funding and terrorism in our neighborhoods," just all this negativity that wasn't there before. It was very shocking to me because these are people we know who are making these comments, people we thought were our friends and were our neighbors.

Opposition to the mosque gave voice and platform to anti-Muslim attitudes, offending Muslims living in the southwest suburbs, especially when the voices were those of their neighbors. The concerns of mosque opponents not only resonated with some statements of government officials about the dangers of Arab and Muslim Americans, but they repeated some of the charges of the most vigorous anti-Muslim activists in the United States. On the positive side, however, a southwest suburban interfaith group emerged and became institutionalized out of the mobilization that arose to support the Orland Park mosque.

Analysis: The Significance of Place

The very different public actions around mosques described here, especially the dissimilarity between the siege in Bridgeview and the ring of protection on the southwest side of the city during the first week after the 9/11 attacks, reveal the significance of place in post-9/11 Arab and Muslim American experiences. In one social context, there was a preexisting organizational capacity to introduce a layer of noise into mass-mediated messages of hatred and suspicion and to organize protective action across racial, ethnic, and religious lines. In another social context, the southwest suburbs, voices of racial bigotry went largely undisturbed (although they were contained by the police), and the mob that organized at a local high school may have initially felt some degree of tacit support for their actions. In the southwest suburbs, two sets of neighbors faced off against each other—one hiding behind locked doors, the other ready for violent action—with armed police poised in the middle. These actions around mosques both expressed and set the moral tone for their neighborhoods in the months and years to follow.

These variations also speak to the contextual meaning of race and the ways in which "difference" can be mobilized—as a force of hatred or a force of solidarity. Precisely because they had been racialized as "others" and largely excluded from participation in local mainstream institutions, Arab and Muslim Americans could easily be symbolically transformed into enemy aliens in the southwest suburbs. On the southwest side, on the other hand, active efforts were undertaken to undermine mainstream messages that promoted hatred and fear and to protect Arabs and Muslims, who were institutionally at least equal participants in a shared community. These efforts did not begin on 9/11 but had been going on for years. While the racialized status of Arab/Muslim Americans made it easier to mobilize solidarity with them among urban people of color and more difficult to do so among suburban whites, in both cases the solidarity had to be mobilized and the interpretations made.

The interwoven character of relationships on the southwest side of the city brought about a sense of safety for Arab Muslims *as Arabs and Muslims,* even though the neighborhood was by other measures not particularly safe. They were well aware of what was happening in the majority-white southwest suburbs and saw that it was not happening on the southwest side. Danger became attached to whiteness. This Arab Muslim woman echoes the sentiments of many others when she says that she felt safer on the southwest side than in the southwest suburbs.

> Actually, I feel safer in this community than going to Eighty-seventh and Roberts Road [suburbs], where it's all Arab. Actually, I don't, at all, feel safe there. I feel that's such a target place. Here, I feel comfortable when I walk up Sixty-fourth Street, but I've been working here for ten years and people know me. It's a mixed neighborhood, and it's kind of like my own place.

Many Arab Muslims on the southwest side interviewed in this study thought the solidarity and relative safety they experienced in that part of the city was "inherent" because they lived among people of color—other Arabs, Latinos, and African Americans, with a mix of whites. They knew their experiences were different from what was happening in the majority-white southwest suburbs, and race seemed to provide a reasonable explanation. It might have been that because of their own historic experiences, African Americans were less likely than others to attack Arab Americans or their homes or businesses. It might have been that, because Islam is more firmly rooted among African Americans, they were less likely to attack a Muslim. Chicago hate crime data showed very low rates of attacks on Arabs/Muslims in African American–majority neighborhoods. The same data, however, showed high rates in predominantly Latino neighborhoods. Perhaps on the southwest side, where Latino, African American, and Arab American youth shared public high schools, there was an awareness of similar racialized status, producing a natural solidarity. It is more likely, however, that such notions are learned.

Defended neighborhoods theory would predict that race matters, not inherently, but at the level of social structure and context. Hate crimes executed to defend against perceived threats to the neighborhood are correlated with the white race, but this construct actually represents "whiteness," a sense of entitlement to cultural hegemony held by some whites that can thrive institutionally in demographic contexts with large white majorities. The southwest side, where Arab Americans have lived for decades (although in the "old days" they were often seen as white), is racially mixed, so there is no white hegemony to defend anymore (as there was in the 1960s and early 1970s). Nonetheless, the neighborhoods of the southwest side are still places whose residents are socially invested: they do not want dangerous terrorists in their community any more than southwest suburbanites do. Defended neighborhoods theory is useful for explaining the varying outcomes found in this study, but what are the social processes at work behind them if we reject the notion of racial inherency, whether for whites or for people of color?

We need to complicate this picture: we need to explain why blacks, whites, and Latinos living among Arabs on the southwest side did not perceive Arabs or Muslims as a threat, or if they did, why they did not act on such perceptions in the persistently violent ways of the southwest suburbs. We further need to ask these questions in light of opinion poll data showing that there were not overwhelming differences in viewpoints across major racial-ethnic groups on a range of matters related to Arabs and Muslims after the 9/11 attacks. Table 6.3 reveals a complex range of attitudes and attitude changes toward Muslim Americans and Islam by whites, nonwhites, blacks, and Hispanics; what is important for our purposes here is that race predicts little across question categories and over time, and that whites did not always hold more negative views than either Hispanics or blacks (Keeter and Kohut 2005).[19] Indeed, the

Table 6.3   Attitudes Toward Muslim Americans and Islam, by Race

Change in Opinion About Muslim Americans After 9/11

Race	March 2001			Mid-November 2001			
	Favorable	Unfavorable	Don't Know	Favorable	Unfavorable	Don't Know	Change in Favorable
White	43%	25%	32	60%	18%	22	+17
Nonwhite	51	22	27	55	16	29	+4
Black	52	24	24	52	19	29	0
Hispanic[a]	48	21	31	56	18	26	+8

Opinion of Islam and Muslim Americans, July 2005

Race	Opinion of Islam			Opinion of Muslim Americans			
	Favorable	Unfavorable	(VOL.) No opinion	Favorable	Unfavorable	(VOL.) Don't Know/Ref	(N)[b]
White	38%	37%	25%	53%	25%	22%	(818)
Nonwhite	44	32	24	61	22	17	(173)
Black	44	35	21	64	26	10	(109)
Hispanic[a]	33	38	29	52	26	22	(63)

Violence and Islam

Race	July 2003			July 2005			
	More Likely to Encourage Violence	Doesn't Encourage Violence More Than Other Religions	Neither/Don't Know/Ref	More Likely to Encourage Violence	Doesn't Encourage Violence More Than Other Religions	Neither/Don't Know/Ref	Change in Encourage Violence
White	45%	41%	14%	37%	46%	17%	-8
Nonwhite	38	42	20	29	56	15	-9
Black	38	46	16	28	56	16	-10
Hispanic[a]	45	35	20	—	—	—	—

Source: Keeter and Kohut (2005).

Note: VOL. indicates that the response option was not offered to the respondents by the interviewer, but rather was recorded if the respondent gave this response.

[a] pp. 66–7. The designation Hispanic is unrelated to the white-black categorization.
[b] pp. 68–9. Sample size applies to "Opinion of Muslim Americans" results. Sample sizes for "Opinion of Islam" results are approximately twice as large.

perpetrator of the first post-9/11 revenge killing in the United States was a Latino, who shot gas station attendant Balbir Singh Sodhi to death in Mesa, Arizona. (Sodhi was a Sikh mistaken for a Muslim.) According to Human Relations Commissioner Gunn, and judging by the neighborhood locations of hate crimes, the perpetrators of the early post-9/11 hate crimes in Chicago were members of all racial groups. While it is compelling to argue, as did a number of study interviewees, that shared experiences with discrimination, dehumanization, stereotyping, and profiling *automatically* produced a "people of color" solidarity between Arabs, Muslims, African Americans, and Latinos (a proportion of the latter two groups being Muslim), I would argue that the embrace of Arab and Muslim Americans as "people like us" had to be socially created.

The Role of Intergroup Contacts

The southwest side of Chicago not only was racially different from the southwest suburbs but could not have been more different in terms of social institutions with its plethora of pan-racial, pan-ethnic, community-based organizations that stressed building community, finding commonalities, and bridging differences. Local institutions embracing these efforts included an areawide youth collaborative, a women's organization, a development corporation, a Muslim action organization, a local YMCA, at least ten churches, two mosques, and a range of ethnic organizations that worked together during times of crisis, which were frequent in these neighborhoods. These were not always easy neighborhoods in which to live; safety, gangs, and street violence were a constant worry (Cainkar 1998). Arab Americans lived in neighborhoods characterized by heterogeneity, and Arab/Muslim American activists in these neighborhoods partnered with African American, Latino, and Euro-American activists to create a space that accepted and was built on diversity.[20]

In the southwest suburbs, there were no organized civic or political efforts that bridged the communities of Arab Americans and non-Arab Americans, who, although neighbors, were by 2001 leading largely separate lives. Two primary sites of intergroup contact in the southwest suburbs were schools and shopping malls, and these were places where Arab American families truly learned that they were not really welcome in the area. "Arabian" kids built social networks with other "Arabian" kids, and these friendship networks ran parallel to those of white kids, periodically spinning off rivalries and fights among boys. Little systematic work at a social or political level had been done to alter this "apartheid"-like situation, aside from occasional consultations with experts to help school staff learn about Arab culture. Alongside reasons of religious training, these animosities and a strong sense that Arab/Muslim American kids needed protection from ridicule and reinforcement of their own human dignity heightened the motivation of Muslims to build their own schools in the southwest suburbs. Antagonism toward Arabs and Muslims was allowed to continue in the southwest suburbs because local sociopolitical norms permitted it. When the 9/11 attacks occurred, the preexisting "us-and-them" social dynamic of the southwest suburbs was easily transformed by the violently inclined into an "us-versus-them" moral order, but only for a short period of time. Collectively organized manifestations of this antagonistic moral order were quashed by police, solidarity reinforcements from other parts of the metropolitan area arrived, and Arab and Muslim American institutions in the area began actively inserting themselves into the lives of the local white community. What remained for years after the attacks was cultural sniping: sporadic but persistent acts of hostility directed by individuals and small groups—until collectively organized efforts resurged again in Orland Park in 2004 to oppose the new mosque, this time channeled into public hearings.

This absence of bridging organizations is unique to neither Chicago's southwest suburbs nor suburbs with significant Arab American populations; rather, it is characteristic of American suburbs in general. Indeed, prior to the large immigration of the late twentieth century and the trend toward immigrant settlement in the suburbs (Singer 2004), American suburbs were largely majority-white places where traditional American social organizations such as the Scouts and baseball leagues built community spirit. New immigrants and their children often found themselves socially barred from these traditional bastions of Euro-American culture—that is, until efforts to bridge gaps between communities were built. Green and his colleagues (1998) predicted that the racial conflict that once characterized cities was likely to move to the suburbs once immigrants and minorities began moving to them. Chicago's southwest suburbs were thus not unique as suburbs in their white cultural hegemony over civic organizations or political power or in their lack of bridging institutions; their uniqueness lay in their large Arab and Muslim American populations and the huge social cleavages that were manifestly exposed in locally flavored responses to the 9/11 attacks.

In sum, when the 9/11 attacks occurred, the mobilization of solidarity across groups that had been well-established practice on the southwest side of the city made it much less likely that Arab and Muslim Americans would be perceived as a threat to the community's way of life. There, Arabs, Muslims, Latinos, African Americans, and whites were not unentangled strangers to each other. The normative tone of the neighborhood discouraged hostilities directed at racial or religious groups, although gang violence often broke these norms. For her part, Sister Zalot thought race had little to do with the intergroup solidarity that characterized the southwest side after 9/11. "I think not. Having been a part of a group where you had to learn to get along with different people is what made a difference." Thomas Pettigrew and Linda Tropp's (2006, 766) meta-analysis of 515 studies of intergroup contact concludes that intergroup contact does reduce prejudice and that its effects translate "beyond participants in the immediate contact situation" to the entire outgroup. It may then be possible to conclude that the work of a host of local community organizations—SWOP, the Southwest Youth Collaborative, the Arab American Action Network, the Latino Organization of the Southwest, the Southwest Development Corporation, Maria High School, the local office of Metropolitan Family Services, local churches and mosques—built bridges across groups and deployed in practice a vision of diversity before 9/11, which after 9/11 gave them interpretive power over mainstream media messages of collective Arab/Muslim guilt for the 9/11 attacks. Their active efforts to mobilize social solidarity immediately after the 9/11 attacks reinforced this vision and set the moral tone for the social order of neighborhood. This moral tone of respect for difference was sorely lacking in the southwest suburbs, both before and after 9/11, and in that void, those who would act on feelings of hatred felt that they had tacit permission to do so.

Conclusion

Two events that occurred around mosques in metropolitan Chicago shortly after the 9/11 attacks, the siege in southwest suburban Bridgeview and the "circle of peace" on the city's southwest side, demonstrated a significant difference in responses to the 9/11 attacks as experienced by Arab/Muslim American communities. These differences correlated with other forms of hate activity: Arab Muslims reported quantitatively more aggression motivated by hate, and more persistent such aggression, in the majority-white southwest suburbs where they lived in substantial numbers, as compared to the racially and ethnically mixed urban neighborhoods where they also lived in substantial numbers, and also as compared to majority-white suburban areas where their presence was proportionately small. These differences highlight the fact that race alone does not predict outcomes. Rather, race intersects with power and perceived entitlements; with definitions of whether a group is "like us" or "not like us"; with the relative size of the group perceived to be the "other" or the outgroup; as well as with perceptions of the threat that the outgroup poses to the community's moral order. In the perceptual field, there is room for a range of interpretations; definitions of outgroups and perceptions of threat are socially created and can be socially deconstructed and undone. Whether they will be created or deconstructed depends on a range of social forces, including media responsibility, organizational action, political interests, and the financial resources tied to those interests.

Hatred was easy to mobilize during the crisis of the 9/11 attacks, especially in the social context of mass-mediated messages that stirred up public anger, widely broadcast statements of key government officials that stoked fear, and preexisting negative attitudes toward Arabs and Muslims, without which the media messages and government statements would have largely fallen flat. Antipathy toward and hatred of Arabs and Muslims were prime materials for some (though not all) talk radio hosts, policy experts, pundits, journalists, and spokespersons for the evangelical Christian right after the 9/11 attacks. For their part, U.S. government officials were calling on Americans to refrain from attacking innocent Arabs and Muslims while at the same time asking the public to be watchful of the Arabs and Muslims in their communities, producing the massive response discussed in chapters 4 and 5. Taken together, these messages created a potent formula for inducing violence under the right set of social conditions.

This study shows that despite seemingly hegemonic messages, those conditions varied. Neighborhoods with significant Arab/Muslim populations showed different hate crime outcomes: depending on preexisting social conditions on the ground, it was easier for groups to mobilize either hatred or solidarity. While white racial dominance has been correlated with a propensity toward hate crimes, the key factor is not numerical superiority per se, but a sense of being entitled to determine whose culture and which values will define the moral order. If strong and organized efforts are brought to bear, this sense of entitlement is something that can be changed, because people can be convinced to see themselves as fundamentally different from or fundamentally similar to others. The history of American society is a history of such changes in social construction, as well as a history of strong resistance to change in some quarters.

As noted earlier, now that active efforts are being made to bring about positive changes in the American public's perceptions of Arabs and Muslims, those who perceive that they have something to lose from such changes have stepped up their own efforts. There are hundreds of examples of such stepped-up efforts, but a poignant one I noticed in early October 2008 was an issue of the *Milwaukee Journal Sentinel* that contained a free DVD entitled *Obsession,* a production designed to provoke fear of Islam and Muslims in the hearts of Americans. Sent to millions of American homes in areas considered contested in the 2008 presidential race (showing its relationship to policy interests), this action revealed that people who have a vested interest in encouraging hostility toward Muslims are extraordinarily well financed. This hate-promoting effort was not without a quick counterresponse. Scholars of Islam and Muslims issued a statement in late October charging that the video distribution was "part of an Islamophobic hate campaign" that fuels "prejudice against Americans who practice their Islamic faith and Muslims worldwide" and that portrays American Muslims "as anti-American and unfit to hold public office."[21] The Muslim Public Affairs Council held a press conference hosted by the Interfaith Alliance in Washington, D.C., on October 7, 2008, with nationally recognized Jewish, Christian, and Muslim leaders speaking out against the distribution of the DVD—which they referred to as an "anti-Muslim film"—to "28 million households in election swing states by a shadowy non-profit group called the Clarion Fund."[22] An accompanying interfaith statement, signed by more than two dozen Christian, Jewish, and Muslim leaders around the country, voiced "deep concern" over the broad distribution of a "divisive and anger-provoking" DVD that promotes "hatred," incites "fear," "dehumanizes Muslims," and furthers "ignorant stereotypes."[23] The duel of discourses is far from over, and a relationship between the interests of those who advance anti-Muslim discourses and their unstated preferences for who runs the American government is demonstrated by the film's selective distribution. Chapter 7 shows the danger of such discourses and the stereotypes they exploit as it examines how ideas about Muslims that play into simplistic dichotomies of civilized and uncivilized, free and unfree, democratic and authoritarian, choice and force, effectively expanded the universe of legitimate post-9/11 hate targets beyond "suspicious" Arab and Muslim men to Muslim American women in hijab.

Chapter 7

Gendered Nativism, Boundary Setting, and Cultural Sniping: Women as Embodiments of the Perceived Cultural Threat of Islam

As I told [a *Chicago Tribune* reporter], instead of doing an article on the mosque, do it on the level of fear in this community because people, especially women with head scarves, are easy targets.
—Arab American Woman Interviewed in Study

I N CHAPTER 6, I argued that the 9/11 attacks constituted a trigger event for the open expression of animosity toward Arab and Muslim Americans living in the southwest suburbs of Chicago, a sentiment that had been building long before the attacks and was related to perceptions associated with their increasing presence in the area. I compared the southwest suburbs to the southwest side of the city, also a place of significant Arab and Muslim American presence, and pointed out that hate actions in the urban area subsided after an initial post-9/11 flare-up, signaling a cleaner, more direct relationship between the 9/11 attacks and the acts of backlash. In the southwest suburbs, acts of harassment, vandalism, petty assault, and other expressions of hatred directed at Arab/Muslim Americans persisted for years after the attacks because they were about matters much larger than 9/11. Rather, they were grounded in notions that Arab and Muslim Americans posed a threat to the existing moral order of the neighborhood.

This chapter identifies some of the social understandings and knowledge tales that underlay the hostile behaviors of southwest suburban neighborhood defenders, informed as they were by meta-narratives circulating within American culture regarding the types of values allegedly held by Arabs and Muslims. It further attempts to explain why their search for visible targets left women as their primary victims. The mob siege on the neighborhood surrounding the Bridgeview mosque during the first few days after 9/11 was a collective, manifest expression of hatred felt by some residents of the southwest suburbs (sentiments articulated in the quotes that open chapter 6), but the mob participants learned rather quickly that communal expressions of hatred were going to face containment by law enforcement. Once this tactic of opposition to the presence of Arab and Muslim Americans was laid to rest, recourse was taken to cultural sniping, which was characterized by the intermittent but targeted actions of individuals and small groups.

Study data indicate that the perceived threat of Arabs/Muslims to the moral order of the neighborhood was not about security and had little to do with terrorism. The perceived threat was cultural, and its targets were gendered: Arab/Muslim women reported experiencing hate encounters at twice the rate of men. The relationship between gender- and place-based interpretations of threat is further supported by the finding that the overwhelming majority of hate actions reported by female study participants occurred in the southwest suburbs (where the majority of incidents overall occurred as well). The targets, however, were not simply Arab/Muslim women; they were women in hijab, who were disproportionately targeted in a place where Arab and Muslim men were readily identifiable. In light of these data (presented in quantitative detail later in this chapter), I conclude that women in hijab symbolized and embodied the perceived threat to the neighborhood's moral fabric. I argue that rather than violence or terrorism, the threat of women in hijab rests in perceptions that these women openly, even proudly, conform to a set of prescriptions and values that are interpreted as un-American, a meaning imputed to them by messages diffused throughout American culture. As perceived adherents to an un-American way of life, American women in hijab are easily transformed into enemy aliens who can be commanded by neighborhood defenders to "go home." The hate crime experts Jack Levin and Jack McDevitt (2002, 78) point out that the selection of victims in neighborhood defense hate crimes is not random; rather, these crimes are targeted at the "types of individuals" who represent the threat. Precision targeting is critically importance to neighborhood crusaders, whose actions are predicated on getting a specific message across.

Neighborhood defense theory explains why the specific social and demographic context of the southwest suburbs might produce a persistent pattern of hate acts, but it is American culture that provides the meanings and interpretations that lie behind these acts. Cultural messages offer the substantive material for claims of threat and assist in efforts to identify targets. Levin and McDevitt (2002, 37) argue that "hatred has long been an integral part of American mass culture, finding expression in art, music, politics, religion, and humor," and that a culture of hate plays a key role in supporting and encouraging hate crime activity. "Stereotypes . . . *justify* hate crimes in the mind of the perpetrator by providing him with the essential dehumanized images of vulnerable individuals" (46). Hatemongers therefore do not need to invent the cultural threat posed by certain groups because, as with all historically subordinated groups, the reasons such groups are said to pose a cultural threat are already scripted for us and socially communicated through gossip, rumors, stories, books, newspapers, cartoons, art, radio, television, film, and the Internet. No matter the medium, the reasons certain groups are to be disliked, shunned, excluded, interned, or expelled are offered to us—we do not have to work for them. Those who engage in such discourses ask that we trust in the truth of the message; we are not required to see the alleged aberrant characteristic in motion. At some eventual point, labeling, profiling, selective perception, provocation, and self-fulfilling prophecies will work together to help that "truth" appear. This is the brilliance of institutional discrimination: whether applied to Catholics, Jews, Muslims, African Americans, Native Americans, Arab Americans, Latinos, Asians, women, gays, or the disabled, systematic human behavior that creates inferior conditions for specific groups is able to produce situations in which, if we look long and hard enough, we may be able to find glimpses of the stereotype. Before and after 9/11, American mass culture possessed substantial resources for fomenting anti-Arab and anti-Muslim hatred (see chapters 3 and 4). A tool kit of messages and interpretations was ready to be mobilized for those seeking to act on hatred. The persistence of these discourses prior to 9/11 had produced a national climate that betrayed the more enlightened possibilities of the American people, a potential that only became evident when the hatred and thirst for revenge expressed by many Americans after 9/11 produced a new counterforce.

Group stereotypes are often gendered, such that men are said to pose one type of threat and women another. Gendered ideas were evident in the ways in which the American government and neighborhood defenders responded to the 9/11 attacks, but the question emerges: Why did one group focus on men and the other on women? The 9/11 attacks, by seeming to prove the stereotype that Arab and Muslim men are inherently violent, gave stronger voice and a wider platform to those whose interests helped construct it. Acting on a stereotype of Arab/Muslim men because it had little knowledge to go on, in part because of the American government's own prior behavior toward Arab and Muslim American communities, government officials after the 9/11 attacks referred to Arab and Muslim American communities as potential beds of suspected terrorists. The Bush administration constructed executive branch domestic security policies based on this notion—even though the 9/11 terrorists were neither Arab or Muslim Americans nor members of these communities (National Commission on Terrorist Attacks Upon the United States 2004)—and focused its policies on men. As recounted in chapter 4, American government agencies conducted widely publicized mass arrests and deported thousands of noncitizen Arab and Muslim men, who were referred to by the government as "terrorists," although they had been cleared of terrorist associations. Not only were the subjects of these policies men, but so were the overwhelming majority of the "suspicious persons" identified in the tens of thousands of "tips" called in by the public. Only two females, both sixteen-year-old girls, were detained and incarcerated on suspicions of being terrorists, and women were wholly excused from the government's special registration program.[1] Arrest, interrogation, incarceration, special registration, and removal were almost wholly implemented on male subjects, although the lives of women and children were nonetheless seriously affected by these measures.

Bill Ong Hing (2002, 4) argues that, like Japanese Americans after the attacks on Pearl Harbor, Arab and Muslim Americans were effectively de-Americanized after 9/11, positioned as foreigners and then denuded of their civil rights: "What has been happening to Muslims, Middle Easterners, and South Asians in the United States in the wake of September 11 is a process of ostracism from the American community—a de-Americanization process—that we have witnessed before. The process often involves two aspects—(1) the actions of private individuals and (2) official government-sanctioned actions."

De-Americanization revolves around notions of perpetual foreignness (Hing 2002) and an implicit lack of national loyalty (Akram and Johnson 2002). According to Hing (2002, 3–4), the actions of government and hatemongers work in tandem. "The message is one of exclusion: 'You Muslims, Middle Easterners, and South Asians are not true Americans' " (3). Whether citizens or noncitizens, the victim community is "forever regarded as immigrant America, as opposed to simply part of America and its diversity" (4). When perceived as non-American, such communities can be easily placed outside the boundaries of constitutional rights and removed from national understandings of social justice (Leiken 2004, 11). Arab and Muslim Americans were well aware that their citizenship had become different from that of other Americans.

> "I have to be cautious as a citizen of this country—that's not something an average American has to do," said an Arab-American Muslim waiting in line at the Al Rasheed meat market on 63rd Street. "After Timothy McVeigh, nobody said everyone with blue eyes and blonde hair is a danger to society." The man declined to give his name or hometown for fear of retaliation from law enforcement. (Winograd 2001)

It appears that Arab and Muslim Americans were de-Americanized in gendered ways: the source of their "perpetual foreignness" was interpreted differently depending on whether they were men or women. From the perspective of hindsight, a division of labor seemed to have evolved: the management of men as potential terrorists was the province of government agencies, while the management of women as perceived flagrant violators of American values was left to private actors.

I reproduce here some of the cultural matter that informed the neighborhood defenders' focus on women and provided them with rationales for their target selection. These include the substantive content of anti-Arab and anti-Muslim cultural discourses, which are nativist because they portray Arabs and Muslims as "enemies of a distinctively American way of life" (Higham 1955, 24), and government jingoisms that revolved around notions of freedom, hatred of freedom, and the needs of Afghani women wearing hijab. I also make note of Joane Nagel's (2003) theory that during times of crisis, when nationalism is mobilized, men and women are expected to conform to hegemonic definitions of masculinity and femininity. If Arab/Muslim men are pinned with being inherently violent and violence is acceptably a masculine trait, then Arab/Muslim men are in fact conforming to gendered standards, suggesting that neighborhood defenders should turn their attention to Arab/Muslim women wearing hijab, who are clearly violating American hegemonic standards of femininity. Arab/Muslim women in hijab should thus be "de-hijabed," or commanded to "go home." However, if Arab/Muslim men are seen as "perpetual foreigners" and as the enemy, extending Nagel's theory to the situation would seem to require that their masculinity not be engaged or rewarded at all; thus, a different type of action is called for: they need to be emasculated and feminized. This type of project is difficult (although not impossible) for private parties in the neighborhood to pursue and is best undertaken in places where the conditions are more appropriate; here, government actors with powers of confinement have far greater leeway.

My first line of argument as to why neighborhood defenders focused on women, however, is far simpler than these. I argue that in the very grounded reality of daily life in the southwest suburbs, there was no data to support the notion that Arab and Muslim men were either violent or terrorists. The stereotype just did not hold up when measured by experiences the defenders had before their eyes. While acknowledging that stereotypes need no confirmation with data, in fact they reduce contrary data to the exceptional; when it came to discerning the immediate threat to the neighborhood, violence was not the problem and men were not its symbols. Furthermore, other vague notions, such as that Arabs and Muslims hate democracy or want to take over the United States, had few visible indicators outside of interpretations centered on the presence or absence of American flags; the meanings imputed to these nongendered objects *were* acted upon. While women in hijab were as identifiable as Arab and Muslim men in the southwest suburbs, it was the meaning of hijab as it was commonly understood that was more culturally salient as something that needed to be fought, rendering Muslim women in hijab the visible targets of neighborhood crusaders.

A Neighborhood Focus on Women in Hijab

There was a fundamental problem with the stereotype that charged Arab and Muslim men living in American communities and walking freely in its public spaces with being terrorist threats: they had little record of the violence they were said to find so irresistible (outside of the fictional creations of filmmakers). Perhaps more than most Americans, Chicago's southwest suburbanites knew this fact the best. While they may have viewed Arab and Muslim Americans in a host of negative ways, they knew from direct experience that their Arab/Muslim neighbors did not live up to the stereotype of being violent. Arab and Muslim Americans could not be pinned with being purveyors of neighborhood violence, community agitation, murder, property crimes, or drug dealing, let alone with violent assault on American institutions. There was no evidence that Arab or Muslim Americans brought down a neighborhood's housing values, neglected their homes, or brought criminal elements into an area, some of the typical charges made against racial-ethnic minorities moving into white neighborhoods. By most standards and on most accounts, Arab and Muslim Americans in the southwest suburbs would be considered desirable neighbors and law-abiding families. The only real evidence that bigots could marshal forth, beyond rhetoric and allegations of secret cells, was in the "truth" of the foreignness and disloyalty symbolized by the hijab.

Common American understandings of the meaning of hijab laid the groundwork for constructing women who wore hijab as a foreign cultural threat that required outcasting after the 9/11 attacks. The cultural threat argument explains why Arab Muslim women were physically victimized and verbally harassed by the public in the southwest suburbs to a much greater degree than Arab Muslim men, and why a woman in hijab was present in the overwhelming majority of such incidents. If the perceived threat to the neighborhood was of terrorists, then men would have been the logical objects of attack, especially in the southwest suburbs where Arab and Muslim men are easily distinguished from the majority-white population. In this study, however, women reported experiencing hate acts at a rate more than double that of men. Sixty-five percent of the women interviewed in the study (30 of 46) reported personally experiencing physical or verbal hate acts, compared to 30 percent of men (17 of 56).

A majority of these experiences occurred in the southwest suburbs. Arab Muslim women were also more likely than Arab Muslim men, by a wide margin, to say that they felt unsafe in certain places: 83 percent of women and 45 percent of men said that there were certain places where they felt unsafe. When men and women were asked to describe threatening places, the most frequent answers were: where many Arabs live, Arab shopping districts, mosques, and southwest suburban shopping malls—in other words, southwest suburban locations of Arab American demographic concentration. Like the proportions of women who said that they felt generally unsafe, the proportion of women who said that they felt unsafe in these specific types of places was much higher than that of men. Although both men and women shared the view that these were zones of unsafety, men mentioned other places not mentioned by women, a topic we return to later in this chapter.

A woman wearing hijab was present in more than 90 percent of hate incidents reported by Arab Muslim women, signaling its important symbolic role in the eyes of neighborhood defenders. Sixty percent of women who reported experiencing hate acts were wearing hijab when the incidents occurred, and an additional 30 percent were in the company of women wearing hijab.[2] In addition, more than half of the men who reported experiencing hate acts were in the company of women wearing hijab when the incidents occurred. Furthermore, when asked which subgroup of Arab Muslims was most affected (in any way) by post-9/11 events, 55 percent of study respondents identified women wearing hijab. Women wearing hijab were more likely than other women and than men to be spit at, to experience another driver's road rage, to have items thrown at their cars, to be followed by strangers, to be subjected to hateful language, and to report home vandalism and sieges.

The hateful experiences reported by women in hijab occurred initially across the metropolitan area, but after the period of heightened post-9/11 backlash tapered down, all but two events reported in this study occurred in the southwest suburbs. The following incident occurred within weeks of the 9/11 attacks near a university campus just west of downtown Chicago. This Arab Muslim woman, who experienced the threat of vehicular assault, reported a new sense of fear attached to wearing hijab, a feeling she had not experienced prior to the attacks.

> Literally, I could not leave my apartment because I was scared to leave and lived in fear. For the first time in my life, I was fearful for my life. When I did go out, I would have things thrown at my car, remarks made. People who used to be friendly with me were not so friendly. Some of them may not have said anything directly to me but were standoffish now. And I understand because I think I'm a reminder of what happened that day. Before, I would walk around and nobody ever said anything to me, but immediately thereafter, especially the couple of days after 9/11,

I would be screamed at, yelled at, "Go back to your country." It was just a very scary time in my life. I actually had a bottle thrown at my car. . . . One time, I was crossing the street here at Paulina, and a man who was driving came to a stop sign and was slowing down. Then I started crossing because I thought he was coming to a full stop. He pressed on the accelerator, and I retracted from crossing the street. He yelled out of his car, "You terrorist." . . . To be honest, I have friends who have considered and have actually taken off their hijab just because they were fearful of their lives. I didn't come to that point where I would consider ripping it off, but I can see why some women did.

While many interviewees spoke of incidents in which a woman's hijab was pulled off, no one in this study personally experienced such an attack. Nonetheless, the Council on American-Islamic Relations in Chicago has taken reports of such incidents, including one as late as 2006, a discouraging sign. The 2006 incident occurred at a McDonald's in southwest suburban Orland Park (the site of a new mosque): an eighteen-year-old man reached from behind and pulled off a woman's head scarf.[3] In another 2006 incident, CAMELS was spray-painted on an Arab American family's lawn in far southwest suburban Tinley Park.[4] While this incident was directed at an entire family, it reveals the persistence of dehumanizing views of Arab and Muslim Americans in the area. The locations of both incidents indicate the movement of hate encounters to areas where the Arab/Muslim presence is newly increasing.

Nativist Discourses Inform Neighborhood Defenders

John Higham (1955, 24) defined nativism as "zeal to destroy enemies of a distinctively American way of life." Higham observed that nativist practices surge when fear binds the nation together; at such times, discourses championing "national homogeneity" establish the boundaries of inclusion (us) and exclusion (them). "Mere difference is not enough to provoke nativist zeal," noted Higham, since hostile views toward the cultures and institutions of strangers and newcomers are a "perennial human experience" (3). It is during times of national crisis and war that a "profoundly intense American feeling" emerges, along with a "persistent conception about what is un-American" (5). During times of national crisis, acts of harassment and violence based in nativist ideas of "who we are not" become directed at perceived cultural threats to the American way of life and are articulated as national defense. In the southwest suburbs, neighborhood defenders latched on to the arguments of those who constructed Arabs and Muslims as a national threat and reconstructed their Arab and Muslim American neighbors as foreigners who posed a threat to the very fabric of American culture. The American culture they were defending was the one in which they chose to live—Euro-American, white, middle-class, Christian, and free. Arab Muslim women wearing hijab were positioned as the countersymbols to this culture, the people "we are not." Hijab was interpreted by them as representative of coercion and female submission, values considered "un-American." Women in hijab were thus symbolic foreigners, to be outcasted in acts of national defense. Women in hijab were commanded to "go home."

Writing in the 1950s, Higham (1955, 6) believed that anti-Catholic nativism, which called for "stiff naturalization laws and exclusion of Catholics and foreigners from public office, completely overshadowed every other nativist tradition."[5] It is instructive, then, to compare nativist assertions concerning Catholics in the 1850s to those made today about Muslims. The following excerpts selected from the archives of the Historical Society of Pennsylvania position Catholics as foreign agents who pose a threat to the American core values of individual freedom and political liberty. Catholics, the nativists said, were unable to practice democracy. Nativists argued that the large migration of Catholics to the United States was a papal plot to subvert American institutions and install in their place an authoritarian Catholic Church.

THINGS WHICH ROMAN CATHOLIC PRIESTS AND ALL TRUE ROMAN CATHOLICS HATE

Providence, July 22, 1854

1. They HATE our Republic, and are trying to overthrow it.
2. They HATE the American Eagle, and it offends them beyond endurance to see it worn as an ornament by Americans.
3. They HATE our Flag, as is manifest by their grossly insulting it.
4. They HATE the liberty of conscience.
5. They HATE the liberty of the Press.
6. They HATE the liberty of speech.
7. They HATE our Common School system.[6]

July 15, 1854

Naturalization Laws

This is our point: ENTIRE AND UNCONDITIONAL REPEAL.
Because it is every day weakening the strength, and destroying the character of the country. America can only be America by keeping it American.[7]

Like the old nativist charges that "they hate our Republic and are trying to overthrow it," modern anti-Muslim discourses quite similarly speak of Muslim plots to take over American institutions and establish authoritarian rule—a leadership style represented as inherent to both

Arabs and Muslims—and similarly include calls for halting their immigration. In a 2002 report for the Center for Immigration Studies, Daniel Pipes and Khalid Durán argue:

> In its long history of immigration, the United States has never encountered so violent-prone and radicalized a community as the Muslims who have arrived since 1965. Because the immigrant Muslim community is so new, it is still very much in formation. Which way will the first generation of immigrant children turn? Will their dual identities as Americans and Muslims be complementary or contradictory? Will they accept or reject the Islamist program of changing the United States? Will they control the urge toward violence? More broadly, will they insist on adapting the United States to Islam, or will they agree to adapt Islam to the United States? Much depends on the answer.

Assertions that Arabs and Muslims are inherently incapable of democracy are common to these discourses, usually accompanied by claims that portray historical trends or current political realities as *culturally inevitable* outcomes. That is, if Arabs and Muslims do not have democratic governments, it has nothing to do with power or global politics and everything to do with cultural proclivities. Such is the case with Bernard Lewis's (1994) assessment of the Muslim "problem with democracy." Lewis asserts that Muslims march behind authority because of their religious beliefs:

> It is not easy to create and maintain free institutions in a region of age-old authoritarian traditions, in a political culture where religion and ethics have been more concerned with duties than with rights, in which obedience to legitimate authority is a religious obligation as well as a political necessity, and disobedience a sin as well as a crime.

These ideas blatantly contradict another oft-asserted trope: the inherent chaos and turbulence of the Arab and Muslim world, a place (reduced to a single unit) "teeming" with people who are ultimately unpredictable and live in the throes of their emotions and discontents. Although it is sociologically illogical to find rampant chaos and disorganization (disobedience) in a place where obedience is sacred and authoritarianism is said to rule, such contradictions are possible in an imagined world of the other, where, unlike other places on earth, there is no growth, no change, no diversity, no human adaptation, and no material for sociological study, except for why things never change. Similar ideas were the hallmark of anti-Catholic nativism in the nineteenth century, when Catholics were portrayed as irrational, emotional, and uncontrollable, at the same time as they were said to be controlled by a love of authoritarianism and the pope.

The following statements, made by talk radio hosts in 2004, also closely mirror earlier discourses about Catholics and reveal much more about American anxieties than they do about the groups targeted by their discourses. This time it is Muslims who are perceived as intending not only to take over American political institutions but also to manipulate attitudes favoring tolerance so as to ultimately destroy American culture and eradicate its core component, freedom of choice. In April 2004, in Tulsa, Oklahoma, the talk radio (1170 KFAQ) host Michael DelGiorno asserted:

> Allah is not the God of this nation, but that is exactly the agenda of Islam: to change our government from within through politics and through tolerance and inclusion—alter our culture.
>
> But make no mistake about it, their goal is not to be one of many gods and one of many religions, it's to be the God and the religion of the entire Earth.
>
> Christians, you better start speaking up and standing up for what's right, it's already too late in Michigan. . . .
>
> How much longer before it's too late right here at home?

Thwarting the planned Muslim takeover of the United States might require drastic action, according to the Boston radio (WTKK-FM) host Jay Severins, who suggested: "I've got an idea, let's kill all Muslims."[8]

A few months prior to his nomination by President George W. Bush to the Board of Directors of the United States Institute of Peace, the neo-conservative Daniel Pipes argued that American Muslims, as well as Muslim visitors and immigrants, need special scrutiny:

> There is no escaping the unfortunate fact that Muslim government employees in law enforcement, the military, and the diplomatic corps need to be watched for connections to terrorism, as do Muslim chaplains in prisons and the armed forces. Muslim visitors and immigrants must undergo additional background checks. Mosques require a scrutiny beyond that applied to churches, synagogues, and temples. Muslim schools require increased oversight to ascertain what is being taught to children.[9]

Mark Krikorian (2002) argues in a *National Review* article entitled "Muslim Invasion?" that the solution to the Muslim "problem" in the United States lies in reducing their immigration and "slowing the growth of the Muslim population." Echoing the statements of Attorney General Ashcroft about terrorists lurking within Muslim American communities, Krikorian argues: "Muslim immigration helps facilitate domestic terrorism, with immigrant communities serving, as Mao might have said, as the sea within which the terrorists swim as fish. The vast majority of Muslim immigrants, of course, are not terrorists; rather, immigrant communities provide unintentional cover for terrorists because of their insularity, just as Italian-immigrant communities generations ago provided cover for the Mafia." Although Krikorian ties the Muslim danger in part to the potential erosion of American support for Israel, he believes, not unlike supporters of Americanization and immigration quotas nearly one hundred years ago, that the Muslim problem can be resolved through reduced immigration accompanied by assimilation.

> U.S. support for Israel is at a crossroads—we can continue with our current policy of high immigration and guarantee a steady erosion of support for Israel; or we can reduce immigration, slowing the growth of the Muslim population and allowing America's powerful assimilative forces to work. We can't have both.

While President George W. Bush called for public tolerance and restraint after 9/11 and delivered a very positive speech about Islam at the Islamic Center in Washington on September 17, 2001, other statements made by President Bush supported the notion that Muslims hate freedom and democracy. For example, in his September 20, 2001, speech to Congress and the American people, President Bush (2001) said:

> Americans are asking, why do they hate us? They hate what we see right here in this chamber—a democratically elected government. Their leaders are self-appointed. They hate our freedoms—our freedom of religion, our freedom of speech, our freedom to vote and assemble and disagree with each other.[10]

Clearly some Americans heard President Bush's earlier call for tolerance, but others latched on to this oft-repeated slogan about Arabs and Muslims hating "our freedom," a slogan vested with increased currency when the Bush administration used it as a rallying cry for its "war on terror" and its invasions and occupations of Afghanistan and Iraq.

The Defense Science Board's 2004 report to the secretary of Defense argues that this discursive narrative contributed significantly to the failure of the Bush administration's war on terror, largely because its dishonesty resulted in the U.S. government commanding little respect among persons in the countries it was claiming to help. The Defense Science Board (2004, 40) wrote:

> Muslims do not "hate our freedom," but rather, they hate our policies. The overwhelming majority voice their objections to what they see as one-sided support in favor of Israel and against Palestinian rights, and the longstanding, even increasing support for what Muslims collectively see as tyrannies, most notably Egypt, Saudi Arabia, Jordan, Pakistan, and the Gulf states. Thus when American public diplomacy talks about bringing democracy to Islamic societies, this is seen as no more than self-serving hypocrisy. . . . Furthermore, *in the eyes of Muslims,* American occupation of Afghanistan and Iraq has not led to democracy there, but only more chaos and suffering. [emphasis in the original][11]

The Defense Science Board (2004, 35) points out that Arabs and Muslims overwhelmingly want freedom and democracy, but that it is U.S. policies that have blocked this potential outcome. The argument of cultural inherency was a smokescreen that stopped Americans from examining matters further. Nonetheless, what people believe to be true is true to them, and when American government officials invoked "us-versus-them" paradigms in their speeches to explain government policies after 9/11, hatred of freedom was a core around which they pivoted. Framed in this way, Arab and Muslim beliefs, values, and culture (as if there were only one) could only be interpreted as profoundly threatening to the American way of life. As a consequence of these types of statements, Arab and Muslim Americans found themselves transformed into not only security threats but also cultural threats, a concept that mobilized neighborhood defenders and focused their attention on places and subjects where the threat appeared greatest.

The Meanings of Hijab

In the dominant Western discourses, wearing hijab is represented as an act of oppression enforced on Muslim women by Muslim men. It is thus interpreted as symbolic of women's submission to patriarchal men, a trait associated with backward societies and cultures, places far less civilized than the United States. Indeed, photos of women in hijab have been central to the image construction of Arab and Muslim societies as places where the way of life lies in opposition to American ideals of freedom and individual liberty. The alleged relationship between the hijab and oppression, and its oppositional bearing to civilized society, American culture, and personal freedom, was a core theme of the U.S. invasion of Afghanistan after the 9/11 attacks. As Lila Abu-Lughod (2002) points out, saving Muslim women was a cultural theme invoked to garner support for American military actions in Afghanistan. Although there was no apparent strategic necessity for such a theme—there was little domestic opposition to the invasion—the theme was part of the government's mixing of military strategies and cultural chauvinism to reinforce ideas about American cultural superiority, often articulated by the government in its "war on terror" dichotomies: the civilized and the barbaric, the free and the unfree, us and them. In the government's construction, women in hijab were symbols of force and barbarism, countersymbols to American civilization and freedom. Put forth as symbols of something Americans should disdain and conquer, American women in hijab became the "them" that neighborhood defenders sought to cast out.

If one believes that where there are women in hijab there is force and authoritarianism and that women wearing hijab are open displays of coerced submission to men, then it follows that Muslim women should

rejoice in being saved from such coercion, whether through military liberation or migration to the West. By their very action of wearing hijab,
then, these American women somehow do not deserve to live in the
United States, because whether forced to wear hijab or choosing to do so,
they are actively rejecting the promises of American freedom. Women in
hijab are thus potent symbols of the victory of tyranny over the ideal of
individual liberty, and even women who freely choose to wear hijab are
acting in a manner unacceptable to American culture. There is no space
for choice when it comes to hijab if it is interpreted as a symbol of force.
Rejecting freedom, American women in hijab cease to be unique persons
with individual dignity; instead, they are interpreted by nativists as symbols of the calculated use of American freedom to take over American
culture, dragging the country into political backwardness and despotism.
Here the echoes of anti-Catholic nativism ring loudly.

Before moving on, it is important to restate the illogic of these social
constructions that debase Muslim women's free will and choice: Muslim
women who *choose* to wear hijab are *using* American freedom to openly
flaunt their *rejection* of American freedom. Constructions such as these that
cast American women in hijab as un-American, even anti-American, in
their motivations explain why neighborhood defenders driven by a "zeal
to destroy enemies of a distinctively American way of life" (Higham 1955,
24) called for Muslims women in hijab to "go home" and systematically
harassed, assaulted, spit on, and followed them.

Arab and Muslim Women: Producers of Terrorists

Themes revolving around the hijab and its relationship to core American
values were primary, but they were not the only ones in American popular culture that singled out Arab/Muslim women as different, even barbaric. As is common to misogynist arguments, purveyors of hatred go after
Arab/Muslim motherhood itself. Anti-women arguments tend to play into
larger stereotypic themes about a group and then focus on women's particular role in producing and reproducing certain cultural outcomes. The
inevitability assigned to cultural traits is thus not inevitable at all, but
deeply the responsibility of women. The case of Arab/Muslim women is
no exception to this pattern: quite compatibly with larger stereotypes
of Arabs and Muslims, misogynist narratives claim that Arab/Muslim
women actively nurture the violent personalities of Arab/Muslim men
by refusing to hug them as children. The following quote, for example,
charges that Arabs and Muslims are cold and harsh with their children
and implies that mothers are fully on board with the cultural plan—
to predispose their children to adulthoods of brutality and barbarism.
Once again, we cannot tell whether women choose or are forced to engage

in this seemingly barbaric behavior, but yet again it does not really matter. This quote, which also conflates Arabs and Muslims to capture both universes in one swoop, was not found on the website of a hate group; it was prominently positioned on the website of the very mainstream Annapurna Center for Self Healing in Washington State.[12] Restating claims made by Howard Bloom (1989) in an *Omni* magazine article entitled "The Importance of Hugging," the quote refers to the Arab (or is it the Muslim?) as a "walking time bomb."

> Could the denial of warmth lie behind Arab brutality? Could these keepers of Islamic flame be suffering from a lack of hugging? . . . In much of Arab society the cold and even brutal approach to children has still not stopped. Public warmth between men and women is considered a sin. And the Arab adult, stripped of intimacy and thrust into a life of cold isolation, has become a walking time bomb. An entire people may have turned barbaric for the simple lack of a hug.[13]

In this particular manifestation of the argument, the role of the kind and loving mother is eviscerated by replacing her with references to totally unrelated norms concerning public displays of affection between unrelated adult males and females. Bloom (1997) lays out this argument more fully in his book *The Lucifer Principle,* where he explains why Islamic societies are "high on the list" of "barbarians." While his argument is clearly an example of Orientalist (and racist) literature that, like others of its genre, uses spurious data to support its argument, it was nonetheless publishable in *Omni* magazine as "scientific" and is representative of a certain track in American culture.

The website of the Global Ideas Bank, which claims to be the "greatest ideas site on the internet today" posts a similar argument, based on Bloom's work (enacting Said's notion that repetition rather than objective data is the hallmark of Orientalist claims), in stating as fact that Muslims treat their children coldly:

> The cultures that treated their children coldly produced brutal adults, according to a survey of 49 cultures conducted by James Prescott, founder of the National Institute of Child Health and Human Development's Developmental Biology Program in the States. . . . Prescott's observations apply to Islamic and other cultures, which treat their children harshly. They despise open displays of affection. The result, he claims: violent adults.[14]

Notions such as these about Arab/Muslim culture, women, and child-rearing form part of the core of the "knowledge tales" discussed in chapter 5. They are the ideas about Arab and Muslim society that flow through American culture, that must be engaged in conversations, that are held by people who will fight for the cultural truths they embrace.

Their transporters "know" that they are true because they read articles and books about them, signaling their own cosmopolitanism and literary reach. Yet in the years I have spent living in and visiting Arab and Muslim-majority countries, as well as the times I have spent among Arab and Muslim Americans, I have witnessed not only *no* harshness toward children but quite the opposite: a greater outpouring of love, affection, and hugging than is found in the white middle-class (Catholic/Christian) American culture I know best. Nonetheless, the diffusion of these ideas in American culture, whether true or not, provided further reason why nativists felt they could rightfully focus their attacks after 9/11 on Arab and Muslim American women, the reproducers of culture, especially in areas where their large number was seen to pose a significant cultural threat to the neighborhood's moral order.

Nagel (2003) points out that when nationalism is mobilized, such as in times of crisis, men and women are expected to conform to hegemonic definitions of masculinity and femininity. In the competition over definitions of who and what is American that emerged after the 9/11 attacks, attacks on women in hijab were acts of cultural sniping taken to affirm the boundary of proper American womanhood. Harassment, rudeness, assaults, vehicular pursuits, and threats of greater violence, framed in utterances of outcasting ("go home"), were belligerent acts of aggression that asserted that American femininity precluded hijab. American feminist support for liberating Afghani women from the burqa reinforced this narrow definition of femininity, which is why so many other women found feminist calls to support the United States invasion of Afghanistan offensive. Ideas about covering versus exposure and force versus choice became binary poles around which the cultural front of the "war on terror" was waged, with women's clothing and bodies on the frontline, and sometimes men's.

Cultural Sniping: Muslim Women in Hijab as Symbols of the Rejection of American Values

> One of my friends was wearing a scarf, but not anymore. Her neighbor put small flags at all of the houses (on the block), and my friend asked her, "Why didn't you put flags in front of our house?" She said, "Because you are Muslim." My friend said, "No, I was born here, my husband was in the Army," and she went out and bought a big flag. A lot of women who wore the scarf stopped. They were afraid someone would attack them.

This quote from an Arab Muslim woman living in the southwest suburbs shows the relationship between being American and wearing hijab as understood by a Euro-American woman: one negates the other. When a flag, the symbol of American nationalism, is denied to the American-born woman wearing hijab, she removes her hijab and purchases a flag, both actions supporting a specific concept of being an American woman.

Many Muslim women, however, refused to stop wearing hijab, even when doing so was suggested to them as protection from attack.

> My husband told me to take it, the hijab, off. I said, "No. I am wearing it for my religion. If I'm not bothering anyone, no one should bother me."

Just as many Arab/Muslim American families bought flags to place on their lawns, making the statement that they too were Americans, many women in hijab bought flags for their cars. Beyond making a statement, they perceived that a car flag was a way to enhance their safety while moving about. Vehicular safety was important because many women reported being cursed or followed while driving.

> Our neighbor was chased by four or five people who were riding in a car. She ran away very quickly to the police station. That really happened. She was very terrified. They had tracked her many times in the past. This is why she didn't go home; she didn't want them to know where she was living. They fled when they saw her heading towards the police station.

"Raghead," a derogatory term for Arab men referring to the head shawl traditionally worn by some men in various Arab countries, was now being shouted at women in hijab:

> One guy, when I was taking groceries out of my car, yelled, "Go back to where you came from, you raghead!" I was in the cul-de-sac by my house. He yelled out of his car. It was scary, but he went away.

The relationship between public safety (or the lack thereof) and wearing hijab was so highly interconnected that Arab Muslim women who did not wear hijab believed that their lack of hijab was the source of their safety. One woman, for instance, when asked whether she felt safe shopping, said that she did, "because I don't wear hijab."

I argue that if fear of terrorists had been behind the public attacks on Arabs/Muslims in the southwest suburbs, one would expect that those attacks would be focused on men. I have concluded, based on a range of study data, that women in hijab were instead the focus of attacks because they were seen to represent a threat to the moral order of the neighborhood that neighborhood crusaders were attempting to thwart. For the sake of comprehensiveness, however, I propose here a few alternative explanations for why harassment and hate acts were focused on women, explanations for which I have little supporting data. Muslims and non-Muslims alike often say that Muslim women in hijab are targeted simply because they are so easily identified as Muslims. Their head scarves provide a level of certainty about their religious faith, but the attack has little to do with gender or with understood meanings of hijab. This explanation is quite plausible for the hate encounters that occurred in other types of areas—for example, in other parts of the Chicago metropolitan area where Arab or Muslim residents are relatively few in number, or in other similar places in the United States—and it may even be applicable to some of those that occurred in the southwest suburbs. As Levin and McDevitt (2002) point out in their book *Hate Crimes Revisited*, there is more than one type of hate crime perpetrator, and hate crimes are perpetrated for a range of reasons, including thrill-seeking, expressing resentment, and fulfilling a higher-order mission. My argument is that the hate activities in the southwest suburbs were mostly tied to defense of the neighborhood's moral order and that women were *chosen* as targets in a place where Arab and Muslim men were easily distinguished from and by the majority-white population, for very specific reasons tied to cultural understandings. It is also possible that some bigots thought out their actions extensively and decided that the government was acting aggressively enough toward Arab and Muslim men so that their own work had to focus strategically on women. The only way to prove or disprove this line of thinking is by studying the perpetrators, which I have not done. Some aggressors may have assumed that women were weaker than men or that women wouldn't strike back, as one male interviewee believed:

> Some of the attacks were against women, some because they wear their veil. Being a woman is being vulnerable, you know, because people look at you as the weaker one than the male. . . . Sometimes maybe women can communicate with others a lot better than men or in a better way, because if somebody talked to an Arab man, they might get defensive, they might be very offended, they might be ready to fight or something. But a woman might do it by talking. It's already happened. Pulling their scarves off and hitting a woman, or spitting on her. Where, if it was a guy, they wouldn't have done that. And it's a guy doing it usually. So, yeah, I think women are more vulnerable than men.

Nativism in the Neighborhood: Flags, Hijabs, and National Boundary Setting

Starting with the siege on the Bridgeview mosque, the breaking of the windows of Arab American stores, and the machete attack on the Arab American gas station attendant who audaciously "claimed to be American," attacks on Arab and Muslim Americans, their property, and their institutions in southwest suburbs were often accompanied by statements rejecting their Americanness and calling for them to "go home." Whether shouted, spray-painted, or symbolized by flag-waving, the message to Arab and Muslim Americans in these areas was not simply to leave the neighborhood but to leave the country.

> My husband, kids, and I were all verbally attacked. That included dirty verbal insults and even hand and finger signs. Many times people would attack us by saying, "What are you doing here? Go back to your country!"

The American flag played a prominent role in these performances of outcasting: the mobs around the Bridgeview mosque waved flags, and interviewees reported that flags were draped from the cars of southwest suburbanites who shouted insults at them. These were not the flags of patriotic Americans expressing national solidarity after the 9/11 attacks; many of these particular flags were the props of southwest suburban bigots symbolically erecting national boundaries. Flags, in turn, played a symbolic role for Arab and Muslim Americans seeking to assert their membership in the nation. Women in hijab placed flags in their cars, and Arab Americans began displaying flags on their lawns. A flag was hung on the Bridgeview mosque while under police protection, and the first prop on the Orland Park mosque construction site was an American flag.

> Some people painted in our driveway GO HOME. People threw firecrackers in our driveway. They must be from the neighborhood. Who else would know who we were? All the Arabs in the neighborhood started putting flags out.

Outcasting the Foreigner: Shopping Malls and Supermarkets as Contested Spaces

There are hundreds of Arab American businesses in the southwest suburbs, especially in the suburbs close to the city border. Few persons who are not Arab or Muslim ever set foot in these businesses. In 2006 I counted more than one hundred Arab American businesses in a two-square-mile area centered on Bridgeview's Harlem Avenue. The Arab American business enclave in Bridgeview approaches institutional completeness: it contains bakeries, restaurants, and shops selling ethnic foods, spices, sweets, and commercial goods such as cookware, videos, clothing, religious materials, and satellite dishes; a wide range of services, including real estate, travel, hair salons, barber shops, communications, entertainment, and so on; an Arab American–owned bank, a mosque, and two Islamic schools. An Arab American church is located in an older, historic setting in the near western suburbs, while another church is located a few miles southeast of Bridgeview. Unfortunately, the extensive institutional and economic presence of Arab Americans did not translate into either safety or power in 2001. Instead, their businesses and institutions were the objects of widespread property damage after 9/11 as assailants broke the windows of at least a dozen southwest suburban Arab American businesses and the mosque was placed under siege.

Arab Americans from the southwest side and the southwest suburbs shop not only in Arabic businesses but also in southwest suburban shopping malls and supermarkets. These were the places where Arab Muslim women said they felt least safe. Malls and supermarkets were repeatedly mentioned by Arab Muslim women as sites of harassment, verbal abuse, and physical assault. Women in hijab reported that it was most often in these types of places that they were spit at, sneezed on, and told to "go home," "go back to your country," or "go back to where you came from." One woman told me, "A group of white people approaching me in a mall would scare me." Southwest suburban shopping malls and supermarkets were key sites for hostile encounters because they were among the few places outside of the block, the public school, and the superstore where suburban whites and Arab/Muslim Americans met and shared space for extended periods of time.

> My mother's friend was walking into the supermarket. Someone tugged at her scarf, shouted at her, and spit at her. This was on Ninety-fifth Street in Bridgeview or Palos Hills.

Unlike the "social seams" described by Jane Jacobs (1961)—places where interactions between members of different racial-ethnic groups symbolically sew their lives together (which characterizes Sixty-third Street)—the experiences of Arab Muslims in southwest suburban malls and supermarkets indicate that they became spaces of heightened contest after 9/11, places where their right to walk freely was often challenged, especially if they were women. Malls and supermarkets were key spaces for boundary setting and the acts of outcasting performed by some members of the southwest suburban white community. Their actions went beyond efforts to deny American cultural citizenship to Arabs and Muslims; they challenged their very right to live in the United States. Since a large proportion of Arab and Muslim Americans living in the southwest suburbs were born in the United States, they first had to be constructed as foreign—de-Americanized—before they could be told to go home.

Since displaying the American flag symbolized loyalty to the United States, many women who wore hijab felt that displaying an American flag was essential to proving that they too were American.

> This girl I was with felt so uncomfortable entering the Home Store in Lemont that the minute we walked in, she said, "Do you have any flags here?" I think people who cover have obviously been affected. They're more aware of people watching them.

In their meta-study of hate crimes, Green, Strolovitch, and Wong (1998, 373) identify an "exclusionary impulse" at the core of neighborhood defense strategies in majority-white residential areas. Such an impulse lies behind the preferences of many whites to live in racially segregated suburbs, where they find comfort in cultural and racial homogeneity (Farley, Danziger, and Holzer 2000; Massey and Anderson 2001). This study shows that under certain conditions (such as the national crises of which Higham speaks), such exclusionary impulses can include a sense of entitlement to national boundary setting: neighborhood groups feel empowered not only to defend the character of the neighborhood but to define who is and who is not American and to take defensive action against persons thus defined as aliens and outsiders. While Green and his colleagues found a correlation between race and the exclusionary impulse behind neighborhood defense, I can only speculate here about the role of race in what I call "national boundary setting." On the one hand, we would expect less organized support for narrow definitions of who and what is American among groups that still experience barriers to inclusion in the United States, principally people of color and members of racial-ethnic minority groups. At the same time, however, countervailing messages on the national front calling for a united stand against the enemy encourage a sense of national "we-ness" that includes everyone except "them"—the members of the "enemy" group.

I argued in chapter 6 that racial demography is given meaning when understood through notions of entitlement. The American government uses themes of American entitlement to support its military campaigns, and the "we-ness" it articulates suggests the inclusivity of most Americans. The communities represented—through images of "our" shared fate—in the government's print and television ads to recruit military conscripts are those of the groups from whom it recruits best: the lower socioeconomic classes and the communities of people of color and minority groups. This study can draw no firm conclusions on the relationship between race-ethnicity and exclusionary national boundary setting. To do so requires comparative analysis of post-9/11 Arab/Muslim experiences across places where they live as a significant group among nonwhite or minority groups. Although this study had such a comparative place, any clean racial or ethnic effect was overridden by the existence of extensive intergroup community organizing whose ethos stressed the equal human dignity of all groups. I do not know what would have been the outcome in the absence of such organizing. Theory development about the role of race-ethnicity in "national boundary setting" during times of national crisis thus remains open to testing.

Mobilizing popular sentiments against exclusionary ways of thinking at the local and national levels is even more important during times of national crisis if hate crimes and, worse, support for programs like internment or concentration camps are to be prevented. Yet these are the very times during which nativism is nurtured by those whose interests are tied to encouraging it and groups that are predisposed, for a range of reasons, to receiving nativist messages are mobilized. In local settings where exclusionary impulses already exist, nativism is mobilized as neighborhood defense, and local and national interests appear to intersect. Neighborhood defense becomes equated with national defense, symbolized by the integral role of flags during the process of acting on hate. On this score—mobilizing popular sentiments *against* nativism and exclusionary ways of thinking—the Bush administration did poorly. At the same time as it condemned popular violence against innocent Arab and Muslim Americans after 9/11, members of the Bush administration made statements that fed into widely held stereotypes, and executive branch staff with preexisting anti-Arab/Muslim prejudices were allowed to determine its domestic security policies. Bush administration statements and policies made it very difficult for many to discern which Arabs and Muslims could be considered "innocent." We cannot have it both ways with good outcome. Persons opposed to racial-ethnic violence and harassment may be more likely to attend to the messages calling for restraint (but they do not need them), while persons who can be propelled to violence may hear more loudly and act on messages invoking negative stereotypes— leaving a group of people in the middle who can be mobilized in either direction by something that shocks their sensibilities.

The Meaning of Hijab to Muslims from a Sociological Perspective

Although Islamic scholars are in considerable agreement on Muslim women's religious duty to wear hijab, as revealed in the Qur'an and Sunna (the traditions and sayings of the prophet), there are varying interpretations of the extent to which women should cover their bodies (hijab) to meet Islamic standards of modesty. There are also different views among persons of Muslim faith on this matter, as well as significant variations from place to place and over time in patterns of usage and styles of hijab. Probably a majority of practicing Muslims today believe that the Qur'an mandates that Muslim women cover their hair (at minimum) in the presence of strangers and certain relatives as an act of modesty and faith in God.[15] Many Muslim women who do not wear hijab say that they believe that wearing hijab is what they should do, but that they have not reached that stage of religious faith or maturity. Other Muslims, both practicing and nonpracticing, believe that it is not mandatory.[16] Some Muslims believe that there is no room for personal choice in this matter, while others cite the Qur'anic injunction: "Let there be no compulsion in religion" (Qur'an, Sura 2, Sûrah al-Baqarah, 256). In the modern era until the past few decades, wearing hijab was largely an urban phenomenon in some Muslim-majority countries and a rural phenomenon in others. Wearing hijab and hijab styles has at times been connected to social class or symbolism around women's domestic roles (Talhami 1996). In Iran and Saudi Arabia, wearing hijab is currently legally mandated for women, and wearing hijab in certain places is explicitly forbidden in Turkey and France, but state intervention in this religious practice is not the norm in Muslim-majority countries. Although many Americans believe that Saudi Arabia, Afghanistan, and Iran are the norm—because that is what they have been most exposed to in popular culture—these three countries are actually deviant cases when it comes to women's legal rights concerning hijab.

Today commitment to fulfilling the religious requirement of hijab is at a higher level than ever before among Arab American Muslim women. Over the past twenty years, the proportion of Muslim American women choosing to wear hijab has increased dramatically, irrespective of whether they are immigrants or American-born (Cainkar 2004d). There are many American-born Muslim women who adopted hijab before their mothers did, or who wear hijab when their mothers do not. Muslim women in this study who wore hijab were as likely to be American-born as immigrants. This distinction, however, was irrelevant to those who assaulted, spit at, followed, and otherwise taunted Muslim women in hijab after 9/11. To the perpetrators of hate acts, women in hijab were all foreigners, symbols of something foreign and un-American.

Muslim men and women interviewed in this study expressed a range of views on hijab. While I did not ask questions about hijab, it came up spontaneously during responses to questions about safety and hate encounters and questions about religious faith after 9/11 (chapter 8), and these responses indicated a range of views. For example, this American-born Arab Muslim woman strongly contests the belief that hijab is mandatory and reports engaging in such a discussion with a woman wearing hijab in a southwest suburban supermarket before 9/11:

> Here's one incident that happened before 9/11, about this Arab woman with a veil on. I was shopping at Jewel, and I heard this guy say, "Hey, I thought Halloween wasn't until tomorrow. Look over there." So I looked, and my heart sunk. I felt so hurt. I didn't even know this woman. I didn't say anything to him. I went over to her and said, "Salaam Aleekum [peace be upon you]." The irony of this, to show the diversity, she's got two kids in the shopping cart with Froot Loops and she's got a veil on, but Froot Loops is the key. I said to her, "I'm a writer, and I write about Muslim women in the Arab world, and I'd like to ask you a question if you don't mind. Why are you wearing the scarf?" She said, "Jozi, my husband." I asked her what she thought. I told her I didn't want to upset her, but I was concerned. She knew I was a Muslim, and she told me I wasn't going to go to Heaven because I didn't have a head scarf on. So I asked her

what she thought, and she answered that it was in the Qur'an. I said, "Habibti, no, it's not. It's misinterpreted. Half of the people who interpret the Qur'an don't interpret it the right way."

Since hijab makes one stand out and brings on the potential for abuse, this southwest suburban, American-born, Arab Muslim man spoke of resisting his immigrant wife's wish to wear hijab, just as he stopped her from putting an Islamic symbol in their home window.

> My wife doesn't wear anything on her head. She wanted to, and that was something I talked with her about. I said, "I don't want you to wear that." We got into an argument over it. She said, "God will punish me." She said that one day she would like to, or one day she might. And I said, "No." Her sister sent her a light with a crescent and a star, and she was talking about putting it in the window, and I said, "Heck, no." My wife is new here. She hasn't been here even five years yet. After 9/11, I felt paranoid. I knew it wasn't a very nice world before 9/11, but it just got a lot worse after.

Some women said their decision to wear hijab went against the grain of family custom. When they began to do so, their parents were upset. "The Arabs my parents knew were more culturally Muslim than religious. When I began to wear the scarf at age twenty-one, my mom was upset." Most interviewees in this study, however, interpreted wearing hijab as a sign of strong religious faith, and they held great respect for *muhajibaat* (women in hijab). They recognized the special challenges posed by wearing hijab in the United States—challenges that were compounded after 9/11.

> I'm not religious. If I was, I would not be ashamed of it. I wore hijab for two years in college. I have respect for those who wear it. It must be stressful in certain situations.

> I have always been reticent to cover my hair. I hope to someday. I am not sure how to make it happen. If I thought about doing it, I would have a second thought about doing it at this time.

For women who did not grow up wearing it, choosing hijab was not a quick decision. Rather, it was the outcome of a process of contemplation and measured timing.

> I started wearing hijab at age twenty-five. I built up to it slowly. It was a personal process. I spent time in Egypt and wore it there. I was comfortable there wearing it. I was not worried about people staring. My mother started wearing it later after *hajj*.

As this woman notes with reference to her mother, some women begin wearing hijab after making the pilgrimage to Mecca (hajj). One American-born woman in hijab noted that cultural practices continue to oppress some Arab and Muslim women and that these need to be acknowledged, but distinguished from the act of wearing hijab.

> Muslim women in general who practice and identify as Muslim have been under fire. We always have to defend ourselves, that we are not oppressed. But at end of day, [some of us are oppressed by culture, not religion]. We have to defend the hijab or stop wearing it.

After repeated attacks on women in hijab were reported across the United States, some Muslim women who had not practiced hijab before 9/11 began doing so, a phenomenon noted by a number of study participants. The decision to wear hijab at such a time reflected not only religious faith and personal strength but also a strong desire to assert the dignity of hijab in the context of its denigration; wearing hijab was an assertion of both resistance and pride to those who sought to seize its dignity. Similar motives under earlier conditions of disparagement in the United States had lain behind assertions of "Black Is Beautiful" and "Chicanismo."

Fadwa El Guindi (1999, 184) has described women's decisions to wear hijab in Egypt as partly an act of resistance. It is, writes El Guindi, a statement of "liberation from imposed, imported identities, consumerist behaviors, and an increasingly materialist culture." Embedded in wearing hijab, she continues, "is imagery that combines notions of respectability, morality, identity, and resistance." In the post-9/11 American context, wearing hijab enhances the visual differences between a purported "us" and "them," while at the same time challenging this dichotomization. Asserting hijab, not negating it, actually works to begin tearing down these constructed boundaries. Choice, according to El Guindi, has always been the variable behind feminist support for and resistance to hijab in Islamic contexts. In the United States, Muslim women are still struggling to get mainstream feminists to hear them. Zeina Zaatari (2005, 84) argues that "my white feminist colleagues often seemed to be more interested in pointing to how horrendous life for women in my part of the world is and in finding ways to 'save' these women than in engaging in actual meaningful dialogue with them or me." Focusing on ideas about choice is a tough challenge in circles where the notion that women should be required to do something that men are not is largely rejected.

Women in Hijab Alter Their Behaviors After 9/11

Some women stopped wearing hijab temporarily after 9/11; many were pressed by their husbands to do so, at least until the situation settled down. Some religious figures, whose authority was accepted by some women and contested by others, issued statements after 9/11 that women who felt in harm's way could refrain from wearing hijab.

Many have stopped wearing hijab. Many men asked their wives to take it off. Some did, some didn't. Fatwas [scholarly opinions on Islamic law] were issued saying it was okay. If you are in extreme physical harm, take it off or wear a cap or stay home. One fatwa was from a sheikh from Mauritania; another was from someone who is a doctor by day and a sheikh by night. He really has no authority to do so.

Some women who wore hijab stayed inside their homes for weeks:

After 9/11, my sister-in-law didn't go out of their house for two weeks, and that's because she wears the veil. She's a widow, and she's the one who cooks and cleans and does everything in the house, and her kids are always working. . . . She's stuck in the house because of what happened.

Other women continued to wear hijab and also to leave the house, but at the same time their husbands assumed many of their usual public tasks.

I have another friend who insisted that his wife take off her hijab, and she refused. She kept going out, but he was worried about her. He would do lots of the errands that she used to do because he was worried.

Many other women carried on with life in hijab, but, aware that they were the potential targets of attack, shifted their patterns of movement in public space and exercised more caution about where they went.

Forest preserves and parks were definitely out. Places where soccer moms go were places I would not go.

Some women who wear hijab reportedly endured extensive stress and anxiety during this period.

One of my friends, immediately after September 11, she was afraid, and she couldn't go out, and she ended up staying home and having psychological anxiety and being treated for that because she almost had a breakdown. She was so afraid for her children and worried about her husband and about what would happen to us in this country.

The perceived danger was a heart-wrenching challenge to some women's commitment to their religious beliefs.

After the events, we have begun to feel less secure than before. And because I wear a veil, I have been living in a conflict: I have been confused about what to do. Should I take off the veil? Keep it on? What to do? If I keep it on, I might endanger myself, and if I take it off, I would endanger my faith. I have been living in fear and anxiety.

Women's Bodies and Clothing: Historic Sites of Ideological Battles

A scholar in Chicago's Arab American community who was interviewed in this study suggests that Muslim women's greater vulnerability to public harassment than men's continues a global historical pattern in which women's bodies and dress are the battlegrounds where larger conflicts are fought. Because of the post-9/11 attacks on women in hijab, this Arab Muslim woman has softened her prior antipathy for it; she now sees the hijab as a woman's choice that must be defended. While she considers the "hijab phenomenon" an "exaggerated response to modernity," she sees women's agency in the choice to wear it. Like others, she maintains that attacks on women in hijab increase the commitment of many women to wearing it.

> [*Have women been affected in any special way?*] Oh, yeah. More vulnerability. They are more subject to harassment. The whole ideological battle is being fought over women's bodies and women's clothing.
>
> The September 11 events made me reevaluate my animosity to Islamic phenomena, like hijab, because, traditionally, I'm hostile to this. Now I'm not that hostile. I want to protect them. I feel like protecting them. I defend them. Actually, I do. I say to people, "It's their choice." I never used to think it was the women's choice. Now I say, "Well, maybe it is their choice and they should be able to wear whatever they want to wear." I probably was much more harsh on them before. So they suffered from my rejection of Islamization, wearing the hijab here in the U.S., I mean. The hijab in Egypt isn't a threat to anybody, it's accepted. Here it's not accepted, and it makes women more vulnerable, which I think now they are beginning to realize.
>
> I think Americans are beginning to adjust to it, and as they do the animus will be taken out of it. I think there's a sense of defiance now about wearing the hijab.

Hijab is about respecting physical modesty, a value that is not alien to other religions. Given the long histories of Judaism, Catholicism, and Orthodox Christianity, the practice of women covering their hair as an act of faith was abandoned relatively recently, and some women of these faiths still practice it. In the 1960s, the Vatican and Western feminists shared the view that veiling was not a practice consistent with modernity. Catholic nuns began taking off their veils. Veiling and rigorous modesty came to be understood in the dominant American culture as retrograde; wearing an expression of one's faith was replaced with the idea that spirituality is a private matter. Nonetheless, some measure of respect or tolerance has been accorded to Jewish women, Amish women, and Catholic nuns who cover their hair because of their religious beliefs. When Muslim women engage in this practice of faith and modesty, however, a different interpretation of their behavior applies that puts them in a potentially dangerous situation.

An Arab American woman who says she has chosen for now not to wear hijab thinks that pointing out religious continuities in wearing hijab would help others see hijab's meaning:

> I was insulted even before September 11. They used to call us "camel jockeys" or the "hijab" and make fun of us. After 9/11, it got worse, and it's still going on. It's mostly women with the hijab who are being attacked verbally. I want to sit with the people and explain about the hijab, and I would say, for example, "Look at the Virgin Mary. We respect the Virgin Mary. What is she wearing? Is she naked? She's wearing something respectable."

But for some Americans, hijab was invested with a host of imputed meanings that symbolized their worst fears: authoritarianism, loss of freedom, and Muslim takeover. They did not invent these fears; they learned them.

The Modesty/Nudity Nexus and the Poles of Force and Choice

Degradation ceremonies pivoting around Muslim beliefs in the dignity of physical modesty and its corollary, private sexuality (what Bloom was actually referring to when he wrongly argued that Muslims don't hug their children), seemed characteristic of the post-9/11 world. These ceremonies were acted out in their most vulgar form when Muslim men were in the captivity of American jailers, whether in the repeated body searches at the Metropolitan Detention Center in Brooklyn, New York (Office of the Inspector General 2003) or the forced nudity to which Iraqi men were subjected at the U.S. military's Abu Ghraib prison. The ideas behind these actions perpetrated against Arab and Muslim men, which were clearly emasculation rituals, emerged from notions similar to those that drove attacks on women in hijab: they were ideas grounded in a "culture war" in which modesty was interpreted as the polar opposite of freedom. The binary of force and choice was another pole around which post-9/11 backlash revolved; Muslim women were perceived as forced to cover their hair, just as Arab/Muslim men were perceived as forced into sexual sublimation. The paradoxical element of this culture war was in the use of force to eradicate choice, whether by pulling off a Muslim woman's head scarf or forcing nudity on a male inmate at Abu Ghraib. To those engaged in such forceful practices, freedom meant "my way or no way"—the absence of choice.

Another twist on the modesty/nudity nexus was one called for by the nationally syndicated radio talk show host Neal Boortz, who has posted "Allah . . . Please save me from your people" across the top of his website. Invoking knowledge tales about Muslims, Boortz called for American women to walk naked en masse in neighborhoods with large Muslim populations—an act that, Boortz claimed, would force Muslim men who saw them to commit suicide. Mixing national defense, religious faith, and culture wars, the logic of this proposed collective action (with patriarchal tones) worked as follows:

> You, too, can help fight terrorism. Solely as a public service Nealz Nuze has agreed to share a plan with you . . . a plan to eliminate possible Islamic terrorist cells in many of America's larger cities. As you may know, it is a sin for a devout Muslim to see any woman other than his wife naked. If he does happen to see another naked woman, he must commit suicide to purge his soul. So, understanding this about devout Muslims, at 4:00 P.M. this coming Saturday, May 1, women in major American cities with large Muslim populations are going to strip naked and walk about their neighborhoods. The plan is to walk about the neighborhood for one hour in an effort to cause any lurking *Al Qaeda* sleepers to end their own miserable lives. Good luck ladies! And thanks for the effort![17]

Attacks on Women in Hijab Decrease in the Southwest Suburbs

Toward the end of data collection for this study, interviewees reported that attacks on women in hijab seemed to be decreasing in the southwest suburbs.

> Actually, I have a sister-in-law who became religious, and she put a scarf on her head. At quite a few places, I was with my brother, his wife, and my wife in the malls, and we'd hear these really nasty remarks, but we'd just keep walking. I have to admit, it's less frequent, thank God. I think people are realizing that it's not polite . . . it's not appropriate.

The banning of hijab in French state schools emerged in interviews and conversations held in the spring of 2004 as a new point of comparison: whereas in France sentiments against the hijab had become institutionalized by the state, Muslim women in the United States were legally free to wear hijab.

> I don't think it's still going on as much. It's very interesting. America, compared to Europe, is more conservative in some areas but progressive in others. Contrasting with what's happening in France, in regard to the head scarf, America is more progressive in that sense than France.

Indeed, U.S. government agencies such as the Department of Justice, the Department of Education, and the EEOC had issued numerous statements, advisories, and brochures supporting the right of Muslim women to wear hijab free from discrimination and advising everyone concerned on how hijab should be managed during security inspections. The government also supported this right in court cases revolving around wearing hijab in public schools, often with the assistance of organizations typically associated with evangelical Christians.[18]

While most study participants felt that voices in the American media bore substantial responsibility for inciting attacks on women in hijab, some credited the media with eventually offering information that promoted new interpretations of reality.

> I think the women with the hijab, with the cover, were affected in the beginning. I think it's much less now because the media helped the people to look at it a little bit different.

In addition to teach-ins, new courses, and new books on Islam, some Arab Muslim women reported personal experiences in which non-Muslims expressed an interest in learning more about Islam and hijab. This is another indicator of the quest for knowledge that was one of the paradoxical outcomes of 9/11: "I really think people are more interested in Islam—what it is, what faith stands for, hijab and why women chose to wear it. They want know about me."

Gendered Insecurity for Men

In answer to questions about where they felt least safe after 9/11, the responses of Arab Muslim men were quite different from those of Arab Muslim women, and they were tied to an understanding of their own gendered vulnerabilities. Men were generally not the objects of attack by neighborhood crusaders seeking to defend the moral order. Instead, their insecurity stemmed from government policies and from the racialized and gendered understandings that they believed members of the American public held about them in places where there were *few* Arabs or Muslims and where they knew no one. The specific places they mentioned included areas that were all white, especially small towns and rural areas where they did not know anyone, and airports. As reported in chapter 5, many men interviewed in this study reported that they had stopped traveling domestically by air after 9/11 because they had come to expect harassment at airport security checkpoints or humiliation on airplanes. One Arab Muslim man said, "I would feel least safe at the airport. I feel like they may give me more special attention. And someone on the plane might go crazy if they find out I'm Arab." Another Arab American man reports his experience as follows:

> I think it's much safer not to travel. People look at you on the plane. I got on a plane after 9/11, I felt bad because people were staring at me. One time, my seat was 26 or 27, and I sat on the aisle and people were turned around looking at me. I don't feel secure, so for that reason I try not to travel. I'm not afraid really, and I feel sorry for the people who lost their lives. But now people are looking at me like I'm going to take my own life, and I feel pretty bad. I never felt that way before.

Some men said they began traveling by automobile instead of airplane. The change from air to auto travel, however, increased their exposure in non-urban areas and rural hinterlands, places considered especially risky because they were associated with intolerance and a perceived greater likelihood of arrest or assault. Such places took on the shape of places of exception: sites of danger where it could be assumed that anything goes. Where one is a stranger and knows no one, the perception is that there is no protection.

> Actually, when I go far away, traveling from state to state by car, or if I go to a shopping mall, or if I end up, like one time, I ended up in the suburbs of Washington, D.C., and there was nobody there with a beard. A lot of people looked at me. I didn't feel safe.

These fears were not wholly imagined. For example, in 2002 John Cooksey, a Republican from Louisiana in the U.S. House of Representatives, made a public call for Arab and Muslim men to be stopped and checked and identified such persons by their clothing: "If I see someone come in and he's got a diaper on his head and a fan belt around the diaper on his head, that guy needs to be pulled over and checked" (Irvin 2006). His narrative revolves around head coverings, but he was not denigrating the Muslim hijab but the kuffiya, the checkered shawl traditionally worn by some Arab men, by calling it a "diaper." Since very few Arab men in the United States wear a kuffiya, we may assume that Cooksey was speaking symbolically, while also displaying a cultural contempt for men who wear "foreign" head coverings. Imagined notions about men who wear certain types of head covering contributed to widespread attacks on Sikh men after 9/11. Cooksey's language indicates that he was calling upon law enforcement, not the public, to handle this task.

Arab Muslim men felt unprotected by the rule of law and feared that an abusive and incommunicado detention could commence more easily in a small town or in a place where they did not know anyone than in an urban area where someone could be found to help them. They feared being beaten, being detained, and being moved from place to place while multiple agencies searched for records of illegal activity, suspicious contacts, or ties to terrorism, and they feared that, in the process, *no one would know.*

> When I go on the road, and I'm driving through Indiana, there are times when I definitely think about the context of being seen as, you know, an

Arab in a predominantly white environment, provoking law enforcement or local residents.

These fears were not unreasonable at the time because they were based on the known experiences of post-9/11 detainees. Human Rights Watch's (2002) report on the arrest and detention of Eyad Alrababah illustrates some of these features. Alrababah was not picked up in a small town but went voluntarily to FBI headquarters in Bridgeport, Connecticut, in September 2001 to report that he had met four of the alleged hijackers. After months of solitary confinement, being moved from jail to jail, and without legal support, he was finally charged with conspiracy and document fraud. He eventually pled guilty to the latter charge and was sentenced to time served. Alrababah's crime was signing a form that falsely certified a New Jersey man as a Virginia resident, permitting the man to obtain a Virginia driver's license. The New Jersey man was not linked to terrorism, and Alrababah was not charged with helping any of the 9/11 hijackers obtain driver's licenses or with knowing their plans. When Human Rights Watch interviewed him, he was still in detention pending deportation. One of his primary complaints was lack of communication with the outside world: "Nobody knows you are there," he told Human Rights Watch (2002, 62–63).

Overall, however, men in the study were only half as likely as women to say that there were places they felt unsafe.[19] This was perhaps due to the fact that Arab and Muslim men's sense of being unprotected was tied to places they could avoid as long as they stayed in large cities, they stayed in places where they knew other people, and they traveled infrequently. Women's experiences were just the opposite: after the initial burst of hate crimes subsided, they were least likely to feel safe in their own neighborhoods or in places where there were many other Arabs and Muslims, a perception brought about by women's negative experiences in the southwest suburbs. While men who were American citizens were safer than men who were not, because the latter were more vulnerable to arbitrary actions of the state and had fewer legal rights during this period, citizenship status had little meaning for women, whose experiences were based on perceived status, and if they wore hijab they were seen as foreigners.

Conclusion

No matter where they were born or what their citizenship status was, Arab Muslims living in the southwest suburbs of Chicago reported being treated as foreigners in their own neighborhoods. Flags were waved at them or denied to them, in both cases expressing the notion that a person could not be American and Arab or Muslim at the same time. They were "de-Americanized," but in specifically gendered ways.

Women in hijab were the ultimate symbols of this foreignness because hijab was understood to represent the un-American values of force and authoritarianism, the opposite of American personal freedom. To some, women in hijab were antifeminists, and even though there were plenty of (white) patriarchal men in the southwest suburbs, symbols interpreted as women visibly heeding the demands of men were viewed as retrograde. Arguments by women that they chose to wear hijab carried little currency with persons who held these views because by the very action of choosing hijab, these Muslim women were seen as blatantly rejecting the promises of American freedom. As such, these women who wore hijab by choice were potentially more dangerous than women who wore hijab because someone had told them to. Whichever way one looked at it, women in hijab were symbols of a potential threat to the cultural and moral order of the neighborhood. In the southwest suburbs, where these interpretations were allowed to flourish because there were few voices to the contrary, women wearing hijab were more likely than men or other women to be spat at, to experience the road rage of other drivers, to have items thrown at their cars, to be followed by strangers, to be subjected to hateful language, and to report home vandalism and sieges.

This imputed foreign status and lesser set of social rights for women was synergistic with federal government policies that abrogated the civil and legal rights of Arab and Muslim men. Public support for the mass arrests, detention without charges, special registration, mass expulsion, wiretapping, and spying without pretext practiced against Arab and Muslim American communities was easier to obtain when these groups were understood as not really loyal Americans. Arab Muslims interviewed in this study understood that the same ideas that encouraged public attacks on them were behind support for reducing immigration from Arab and Muslim countries and limiting their civil rights in the United States. This support was shown in polls conducted in 2002 that found that nearly 60 percent of Americans favored reducing the number of immigrants from Muslim countries (CNN/Gallup/*USA Today* poll, March 2002), that a majority of Americans felt there were "too many" immigrants from Arab countries (Jones 2002), and that a majority of Americans favored racial profiling "directed at Arabs and Muslims" (Cole and Dempsey 2002). Arab Muslims understood well that they had been socially constructed as a monolithic group that at best posed a threat to American culture, and at worst was the enemy within.

The immigration scholar Oscar Handlin (1951) called nativism a threat to democracy and a victory for conformity. He asserted that when the scope of the founding freedoms becomes rigid and conscribed, democratic society is endangered. By showing that force was used to compel Arabs and Muslims to shake off their perceived values and adopt the values and customs held by others, I make this very point: freedom cannot be obtained through coercion, and rigid constructions of who or what is American are not only undemocratic but authoritarian. Muslim American women are now skillfully casting their right to wear hijab as a civil rights struggle whose victory is essential to a robust American democracy and whose defeat would signal the triumph of hatred and authoritarianism over democracy. Indeed, hatred and authoritarianism are precisely the attributes that were inscribed on *their* bodies by those who sought their social exclusion (or religious conversion). What has unfolded since the 9/11 attacks is yet another struggle to determine who and what is American and who will have the power to define these boundaries. Gary Gerstle (1999, 290), however, has persuasively argued that "Americanization" *is* shaped by coercion, exclusion, and restriction and that the national community is a "structure of power that circumscribes choice and shapes the identities to which individuals and groups can aspire." The forces of hatred and exclusion that erupted after 9/11 spurred the mobilization of Arab and Muslim Americans and brought forth a host of supporters, producing some of the paradoxical outcomes discussed earlier in this book. In the final chapter, we look at some of the outcomes of the post-9/11 period, including shaping, for Arab and Muslim American organizing, for their views of their future in the United States, and for their religious faith.

Chapter 8

Conclusion:
Insiders/Outsiders in America

> They [Muslims] have a good future. There are some coming out of post-9/11 stronger, more determined—to change this concept and make themselves more visible and open, especially in political elections.
> —Anonymous Arab American man

UPON FINAL analysis, the post-9/11 experience for Arab and Muslim Americans reveals a paradoxical historical moment. At the same time as members of these groups have since 9/11 experienced extensive institutional discrimination, government targeting (mainly focused on men), and public attacks (largely focused on women and Islamic religious institutions), they have also experienced enhanced civic inclusion. Arab Americans and Muslim Americans, their organizations and institutions, have become visible players in the American public square to a greater degree than at any previous time in American history—with the significant exception of African American Muslims, who have a decades-long history of engagement in American society (Nimer 2005; Moore 2003; Chicago Council on Global Affairs 2007; Jackson 2004). This civic inclusion is by no means evenly distributed across the nation, nor is it uncontested, but it is nonetheless measurable. This perhaps unexpected positive outcome of post-9/11 events emerged from the dialectic that was put into motion when state repression, public attacks, and popular vilification rather quickly reached a level that was intolerable to Arab and Muslim Americans, to a sector of American civic institutions, and to many individuals in the United States. Individuals and groups mobilized in response to these excesses, and in the process a wide range of new sociopolitical intersections emerged between activists, advocacy organizations, political leaders, philanthropists,, and Arab and Muslim Americans. At their meeting point, there was a symbolic convergence of "us" and "them" and a new, more inclusive configuration of who "we" are.

The wave of government arrests and calls for "Americans" to be watchful of their Arab and Muslim neighbors in the immediate post-9/11 period required that Arab and Muslim Americans vociferously defend their right to live in the United States in possession of the same civil rights as other Americans. The broad support they received for claiming their rights pulled them in from the margins of social exclusion and forged a new level of individual and organizational integration into American society. As this book journeyed through numerous aspects of the post-9/11 Arab/Muslim American experience, the work of many individuals and groups left a handprint on this story: human rights organizations investigating abuses of prisoners; private philanthropies supporting community defense work; civil rights attorneys defending the falsely accused; immigrant coalitions marching in protest against government excesses; Japanese American and other ethnic organizations calling for an end to collective profiling; community organizers conducting civil rights teach-ins and special registration monitoring; mosques organizing open houses; neighborhood organizations forming mosque defense committees; interfaith groups speaking out against hate crimes; school girls exchanging solidarity visits; and local and national Arab and Muslim American organizations taking on a broader range of tasks than ever before under the new emergency conditions.

To the degree that Arab and Muslim Americans and their organizations shared in mobilizations with mainstream institutions, their communities and organizations became, broadly speaking, less isolated and more permeable, and thus "much more subject both to influencing and being influenced by the larger society" (Orum 2005, 926). Chapter 6 showed that at the micro level, in spatial zones where Arab and Muslim American institutions had been socially connected in positive ways to groups outside of their own prior to the attacks, they experienced greater relative safety after the attacks. In places where Arab and Muslim institutions, even if internally robust, were fairly impermeable prior to 9/11—a term defined by Anthony Orum (926) as "cut-off and isolated from influences outside themselves"—safety was not assured. Post-9/11 mobilizations in support of Arabs and Muslims changed these conditions, although slowest to change were local southwest suburban institutions. Nonetheless, the support and opposition that Muslims encountered in 2004 over a permit to build a mosque in Orland Park showed evidence of stronger intergroup relationships despite the persistence of traditional sources of antipathy.

In this final chapter, I look at some of the ways in which Arab Muslim Americans contextualized their post-9/11 experiences and came to understand their religious faith, their future in American society, the actions they needed to take to improve their collective conditions, and their overall possibilities for being fully embraced by an American "we." I also look at some of the ways in which external events and groups, acting in both constructive and obstructive ways, have shaped these understandings. The overwhelming majority of Arab Muslims interviewed in this study said that their religious faith deepened during the post-9/11 years because their own questions of faith brought about a deeper knowledge and appreciation of Islam. A majority also said that they saw the future for Arabs and Muslims in American society as positive. They took this view because they interpreted their experiences as another chapter in the American story of the fight for social inclusion that all racial, ethnic, and religious minority groups have to wage. Modeled after the tactics of these groups, the paths of agency were thus defined and clear: claiming civil rights, voting, being politically active around domestic issues, attending rallies, and working in coalitions with others. American philanthropies weighed in with the financial support needed to move community institutions forward in precisely these ways. The social relationships, financial support, and mobilizations that were the bridges to greater Arab and Muslim American social inclusion also held the power to define the terms of engagement, that is, to shape their tactics and messages. As noted at the close of chapter 7, Gerstle (1999, 290–91) argues that Americanization has always been shaped by a "mixture of opportunity and coercion" and by a "structure of power that circumscribes choice and shapes the identities to which individuals and groups can aspire." There is evidence of both opportunity and coercion in the activities of Arab American and Muslim American organizations in the post-9/11 era.

Inclusion Is a Struggle

> Regardless of the cause for a more politically conscious Muslim community, there are more politically active Muslims engaging in proactive discourse and professional activism than there were ten years ago.
> —CAIR-Chicago, December 11, 2006

The majority of Arab Muslims interviewed in this study framed their post-9/11 experiences in the context of the historical experiences of other racial and religious minority groups and their struggles for social and political incorporation. In this context, the majority also believed, like other groups in the United States that have faced and fought social exclusion, nativism, hate crimes, and stereotyping, that the eventual outcome of the harrowing Arab and Muslim American post-9/11 experience would be positive. Sixty-nine percent of Arab Muslims interviewed (70 of 102) said that they were positive about the future for Arabs and Muslims in the United States, while 23.5 percent (24 of 102) had a negative outlook and 9 percent (9 of 102) were uncertain. Of those with a positive view, many spoke of the current period as emblematic of a larger

American history that "swings" against certain groups and retracts their rights, but eventually swings the other way.

> I like to base things on history. If you go through history, you see other groups targeted as the enemy. I like to think, as a people, the community will build. 9/11 has opened people's eyes as to who Arabs, Muslims are. We will be more integrated in the society. A lot of people are making the effort. This is Arabs' and Muslims' rite of passage. Every group has gone through this. I hope we can move on and be active participants in society at all levels.

> I think there is a great future. I think there are swings, and now it's swung too far [against civil liberties], but it's going to come back, and when it comes back, there'll be much, much more knowledge and appreciation of Islam among the American public than there was before.

Most of these respondents believed that positive change requires constant effort, and they placed much of the burden of this effort on Arab and Muslim Americans, who, they believe, need to organize and claim their rights.

> The Arabs and Muslims are not going to disappear, and they are going to assert themselves, probably more. I am confident and hopeful that this atmosphere will disappear sooner hopefully than later, because if you look at the American system in general, and government policies in general, you see swings from extreme right to extreme left, and I think this is one of those swings.

> We have to be more vocal and involved. I would be more willing to go to a protest or a rally. We need to say what we need to say. We don't have the luxury to be quiet anymore.

Reclaiming the narrative on Islam was seen as an essential component of organized efforts.

> Listen, if all Muslims in America don't take a basic one track in their life or stand on a solid cornerstone, they won't have any future, and maybe America would kick them all out. . . . We need more institutions and associations in this country, to be united more and more. We need to let them know what Islam is and that we are against what happened. We are against those explosions and terrorist acts which do not belong to Islam. . . . There is something in this world called reasoning. We can use it, but not violence.

Reaching this conclusion about the positive future for Muslims and the need for increased Muslim activism was often framed by the notion of struggle.

> I struggle. I'm concerned about how my religion is being perceived by others and what effect it will have. I see Muslims voting, more represen-

tation, more people standing up for what they believe in. Hopefully it's done in a constructive manner on all sides. I have hope.

A few of those with a positive outlook held a more passive view about the Muslim American role in effecting positive change, believing that it was up to the American people to change their attitudes toward Muslims. While this view was not characteristic of the immigrant generation, it was expressed only by immigrants.

> There will be a place for Muslims in this country one day. Why not? It depends on American people and how they will change their thinking about the Muslim people.

Nearly one-quarter of respondents, however, had a negative outlook on the future for Arabs and Muslims in American society. Instead of seeing the Arab and Muslim experience as part of the ongoing American story of prejudice, racism, xenophobia, and nativism waged against new and different groups of people that gets righted over time after a period of struggle, they framed American anti-Arab and anti-Muslim attitudes in the context of the larger global activities of the U.S. government, for which they saw little hope for change. In other words, it was not domestically grounded racialized or religious fears that explained the subaltern position of Arab and Muslim Americans; rather, it was American foreign policies in general and the Bush administration's global "war on terror" that drove these American fears, incited animosities, and provoked intergroup conflict. Viewed from this perspective, little could be done to effect positive change on the domestic front without a major shift in American foreign policy.

> I see a black picture for the entire U.S., not just for Muslims. The way that they are looking for these incidents, terror attacks, they are increasing culture clash, and bringing conflicts between races and religions.

> We can't imagine anything good. Are we the next casualty? As many casualties in the news, now new casualties among Arab Americans sacrificed in the name of fighting terrorism.

The Terms of Engagement and Shaping Power

By the time of the 9/11 attacks, relationships between the secular and faith-based organizations operating within Chicago's Arab American community were fairly well coordinated. The wide popular appeal of Arab American secular institutions had begun to wane in the Chicago metropolitan area (and elsewhere) in the early 1990s, leaving a void that many Arab Muslims filled with stronger faith-based affiliations. This change was in part a response to frustration; the perception was that years of playing according to the American rules of the game had led to few positive outcomes for Arab and Muslim Americans and for Arabs and Muslims overseas. The switch-over to faith-based organizations did not signal a banal, pedestrian search for a new way to organize time, thought, and energy. Rather, a deep, almost collective yearning drove the focus on faith. Although I have written about this change in more detail elsewhere (Cainkar 2004d), the most succinct way I can accurately describe the hope that comes with faith is through the words of W. E. B. Du Bois (1995 [1903], 274):

> Through all the sorrow of the Sorrow Songs there breathes a hope—a faith in the ultimate justice of things.

Faith that justice would ultimately prevail was a stirring that rose and spread throughout Chicago's Arab Muslim community in the 1990s. While not unconnected to global Islamic revival, this surge in faith was very local in its palpability and meaning. It had everything to do with human integrity and nothing to do with violence—a crucial point to make in the context of alternative explanations that equate these changes with terrorism and a growing "Muslim problem" in the United States (see chapter 7). Recognizing and respecting these changes, the secular Arab American Action Network on Sixty-third Street had begun coordinating its youth programs with the Inner City Muslim Action Network (IMAN) and administering some of its social service programs at its satellite location at the Bridgeview Mosque Foundation.

The response of these organizations to their communities' post-9/11 predicament was largely to employ strategies and tactics similar to those used by historically excluded groups: public protest, community organizing, voter registration and voting, crafting a targeted message, expanding solidarity networks, hosting educational and cultural forums, and appropriating the narrative of self-definition. This work was aided by financial support for institutional capacity building and leadership development. These activities largely reflected what philanthropic organizations were prepared to fund as well as the organizing agendas of local coalitions. The embrace of Arab and Muslim American communities by a strong immigrants rights coalition in metropolitan Chicago—the Illinois Coalition for Immigrant and Refugee Rights (ICIRR)—sharply defined many of the terms of engagement, since the coalition's electoral legalization agenda requiring voter registration and get-out-the-vote campaigns seemed to intersect with Arab and Muslim American needs for legal defense and citizenship rights. The same shaping power was held by the Alinsky-esque United Power for Action and Justice coalition, which stepped up its leadership development work in faith-based communities, including the Bridgeview Mosque Foundation and the Council of Islamic Organizations of Greater Chicago.

Interviewees who held the view that the Arab and Muslim American predicament was secondarily about social exclusion in the United States and primarily connected to U.S. foreign policies believed that electoral work, voting, and domestic issue campaigns were not likely to produce the changes needed to halt the defamation and political exclusion of Arab and Muslim Americans. They were not optimistic about the Arab and Muslim American future and believed that more effort should be put into direct action organizing that would frame domestic issues in a global context. Activists who took this perspective were not passive: they cooperated in a wide range of activities organized around the multiple and complex needs of Arab and Muslim Americans and other immigrant and disenfranchised communities, but their hearts lay elsewhere. According to this Arab American activist:

> We were forced to reach out to other organizations and communities for support. This helped us build networks with some entities we did not have relationships with. Despite the hundreds of incidents of discrimination and racism this community has endured, there have been as many if not more of people reaching out in solidarity. People are learning a lot more about world geography and basic history. On some level this is positive. Also, I think on some level that there is a realization in some places, even among those not politically astute, that there is a broader worldview that came out of 9/11. Some do see us [the U.S. government] as having plans for world hegemony. A large percentage of people especially in the Third World are resentful of us. Not in the way the administration describes it—as jealous of our way of life—but due to the subjugation and oppression of American policies. We need to have education about the community and what it's facing now put in a historical perspective. Provide a geopolitical analysis of Afghanistan, Iraq, Palestine resistance. . . .
>
> I still believe that faith-based institutions are important and play an important role, but I believe that the more important institutions are not only those that provide faith-based support or direct social services. I think most important are those providing advocacy, trying to develop organizing campaigns and leadership from amongst affected immigrants to resist anti-immigration legislation and the criminalization of Arabs and Muslims. We need a stronger low-cost, free legal service. We need legal clinics around immigration issues, deportations. Some in the community feel the need for more concentrated electoral work. I feel the problem in the U.S. is systematic. I don't feel one party is naturally inclined to be more supportive of our issues than the other. I would rather see community resources go into direct action organizing campaigns than voter registration and political campaigns.

New relationships and permeabilities of Arab and Muslim American institutions and the shaping power of post-9/11 solidarities were also evident in other activities. For example, the two featured themes of the

Bridgeview Mosque Foundation's open house Ramadan iftar of 2007 were Islamic perspectives on the importance of voting and political participation and its perspectives on environmentalism and global warming, for which an imam was brought from Washington to speak on the Qur'anic bases of Muslim environmentalism. Shaping is indicated by the acquiescence of most Arab and Muslim American institutional leaders to demands that they publicly denounce violence committed by Arabs and Muslims anywhere in the world, despite arguments by some of these leaders that doing so amounts to de facto acceptance of claims that all Arabs and Muslims can justifiably be held accountable for the actions of any Arabs and Muslims. While major Arab and Muslim American organizations have issued such statements of condemnation, they have received little media attention, leaving space for those who oppose their civic integration to continue arguing that these organizations support terrorism. Arab and Muslim American organizations were also advised by some outside supporters to subordinate claims related to U.S. foreign policies perceived as unjust or wrong-minded to claims and activities associated with "becoming American." Work on behalf of the people of Palestine, Kashmir, Afghanistan, Iraq, or Lebanon, the tortured, or those held at Guantánamo Bay was to be sublimated to voter registration, leadership development, capacity building, and civil and immigrant rights. The federal government's closure of five major Muslim American charities largely redirected Muslim American philanthropic energies from overseas to needy local groups. Asserting its rightful place in the local community after the social isolation that allowed hatemongers to believe they could lay siege to the mosque in the days after 9/11, the Bridgeview Mosque Foundation opened a community food pantry in March 2005. This charitable venture has served up to 150 needy families per week, at least half of whom are non-Muslims, including low-income residents of the nearby trailer park, the very place from which it was suspected that the first post-9/11 attacks on the mosque emanated (see chapter 2). A quote found on the Mosque Foundation website expresses the transformative relationship-building power of this effort: "Maybe whatever they might have thought about Muslims before they stepped into the Food Pantry is changed when they step out. I hope that they see the true kindness and generosity of Islam when they see all these ladies wearing hijab eager to help them."[1]

Another significant engagement after 9/11 brought representatives of Arab and Muslim American communities into regular meetings with local representatives of federal law enforcement, the U.S. Justice Department, and the Department of Homeland Security, an activity not opposed by Arab and Muslim American leaders, but one that contained within it a number of implicit assumptions about the character of their communities. Such meetings, sometimes called "roundtables," began to be held

across the country in 2002 in cities with large Arab or Muslim populations and were framed as opportunities "to get to know one another."
They were the federal government's response to charges that it was
alienating Arab and Muslim Americans instead of making them allies in
the fight against terrorism. As discussed in chapter 4, local-level participants on both sides of the table were frustrated by actions taken at the
top levels of the Bush administration that were counterproductive to
their own. In 2007 the Chicago office of the FBI organized a Youth
Academy for the tenth grade of Universal School, a Muslim school in
suburban Bridgeview, where students met with FBI agents for a class
period twice weekly to learn about FBI work on terrorism, cyber crime,
and civil rights. Similar relationship-building efforts on the national
level include the American-Arab Anti-Discrimination Committee's
active promotion of FBI careers for Arab Americans.

Persistent Voices of Exclusion

While these significant social changes were occurring, voices of anti-
Muslim nativism and anti-Arab dehumanization continued to roar, keeping alive a countervailing social impulse to isolate Arab and Muslim
Americans as "outsiders" in American society by arguing that they are
persons "who cannot be trusted to live by the rules" (Becker 1963, 1).
Their discourses and narratives were working in the opposite direction of
those who were building bridges to the mainstream, producing a bifur-
cated social environment. These were not isolated individuals; among
them were elected officials, candidates for office, wealthy patrons, and
media personalities. A few examples will make this point. In 2004, U.S.
Congressman Peter T. King (R-N.Y.) claimed on nationally syndicated
radio that 85 percent of American Muslim religious leaders are "an enemy
living amongst us" and that "no [American] Muslims" cooperated in the
"war on terror."[2] "Islamo-Fascism Awareness Week" in the fall of 2007
was a national speaking tour about the dangers of Islam sponsored by
David Horowitz's Freedom Center, which called its visit to two hundred
college and university campuses "the biggest conservative campus
protest ever, a wake-up call for Americans."[3] Similarly oriented anti-
Arab/Muslim groups and personalities, whose websites often reveal the
relationship between these views and their foreign policy perspectives,
worked to create a national uproar over the intention of newly elected
Muslim American congressman Keith Ellison (the first African American
to be elected to national office from Minnesota and the first Muslim
in Congress) to take his oath of office during a private ceremony with
his hand on a Qur'an. The lecturer and talk-show host Dennis Prager
claimed that Ellison's act "undermines American civilization."[4] Mary
Grabar, another conservative commentator, said, "Keith Ellison wants to

govern in a country whose values he rejects," and, "by rejecting the Bible, he rejects our country's principles of reason and free will."[5] Being Muslim was thus characterized as rejecting the promise of American freedom, similar to the way in which wearing hijab was interpreted. Arab American Institute president Dr. James Zogby, who pointed out that some Jewish members of Congress have used the Torah in the optional private ceremony, argued in turn that the core value at stake *is* individual freedom. "Objections to Ellison's desire to use the Quran during a personal, unofficial and optional event are outright displays of anti-Muslim bias and are contrary to the core values of individual freedom upon which our nation was founded."[6] As pointed out in chapter 7, some American groups openly advocate the use of coercion to impose respect for values like freedom; while seemingly contradictory, Gerstle (1999) describes this pattern as characteristic of American history.

"Fear and Mistrust of Muslims Runs Deep" was the title of a Reuters article (Debusmann 2006) about talk radio host Jerry Klein's (630 WMAL) November 2006 show, when his switchboard was jammed with callers after he suggested that all Muslims in the United States be identified with a crescent-shaped tattoo or armband. Some callers were angry about his statement, while others thought it was a great idea; some demanded that stronger measures be taken against American Muslims. At the end of the show, Klein revealed that he had perpetrated a hoax, stating, "What you just did was show me how the German people allowed what happened to the Jews to happen." A surge of anti-Muslim statements characterized a number of electoral campaigns, moving such sentiments out of the province of blogs, websites, conservative media personalities, and shock jocks and into popular use to build support for certain candidates. In Illinois, a candidate for the Eighth Congressional District, who was the head of his ward's Republican Committee, told the suburban *Chicago Daily Herald*'s editorial board that he had no problem with the government placing human monitors in mosques, explaining, "For years I've been distrustful of Islam" (Davis 2004). Charges of Muslim American disloyalty were part of a number of 2007 political campaigns, in some cases sparking the criminalization and return of Muslim American campaign donations.[7] A 2007 Rudy Giuliani–approved presidential campaign advertisement referred to Muslims as "a people perverted."[8] The most substantial resurgence of anti-Muslim sentiment, however, was in the 2008 presidential campaign, when assertions that being Muslim means being anti-American were used to build public fear of presidential candidate Barack Obama, who, although not Muslim, is the biological son of a Muslim man. This fear was leveraged and augmented with distribution of the anti-Muslim film *Obsession* to 28 million American households located in contested areas for the 2008 presidential race, and it reached its peak in the final six weeks of the campaign.

These types of deprecating discourses have not been reserved for Muslims alone; Arabs have faced their share of dehumanization, with little institutional rebuke. One can compare the extensive institutional censure (although not uncontested) that followed MSNBC shock jock Don Imus's degrading statements about Rutgers's female African American basketball players on his April 2007 *Imus in the Morning* radio show, for which both Imus and producer Bernard McGuirk were fired, to the absence of institutional backlash for the opinions openly aired on Imus's show that Palestinians are "stinking animals" and it is permissible to "kill them all" (once the counterposed symbol of civility, the American, leaves the scene). The following dialogue between Imus, McGuirk, and Imus's guest, the sports anchor Sid Rosenberg, was aired on Imus's November 12, 2004, show:

DON IMUS:	They're [Palestinians] eating dirt, and that fat pig wife [Suha Arafat] of his is living in Paris.
SID ROSENBERG:	They're all brainwashed, though. That's what it is. And they're stupid to begin with, but they're brainwashed now. *Stinking animals.* They ought to drop the bomb right there, *kill 'em all right now.*
BERNARD MCGUIRK:	You can just imagine standing there.
ROSENBERG:	Oh, *the stench.*
IMUS:	Well, the problem is that we have Andrea [Mitchell, *NBC News* chief foreign affairs correspondent] there. We don't want anything to happen to her.
ROSENBERG:	Oh, she's got to get out. Just warn Andrea, get out, and then drop the bomb, *kill everybody.*
MCGUIRK:	It's like the worst Woodstock.
ROSENBERG:	Look at this. Look at these *animals. Animals!* [emphasis added][9]

Freedom of speech is a core American value, but according to one study of normative social patterns, hate speech is not socially tolerated when it is directed against groups that have fought for and won an accepted social status, groups that we might call "insiders" (Gould 2005). Measured by this standard, the level of social tolerance for hate speech directed against Arab and Muslim Americans indicates that their marginal insider/outsider status continues despite post-9/11 progress. Public opinion polls showing that anti-Muslim sentiments persist among the American population support this conclusion. A 2006 Gallup poll (*Washington Post*–ABC News) found that 39 percent of American respondents favored the requirement that Muslims carry special identity cards, 51 percent believed that Muslims are not loyal to the United States, and 25 percent said that they would not want a Muslim neighbor.

Another 2006 poll (CAIR) showed that less than half of the American population has a positive view of Islam.

Freedom-Lover/Freedom-Hater

That Muslims inherently hate freedom is a core argument of anti-Muslim groups, but as Georgetown professor John Esposito argues, this charge does not match reality on the ground. Citing a 2006 Gallup World Poll, Esposito notes:

> Large numbers of Muslims cite the West's technological success and its liberty and freedom of speech as what they most admire. When asked if they would include a provision for Freedom of Speech, defined as allowing all citizens to express their opinion on political, social and economic issues of the day if they were drafting a constitution for a new country, overwhelming majorities (94% in Egypt, 97% in Bangladesh, 98% in Lebanon etc.) in every country surveyed responded yes, they would.[10]

My study found similar views. When interviewees were asked, "What are the two best things about the United States?" the overwhelming majority cited "freedom" as their first response: "We still have the freedom to speak our minds, which is the very health and heart of the American people." Many, however, qualify this response with the opinion that the American government is reducing such freedom.

> It's the freedom to come and go as you please, and openness to say what you feel. Well, that used to be. The First Amendment rights have waned since 9/11. There's a lot of good things about this country, but it's disintegrating.

> Freedom and democracy are good things, although that has become less since 9/11.

The second most common response to this question cited opportunities for work and study and for making a living, while the third most common was about diversity and pluralism.

> The best thing about the U.S. is it's really a melting pot. I have lived in different places in the world, and as a foreigner it is a much more welcoming society than any other society I have been in.

Anti-Arab/Muslim groups whose arguments are based on stereotypes and social constructions continue to erect barriers to the full social and political incorporation of American Arabs and Muslims. When some of them identify what Muslims must do to be considered for membership in the American nation, the "cleansing hoops" are usually so tied to condemnations of the Qur'an and derisions of the prophet Mohammed that they largely require Muslims to become not Muslim at all to be American. Arabs and Muslims, of course, are not the first groups to face coercive pressures to take on the often impossible task of un-becoming who they are; African Americans and Asians could not become white, Slavs could not become Nordic, and Roman Catholics and Jews would not become Protestants. As we see here, however, 9/11 and its aftermath produced the opposite response in a majority of the Arab American Muslims interviewed in this study: for them, the events of this period brought on a soul-searching from which they emerged more deeply Muslim.

A Test of Faith

The 9/11 attacks and their aftermath shook the religious faith of the majority of Arab Muslims interviewed in this study, some of whom referred to what they went through as a "test of faith." Only 16 percent of the Arab Muslims interviewed said that they experienced no changes in their religious faith after 9/11. Of the 84 percent who reported changes in their religious faith, a number of factors were cited, including the 9/11 hijackers' use and abuse of Islam to justify their actions, the treatment Muslims received from the American government, the broadly hostile reactions of the American public, the allegations of anti-Muslim activists and spokespersons, the questions from non-Muslims they could not answer, and their own questioning of what they had been taught about Islam. The substantial government, media, and public attention focused on Islam and Muslims awakened in them a process of Muslim self-discovery. Seventy percent of the Arab Muslims interviewed, and more than 80 percent of those who reported changes in their religious faith, said that they emerged from these post-9/11 tests of faith with positive changes in their faith, while 14 percent of all persons interviewed reported negative changes. Of the persons reporting positive changes, 76 percent described having deeper religious convictions and a stronger Muslim identity.

> It's affirmed it. It's made it stronger. Like I said, it's a big test for us. When a lot has happened to you and your faith is tested, it's made me stronger and I'm more inclined to read more. I want to know what's out there and what people are writing about us. I've had a lot more confidence in challenging certain websites that get posted, making comments, etc. I feel a lot more informed just because I have taken initiative to be more informed post-9/11.

As discussed in chapter 5, many interviewees reported an increased desire to learn about their faith so that they could answer the questions posed to them by non-Muslims about Islam.

The flow of unexpected questions encouraged me to learn more about my faith.

There is no question that, being intellectually inclined, I became more critical of my faith, but to a pleasant conclusion, I guess. More reaffirming. It has affected my faith in that it made me look for certain answers that I did not necessarily need, but I needed to supply the answers for others.

Others indicated that the events of 9/11 and their aftermath caused them to question God's plan for Muslims.

I started questioning God a little more. This whole Muslim fiasco . . . I asked myself, why, how, where, and when? . . . So much is going against Islam, I started to question if we are wrong. How it could be if we are so righteous and good and divine in our ways? Why? Do we have it wrong now? Maybe our turn is in the afterlife?

Some, particularly those born in the United States or who migrated at an early age, questioned what they had been taught about Islam.

Well, I do have to admit, I think that on 9/11 and a year after, a lot of things were really shaken for me. I think when people asked, "Why were you withdrawn?" or "Where have you been?" I usually say it's because of my family, but I really think it's because I felt there was such internal chaos for me that my faith, my belief, all of that, things were just out of order. It took me a while to get things back in sync to feel comfortable. I wouldn't say I was questioning my religious belief, I would say I was questioning what I was taught. That's what was a lot of the issue. You know, you think of all the paradigms like "Oh, my God. Everything I was taught was wrong." Or you just begin to think your foundation is just not correct, so definitely, I think a year or two of internal struggle of "what are my beliefs."

Again, I'm not questioning, okay, I need to be another religion, but just questioning what was I taught. It was hard, I mean, I remember going around Ramadan time and standing behind an imam and just watching everything he was saying and even the verses that were being read and how they were interpreted, not the actual verse but the interpretation of the verses. I think that really shook things up.

Arab Muslims who questioned what they had been taught about Islam said that they felt they had been trained to focus too much on the "small things," which often made them judgmental toward other Muslims. For example, they were taught that one should judge a Muslim woman's faith by the degree to which she covers herself or that one shows one's faith by saying, "Allahu akhbar," instead of clapping. Religion was taught more as a set of rules that set them apart from others than as a deep and meaningful value system, which would have given them a stronger grounding and allowed them to focus on what they shared with others in the society in which they lived. To remedy these deficits and to find the answers to their questions, they consulted the Qur'an directly as well as the teachings of various Muslim scholars. Here they found Islamic perspectives on issues that really mattered to them, like social justice, human equality, racism, sexism, and how to face personal struggles. This engagement with Islamic scripture and theology made them stronger Muslims.

> My faith has become a hundred times stronger after 9/11. After 9/11, I really felt a closeness ironically with my religion that I had not had prior to [9/11], and I opened the Qur'an consistently for the first time and read it. If I could add this, the things that I questioned, the things that I thought were oppressive specifically to me and my gender, I went in search of. And these are the things that I sought out and read, and then I went and found out why it said it, until I not necessarily agreed but was satisfied with the reason. And that gave me peace with my religion.

Some called for a more "sophisticated" Islamic education that would be more deeply spiritual, be focused on Islamic values, and provide meaning for life in the United States.

> I think I had a big crisis. On the issue of the suicide bombing and the justifications that are promoted with that by some Islamic scholars. I lost respect for a number of religious leaders and scholars who I used to look up to and admire. I shifted gears religiously quite a bit to more of a Sufi orientation. Because 9/11 and other factors sort of shifted my thinking to a more essential perspective on what Islam is all about, which is simply a challenge for human beings to lead a spiritual, religious life that creates a more divine presence, to lead a more upright life. I think there needs to be increased religious education in a way that is sophisticated, spiritually oriented, and is reconciled with our identity as Americans.

As mentioned in chapter 5, many Arab Muslims who were not literate in Arabic, or whose children were not, wanted to learn or teach their children Arabic so that they would be able to consult the Qur'an in Arabic on their own.

> I yearn more for my roots, and my religious spiritual roots personally. After 9/11, I felt like I stuck out, [was] more scrutinized, and that brought out a lot of self-scrutiny too. I felt that had gone dormant, my relationship with my religion and culture, both. And I felt also that I must under all circumstances make sure that my children also experience a spiritual journey to exploring their Muslim faith. They needed to know more about it. They needed to know; they need to be able to defend their beliefs. I went about actively seeking tutors, language tutors, so that they would feel more comfortable picking up a Qur'an and reading it in Arabic rather than a translation.

Among the 14 percent of Arab Muslims who said they experienced negative changes in their religious faith after 9/11, some were more guarded about their beliefs and less inclined to share them publicly for fear of how they would be perceived:

> I don't know if I want to confront people who have these misconceptions about my faith. They'll see me as an extremist, reinterpret. I stay away from discussing my religious beliefs in public.

Others said that they were wary of engaging in activities with other Muslims, including praying at a mosque, because they feared the spotlight of the government.

> It made me become more cautious and at the same time more fearful, cautious of who I am around and situations I may put myself in. People have gone through various emotions and lost trust and faith in people.

> I have lessened my visits to the mosque after the events, in fear of being subject to questioning or something that I don't like. I want to be on the safe side in every step of my life.

Driven by the answers they found in their quest for deeper knowledge, the majority of the Arab Muslims interviewed in this study had a stronger appreciation for Islam after this spiritual journey. They emerged from the post-9/11 period with better skills, both to practice their religion and to explain it to others in the United States.

Conclusion

Arab and Muslim Americans enter the future in a different and better domestic sociopolitical position than they occupied on September 11, 2001. Their heightened state of social and civic engagement, which emerged out of the relationships, solidarities, and coalitions formed in their defense, should at minimum provide them with better protection from public attack and mass arrest should another event occur that some might use to provoke notions of collective responsibility. Theoretically, in many places the relationships are in place to block the types of major assaults on Arab and Muslim American civil rights and public safety that occurred in the years following the 9/11 attacks. Unfortunately, however, these very changes in Arab and Muslim American social status have exposed segments of the American population that rely on anti-Arab and anti-Muslim sentiments for their own benefit, parts of which are well organized, well financed, and invested in inciting public fears. While these groups existed before 9/11, they were then able to capitalize on the public's passivity and lack of knowledge and on Arab and Muslim social exclusion to get their defamatory messages across with little protest from mainstream institutions. Now they work in an environment in which their discourses and actions are contested by a sizable and more knowledgeable sector of the American population; this is a significant change.

Sociologists recognize that the social and political inclusion of subordinated groups requires the removal of structural barriers. Just as African Americans, Native Americans, Asian Americans, Latinos, Jews, Catholics, women, and other groups have challenged legal and customary barriers to social, economic, and political equality in the United States, so must Arab and Muslim Americans. The structural barriers faced by Arab and Muslim Americans, in addition to those associated with race and religion, are tied to domestic and global political interests that gain from constructing them as deviants, outsiders, and as inherently violent.[11] These groups rely on fear, conflict, violence, and strife to prove their arguments. While many journalists, media personalities, entertainers, academics, filmmakers, and elected representatives oppose these divisive messages, their voices must struggle within a cacophony of allegations of threat and incitements of fear. Consequently, despite the recent structural advances of Arab and Muslim Americans, their social and political incorporation has been stalled by parties who continue to argue that "they" can never be part of "us," using social constructions such as "they hate 'our' values." It is useful here to revisit the words of southwest suburban Orland Park Baptist minister Lyons and of a resident of the town, because their statements indicate how damaging these social constructions are; beyond the podiums and platforms of speakers like these, such words are used on an everyday, grounded level to deny people's fundamental rights in the United States.[12]

> Now, as a Christian, a Baptist, and an American, I'm a firm believer in religious liberty and favor any religious group buying property or erecting a house of worship, but liberty has limits! No group that jeopardizes our personal safety or our national security is deserving of our tolerance.

> We don't hate you. We have no ill feelings for you. I think what's happened today is because of what's going on in America and because our boys are losing their lives every day [loud clapping]. We care about America. We care about what's going on because we don't want to bring it here. We're not saying that you'll bring it, but you must understand, that *because you're tied in with this religion* and a possible mosque in Orland Park, it will come to our doorstep. . . . If there is trouble in Orland Park, it will be our police force that will have to take the brunt of it. It'll be our fire department who will have to come in and take care of the problem. It will be our tax dollars that will have to take care of this problem. [emphasis added]

As long as arguments that Arabs and Muslims are fundamentally different from "us" are socially tolerated in the United States and continue to hold a significant place in American culture, whether referring to Arabs and Muslims inside or outside the United States, it is difficult to pronounce that the road ahead will be smooth for Arab and Muslim Americans.

Notes

Chapter 1

1. In this book, I use the term "Arab Muslims" to refer to the group of individuals who were interviewed for this study and for whom study data may be most appropriately extrapolated. On the other hand, because Arab American and Muslim American post-9/11 experiences shared many features, for reasons explained in this book I use the terms "Arabs and Muslims," "Arabs/Muslims," and "Arab Americans and Muslim Americans" to refer to this larger group. Empirical study would need to determine the ways in which different Muslim subgroups had varying and shared experiences. I suspect that African American Muslims and European Muslims had some experiences that differed from the narrative reported in this book; the experiences of black African immigrant Muslims may be more nuanced, depending on their country of origin and social class. This study, I believe, represents best the experiences of those who most closely approximate the physical features of the "terrorist phenotype" that Americans had come to understand—in other words (excuse the term), "brown" Muslims, as well as those who could be most unambiguously cast as "foreigners" because policies and public behavior were heavily driven by stereotypes and notions of foreignness. This group included Arabs, South Asian Muslims, and some West Asian Muslims (for example, Iranians and Afghanis)—the groups most often captured under the social construction "Middle Easterner." The same need for empirical examinations of differences in experience applies to Arab Christians and Muslims. The Detroit Arab American Survey (Baker et al. 2004) and the work of Jen'nan Ghazal Read (2008) begin to address these matters using survey data.

2. Life history profiles conducted with a small sample of Arab Muslim Americans in 2008 revealed that for some the fear of internment camps had not gone away (see chapter 2).

3. *Hijab* is a composite term meaning a modest form of dress and manner appropriate for a Muslim woman. There is variation in interpretation about which parts of women's bodies should be covered to meet an Islamic standard of modesty. There is general agreement that hijab requires women to

cover their hair. In this book, I use the word "hijab" to mean "head scarf" because this is the most common form of covering worn by the women described here, and because the women against whom hostile acts were perpetrated were wearing head scarves alone, or head scarves and full-length coats.

4. I use the words "hate acts" and "hate encounters" in this book instead of "hate crimes" to cover more broadly those actions that might not be considered a crime, such as spitting, sneezing in someone's face, and hand signals.

5. This finding could mean that the government's aggressive and widely publicized efforts focused on men reduced the public's propensity to attack men and shifted their focus to women.

6. The United States is different in this regard from France and Turkey, where the hijab is outlawed in certain places, and from Saudi Arabia and Iran, where it is mandatory.

7. This definition of social capital is adapted from that of Harvard's Saguaro Seminar, "Civic Engagement in America," available at: http://www.hks. harvard.edu/saguaro/glossary.htm (accessed July 21, 2008).

8. Whether this enhanced social and political integration of Arab and Muslim Americans raised the activity level of those who opposed their embrace should be studied.

9. Funder reluctance to support many Arab and Muslim American organizations because of political concerns long predated 9/11. See chapter 3 for an explanation of the sociopolitical context in which these actions occurred. The charges to which they felt vulnerable were trumpeted in the 2008 claims that the presidential candidate Barack Obama supported terrorism because a foundation on whose board he served, the Woods Fund, approved a post-9/11 community-organizing grant to the Sixty-third Street–based Arab American Action Network in Chicago after its community center was set on fire by an arsonist.

10. See "McCain Supporter: 'Obama Is an Arab,' " October 10, 2008, available at: http://www.youtube.com/watch?v=0YIq5Q15L1o (accessed November 20, 2008).

11. I believe John McCain's intent was fair-minded, despite his choice of words. See "Ben Affleck Rejects Use of Arab/Muslim as Slur," *Politically Incorrect with Bill Maher,* October 20, 2008, available at: http://www.youtube.com/watch?v=-qwsSDE2sdo&NR=1 (accessed November 20, 2008).

12. "What If He Were Muslim? Colin Powell on Muslim Americans," *Meet the Press,* October 19, 2008, available at: http://www.youtube.com/watch?v=dYELqbZAQ4M&NR=1 (accessed November 20, 2008). See also "Campbell Brown: So What if Obama Was a Muslim or an Arab?" (accessed October 13, 2008) available at: http://www.youtube.com/watch?v=_ LXMMmfd1lw.

13. "Student Attacked: I Was Victim of Hate Crime Last Week," *Chicago Sun-Times,* October 10, 2008; Debra Horan, "Villa Park Mosque Vandalized for Fourth Time," *Chicago Tribune,* October 10, 2008. The western suburbs constitute a very different context for hate acts than the southwest suburbs described in chapters 6 and 7.

14. "Favorable ratings of Muslim Americans rose from 45 percent in March 2001 to 59 percent in November 2001 before falling slightly to 54 percent in March 2002" (Keeter and Kohut 2003, 185; see also table 6.3 and related note).

15. Essentialized notions informed Bush administration policies and actions for a much longer period of time than they did the behavior of the American public at large.

16. Evelyn Alsultany (2008; personal communication, July 20, 2008) would put television shows such as *24*, *The Guardian, Seventh Heaven, The Education of Max Bickford*, and *The Practice* in this sympathetic genre.

17. Examples of this stigma could be located in critical caricatures representing Obama as a Muslim; in the request by Michigan organizers that women in hijab not be positioned near or behind Obama at a public event, an incident for which Obama personally apologized; and by Obama campaign flyers entitled "Barack Obama Is Not a Muslim."

18. Detailed explorations of the history and experiences of Arab Americans in metropolitan Chicago can be found in my chapter on Arabs in Koval et al. (2006), in my chapter on Arab Americans in Suleiman (1999b), and in Hanania's *Arabs of Chicagoland* (2005).

19. Of the more than 60 percent of Palestinians living in diaspora, the vast majority reside in Arab countries, some of which have offered them citizenship. Jordan gave citizenship to the majority of refugees landing there after the 1948 and 1967 wars and dispersions. It also gave Jordanian citizenship to Palestinians living on the West Bank and in East Jerusalem between 1948 and the early 1990s. Israel gave citizenship to the few hundred thousand Palestinians who managed to stay and hold on to their land after its creation. Lebanon offered citizenship to some (relatively few) Palestinian refugees, mostly Christians. Palestinians lived in relatively large numbers in Arab Gulf countries until 1990 but were rarely accorded citizenship. The majority of immigrants to the United States listed as Kuwaiti or Saudi by country of birth or last permanent residence are Palestinians who migrated to these countries for work and then came to the United States in a third migration. Palestinians are also hidden within Israeli, Lebanese, and, to a lesser extent, Syrian and Yemeni migration. Most Palestinians living in Gaza, Lebanon, Syria, and Egypt have no passports, rendering migration difficult.

20. Somalia is a member of the League of Arab States, although Somalis are not necessarily Arabs.

21. A smaller number of Arabs have migrated to the United States from other countries. During World War I, the largest number of Arab immigrants to the United States came from Central and South America (Cainkar 1988).

22. Immigration and Naturalization Service country of birth data, 1972 to 1999.

23. The 1980 U.S. census counted 25,288 persons of Palestinian ancestry in the United States, while a 1984 Census Bureau study using migration and natural increase data estimated that there were at least 87,700 Palestinians in the United States, a 350 percent difference. In 1986 the demographer Janet Lippman Abu-Lughod estimated that there were 130,000 Palestinians in the United States, while four years later the 1990 census counted only 48,019, a 270 percent difference.

24. See EPIC, "Freedom of Information Documents on the Census: Department of Homeland Security Obtained Data on Arab Americans from Census Bureau," available at: http://epic.org/privacy/census/foia/ (last updated September 17, 2004; accessed July 23, 2008).

Chapter 3

1. At one time, the sociologist Robert Park considered Japanese Americans unassimilable. See Stanford Lyman (1972) in Hilary Conroy and Scott Miyakawa's *East Across the Pacific*.
2. Eighty percent of Palestinian respondents identified as white (Shryock 2008).
3. On U.S. Census Bureau products, Arabs who can be identified as Arabs by the Census Bureau (such as by language, place of birth, or ancestry) are recoded as white if they check "other," the only viable alternative category according to Arab Americans. In this study, I asked participants: "There have been discussions about whether Arabs are white or not, with different points of view. Do you think Arabs are white, not white, or what?"
4. Author's field notes from Orland Park public hearings, 2004.
5. U.S. Congress, Immigration Act of 1917, February 5, 1917, 39 Stat. 874.
6. Between 1916 and 1919, cross-Atlantic travel was limited by war. More than 90 percent of Arab immigrants came to the United States from other countries in the Americas. When Arabs initially boarded ships for "America," their destinations included the Caribbean and South, Central, and North America, all sites of historic Arab communities.
7. See note 5.
8. The Asia Barred Zone was defined by Congress as follows: "South of the 20th parallel latitude north: West of the 160th meridian of longitude east from Greenwich: North of the tenth parallel of latitude south: Or who are natives of any country, province, or dependency situated on the continent of Asia: West of the 110th meridian of longitude east from Greenwich and east of the 50th meridian of longitude east from Greenwich and south of the 50th parallel of latitude north; except that portion of said territory situated between the 50th and the 64th meridians of longitude east from Greenwich and the 24th and 38th parallels of latitude north."
9. Quotas were based on racialized notions of superior and inferior whites.
10. The 1925 case of John Mohamad Ali was decided in accordance with the criteria used by justices in the 1923 Supreme Court decision *United States v. Thind,* who concluded that Asian Indians were not white, based on the "common man's understanding" of whiteness. Marian Smith (2002) notes: "Facing proceedings to cancel his 1921 naturalization, John Mohamad Ali told the U.S. District Court in Detroit in 1925 that though born in India, he was not East Indian or Hindu. Rather, he was properly Arabian, for his ancestors originated in Arabia. The court replied that Ali's ancient ancestry was not at issue. Ali had dark skin and fit all other criteria that had disqualified *Thind* from naturalization." Smith argues that the court's decision left vague the issue of the eligibility of Arabs for naturalization, renewing the "controversy over the eligibility of those peoples who bordered on the barred zone."

11. Smith (2002) references "Matter of S——" (exclusion proceedings, 56071/165, October 18, 1941, 1 I&N 178–79); U.S. Department of Justice (1943).

12. The Roberts Commission was led by Owen J. Roberts. The commission had been charged by executive order on December 18, 1941 with the task of ascertaining the facts surrounding the attacks by the Japanese armed forces on Hawaii on December 7, 1941.

13. *Korematsu v. United States* 323 U.S. 214 (1944).

14. Personal conversation with the historian Elliot Barkan, May 2006.

15. This group of immigrants was relatively unknown to scholars until Yemeni immigrant Nagi Daifullah was killed in 1973 by a county sheriff while organizing for Cesar Chavez and the United Farm Workers.

16. See the Arab American Institute website: http://www.aaiusa.org/foundation/34/census-information-center (accessed November 5, 2007).

17. These data are Arab American Institute tabulations of the 2000 census; they combine all persons from Arab countries, whether ethnically Arab or not, and include Sudanese and Somalis.

18. Author's interviews with founding members of the Association of Arab American University Graduates: Ibrahim Abu-Lughod, Sofia and Hassan Haddad, Ghada Talhami, and Elaine Hagopian.

19. Scholars have debated whether this strong support for Israel was largely tied to American anti-Communist designs or based on a special relationship independent of them (see, for example, Rubenberg 1989).

20. http://www.aaug-asq.org/about_the_aaug.htm (accessed October 30, 2007).

21. The archives of the American-Arab Anti-Discrimination Committee provide a wealth of such documentation.

22. Space was extended, for example, to women, gays, and the disabled. Because Muslims were not a "racial" group, they found more open access to the space of claims-making than Arab Americans.

23. The spring 2005 issue of the *MIT Electronic Journal of Middle East Studies* is a tremendous compilation of essays by Arab American feminists describing their experiences with social and political exclusion, stereotyping, and silencing.

24. See Tracked in America, "Abdeen Jabara: Targeting Palestinian Activists," available at: http://www.trackedinamerica.org/timeline/civil_rights/jabara/ (accessed August 12, 2008).

25. According to INS data, more Palestinians were admitted on student visas than as quota immigrants in the 1980s (Cainkar 1988).

26. Immigration Act of 1990. See PL 101-649.

27. Drawing on survey data collected from an Arab mosque and an Arab church, Read (2008) finds that Muslim Arab Americans are more likely to define and perceive themselves as a minority group, while Christian Arab Americans are able to use their religious identity as a bridge to the cultural mainstream. For example, one-third of Christian respondents reported that other people consider them "white," while Muslims were much more likely to report that others perceive them as a minority group—either as "Arab" (54.3 percent), "Hispanic" (16.8 percent), or "Asian" (13.3 percent). Correspondingly,

Muslims were three times as likely to say that they had experienced discrimination "fairly often" or "very often" since 9/11 (38 percent compared to 12 percent of Christians).

28. Issues of Arab Americans and racial identity are examined further in Jamal and Naber's *Race and Arab Americans Before and After 9/11: From Invisible Citizens to Visible Subjects* (2008).

29. Since these are open-ended questions, some persons offered responses that fell into multiple categories.

30. The DAAS (Baker et al. 2004, 16) reports that persons born in the United States were more likely to check the "white" box than those not born in the United States—again suggesting that socialization may play a role in response patterns (which I argue in this chapter and in Cainkar 2008).

31. These scholars are not usually clear about the scope of the term "Muslim Americans." They do not seem to imply citizenship when invoking "American" but rather a sense of permanent residence. With regard to size estimates, Haddad (2004) reported the following estimates: B'nai Brith, 2 million; W. Dean Muhammed (Muslim American Society), 11 million; the Council on American Islamic Relations, 7 million. Ilyas Ba-Yunus and Kassim Kone estimate 5.7 million in Bukhari, Nyang, Ahmad, and Esposito (2004). The religion scholar Jane Smith (1999) estimates 6 million, while the survey researcher Tom Smith (2001) estimates 1.88 million.

32. See Association of Religion Data Archives (ARDA), "United States: Muslim Estimates—Rates of Adherence per 1,000 Population (2000)," available at: http://www.thearda.com/mapsReports/maps/map.asp?alpha=0&variable =24&state=101&variable2=617&GRP=1&Var2=617 (accessed July 9, 2008).

33. Counting persons by religious affiliation is prohibited in U.S. census data collection. This method of measurement would exclude a significant proportion of Muslims, including most African American Muslims, European-origin Muslims, and Muslims from countries in which they are a religious minority (U.S. Bureau of the Census 2000).

34. The grouping of immigrant generations into one category, "immigrant Muslims," leaves much to be desired from a sociological perspective, since immigrants and their native-born children lead quite different lives. The category "immigrant Muslims" is often used by scholars of European Muslims to describe multiple generations—a practice that displays more than anything the outsider status of Muslims in Europe—as well as by politically motivated analysts whose perspectives gain credence by blurring distinctions.

35. In a question-and-answer session following a 1963 speech at Western Michigan University, the Reverend Martin Luther King Jr. amplified this remark: "We must face the fact that in America, the church is still the most segregated major institution in America. At 11:00 on Sunday morning when we stand and sing and Christ has no east or west, we stand at the most segregated hour in this nation. This is tragic." See Western Michigan University Libraries, Archives and Regional History Collections, http://www.wmich.edu/library/archives/mlk/q-a.html (accessed May 26, 2008).

36. This concept emerged more than once in protests against the construction of a new mosque in Orland Park, Illinois (author's field notes from Orland Park public hearings, 2004).

37. Emerson's biases have been the subject of much criticism over the past decade, yet he still appears as a national media personality and has been called on by Congress to testify as a terrorism expert as recently as the summer of 2008. An article by John Sugg (1999) notes: "A *New York Times* review (5/19/91) of his 1991 book *Terrorist* chided that it was 'marred by factual errors . . . and by a pervasive anti-Arab and anti-Palestinian bias.' His 1994 PBS video, *Jihad in America* (11/94), was faulted for bigotry and misrepresentations—veteran reporter Robert Friedman (*The Nation*, 5/15/95) accused Emerson of 'creating mass hysteria against American Arabs.' . . . Emerson's most notorious gaffe was his claim that the 1995 Oklahoma City bombing showed 'a Middle Eastern trait' because it 'was done with the intent to inflict as many casualties as possible' (CBS News, 4/19/95)."

38. Poll data from the Pew Research Center for the People and the Press and the Pew Forum on Religion and Public Life; see Keeter and Kohut (2003).

Chapter 4

1. Michael E. Rolince, former FBI special agent in charge of counterterrorism and Section Chief of the International Terrorism Operations Section, told the Muslim Public Affairs Council (MPAC) in 2005 that after "about half a million FBI interviews . . . I'm not aware, and I know 9/11 about as well as anybody in the FBI knows 9/11 . . . of any single person in your community who had they stepped forward could have provided a clue to help us get out in front of this. The reality of that attack is that nineteen people came here with what they needed. . . . This is important because your community gets painted as not doing enough and that you could have helped." Michael E. Rolince, speech delivered at the workshop "Muslim–Law Enforcement Partnership," MPAC convention, Long Beach Convention Center, Long Beach, Calif., December 17, 2005, audio file available at: http://www.mpac.org/multimedia/audio (accessed June 10, 2007). This remark is found at the question-and-answer section at the end of the recording.

2. Private conversation, November 15, 2008, Detroit, Mich.

3. See the Social Science Research Council (SSRC) Project on Reframing the Challenge of Migration and Security. Frustrations with "Washington" were repeatedly reported by various local-level federal law enforcement authorities in meetings between them, the project's consulting scholars, and members of Arab and Muslim American communities. See SSRC, "Reframing the Challenge of Migration and Security," available at: http://programs.ssrc.org/gsc/gsc_activities/migration/ (accessed December 10, 2008).

4. I highly recommend this incredible documentary for anyone who wants up-close-and-personal reports of post-9/11 detainees and their experiences.

5. Limited interviews with Arab American Christians produced the same findings, because post-9/11 U.S. government policies targeting Arabs did not distinguish between Christians and Muslims.

6. Muslim Civil Rights Center, "General Survey," November 2002. The study sample was 61 percent South Asian, 10 percent American, and the rest Arab and other. The percentage immigrant was not specified.

7. My initial estimate of at least 100,000 was derived as follows: nearly 83,000 persons living in the United States underwent special registration. It could be safely assumed that at least 20,000 more Arabs and Muslims nationwide were affected by one or more of the other post-9/11 national security initiatives, such as FBI interviews, wiretapping, or detention. More recent reports indicate that these numbers could be much higher.

8. The term "investigation dragnet" is used by the Council on American-Islamic Relations in its 2004 report (CAIR 2004).

9. Human Rights Watch, "Scores of Muslim Men Jailed Without Charge; Justice Department Misused Material Witness Law in Counterterrorism Efforts," press release, June 26, 2005, available at: http://hrw.org/english/docs/2005/06/27/usdom11213.htm.

10. Quoted in ACLU, "U.S.: Scores of Muslim Men Jailed Without Charge," press release, June 27, 2005, available at: http://www.aclu.org/safefree/detention/17616prs20050627.html (accessed November 2006).

11. See note 10.

12. Quoted in ACLU, "Justice Department May Be Using Controversial Patriot Act Powers After All, Letter Reveals," press release, May 20, 2004, available at http://www.aclu.org/safefree/patriot/17399prs20040520.html (accessed September 10, 2008).

13. Data received from the Immigration and Naturalization Service (now defunct).

14. "Non-immigrant aliens" includes all immigrants who are inspected by the INS upon entry to the United States and are not U.S. citizens, permanent residents, applicants for permanent residency, or applicants for asylum. The rule for special registration excludes non-immigrants who are diplomats, persons working with international organizations, and a few other narrow categories of non-immigrants (categories A and G). I would like to thank the attorneys Susan Compernolle and Jeanne Butterfield for their technical assistance on the development of this section.

15. Carol Hallstrom, Department of Homeland Security, Community Relations, Chicago; see also Swarns (2003). Because the program worked by country of nationality and citizenship, the swoop included Iranian and Arab Jews, Iranian Baha'is, and Arab Christians.

16. During the Palmer Raids, 556 foreign nationals were deported.

17. Under Operation Wetback in 1954, more than 1 million U.S. citizens and noncitizens of Mexican descent were deported to Mexico.

18. U.S. Department of Homeland Security, "Fact Sheet: US-VISIT Program," May 19, 2003, available at: http://www.dhs.gov/xnews/releases/press_release_0155.shtm.

19. National Council of Pakistani Americans, February 15, 2003.

20. Posted February 25, 2003, on the special registration list-serve by Patrick Giantonio of Vermont Refugee Assistance.

21. 67 FR (Federal Register) 61352. Visitors who fit other criteria included persons who consular officials or INS inspecting officers had "reason to believe"

were nationals or citizens of a designated country, and other non-immigrants who met or were believed to meet "preexisting criteria" specified by the attorney general. Some of these criteria were published in the Federal Register.

22. 58 FR 68157 and 58 FR 68024. Reno removed 8 CFR (Code of Federal Regulations) 264.3 (Thornburg) and added 8 CFR 264.1(f). It was one paragraph at the time and is now thirteen. The 1996 expansion is at 61 FR 46829.

23. 56 FR 1566. This registry was during the 1990 to 1991 Gulf War period. The government's stated reasons for registry included: the Iraqi theft of Kuwaiti travel documents, the "potential for anti-U.S. terrorist-type activities" because of "U.S. condemnation of and economic sanctions against the Iraqi invasion of Kuwait," and "securing information on terrorists."

24. INS Special Registration Q&A, December 23, 2002.

25. See the Commission Inquiry press release (September 18, 2006) of the Arar Commission at: http://ensign.ftlcomm.com/loosends/flag/Release Sept18.pdf (accessed July 12, 2008).

26. Persons not inspected by the INS upon entry (EWIs, for "entered without inspection") were not covered by this special registration program. However, Ashcroft's final rule of August 12, 2002 (8 CFR 264.1), reads: "nonimmigrant aliens . . . who have already been admitted to the U.S. or who are otherwise in the U.S."

27. Ashcroft invoked the authority of a discretionary ten-day notice clause contained in 1981 immigration legislation that canceled annual address reporting for permanent residents and quarterly address reporting for visitors, but that permitted the attorney general (AG) to require "natives of any one or more foreign states, or any class of group thereof," to notify the AG of their current address and "such additional information as the Attorney General may require" (P.L. 97-116; December 29, 1981; Immigration and Nationality Act Amendments of 1981).

28. 8 CFR 214.1.

29. 8 CFR 264.1(f)(9). This presumption can be overcome. Consular officials are initially in charge of making this determination.

30. As reported by Canadian Broadcasting System News on January 13, 2003, a "Canadian passport 'meant nothing' to U.S. immigration officials."

31. 67 FR 70526.

32. Attorney General John Ashcroft, press release, February 14, 2003. Armenia had been included in the initial Federal Register notice for this group, but was removed two days later after protest from the Armenian government. When similar protests from other governments produced no such change, it became clear that the special registration program was designed for Arabs and Muslims.

33. 68 FR 2363.

34. Email from the Arab American Action Network, April 20, 2003.

35. A comment sent to Attorney General Ashcroft on the proposed special registration rules asserted that judges had determined in prior cases that the veracity of "immaterial" information cannot be used as a basis for determining maintenance of status. Attorney General Ashcroft replied that in the case

of special registration, "information that aliens are required to provide *is* material to their immigration status" (emphasis in original); 67 FR 52588.

36. Notices posted February 28, 2003, on the Yahoo groups special registration list-serve.

37. The law requiring aliens to carry their registration documents with them at all times is still on the books. This would mean that carrying one's passport bearing registration information is mandatory, although this rule is not currently enforced.

38. Over the years the meaning of "registry" has changed and loosened up. The photos used to apply for visas are considered part of registry, the fingerprint rule was waived for most nationals, and the Form I-94 (Arrival-Departure Record) or other specified forms processed upon entry to the United States became evidence of "registry."

39. From 1903, 1917, 1918, 1920, and 1940 laws.

40. U.S. House of Representatives, Judiciary Committee, "Need for Legislation," report 97-264, October 2, 1981.

41. P.L. 97-116. Immigration and Nationality Act Amendments of 1981. December 29, 1981.

42. 1940 Smith Act, section 32(c)5 (now section 263). The Smith Act permitted "special regulations for the registration and fingerprinting" of: alien crewmen, holders of border-crossing identification cards, aliens confined to institutions, aliens under order of deportation, and aliens of any other class not lawfully admitted to the United States for permanent residence.

43. Just as Ashcroft made males from the designated countries who were age sixteen or older a class of people for special registration.

44. American Civil Liberties Union (ACLU), "ACLU to Provide Legal Help to Muslims and Arabs Caught Up in New Round of FBI Questioning," August 5, 2004, available at: http://www.aclu.org/safefree/general/18508prs20040805.html; see also Anderson (2004) and Moore (2004).

45. See JACL (2001). The JACL soon issued another statement protesting Ashcroft's detention policies; see John Tateishi, JACL National Executive Director, "JACL Statement on the DOJ's Detention Policies," November 2001, available at: http://www.asianchamber.org/viewArticle.php?articleId=12.

46. A similar representation is found in academia, where research and pedagogy on South and West Asians is underrepresented.

47. See CAIR–New York, www.cair-ny.com/Homepage/List/params/list/1525/default.aspx (posted February 17, 2003; accessed October 5, 2008).

48. The government swiftly deported his brother Husseyn in June 2007 for a visa violation.

49. See, for example, the reports by Human Rights Watch, the Council on American-Islamic Relations, the U.S. Department of Justice, and the Office of the Inspector General in the bibliography; see also ADC (2003); Tsao and Gutierrez (2003); Salaita (2006); Cainkar (2003a, 2003b, 2004a, 2004b, 2004c, 2004d, 2005a, 2005b, 2006, 2008); Cole (2003); Hagopian (2004); Naber (2006); Baker et al. (2004).

50. Protecting "our people and their freedoms" was part of the Department of Homeland Security's mission. The DHS was created in 2002, merging for-

merly disaggregated (nonmilitary) government agencies, to implement a "unified national effort to secure America" while safeguarding "our people and their freedoms." Its mission includes: "We will ensure safe and secure borders, welcome lawful immigrants and visitors, and promote the free-flow of commerce." One of its strategic goals is protection: "Safeguard our people and their freedoms, critical infrastructure, property and the economy of our Nation from acts of terrorism, natural disasters, or other emergencies"; see www.dhs.gov/dhspublic (accessed May 3, 2006).

Chapter 5

1. Efforts to impugn persons with counternarratives can be read to this day on websites such as CAIR Watch (http://www.americansagainsthate.org/cw/) and Campus Watch (http://www.campus-watch.org/), among countless others.
2. This information is based on meetings sponsored by the Social Science Research Council (SSRC) for the project Reframing the Challenge of Migration and Security, funded by the Carnegie Corporation. See http://programs. ssrc. org/gsc/gsc_activities/migration/ (accessed December 10, 2008).
3. Reported during SSRC meetings for Reframing the Challenge of Migration and Security and in background research.
4. Since I did not interview anyone under age eighteen for this study, reports on the experiences of youth come largely from parents and community leaders.
5. Dr. Samirah received legal support from Chicago's Heartland Alliance to challenge his de facto deportation. The Supreme Court declined to hear his appeal in June 2004. His petition for a writ of certiorari is available at: http://www.usdoj.gov/osg/briefs/2003/0responses/2003-1085.resp.html (accessed September 17, 2008).
6. Quote located in "Statement" in part 2 of Sabri I. Samirah's petition for a writ of certiorari; see note 5.
7. Christina Abraham, CAIR-Chicago civil rights coordinator, press release, June 19, 2007.
8. In the lawsuit *Bavi v. Mukasey*, the ACLU of Southern California, the National Immigration Law Center, the Asian Pacific American Legal Center, and Munger, Tolles & Olson ask a federal judge to enforce time limits on name checks for people in the naturalization process. Attorney General Michael Mukasey and the FBI, which conducts the checks, and the U.S. Citizenship and Immigration Service (USCIS), which oversees the naturalization process, are named as defendants. See ACLU, "Groups Sue to Stop Excessive Citizenship Delays," December 5, 2007, available at: http://www.aclu.org/immigrants/gen/33279prs20071205.html (accessed December 11, 2008).

Chapter 6

1. Illinois Advisory Committee to the U.S. Commission on Civil Rights (2003). At the time of the report (2003), the defendant had agreed to plead guilty to aggravated battery, unlawful use of a weapon, and a hate crime, according to the Cook County State's Attorney's Office.

2. Testimony of the Arab American journalist Ray Hanania at the hearings of the Illinois Advisory Committee to the U.S. Commission on Civil Rights (2003).

3. I use the term "hate encounters" to describe incidents in which perpetrators engaged in offensive activities motivated by feelings of prejudice toward a person or persons with the ascribed status of Arab or Muslim, without addressing whether the activity qualifies as a crime or not.

4. Personal communication with Christina Abraham, human rights coordinator, CAIR-Chicago, November 26, 2006.

5. Gunn's numbers do not match those that the city of Chicago reported to the FBI, shown earlier, but the pattern is the same.

6. Whether the arson of the building housing the Arab American Action Network, located above a small local business, was a hate crime or was perpetrated to collect insurance by the small business owner was not resolved as of this writing. It is not discussed further in this chapter, although whatever its source, it was a major setback for the Arab American community organization in a time of heightened need. A number of local foundations contributed emergency money to the organization after the fire, including the Woods Fund, the Crossroads Fund, the Field Foundation, the Tides Foundation, and the Four Freedoms Fund.

7. Assuming significant undercounting, this proportion is probably higher.

8. See chapter 1 for qualitative explanations for undercounting; see also Arab American Institute Foundation, "Quick Facts About Arab Americans," available at: http://www.aaiusa.org/page/file/8e66571fbe9d44abed_bsomvyjkp.pdf/quickfacts.pdf.

9. See chapter 1 for more information about this highly controversial product assembled by Census Bureau staff in 2003; see also Electronic Privacy Information Center (EPIC), "Department of Homeland Security Obtained Data on Arab Americans from Census Bureau," July 2004, available at: http://epic.org/privacy/census/foia/ (accessed June 2007). Peoria is home to a historic and largely second- and third-generation Lebanese population.

10. The description of Arab Americans' local civic and political status is based on my field research.

11. Land for the Bridgeview mosque was purchased in 1982, before Arabs and Muslims had a significant demographic presence in the area.

12. I have not been able to confirm reports that a talk radio host inspired or called for the march.

13. See Chambers (2003) for a discussion of United Power for Action and Justice.

14. See United Power for Action and Justice at: http://www.united-power.org/node/54 (accessed February 22, 2009).

15. Recorded by the author at the April 2004 Orland Park public hearing.

16. Recorded by the author at the April 2004 Orland Park public hearing.

17. In fact, the city council voted to annex the property slated for the mosque to the city of Orland Park.

18. Part of a study of conflicts over mosques in the Chicago suburbs funded by Chicago Community Trust.

19. In chapter 1, I comment on another aspect of this poll data—that attitudes toward American Muslims were generally more favorable two months after the 9/11 attacks than they were six months prior to and six months after them. I believe these measures of attitudinal changes indicate that people's opinions on a subject can vary according to changes in larger social contexts, irrespective of any perceived actual changes in the subject. I believe that the increase in favorable views as of November 2001 (or the less unfavorable views among African Americans, for whom the percentage holding favorable views stayed the same) may reflect less a change in perspectives on Muslim Americans than a distaste for the profiling and hate acts perpetrated against Muslim Americans by the government and the public. Interpreted in this way, those views might be seen as a measure of the recognition of Muslim Americans as Americans who possess the same rights as others.

20. For example, in the past few years more than half of the participants in the Arab American Action Network's summer camp and after-school tutoring have been African American.

21. The statement was posted on the Sociology of Islam list-serve on October 8, 2008 (SOCIOLOGY_OF_ISLAM@listserv.vt.edu).

22. Muslim Public Affairs Council (MPAC), "Interfaith Leaders to Speak Out Against Anti-Muslim DVD," press release, October 8, 2008, available at: https://app.e2ma.net/app/view:CampaignPublic/id:2785.1386437488/ri d:538abfd1c2a577c06676aa129632faad (accessed October 8, 2008).

23. Muslim Public Affairs Council (MPAC), "Statement from American Religious Leaders in Response to Mass Distribution of 'Obsession,' " press release, October 6, 2008, available at: http://www.mpac.org/article.php?id=711 (accessed October 8, 2008).

Chapter 7

1. These are the only female cases that received significant national press attention; there may be others of which I am not aware; see Bernstein (2005).

2. Women wearing hijab constituted 46 percent of the female sample.

3. The perpetrator was initially charged with a hate crime, but the state's attorney lowered the charge to battery. The man pled guilty to battery and was sentenced to perform community service with CAIR-Chicago.

4. The defendant in this case was acquitted because the family was unsure as to whether it could positively identify him; the perpetrator was wearing a ski mask at the time of the incident.

5. This conclusion about anti-Catholic nativism is largely possible because Higham viewed exclusionary actions against persons seen as nonwhite as a different form of nativism, which he called racial nativism. One form of nativism (racial) was about "who we are," and the other form of nativism (anti-foreign) was about "who we are not" (Higham 1955, 9).

6. "The Anti-Catholic Press, 1854: *The Know-Nothing: and American Crusader,* 29 July 1854," available at Historical Society of Pennsylvania, http://www. hsp.org/files/anticatholicpress.pdf (accessed July 2007).

7. "The Anti-Catholic Press, 1854: *The Know-Nothing: and American Crusader,* 15 July 1854," available at Historical Society of Pennsylvania, http://www.hsp.org/files/nativistpress.pdf.

8. Muslim Civil Rights Center. Reported on April 22 and 30, 2004, references 1891, 1859.

9. Quoted in *Jerusalem Post,* January 22, 2003, p. 9.

10. President Bush's September 17, 2001, speech at the Islamic Center of Washington, D.C., focuses on Islam as a religion of peace and solace. See http://www.pbs.org/newshour/bb/military/terroristattack/bush_speech_9-17.html.

11. The Defense Science Board is a federal advisory committee that was established to provide independent advice to the secretary of Defense. See also Regan (2004).

12. The Defense Science Board (2004, 17) describes the simplifying function of the conflation that subsumes complex and different matters into one rubric: "The Global War on Terrorism replaced the Cold War as a national security meta narrative. Governments, media, and publics use the terrorism frame for cognitive, evaluative, and communication purposes. For political leaders, it is a way to link disparate events; identify priorities, friends, enemies, victims, and blame; and shape simple coherent messages. For journalists and news consumers the terrorism frame conflates and appears to make sense of diverse national security stories—Al Qaeda, Jihadists, Iraq, Afghanistan, Israel, Iran, Chechnya, Indonesia, Kashmir, the Philippines, Kenya, Spain."

13. Annapurna Center for Self Healing, "Explorations: The Importance of Hugging," available at: http://theannapurna.com/hugging.html (accessed July 2007).

14. See Global Ideas Bank, "Lack of Touching Leads to Violence?" available at: http://www.globalideasbank.org/site/bank/idea.php?ideaId=35 (accessed July 25, 2007).

15. See, for example, the Sound Vision website for further religious information on hijab: http://www.soundvision.com/info/hijab/.

16. I am unaware of any research on this question that comprehensively surveys a representative sample of 1.2 billion Muslims.

17. From Neil Boortz's website: http://boortz.com/ (accessed September 2006).

18. See, for example, *Hearn vs. Muskogee Public School District,* District Court for the Eastern District of Oklahoma, C.A. no: CIV 03-598-S.

19. It may also be true that men are generally less likely than women to admit feeling afraid or unsafe. Study data, on the other hand, show that women experienced twice the rate of harassment as men, lending support to men's perception of greater safety.

Chapter 8

1. Connie al-Ramahi, food pantry volunteer, quoted in "Mosque Foundation Food Pantry Celebrates Tenth Anniversary," September 6, 2007, available at: http://www.mosquefoundation.org/articles/articletype/articleview/articleid/24/pageid/14.aspx (accessed December 16, 2008).

2. King made those remarks February 9, 2004, on *The Sean Hannity Show*, a nationally syndicated radio program. The Democratic National Committee (DNC) condemned King's remarks as hate-filled.

3. See Terrorism Awareness Project, "Islamo-Fascism Awareness Week," available at: http://www.terrorismawareness.org/islamo-fascism-awareness-week/ (accessed December 6, 2007).

4. On November 28, 2006, conservative columnist Dennis Prager said: "America, not Keith Ellison, decides what book a congressman takes his oath on"; available at: http://townhall.com/columnists/DennisPraer/2006 (accessed December 12, 2006). Prager went on to say in his column: "Keith Ellison, D-Minn., the first Muslim elected to the United States Congress, has announced that he will not take his oath of office on the Bible, but on the bible of Islam, the Koran. He should not be allowed to do so—not because of any American hostility to the Koran, but because the act undermines American civilization."

5. Conservative columnist Mary Grabar said on December 11, 2006: "It's not just about the Koran or the Bible." Available at: http://townhall.com/columnists/MaryGrabar/2006 (accessed December 12, 2006).

6. Arab American Institute, "AAI Condemns Prejudiced Attacks on Ellison, Asks Congressional Leaders to Come to His Defense," press release, December 5, 2006.

7. See, for example, "Hillary Takes Cash from Terror Suspects," WorldNetDaily, November 4, 2007, available at: http://www.worldnet daily.com/news/article.asp?ARTICLE_ID=58449; and "Over $100,000 in Oklahoma Campaign Donations Linked to Muslim Activist," LibertyPost.org, November 2, 2007, available at: http://www.libertypost. org/cgi-bin/readart.cgi?ArtNum=205367 (both accessed December 7, 2007).

8. See "Rudy Giuliani TV Ad 'Ready,' " available at: http://www.youtube.com/watch?v=y2iFhGtKO-Q (accessed January 3, 2008).

9. See transcript at Media Matters for America, November 19, 2004, available at: http://mediamatters.org/items/200411190009 (accessed December 1, 2007).

10. John L. Esposito, "Muslims and the West: A Culture War?" available at: http://www.unaoc.org/repository/3840Muslims%20and%20the%20West %20A%20Culture%20War,%20J.%20Esposito.doc.pdf (accessed December 6, 2007). See also Esposito and Mogahed (2008).

11. American Muslim incorporation is facilitated by the value of religious freedom in American society, but complicated by the fact that Muslim Americans are largely not members of the dominant white social group: more than 80 percent of Muslims in the United States are of African American, African, Arab, or Asian heritage.

12. Recorded by the author at the April 2004 Orland Park public hearing.

References

Abdulhadi, Rabab, Nadine Naber, and Evelyn Alsultany, eds. 2005. "Gender, Nation, and Belonging: Arab and Arab-American Feminist Perspectives." *MIT Electronic Journal of Middle East Studies*, Special Issue 5(spring). Available at: http://web.mit.edu/cis/www/mitejmes/issues/200507/MITEJMES_Vol_5_Spring.pdf.

Abowd, Mary. 2002. "Arabs Still Reeling from 9/11 Backlash." *Chicago Reporter*, December 1.

Abraham, Nabeel. 1994. "Anti-Arab Racism and Violence in the United States." In *The Development of Arab-American Identity*, edited by Ernest McCarus. Ann Arbor: University of Michigan Press.

Abraham, Sameer Y., and Nabeel Abraham, eds. 1983. *Arabs in the New World: Studies on Arab-American Communities*. Detroit: Wayne State University Press, Center for Urban Studies.

Abu-Laban, Baha, and Michael W. Suleiman, eds. 1989. *Arab Americans: Continuity and Change*. Monograph Series no. 24. Belmont, Mass.: Association of Arab-American University Graduates (AAUG).

Abu-Laban, Sharon McIrvin. 1989. "The Coexistence of Cohorts: Identity and Adaptation Among Arab-American Muslims." *Arab Studies Quarterly* 11 (spring/summer): 45–63.

Abu-Lughod, Janet. 1986. "The Demographic War for Palestine." *The Link* 19(5): 1–14.

Abu-Lughod, Lila. 2002. "Do Muslim Women Really Need Saving? Anthropological Reflections on Cultural Relativism and Its Others." *American Anthropologist* 104(3): 783–90.

———. 2007. "The Dangers of the Circulation of a Transnational Dialect of Rights." Paper presented to the annual meeting of the Middle East Studies Association (MESA). Montreal (November 17).

Ahmed, Ismael. 1975. "Organizing an Arab Workers Caucus." *MERIP* (Middle East Research and Information Project) *Reports* 34(January): 17–22.

Akram, Susan M., and Kevin R. Johnson. 2002. "Race, Civil Rights, and Immigration Law After September 11, 2001: The Targeting of Arabs and Muslims." *New York University Annual Survey of American Law* 58(3): 295–355.

———. 2004. "Race and Civil Rights Pre–September 11, 2001: The Targeting of Arabs and Muslims." In *Civil Rights in Peril: The Targeting of Arabs and Muslims,* edited by Elaine C. Hagopian. Chicago: Haymarket Books.

Al-Qazzaz, Ayad. 1975. "Images of the Arab in American Social Science Textbooks." In *Arabs in America: Myths and Realities,* edited by Baha Abu-Laban and Faith T. Zeadey. Wilmette, Ill.: Medina University Press International.

Alsultany, Evelyn. 2008. "The Prime-Time Plight of the Arab Muslim American After 9/11: Configurations of Race and Nation in TV Dramas." In *Race and Arab Americans Before and After 9/11: From Invisible Citizens to Visible Subjects,* edited by Amaney Jamal and Nadine Naber. Syracuse, N.Y.: Syracuse University Press.

Al-Tahir, Abdul Jalil. 1952. "The Arab Community in the Chicago Area: A Comparative Study of the Christian-Syrians and the Muslim Palestinians." Ph.D. diss., University of Chicago.

American-Arab Anti-Discrimination Committee (ADC). 2003. "Report on Hate Crimes and Discrimination Against Arab Americans: The Post–September 11 Backlash—September 11, 2001, to October 11, 2002." Washington: ADC Research Institute.

Anderson, Curt. 2004. "Seven al-Qaida Suspects Sought in Attack Plan." *Chicago Tribune,* May 26.

Anderson, Elijah. 1990. *Street Wise: Race, Class, and Change in an Urban Community.* Chicago: University of Chicago Press.

Arab American Institute Foundation (AAIF). 2003. "Fact Sheet: States' Rank by Arab American Population (Illinois)." Washington: AAIF.

Ashcroft, John. 2001a. "September 11, 2001: Attack on America: Attorney General Remarks; September 18, 2001." Press briefing, FBI headquarters. Available at: http://avalon.law.yale.edu/sept11/doj_brief020.asp.

———. 2001b. "September 11, 2001: Attack on America." Prepared remarks; for the U.S. Conference of Mayors, October 25. Available at: Avalon Project, Yale Law School, http://avalon.law.yale.edu/sept11/doj_brief003.asp.

Aswad, Barbara C. 1974. *Arabic-Speaking Communities in American Cities.* Staten Island, N.Y.: Center for Migration Studies of New York.

———. 1993. "Arab Americans: Those Who Followed Columbus." *Middle East Studies Association Bulletin* 27(1): 1–22.

Awad, Gary. 1981. "The Arab Americans: An Invisible Minority Awakened." *The News Circle/Arab-American Affairs* (March): 31–32.

Bagby, Ihsan A. 2005. "Imams and Mosque Organization in the United States: A Study of Mosque Leadership and Organizational Structure in American Mosques." In *Muslims in the United States: Identity, Influence, Innovation,* edited by Philippa Strum. Washington: Woodrow Wilson International Center for Scholars.

Bagby, Ihsan, Paul M. Perl, and Bryan T. Froehle. 2001. "The Mosque in America: A National Portrait: A Report from the Mosque Study Project." Washington, D.C.: Council on American-Islamic Relations.

Baker, Wayne, Sally Howell, Amaney Jamal, Ann Chih Lin, Andrew Shryock, Ronald Stockton, and Mark Tessler. 2004. "The Detroit Arab American Study: Preliminary Findings and Technical Documentation." Ann Arbor: University of Michigan, Institute for Social Research.

Barlow, Elizabeth, ed. 1994. "Evaluation of Secondary-Level Textbooks for Coverage of the Middle East and North Africa." 3d ed. Tucson, Ariz.: Middle East Studies Association.

Bassiouni, M. Cherif, ed. 1974. *The Civil Rights of Arab-Americans: "The Special Measures."* Information Paper Series no. 10. North Dartmouth, Mass.: Association of Arab-American University Graduates.

———. 1991. *The Civil Rights of Arab-Americans: The FBI and the Civil Rights of Arab Americans.* ADC Issues 5. *ADC Times* (January–February).

Bawardi, Hani. 2007. "Looking Beyond September 11: 'New Syria' U.S.A. and Arab American Political Activism from 1915 to 1950." Public lecture given at the Race and Ethnic Studies Institute, Texas A&M University, College Station (February 10).

Bazian, Hatem. 2004. "Virtual Internment: Arabs, Muslims, Asians, and the War on Terrorism." *Journal of Islamic Law and Culture* 9(1): 1–26.

BBC News Online. 2002. "Mass Arrests of Muslims in LA." December 19, 2002. Available at: http://news.bbc.co.uk/2/americas/2589317.stm.

Becker, Howard S. 1963. *Outsiders: Studies in the Sociology of Deviance.* New York: Free Press.

Bergen, Peter, and Katherine Tiedemann. 2008. "Disappearing Act: Rendition by the Numbers." *Mother Jones* (March 3). Available at: http://www.motherjones.com/news/feature/2008/03/disappearing-act.html (accessed September 10, 2008).

Bernstein, Nina. 2005. "A Girl in Exile: After the FBI Pegged Her as a Potential Suicide Bomber, the 16-Year-Old Daughter of Bangladeshi Immigrants Living in New York Was Forced to Leave the United States." *New York Times Upfront,* November 14. Available at: http://findarticles.com/p/articles/mi_m0BUE/is_/ai_n17211139 (accessed November 7, 2008).

Bisharat, Mary. 1975. "Yemeni Farmworkers in California." *MERIP* (Middle East Research and Information Project) *Reports* 34(January): 22–26.

Blackistone, Kevin. 1981. "Arab Entrepreneurs Take Over Inner City Grocery Stores." *Chicago Reporter,* May.

Bloom, Howard. 1989. "The Importance of Hugging." *Omni* (February).

———. 1997. *The Lucifer Principle: A Scientific Expedition into the Forces of History.* New York: Atlantic Monthly Press.

Bollag, Burton. 2004. "U.S. Shuts Out Muslim Scholar, Raising Fears for Academic Freedom." *Chronicle of Higher Education* (September 10).

Boosahda, Elizabeth. 2003. *Arab-American Faces and Voices: The Origins of an Immigrant Community.* Austin: University of Texas Press.

Bragdon, Ann Louise. 1989. "Early Arabic-Speaking Immigrant Communities in Texas." *Arab Studies Quarterly* 11(spring/summer): 83–101.

Bukhari, Zahid H. 2003. "Demography, Identity, Space: Defining American Muslims." In *Muslims in the United States: Demography, Beliefs, Institutions,* edited by Philippa Strum and Danielle Tarantolo. Washington: Woodrow Wilson International Center for Scholars.

Bukhari, Zahid H., Sulayman S. Nyang, Mumtaz Ahmad, and John L. Esposito, eds. 2004. *Muslims' Place in the American Public Square: Hopes, Fears, and Aspirations.* Walnut Creek, Calif.: AltaMira Press.

Bush, George W. 2001. "President Declares 'Freedom at War with Fear': Address to a Joint Session of Congress and the American People," September 20. Available at: http://archives.cnn.com/2001/US/09/20/gen.bush.transcript.

————. 2003. State of the Union Address. Available at: http://www.cnn.com/2003/ALL POLITICS/01/28/sotu.transcript (accessed March 8, 2009).

Butterfield, Jeanne A. 1999. "Do Immigrants Have First Amendment Rights?" *Middle East Report* 212(fall): 4–7.

Cainkar, Louise. 1988. "Coping with Culture, Change, and Alienation: The Life Experiences of Palestinian Women in the United States." Ph.D. diss., Northwestern University.

————. 1998. *Meeting Community Needs, Building on Community Strengths: Chicago's Arab American Community.* Chicago: Arab American Action Network, 1998.

————. 1999. "The Deteriorating Ethnic Safety Net Among Arab Immigrants in Chicago." In *Arabs in America: Building a New Future,* edited by Michael W. Suleiman. Philadelphia: Temple University Press.

————. 2003a. "Assessing the Need, Addressing the Problem: Working with Disadvantaged Muslim Immigrant Families and Communities." Baltimore: Annie E. Casey Foundation (November).

————. 2003b. "The Treatment of Arabs and Muslims in Race and Ethnic Studies Textbooks." Paper presented to the annual meeting of the American Sociological Association. Atlanta (August 16–19).

————. 2004a. "The Impact of 9/11 on Muslims and Arabs in the United States." In *The Maze of Fear: Security and Migration After 9/11,* edited by John Tirman. New York: New Press.

————. 2004b. "Introduction: Global Impacts of September 11." *Journal of Comparative Studies of South Asia, Africa, and the Middle East* 24(1): 155–58.

————. 2004c. "U.S. Muslim Leaders and Activists Evaluate Post-9/11 Domestic Security Policies." Background paper. New York: Social Science Research Council, Reframing the Challenge of Migration and Security Project (October). Available at: http://programs.ssrc.org/gsc/publications/gsc_activities/migration/cainkar.pdf.

————. 2004d. "Islamic Revival Among Second-Generation Arab-American Muslims: The American Experience and Globalization Intersect." *Bulletin of the Royal Institute for Inter-Faith Studies* 6(2): 99–120.

————. 2005a. "Space and Place in the Metropolis: Arabs and Muslims Seeking Safety." *City and Society* 17(2): 181–209.

————. 2005b. "Violence Unveiled." *Contexts* 4(4): 67.

————. 2006. "Immigrants from the Arab World." In *The New Chicago: A Social and Cultural Analysis,* edited by John P. Koval, Larry Bennett, Michael I. J. Bennett, Fassil Demissie, Roberta Garner, and Kiljoong Kim. Philadelphia: Temple University Press.

————. 2008. "Thinking Outside the Box: Arabs and Race in the United States." In *Race and Arab Americans Before and After 9/11: From Invisible Citizens to Visible Subjects,* edited by Amaney Jamal and Nadine Naber. Syracuse, N.Y.: Syracuse University Press.

Cainkar, Louise, Ali Abunimah, and Lamia Raei. 2004. "Migration as a Method of Coping with Turbulence Among Palestinians." *Journal of Comparative Family Studies* (special issue on the Middle East) 35(2): 229–40.

Chambers, Edward T. 2003. *Roots for Radicals: Organizing for Power, Action, and Justice.* New York: Continuum.

Chang, Nancy, and Alan Kabat. 2004. "Summary of Recent Court Rulings on Terrorism-Related Matters Having Civil Liberties Implications." New York: Center for Constitutional Rights.

Chicago Council on Foreign Relations (CCFR). 2002. "A Post–September 11 Curriculum for the Chicago Public Schools," by Louise Cainkar. Chicago: CCFR.

Chicago Council on Global Affairs (CCGA). 2007. "Strengthening America: The Civic and Political Integration of Muslim Americans." Task Force Series. Farooq Kathwari and Lynn M. Martin, cochairs; Christopher B. Whitney, project director. Chicago: CCGA.

Chishti, Muzaffar A., Doris Meissner, Demetrios G. Papademetriou, Jay Peterzell, Michael J. Wishnie, and Stephen W. Yale-Loehr. 2003. "America's Challenge: Domestic Security, Civil Liberty, and National Unity After September 11." Washington, D.C.: Migration Policy Institute (MPI).

Clemetson, Lynette. 2004. "Homeland Security Given Data on Arab-Americans." *New York Times*, July 30, p. A14.

Cole, David. 2003. *Enemy Aliens*. New York: New Press.

———. 2006. "Are We Safer?" *New York Review of Books* 53(4): 15–18.

———. 2007. "Anti-Terrorism on Trial." *Washington Post*, October 24.

Cole, David, and James Dempsey. 2002. *Terrorism and the Constitution: Sacrificing Civil Liberties in the Name of National Security*. New York: New Press.

Congressional Record. 1917. 64th Cong., 2nd sess. Vol. 54, pt. 2. Washington: Government Printing Office.

Council on American-Islamic Relations (CAIR). 2002. "The Status of Muslim Civil Rights in the United States: Stereotypes and Civil Liberties." Washington, D.C.: CAIR.

———. 2004. "The Status of Muslim Civil Rights in the United States: Unpatriotic Acts." Washington, D.C.: CAIR.

Council on American-Islamic Relations (CAIR)–Chicago. 2007. "Report: Citizenship Delays Were Top Issue for U.S. Muslims in 2006" (June 16). Available at: http://chicago.cair.com/presscenter.php?file=ps_civilrights 06192007 (accessed September 15, 2008).

Curtis, Edward E. 2002. *Islam in Black America: Identity, Liberation, and Difference in African-American Islamic Thought*. Albany: State University of New York Press.

Davidson, Lawrence. 1999. "Debating Palestine: Arab-American Challenges to Zionism, 1917–1932." In *Arabs in America*, edited by Michael W. Suleiman. Philadelphia: Temple University Press.

Davis, Jon. 2004. "Muslims Denounce Candidate's Remarks." *Daily Herald*, October 2.

Debusmann, Bernd. 2006. "In U.S., Fear and Mistrust of Muslims Runs Deep." Reuters, December 1.

Defense Science Board. 2004. *Report of the Defense Science Board Task Force on Strategic Communication*, Washington: Department of Defense (September). Available at: http://www.acq.osd.mil/dsb/reports/2004-09-Strategic_ Communication.pdf (accessed August 10, 2007).

Du Bois, W. E. B. 1995. *The Souls of Black Folk: Essays and Sketches*. New York: Signet (originally published in 1903).

Eck, Diana L. 2002. *A New Religious America: How a "Christian Country" Has Become the World's Most Religiously Diverse Nation.* New York: Harper San Francisco.

Eggen, Dan, and Julie Tate. "U.S. Campaign Produces Few Connections on Terrorism Charges." *Washington Post*, June 12, p. A01.

El Guindi, Fadwa. 1999. *Veil: Modesty, Privacy, and Resistance.* New York: Berg.

Elkholy, Abdo A. 1966. *The Arab Moslems in the United States: Religion and Assimilation.* New Haven, Conn.: College and University Press.

Equal Employment Opportunity Commission (EEOC). 2002. "EEOC Provides Answers About Workplace Rights of Muslims, Arabs, South Asians, and Sikhs." Washington: EEOC (May 15).

Esposito, John L., and Dalia Mogahed. 2008. *Who Speaks for Islam? What a Billion Muslims Really Think.* Washington, D.C.: Gallup Press.

Fanon, Frantz. 1961. *The Wretched of the Earth.* Oxford: Oxford University Press (originally published in 1953).

Farley, Reynolds, Sheldon H. Danziger, and Harry J. Holzer. 2000. *Detroit Divided.* New York: Russell Sage Foundation.

Fasenfest, David, Jason Booza, and Kurt Metzger. 2004. "Living Together: A New Look at Racial and Ethnic Integration in Metropolitan Neighborhoods, 1990–2000." Living Cities Census Series 1–4. Washington, D.C.: Center on Urban and Metropolitan Policy.

Fay, Mary Ann. 1984. "Old Roots—New Soil." In *Taking Root, Bearing Fruit: The Arab-American Experience,* edited by James Zogby. Washington, D.C.: ADC Research Institute.

Fine, Gary Alan. 1996. "Reputational Entrepreneurs and the Memory of Incompetence: Melting Supporters, Partisan Warriors, and Images of President Harding." *American Journal of Sociology* 101(5): 1159–93.

Fine, Gary Alan, and Irfan Khawaja. 2005. "Celebrating Arabs and Grateful Terrorists: Rumor and the Politics of Plausibility." In *Rumor Mills: The Social Impact of Rumor and Legend,* edited by Gary Alan Fine, Veronique Campion-Vincent, and Chip Heath. New Brunswick, N.J.: Transaction Publishers.

Foucault, Michel. 1979. *Discipline and Punish: The Birth of the Prison.* New York: Vintage Books.

Franklin, Stephen, and Don Terry. 2001. "Muslims Battle Fear, Frustration—Families, Children, Become Targets of Anti-Arab Anger." *Chicago Tribune,* September 16.

Friedlander, Jonathan, ed. 1988. *Sojourners and Settlers: The Yemeni Immigrant Experience.* Salt Lake City: University of Utah Press.

Fuchs, Penny Bender. 1995. "Jumping to Conclusions in Oklahoma City?" *American Journalism Review* 17(5): 11–12. Available at: http://www.ajr.org/article.asp?id=1980.

Fuquay, Michael. 2001. "The Most Segregated Hour." Beliefnet (January). Available at: http://www.beliefnet.com/Entertainment/Books/2001/01/The-Most-Segregated-Hour.aspx (accessed December 11, 2008).

Georgakas, Dan. 1975. "Arab Workers in Detroit." *MERIP* (Middle East Research and Information Project) *Reports* 34(January): 13–17.

Gerstle, Gary. 1999. "Liberty, Coercion, and the Making of Americans." In *The Handbook of International Migration: The American Experience,* edited by Charles

Hirschman, Paul Kasinitz, and Josh DeWind. New York: Russell Sage Foundation.

Ghareeb, Edmund, ed. 1983. *Split Vision: The Portrayal of Arabs in the American Media.* Washington, D.C.: American-Arab Affairs Council.

Goffman, Erving. 1986. *Stigma: Notes on the Management of Spoiled Identity.* New York: Touchstone Books.

Gould, Jon. 2005. *Speak No Evil: The Triumph of Hate Speech Regulation.* Chicago: University of Chicago Press.

Gourevitch, Alex. 2003. "Detention Disorder." *The American Prospect* (January 31). Available at: http://www.prospect.org/cs/articles?article=detention_disorder.

Green, Donald P., Laurence H. McFalls, and Jennifer K. Smith. 2001. "Hate Crime: An Emergent Research Agenda." *Annual Review of Sociology* 27(August): 479–504.

Green, Donald P., Dara Z. Strolovitch, and Janelle S. Wong. 1998. "Defended Neighborhoods, Integration, and Racially Motivated Crime." *American Journal of Sociology* 104(2): 372–403.

Gualtieri, Sarah. 2004. "Strange Fruit? Syrian Immigrants, Extralegal Violence, and Racial Formation in the Jim Crow South." *Arab Studies Quarterly* 26(3): 63–85.

Haddad, Yvonne Yazbeck. 2004. *Not Quite American? The Shaping of Arab and Muslim Identity in the United States.* Edmondson Lecture Series. Waco, Tex.: Baylor University Press.

Haddad, Yvonne Yazbeck, and Adair T. Lummis. 1987. *Islamic Values in the United States: A Comparative Study.* New York: Oxford University Press.

Hagopian, Elaine, ed. 2004. *Civil Rights in Peril: The Targeting of Arabs and Muslims.* Chicago: Haymarket Books.

Hanania, Ray. 2005. *Arabs of Chicagoland.* Images of America series. Charleston, S.C.: Arcadia.

Handlin, Oscar. 1951. *The Uprooted: The Epic Story of the Great Migrations That Made the American People.* Boston: Little, Brown.

Henderson, Nicole, Christopher W. Ortiz, Naomi F. Sugie, and Joel Miller. 2006. "Law Enforcement and Arab American Community Relations After September 11, 2001." New York: Vera Institute of Justice (June).

Hentoff, Nat. 2002a. "A Citizen Shorn of All Rights." *Village Voice,* December 27.

———. 2002b. "Jews Rise Against Ashcroft War: 'It Shouldn't Be Happening Here.' " *Village Voice,* April 2. Available at: http://www.villagevoice.com/news/0214,hentoff,33512,6.html (accessed November 20, 2007).

Higham, John. 1955. *Strangers in the Land: Patterns of American Nativism, 1860–1925.* New Brunswick, N.J.: Rutgers University Press.

Hing, Bill Ong. 2002. "Vigilante Racism: The De-Americanization of Immigrant America." *Michigan Journal of Race and Law* 7(2): 441–56.

Hirschman, Charles. 2003. "The Role of Religion in the Origins and Adaptation of Immigrant Groups in the United States." Paper for Conference: *Conceptual and Methodological Developments in the Study of International Migration.* Center for Migration and Development, Princeton University. Princeton, N.J. (May 23–25).

Hitti, Philip K. 1924. *The Syrians in America.* New York: George H. Doran.

Hooglund, Eric, ed. 1987. *Crossing the Waters: Arabic-Speaking Immigrants to the United States Before 1940.* Washington: Smithsonian Institution Press.

Howell, Sally, and Andrew Shryock. 2003. "Cracking Down on Diaspora: Arab Detroit and America's 'War on Terror.' " *Anthropological Quarterly* 76(3): 443–62.

Hughes, Everett C. 1945. "Dilemmas and Contradictions of Status." *American Journal of Sociology* 50(5): 353–59.

Human Rights Watch. 2002. "Presumption of Guilt: Human Rights Abuses of Post–September 11 Detainees." *Human Rights Watch* 14(4): 12.

———. 2005. "Witness to Abuse: Human Rights Abuses Under the Material Witness Law Since September 11." *Human Rights Watch* 97(2). Available at: http://www.aclu.org/safefree/detention/17616prs20050627.html (accessed November 2006).

Hunter, Albert. 1974. *Symbolic Communities: The Persistence and Change of Chicago's Local Communities.* Chicago: University of Chicago Press.

Huntington, Samuel. 1996. *The Clash of Civilizations and the Remaking of World Order.* New York: Free Press.

Hurh, Won Moo. 1998. *The Korean Americans (The New Americans Series).* Westport, Conn.: Greenwood Press.

Ignatiev, Noel. 1995. *How the Irish Became White.* New York: Routledge.

Illinois Advisory Committee to the U.S. Commission on Civil Rights. 2003. "Arab and Muslim Civil Rights Issues in the Chicago Metropolitan Area Post–September 11" (May). Available at: http://www.usccr.gov/pubs/sac/il0503/main.htm (accessed July 23, 2007).

Irvin, Clark Kent. 2006. "The Usual Suspects." *New York Times*, June 27.

Isikoff, Michael. 2003. "The FBI Says, Count the Mosques." *Newsweek*, February 3.

———. 2004. "Preliminary Reflections on Islam and Black Religion." In *Muslims' Place in the American Public Square: Hopes, Fears, and Aspirations*, edited by Zahid H. Bukhari, Sulayman S. Nyang, Mumtaz Ahmad, and John L. Esposito. Walnut Creek, Calif.: AltaMira Press.

Jacobs, Jane. 1961. *The Death and Life of Great American Cities.* New York: Random House.

Jamal, Amaney. 2008. "Civil Liberties and the Otherization of Arab and Muslim Americans." In *Race and Arab Americans Before and After 9/11: From Invisible Citizens to Visible Subjects*, edited by Amaney Jamal and Nadine Naber. Syracuse, N.Y.: Syracuse University Press.

Jamal, Amaney, and Nadine Naber, eds. 2008. *Race and Arab Americans Before and After 9/11: From Invisible Citizens to Visible Subjects.* Syracuse, N.Y.: Syracuse University Press.

Japanese American Citizens League (JACL). 2001. "JACL Urges Caution on Aftermath of Terrorist Attack." Press release (September 12).

Jarmakani, Amira. 2005. "Mobilizing the Politics of Invisibility in Arab American Feminist Discourse." *MIT Electronic Journal of Middle East Studies* 5(spring): 130–39. Available at: http://web.mit.edu/cis/www/mitejmes/issues/200507/MITEJMES_Vol_5_Spring.pdf.

Jones, Jeffrey M. 2002. "Effects of September 11 on Immigration Attitudes Fading, but Still Evident." Gallup News Service, August 8, 2002. Available at: www.gallup.com/poll/6565/Effects-Sept-Immigration-Attitudes-Fading-Still-Evident.aspx.

Joseph, Suad. 1999. "Against the Grain of the Nation—The Arab-." In *Arabs in America: Building a New Future*, edited by Michael W. Suleiman. Philadelphia: Temple University Press.

Karim, Karim. 2000. *Islamic Peril: Media and Global Violence.* Montreal: Black Rose Books.

Kaushal, Neeraj, Robert Kaestner, and Cordelia Reimers. 2007. "Labor Market Effects of September 11 on Arab and Muslim Residents of the U.S." *Journal of Human Resources* 42(2): 275–308.

Keeter, Scott, and Andrew Kohut. 2003. "American Public Opinion About Muslims in the United States and Abroad." In *Muslims in the United States: Demography, Beliefs, Institutions,* edited by Philippa Strum and Danielle Tarantolo. Washington: Woodrow Wilson International Center for Scholars.

———. 2005. "American Public Opinion About Muslims in the United States and Abroad." In *Muslims in the United States: Identity, Influence, Innovation,* edited by Philippa Strum. Washington, D.C.: Woodrow Wilson International Center for Scholars.

Khalidi, Rashid. 1993. "Consequences of the Suez Crisis in the Arab World." In *The Modern Middle East: A Reader,* edited by Albert Hourani, Philip S. Khoury, and Mary C. Wilson. Berkeley: University of California Press.

Koval, John P., Larry Bennett, Michael I. J. Bennett, Fassil Demissie, Roberta Garner, and Kiljoong Kim, eds. 2006. *The New Chicago: A Social and Cultural Analysis.* Philadelphia: Temple University Press.

Krikorian, Mark. 2002. "Muslim Invasion? What Increased Muslim Immigration Could Mean for U.S. Israeli Policy—and American Jews." *National Review,* April 17. Available at: http://www.nationalreview.com/comment/comment-krikorian041702.asp (accessed October 14, 2008).

Kurzman, Charles. 2002. "Bin Laden and Other Thoroughly Modern Muslims." *Contexts* 1(4): 13–20.

Lait, Jack, and Lee Mortimer. 1950. *Chicago Confidential.* New York: Crown.

Leiken, Robert S. 2004. *Bearers of Global Jihad? Immigration and National Security After 9/11.* Washington: Nixon Center.

Leonard, Karen Isaksen. 2003. *Muslims in the United States: The State of Research.* New York: Russell Sage Foundation.

Levin, Jack, and Jack McDevitt. 2002. *Hate Crimes Revisited: America's War on Those Who Are Different.* Boulder, Colo.: Westview Press.

Lewis, Bernard. 1994. "Why Turkey Is the Only Muslim Democracy." *Middle East Quarterly* 1(1): 41–49. Available at: http://www.meforum.org/article/216.

Lichtblau, Eric. 2008. "Inquiry Targeted 2,000 Foreign Muslims in 2004." *New York Times,* October 30. Available at: http://www.nytimes.com/2008/10/31/us/31inquire.html (accessed March 8, 2009).

Lipset, Seymour Martin, and William Schneider. 1977. "Carter vs. Israel: What the Polls Reveal." *Commentary* 64(5): 21–29.

Lipton, Eric. 2004. "Panel Says Census Move on Arab-Americans Recalls World War II Internments." *New York Times,* November 10.

Little, Douglas. 2002. *American Orientalism: The United States and the Middle East Since 1945.* Chapel Hill: University of North Carolina Press.

Lyman, Stanford M. 1972. "Generation and Character." In *East Across the Pacific: Historical and Sociological Studies of Japanese Immigration and Assimilation,* edited by Hilary Conroy and T. Scott Miyakawa. Santa Barbara, Calif.: ABC-CLIO.

Majaj, Lisa Suhair. 1999. "Arab-American Ethnicity: Location, Coalitions, and Cultural Negotiations." In *Arabs in America: Building a New Future,* edited by Michael W. Suleiman. Philadelphia: Temple University Press.

Mamdani, Mahmood. 2002. "Good Muslim, Bad Muslim: An African Perspective." Available at the Social Science Research Council website, http://www.ssrc.org/sept11/essays/mamdani.htm (accessed December 10, 2008).

———. 2004. *Good Muslim, Bad Muslim: America, the Cold War, and the Roots of Terror.* New York: Pantheon.

Mangaliman, Jessie. 2003. "Role in Registration Worries Ethnic Media." *San Jose Mercury News,* January 20, p. 31.

Massey, Douglas, and Elijah Anderson, eds. 2001. *Problem of the Century: Racial Stratification in the United States at Century's End.* New York: Russell Sage Foundation.

McAlister, Melani. 2005. *Epic Encounters: Culture, Media, and U.S. Interests in the Middle East Since 1945.* Updated edition. Berkeley: University of California Press.

McCarus, Ernest, ed. 1994. *The Development of Arab-American Identity.* Ann Arbor: University of Michigan Press.

McVeigh, Rory, Michael R. Welch, and Thoroddur Bjarnason. 2003. "Hate Crime Reporting as a Successful Social Movement Outcome." *American Sociological Review* 68(6): 843–67.

Michalak, Laurence O. 1983. "Cruel and Unusual: Negative Images of Arabs in American Popular Culture." Washington, D.C.: ADC Research Institute.

Middle East Studies Association (MESA), with Bernard Lewis, Edward Said, Leon Wieseltier, and Christopher Hitchens. 1987. "The MESA Debate: The Scholars, the Media, and the Middle East." Special document. *Journal of Palestine Studies* 16(2): 85–104.

Mitchell, Timothy. 1988. *Colonising Egypt.* New York: Cambridge University Press.

Moore, Kathleen M. 2003. "Open House: Visibility, Knowledge, and Integration of Muslims in the United States." In *Muslims in the United States: Demography, Beliefs, Institutions,* edited by Philippa Strum and Danielle Tarantolo. Washington: Woodrow Wilson International Center for Scholars.

Moore, Solomon. 2004. "FBI Eases Up; Muslims Still Feel Pain." *Los Angeles Times,* November 6.

Naber, Nadine. 2000. "Ambiguous Insiders: An Investigation of Arab American Invisibility." *Ethnic and Racial Studies* 23(1): 37–61.

———. 2006. "The Rules of Forced Engagement: Race, Gender, and the Culture of Fear Among Arab Immigrants in San Francisco Post-9/11." *Cultural Dynamics* 18(3): 235–67.

———. 2008. "Introduction: Arab Americans and U.S. Racial Formation." In *Race and Arab Americans Before and After 9/11: From Invisible Citizens to Visible Subjects,* edited by Amaney Jamal and Nadine Naber. Syracuse, N.Y.: Syracuse University Press.

Naff, Alixa. 1985. *Becoming American: The Early Arab Immigrant Experience.* Carbondale: Southern Illinois University Press.

Nagel, Joane. 2003. *Race, Ethnicity, and Sexuality: Intimate Intersections, Forbidden Frontiers.* New York: Oxford University Press.

National Commission on Terrorist Attacks Upon the United States (9/11 Commission). 2004. *The 9/11 Commission Report: Final Report of the National Commission on Terrorist Attacks Upon the United States.* New York: W. W. Norton.

Newhart, Dave, and Ana Mendieta. 2001. "Ethnic Tensions Boil Over: Arab Americans Here Face Protest Marches, Assaults." *Chicago Sun-Times,* September 14.

New York University (NYU). 2005. "Terrorist Trials: A Report Card." New York: NYU, Center on Law and Security (February).

Nimer, Mohamed. 2005. "American Muslim Organizations: Before and After 9/11." In *Muslims in the United States: Identity, Influence, Innovation,* edited by Philippa Strum. Washington: Woodrow Wilson International Center for Scholars.

Nyden, Philip, Michael Maly, and John Lukehart. 1997. "The Emergence of Stable Racially and Ethnically Diverse Urban Communities: A Case Study of Nine U.S. Cities." *Housing Policy Debate* 8(2): 491–534.

Office of the Inspector General. 2003. "Supplemental Report on September 11 Detainees' Allegations of Abuse at the Metropolitan Detention Center in Brooklyn, N.Y." Washington: U.S. Department of Justice, Office of the Inspector General (December).

Omi, Michael, and Howard Winant. 1994. *Racial Formation in the United States: From the 1960s to the 1990s.* 2d ed. New York: Routledge.

Orfalea, Gregory. 1988. *Before the Flames: A Quest for the History of Arab Americans.* Austin: University of Texas Press.

———. 2006. *The Arab Americans: A History.* Northampton, Mass.: Olive Branch Press.

Orum, Anthony. 2005. "Circles of Influence and Chains of Command: The Social Processes Whereby Ethnic Communities Influence Host Societies." *Social Forces* 84(2): 921–39.

Paral, Rob. 2004. "A Statistical Portrait of Persons with Arab, Middle Eastern, and Turkish Ancestry in Illinois." Unpublished paper. Institute for Metropolitan Affairs, Roosevelt University.

Parrillo, Vincent N. 1997. *Strangers to These Shores: Race and Ethnic Relations in the United States.* Boston: Allyn & Bacon.

Pettigrew, Thomas F., and Linda R. Tropp. 2006. "A Meta-Analytic Test of Intergroup Contact Theory." *Journal of Personality and Social Psychology* 90(5): 751–83.

Pipes, Daniel, and Khalid Durán. 2002. "Muslim Immigrants in the United States." Backgrounder Series. Washington, D.C.: Center for Immigration Studies (August). Available at: http://www.cis.org/articles/2002/back802.html.

Purdy, Matthew, and Lowell Bergman. 2003. "Unclear Danger: Inside the Lackawanna Terror Case." *New York Times,* October 12.

Read, Jen'nan Ghazal. 2004. *Culture, Class, and Work Among Arab-American Women.* New York: LFB Scholarly Publishing.

———. 2008. "Discrimination and Identity Formation in a Post-9/11 Era: A Comparison of Muslim and Christian Arab Americans." In *Race and Arab Americans Before and After 9/11: From Invisible Citizens to Visible Subjects,* edited by Amaney Jamal and Nadine Naber. Syracuse, N.Y.: Syracuse University Press.

Regan, Tom. 2004. " 'They Hate Our Policies, Not Our Freedom': Pentagon Report Contains Major Criticisms of Administration." *Christian Science Monitor,* November 29. Available at: www.csmonitor.com/2004/1129/dailyUpdate.html (accessed November 30, 2004).

Rieder, Jonathan. 1985. *Canarsie: The Jews and Italians of Brooklyn Against Liberalism.* Cambridge, Mass.: Harvard University Press.

Robinson, Mike. 2006. "Illinois Man Who Wrecked Muslim Family's Van Going Back to Jail." Associated Press, August 22.

Roediger, David. 1991. *The Wages of Whiteness: Race and the Making of the American Working Class.* New York: Verso.

Rood, Justin. 2007. "FBI Terror Watch List 'Out of Control.' " ABC News, June 13. Available at: http://blogs.abcnews.com/theblotter/2007/06/fbi_terror_watc. html (accessed June 2007).

Roy, Olivier. 1994. *The Failure of Political Islam.* Cambridge, Mass.: Harvard University Press.

Rubenberg, Cheryl. 1989. *Israel and the American National Interest.* Urbana: University of Illinois Press.

Said, Edward W. 1978. *Orientalism.* New York: Vintage Books.

———. 1997. *Covering Islam: How the Media and the Experts Determine How We See the Rest of the World,* revised ed. New York: Vintage Books.

Salaita, Steven. 2006. *Anti-Arab Racism in the USA: Where It Comes From and What It Means for Politics Today.* London: Pluto Press.

Salem, Lori Anne. 1999. "Far-Off and Fascinating Things: Wadeeha Atiyeh and Images of Arabs in the American Popular Theater, 1930–1950." In *Arabs in America: Building a New Future,* edited by Michael W. Suleiman. Philadelphia: Temple University Press.

Saliba, Therese. 1999. "Resisting Invisibility: Arab Americans in Academia and Activism." In *Arabs in America: Building a New Future,* edited by Michael W. Suleiman. Philadelphia: Temple University Press.

Samhan, Helen Hatab. 1999. "Not Quite White: Race Classification and the Arab-American Experience." In *Arabs in America: Building a New Future,* edited by Michael W. Suleiman. Philadelphia: Temple University Press.

Saytanides, Adam. 2003. "In Pakistan, She Would Be Dead." *Chicago Reader,* February 28.

Schmitt, Gary. 2003. "Power and Duty: U.S. Action Is Crucial to Maintaining World Order." *Los Angeles Times,* March 23. Available at the Project for a New American Century website: http://www.newamericancentury.org/global-032303.htm (accessed November 29, 2007).

Shaheen, Jack G. 1984. *The TV Arab.* Bowling Green, Ohio: Bowling Green State University Popular Press.

———. 2001. *Reel Bad Arabs: How Hollywood Vilifies a People.* Northampton, Mass.: Olive Branch Press.

Shane, Scott, and Lowell Bergman. 2006. "FBI Struggling to Reinvent Itself to Fight Terror." *New York Times,* October 10.

Shohat, Ella, and Robert Stam. 1994. *Unthinking Eurocentrism: Multiculturalism and the Media.* New York: Routledge.

Shryock, Andrew. 2008. "The Moral Analogies of Race: Arab American Identity, Color Politics, and the Limits of Racialized Citizenship." In *Race and Arab Americans Before and After 9/11: From Invisible Citizens to Visible Subjects,* edited by Amaney Jamal and Nadine Naber. Syracuse, N.Y.: Syracuse University Press.

Singer, Audrey. 2004. "The Rise of New Immigrant Gateways." Washington, D.C.: Brookings Institution, Center on Urban and Metropolitan Policy.

Siskind, Greg. 2003. "Letter from Leila Laoudji." *Siskind's Immigration Professional's Bulletin* (June). Memphis, Tenn.: Immigration Law Offices of Siskind, Susser, Haas & Devine, Attorneys at Law. Available at: http://www.visalaw.com/sip/june2003.htm.

Slade, Shelly. 1981. "The Image of the Arab in America: Analysis of a Poll on American Attitudes." *Middle East Journal* 35(2): 143–62.

Smith, Daniel. 2001. "When 'For a While' Becomes Forever." *Weekly Defense Monitor* 5(37). Available at: http://www.cdi.org/weekly/2001/issue37.html#1.

Smith, Jane I. 1999. *Islam in America.* New York: Columbia University Press.

Smith, Marian L. 2002. "Race, Nationality, and Reality: INS Administration of Racial Provisions in U.S. Immigration and Nationality Law Since 1898: Parts 1, 2, and 3." *Prologue* 34(2). Available at: http://www.archives.gov/publications/prologue/2002/summer/immigration-law-1.html.

Smith, Tom W. 2001. "Estimating the Muslim Population in the United States." New York: American Jewish Committee (October).

Sobel, Richard. 2001. "Anti-Terror Campaign Has Wide Support, Even at the Expense of Cherished Rights." *Chicago Tribune,* November 4.

Southwest Organizing Project (SWOP). 2009. "Mission, History and Vision. Available at: http://www.swopchicago.org/display.aspx?pointer=5648 (accessed May 8, 2009).

Stockton, Ronald. 1994. "Ethnic Archetypes and the Arab Image." In *The Development of Arab-American Identity,* edited by Ernest McCarus. Ann Arbor: University of Michigan Press.

Sugg, John F. 1999. "Steven Emerson's Crusade: Why Is a Journalist Pushing Questionable Stories from Behind the Scenes?" FAIR (Fairness and Accuracy in Reporting), *Extra!* (January–February). Available at: http://www.fair.org/index.php?page=1443.

Sula, Mike. 2003. "Instant Prisoner." *Chicago Reader,* February 28.

Suleiman, Michael W. 1988. "The Arab Tradition in North America." Introduction to special double issue. *Arab Studies Quarterly* 11(spring/summer): 1–13.

———, ed. 1999. *Arabs in America: Building a New Future.* Philadelphia: Temple University Press.

Suttles, Gerald D. 1968. *The Social Order of the Slum: Ethnicity and Territory in the Inner City.* Chicago: University of Chicago Press.

Swarns, Rachel L. 2003. "Thousands of Arabs and Muslims Could Be Deported, Officials Say." *New York Times,* June 7.

Takaki, Ronald. 1989. *Strangers from a Different Shore: A History of Asian Americans.* Boston: Little, Brown.

Talhami, Ghada Hashem. 1996. *The Mobilization of Muslim Women in Egypt.* Gainesville: University Press of Florida.

Terry, Don, and Noreen S. Ahmed-Ullah. 2001. "Protesters Turn Anger on Muslim Americans." *Chicago Tribune,* September 14.

Terry, Janice J. 1999. "Community and Political Activism Among Arab Americans in Detroit." In *Arabs in America: Building a New Future,* edited by Michael W. Suleiman. Philadelphia: Temple University Press.

Tirman, John, 2005. "Security the Progressive Way." *The Nation,* April 11.

Trahan, Jason, and Tanya Eiser. 2008. "Holy Land Foundation Defendants Guilty on All Counts," *Dallas Morning News,* November 25.

Transactional Records Access Clearinghouse (TRAC). 2003. "Criminal Terrorism Enforcement Since the 9/11/01 Attacks." Syracuse, N.Y.: TRAC.

Tsao, Fred, and Rhoda Rae Gutierrez. 2003. *Losing Ground: The Loss of Freedom, Equality, and Opportunity for America's Immigrants Since the September 11 Attacks.* Chicago: Illinois Coalition for Immigrant and Refugee Rights (ICIRR).

U.S. Bureau of the Census. 1993. *1990 Census of Population: Ancestry of the Population in the United States.* Report CP-3-2. Washington: U.S. Government Printing Office.

———. United States Census 2000. Available at: http://www.census.gov/main/www/cen2000.html.

U.S. Commission on Wartime Relocation and Internment of Civilians. 1983. "Personal Justice Denied." Washington: U.S. Government Printing Office.

U.S. Department of Justice. Immigration and Naturalization Service (INS). 1943. "Central Office View on the Racial Qualifications for Entry and Naturalization with Respect to Persons of the Arabian Race." Instruction 168. Philadelphia: INS (September 9).

———. Various years. Yearbook of Immigration Statistics. Washington D.C.: U.S. Government Printing Office.

U.S. Department of State. 1950. "Palestine Refugee Program." Publication 3757. Washington: U.S. Department of State (February).

Waters, Mary C. 1990. *Ethnic Options: Choosing Identities in America.* Berkeley: University of California Press.

Wedam, Elfriede. 2005. "If We Let the Market Prevail, We Won't Have a Neighborhood Left: Religious Agency and Urban Restructuring on Chicago's Southwest Side." *City and Society* 17(2): 211–33.

Winograd, Ben. 2001. "A New Fight for Peace." *Daily Northwestern,* October 3.

Woods, John E. 1996. "Imagining and Stereotyping Islam." In *Muslims in America: Opportunities and Challenges,* edited by Asad Husain. Chicago: International Strategy and Policy Institute.

Yale Law School and the American-Arab Anti-Discrimination Committee (ADC). 2008. "Joint Press Release: ICE Targets Immigrants from Muslim Majority Countries Prior to 2004." Available at: http://www.adc.org/PDF/frontline.pdf (accessed March 8, 2009).

Yang, Fenggang, and Helen Rose Ebaugh. 2001. "Transformations in New Immigrant Religions and Their Global Implications." *American Sociological Review* 66(2): 269–88.

Yee, James, and Aimee Malloy. 2005. *For God and Country: Faith and Patriotism Under Fire.* New York: Public Affairs.

Zaatari, Zeina. 2005. "In the Belly of the Beast: Struggling for Non-violent Belonging." *MIT Electronic Journal of Middle East Studies* 5(spring): 75–87. Available at: http://web.mit.edu/cis/www/mitejmes/issues/200507/MITEJMES_Vol_5_Spring.pdf.

Zaghel, Ali. 1977. "Changing Patterns of Identification Among Arab Americans: The Palestinian Ramallites." Ph.D. diss., Northwestern University.

Zogby, James, ed. 1984. *Taking Root, Bearing Fruit: The Arab-American Experience,* vol. 1. Washington, D.C.: ADC Research Institute.

Index

Boldface numbers refer to figures and tables.

311